Practical
Investigation
Techniques

CRC Series in
Practical Aspects of Criminal and Forensic Investigations

Vernon J. Geberth, BBA, MPS, FBINA, *Series Editor*

Practical Investigation Techniques
Kevin B. Kinnee

Practical Aspects of Kinesic Interview and Interrogation Techniques
Stan Walters

Practical Homicide Investigation: Tactics, Procedures,
and Forensic Techniques, Second Edition
Vernon J. Geberth

The Counter-Terrorism Handbook: Tactics, Procedures, and Techniques
Frank Bolz, Jr., Kenneth J. Dudonis, and David P. Schulz

Forensic Pathology
Dominick J. Di Maio and Vincent J. M. Di Maio

Interpretation of Bloodstain Evidence at Crime Scenes
William G. Eckert and Stuart H. James

Tire Imprint Evidence
Peter McDonald

Practical Drug Enforcement: Procedures and Administration
Michael D. Lyman

Practical Aspects of Rape Investigation: A Multidisciplinary Approach
Robert R. Hazelwood and Ann Wolbert Burgess

The Sexual Exploitation of Children: A Practical Guide
to Assessment, Investigation, and Intervention
Seth L. Goldstein

Gunshot Wounds: Practical Aspects of Firearms, Ballistics, and Forensic Techniques
Vincent J. M. Di Maio

Friction Ridge Skin: Comparison and Identification of Fingerprints
James F. Cowger

Footwear Impression Evidence
William J. Bodziak

Practical Fire and Arson Investigation
John J. O'Connor

The Practical Methodology of Forensic Photography
David R. Redsicker

Practical Gambling Investigation Techniques
Kevin B. Kinnee

Practical Aspects of Interview and Interrogation
David E. Zulawski and Douglas E. Wicklander

Practical Investigation Techniques

Kevin B. Kinnee

CRC Press

Boca Raton   Ann Arbor   London   Tokyo

Library of Congress Cataloging-in-Publication Data

Kinnee, Kevin B.
    Practical investigation techniques / by Kevin B. Kinnee.
        p. cm. — (Practical aspects of criminal and forensic investigations)
    Includes bibliographical references and index.
    ISBN 0–8493–8151–7
       1. Criminal investigation—United States. I. Title. II. Series: CRC series in practical
aspects of criminal and forensic investigations.
HV8073.K4744 1994
363.2′5—dc20   93–51085
                                                        CIP

© 1994 by CRC Press, Inc.

No claim to original U.S. Government works
International Standard Book Number 0–8493–8151–7
Library of Congress Card Number 93–51085
Printed in the United States of America 2 3 4 5 6 7 8 9 0
Printed on acid-free paper

Editor's Note

This textbook is part of a series entitled "Practical Aspects of Criminal and Forensic Investigation". This series was created by Vernon J. Geberth, a retired New York City Police Department Lieutenant Commander, who is an author, educator, and consultant on homicide and forensic investigations.

This series has been designed to provide contemporary, comprehensive, and pragmatic information to the practitioner involved in criminal and forensic investigations by authors who are nationally recognized experts in their respective fields.

Preface

Traditionally, law enforcement has depended on on-the-job training as a method to develop new investigators. This presents an inherent problem. For example, if a new investigator is afforded the opportunity of working with an investigator/instructor who is knowledgeable, he or she will probably eventually learn the proper investigative techniques. However, in most cases the information is presented in a hit-or-miss manner and may not necessarily represent the preferred or most efficient method to conduct an investigation.

I remember when I was transferred to the Investigative division. There was a scarcity of information to draw upon to learn my new assignment. Instead, I was informed that I would learn by my mistakes. Today, learning from one's mistakes can cost police agencies millions of dollars in lawsuits.

I decided, therefore, to prepare this book to provide new, as well as veteran, officers with an instructional book geared toward establishing a practical standard for conducting a wide range of criminal investigations. I sincerely hope that the information and checklists within this book will assist police officers and investigators in this pursuit.

Kevin B. Kinnee

Foreword

I have been a police officer for 23 years and have been transferred into jobs that I have had to learn by trial and error. I would have appreciated having a book like this to help me through those changes. Sergeant Kinnee brings a vast amount of work experience to this book. Most books are written by someone after compiling information from people who have been there, but Sergeant Kinnee *has* been there. The back-to-basics approach to the book is refreshing. It causes you to think and to be creative. The book gives you ideas and tips that, coupled with your own experience, will enhance your investigative skills.

Terry Hall
Unit Supervisor
Criminal Intelligence Section

The Author

Kevin B. Kinnee, an 18-year veteran of law enforcement with the Indianapolis Police Department, has spent the last nine years in investigations. Kinnee's broad base of experience is a result of his involvement in over 700 investigations into such areas as vice/narcotics, property recovery, major gambling operations, murder for hire, and organized crime. He has assisted in federal, state, and local investigations and has been detailed to the state police, the Federal Bureau of Investigations, and the U.S. Treasury Department. Kinnee is a certified instructor who has toured the country to conduct seminars for Internal Revenue Service criminal investigators, state and federal criminal intelligence officers, and local law enforcement agencies.

Acknowledgments

I wish to acknowledge and thank all the people and organizations that have contributed to this book. I have listed them in alphabetical order and apologize to anyone whom I may have inadvertently omitted.

Greg Arkins, Jim and Cheryl Alsup, Mike Bates, Mike Beaver, Tom Black, Joseph Brannon, Chief Donald Christ, the Chicago Tribune, the Drug Enforcement Agency, Steve DuBois, Emmitt Carney, Joseph Fyffe, the FBI Laboratory, *Fortune* Magazine, Vernon J. Geberth, Wyonne Hale, Earnest R. Hudson, Jr., Terry Hall, the Indianapolis Police Department Training Staff, International Investigators, Sandra Kinnee, Rundell H. Kinnee, Ellen J. Kinnee, Robby Milam, Marion County Prosecutor's Office, the New York Times, Police Executive Research Forum, William Reardon, the Senate Subcommittee on Governmental Affairs, William S. Sessions, Special Agent Kier Boyd, Special Agent R. Phillip Harker, Special Agent Walt Sirene, Tim Viles, Department of Justice, *U.S. News and World Report,* Tim Wilcox, U.S. Postal Service, and the Public Agency Training Council.

Contents

Chapter 3
Civil Forfeiture 45

Chapter 4
Shoplifting 49

Chapter 5
Case Examples of Informants 55

Chapter 18
Illegal Gambling 225

Chapter 21

Interviews and Interrogations 343

This book is dedicated to my father
Rundell H. Kinnee
(1923–1993)

and to my mother
Ellen J. Kinnee

I also wish to give special thinks to

- Vernon Geberth, Series Editor, and Jim Alsup. Without their help, this book would never have been written.

- The present members of the Special Task Team: Lieutenant William Reardon, Detective Michael Bates, Detective Steve DuBoise, and Detective Wyonne Hale.

- My wife Janet and my sons, Kevin, Jimmy, and Greg.

- Denise Thomas and Sandra Kinnee.

Many thanks for your help.

Introduction

MOTIVATION FOR TODAY'S CRIME

Never before has there been a more compelling force that has pushed people to commit crime: today's major force behind property crime is narcotic addiction. Crack, to be specific, has changed the way we look at how crimes occur. The low cost of ''rock'' and the willingness of dealers to accept stolen property in payment for drugs is central to our nation's crime problem.

If a dealer accepts property for drugs he can substantially increase his profit and diversify his operation. You now see dealers investing in property, which leads to fencing, dealing, and money laundering. You, as the investigator, must look at specific crimes and determine the motivation that drives the criminal.

INTERRELATIONSHIP OF CRIME AND DRUGS

In modern-day society, the impact of drug usage on reported crime is the most important change in the past 10 years. With the advent of crack and other cheap drugs there has been an astronomical increase in the number of crimes committed to subsidize the addicts' needs. With this in mind, investigators must see beyond their day-to-day work and identify where the money and drugs come from and go to. The investigator must identify businesses that lend themselves to money laundering, such as video arcades, car dealerships, taverns, restaurants, ''dirty'' book stores, vending companies, pay parking lots, car washes, loan companies, loan services, produce companies, churches, fast food locations, and wholesale companies.

In addition to businesses that lend themselves to money laundering, the investigator needs to identify the businesses that lend themselves to the buying and selling of stolen property. These include pawn shops, car washes, flea markets, taverns, dope dealers, fences, auctions, variety stores, store front businesses, and out-of-state businesses.

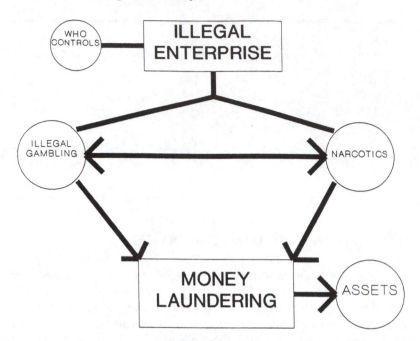

Figure 1.1. Questions that need to be asked when conducting an investigation: Who controls the enterprise? What illegal activities are they involved in? How is the money laundered? What is purchased with the money?

Keep in mind that the property taken, be it a stolen car or items from a burglary, must go somewhere. You can eat only so many VCRs. You must identify where the stolen goods go and how you can stop the flow. For example, stop by a flea market as they set up to open. The people who cover the license plates on their vehicles should be targeted for investigation. A helpful chart is provided in Figure 1.1.

Important: Before you conduct your investigation using the techniques listed here, contact your prosecutor or legal advisor to get input from them. **Do not** be the one who sets a precedent that holds back all law enforcement.

- If there is a doubt .... Do *not* do it.
- Be creative .... Do *not* put blinders on.
- If a law limits you .... Lobby for change.

STEPS NEEDED TO CONDUCT A SUCCESSFUL INVESTIGATION

In order to be successful in the area of diversified investigations, the first thing that must be done is to transform the investigator from a specialist in single-crime investigations (vehicle theft, burglary, robbery) to one who steps beyond his station and observes crime on a continuum.

The investigator must view crime and the motivation for committing the crime on the same level. For example:

Crime — Motivation — Money — Stages
Crime — Motivation — Drugs — Stages

Crime: Burglary. **Motivation:** Drug habit. **Stages:** Stolen property taken to a fence for currency, or currency taken to a drug dealer for drugs.

The diversified investigator needs to view each stage the criminal goes through as a point where law enforcement can inject itself and have an impact on overall crime.

Each stage consists of separate criminal acts, and the investigator needs to know how to conduct an investigation that will encompass all involved. If the investigator cannot catch a burglar in the act, he may be able to "take off" (raid) the fence or drug dealer and work back to identify the burglar.

In addition to the investigator being trained in the diversified approach to investigations, he needs to impact the criminals in such a way as to put them out of business. This can only be done by targeting the criminals in a three-prong attack: *criminal charges, forfeiture of assets through the civil process,* and *use of state and federal IRS.*

Listed below are the motivations for various crimes:

- Shoplifting .... Money or drugs
- Vehicle theft .... Money or drugs
- Credit card fraud .... Money or drugs
- Check fraud .... Money or drugs
- Theft .... Money or drugs
- Internal theft .... Money or drugs

As you can see above, you can impact each of the crimes listed by attacking at any of three levels: (1) the crime itself, (2) where they sell the property (fence), or (3) where they trade for drugs.

ADMINISTRATORS: HOW TO GET PERMISSION TO CONTINUE

Law enforcement administrators have a responsibility to the general public to get the best law enforcement coverage for the money spent. They do this by prioritizing demands for service based on what is viewed at the public's need. With this in mind, you must present the best defense to your administrator. You need to answer the question: "Why should I take manpower and money away from other programs so you can conduct your investigation?".

The best way to answer this question is to show how your investigation will have a major impact on future reported crime. For example you receive information that a fencing operation in your area is buying stolen property from ten burglars. You identify, through sources, that the average burglar commits two burglaries per week. (This source may be the national or state average.) With this information, and the knowledge that in your area the previous year there were 7,000 burglaries, you can request permission to conduct the investigation.

Request that the manpower be committed for the period you feel is necessary, and add the following: By conducting this investigation I will have the ability to impact one seventh of the burglaries in the area. Our intent is to close the fence, identify the ten burglars, and put them out of business.

Here is how you calculate the impact that your investigation could have:

10 burglars × 2 burglaries each week × 52 weeks
Total: 1,040 burglaries per year
Yearly average: 7,000 burglaries
Impact: 1/7 of known burglaries

MIND SET OF THE INVESTIGATOR

The modern-day investigator must be as diverse as the crimes that face him or her. The investigator's mind set is the key to success. The criminal investigator must be creative to defeat all attempts at preventing the investigations from continuing. He or she must be a problem solver and must be able to see beyond their station. The investigator must face challenges as a game and must be determined to win.

CREATIVITY IN LAW ENFORCEMENT

Creativity, without a doubt, is the most important characteristic that an investigator must have. To be creative and have the ability to come up with new ideas and new ways to attack a problem is far more important than any basic training. Because of the nature of law enforcement, creativity is generally suppressed. Officers are indoctrinated in general orders, rules, regulations, and very narrow rules of conduct that are acceptable to the group. By the time an officer serves his time in the trenches and becomes an investigator, he has formed a very regimented way of doing things. To be successful in investigations, this way of thinking must be realigned.

Every day I hear officers say, "We couldn't get in on them, so we left" or "They are suspicious of us, so we won't be able to continue the investigation."

My philosophy is simple:

- Identify the target.
- Create an atmosphere of trust.
- Infiltrate the organizations using a police officer or informant.
- Make it too costly to continue business.

This book is intended to assist investigators in the process of **identifying, isolating,** and **eliminating the illegal organization.**

ROLE OF THE INVESTIGATOR

The investigator has the responsibility to investigate those crimes that are brought to his attention by whatever means available. The normal investigation has two stages: the preliminary investigation and the follow-up investigation. In each stage, the investigator must pay close attention to the facts and make critical decisions that will affect the duration and impact of each case. The investigator must always look for patterns and motivation for the crimes no matter what stage he or she is in.

CRIMINAL INVESTIGATOR

The criminal investigator collects evidence to identify and locate a perpetrator and gathers enough evidence to arrest and convict the subject involved. The tools used by the investigator are diverse, and one never stops finding new ways to uncover facts that will help. Four basic tools used by investigators to uncover facts about a given case are

- Source information
- Interrogations and interviews
- Observations
- Background investigations

We will cover these areas in following chapters. Of them, however, the most important area in which the investigator needs to be proficient is "backgrounding" an investigation, for this is where your success will be measured. This is the point where all investigators vary in the depth and quality of their investigations. This book may not motivate the investigator to do a quality investigation, but it will provide him or her with the knowledge and ability to conduct a thorough short- or long-term investigation. What is done with the information provided is up to you.

Areas to be covered in this text include:

- Receipt and function of complaints
- Background checks
- Probable cause development
- Warrants
- Development of case charts
- Property crimes/property recovery
- Informants
- Surveillance
- Infiltration of organized groups
- Planning and execution of raids
- Legal considerations
- Summaries and case studies

HOW TO IDENTIFY TARGETS

Begin with intelligence gathering (Figure 1.2).

Patrol Districts

Request information from all patrol districts in your area. Request the name and addresses of all locations where stolen property is suspected of being dealt. Request the names and addresses of suspects and what crimes they are committing. Conduct a background on each location and person, and establish a priority list of suspect targets.

Computer Search—Patterns of Criminal Behavior

Select a specific type of crime, such as larceny from a vehicle. Identify patterns which isolate conditions, such as day of the week and the time of day. Identify patterns which lend themselves to tactical situations, such as the surveillance of a given area to apprehend perpetrators (Figures 1.3A and B). Analysis of this data should identify the location where the offense is most likely to occur, the day of the week, and the time of day. This type of intelligence will greatly enhance your chance of success.

Business Community

Contact organizations in the business community, such as retail merchants' associations, and give them information on what your team can do to assist in the area of loss prevention. Provide officers to speak at meetings and to promote a

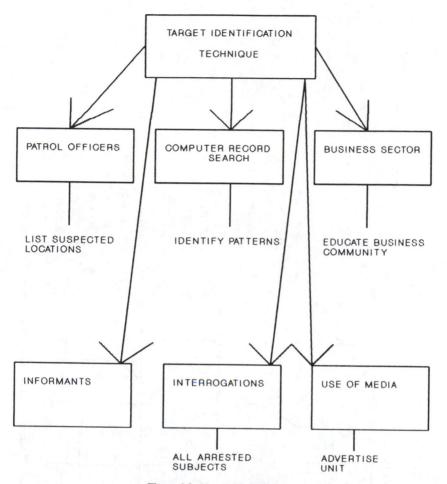

Figure 1.2. How to identify targets.

working relation with businesses in attendance. Follow up with personal contact with those businesses in the community that lend themselves to shoplifting and other criminal activities, such as check fraud and credit card fraud. Identify ways in which these businesses can assist your team in being injected into the chain between the thief and the fence or drug dealer.

Advertise Unit's Existence

Use the media to advertise your existence. Whenever possible, take the media with you on raids. Pass the word through informants that persons providing information can receive payment for their assistance. Inform other agencies (both public and private) as to what your unit does and what it can offer them.

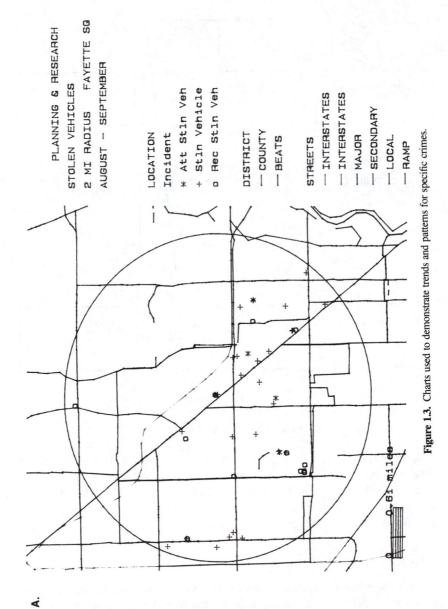

Figure 1.3. Charts used to demonstrate trends and patterns for specific crimes.

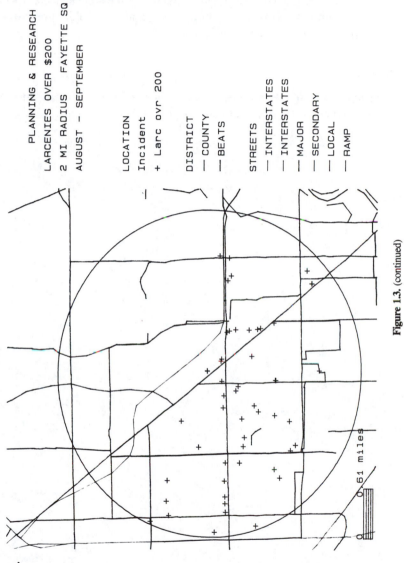

Figure 1.3. (continued)

Interviews

Read daily arrest reports and identify subjects who should be interviewed. Request notification when a specific arrest is made so an interview can be conducted before transport to jail. This is often accomplished by having store detectives call you at the time of arrest. Shoplifters are a great source of information—most can give you a fence and a drug dealer.

Informants

Develop a string of informants that will provide you with a constant flow of information about new targets, i.e., Crimestoppers of the Pawn Unit.

2

Receipt and Validation of Information

Information is received by investigators from several sources within the law enforcement community and outside sources (Figure 2.1). Each source has to be handled in the same way to validate the truthfulness and accuracy of the information.

The credibility of the investigator and the agency he or she represents is at stake, not to mention the possible liability if the investigator fails to do a complete background before acting on the information received. (Remember that your actions could place limits on officers all over the United States if a court rules on your errors.)

SOURCES OF INFORMATION: OUTSIDE LAW ENFORCEMENT SOURCES

For sources of information, look to good citizen organization (Block Club), informants, cooperating individuals, other governmental entities, and private business entities.

A determination as to motivation for information must be made early. Why is this person or organization providing information and what do they have to gain?

Reasons for Informing

- To keep out of jail
- Fear
- Revenge (worst reason)
- Eliminate competition
- Money
- To better society

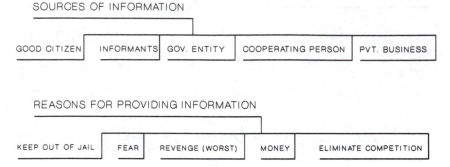

Figure 2.1. This chart demonstrates sources of information and the reason the information has been provided. It is important to know the reason why the source is providing the information in order to protect the officer and the agency.

If you use an informant in your investigation, always check his criminal history first. If there is something that will cause you a problem in court, you must consider it now, not after he is used. If the informant's prior arrests are worse than your target's, you may have a problem convincing a jury to convict your target.

An Informant

The following is from a subject who wanted to be our informant. He even provided us with his resumé.

Mike:

It is probably not necessary to restate this but please watch out for yourself first on this investigation since your career will be on the line. However, if we can bust this one it will make Watergate look like a tea party and you could possibly become the next governor and at long last bring some sanity to Indiana and I can do a fast fade and I can die in peace. On 20 Jan. I lost the sight in my right eye and the left eye could go just as easily. I would look a bit foolish as a retarded Spook peddling pencils out of a tin cup. One good thing about having one eye—the ladies only look half as old!

As you probably know, the Trons boys are the powers to be in town. They began playing games with me and I told them, "If you think Tricky Dick was bad news—wait 'til I get on your ass!" They backed up fast. Those two clowns have heavy duty activity on all four sides of their compound but never are touched, and they get a piece of everything that moves in town and beyond. John has been an FBI fink since Christ was a corporal and he knew that I knew so we waltzed each around for a while then I let the FBI know he was giving them small change and proof he was a capital offender. He was too badly injured to do the job but he had it done and I am afraid my son did it. That story about the job in Detroit was horseshit. My son and another kid were tried for attempted murder—John threatened to kill him and he didn't show. Now the Bureau is jumping up and down on his ass and he is in a panic. Jim D's and a joint in

Pensacola were due for a heavy IRS going over and I panicked him into cutting a deal with the FBI then caught five bar owners and gave them the word—"We pay our people!" I've seen cockroaches scatter but this was a laff riot. That idiot at the ABC Lounge has been a DEA fink for a long time. His wife was humping everything that moved and he was trying to sell ASAP. I gave the DEA the word and they pumped some money into the operation but he closed anyway.

I think, but am not sure, that the Trons have reached into Carmel and are dealing with P.C. and his deputy. In order to get him off my case I called the Prosecutor and threatened to lay a civil rights violation suit on the county. When I went to see P.C., I nearly laffed in his face. Fifty-two officers, 41 years old, and a Brigadier General and his deputy a full colonel! I've seen self aggrandizement in my time but this tops them all. If you can get me his home address please do. I want to see how far above this income he is living. When I went to get my car out of impound there was an elderly woman sitting behind a computer screen. I asked, "How is his wife running the place?" She said, "Oh, just fine." You talk about panic in the streets—the gang that couldn't shoot straight could not possibly top this!

One place to check out on Mr. John is the Department of Corrections. My younger son was very close to this mess and has said nothing but the older boy has been telling me for years.

I was in Albuquerque in December and took care of the big time cocaine dealer who got my stepdaughter hooked. He has been operating out of two miniature golf courses since the day I moved into my home on 1 Aug. '79 so everyone from the Mayor on down is on the take as well as DEA. I'll finish that story at a later time.

Mike, I may be old but as you can see from the resume I was well trained and can still function.

I hope to God I'm not wrong in confiding in you. I more than likely have a contract on my butt—but dems de breaks!

J. Doe

Resumé Accompanying Letter

Objectives
Administrator, Technical Writer, Expeditor, Trouble Shooter, Investigator, Infiltration, Covert/Overt Operations.

Experience
Served six years as Military Policeman, thirteen years as a Special Agent and Collection Agent with Army Intelligence. Supervised up to forty-nine individuals while they were engaged in academic programs and administrative functions. Operated independently while engaged in personal security investigations and controlled foreign nationals in the collection of information. Have written operations and information reports while serving as Desk Officer, Scientific, and Technical Collection Service. Served as Confinement Facility Chief Clerk and Chief Clerk, Provost Marshal Central Files Division. Worked part-time for a total of three years as an automobile and retail salesman during periods of assignment in the continental United States. Also kept books for one and one half years for two bars and a restaurant.

Operations Improvement Skills
By using the skills learned in administration, covert and overt operations, planning and personnel management, I applied them in devising the best means to obtain results in gathering, reviewing, editing, reporting, and applying information received to the successful accomplishment of the overall mission. Established liaison and advised commanders from unrelated branches on the conduct of unorthodox methods of operations.

Negotiations
Served as point of contact for liaison and protocol between military commanders, civilian agencies, and foreign nationals. Presented operational briefings to a major command for justification and authorization for the expenditure of funds. Located, assessed, recruited, and trained individuals, and negotiated with the individual concerning contractual agreements.

Operational Planning Management
Prepared plans for operations in Europe and southeast Asia to obtain intelligence, using both human and fiscal resources on hand. Planned for the acquisition of new resources, obtaining required logistics and services.

Education
Graduated from Arsenal Technical Schools, Indianapolis, Indiana, 1951. Completed the following civilian and military schools.

> Kansas State University, 1961 (one semester)
> Indiana University, Purdue University at Indianapolis, 1977 (two semesters)
> Military Police School, 1956 (8 weeks)
> Army Intelligence School, Baltimore, 1962: Army Intelligence, Area Intelligence Specialist course (21 weeks)
> Army Intelligence School, 1966: Special Agent/Investigator course (15 weeks)
> Central Intelligence Agency School, 1967: Tradescrafts course (5 weeks)
> Successfully completed U.S. Army, General Education Tests for 30 college credit hours, 1957
> German language school (18 weeks)
> Defense Against Sound Equipment, Red Stone Arsenal, AL; Ft. Holabird, MD (17 weeks)

Date Available
Open

Salary History
Annual wages: 75K per annum

Note: Published writer. Desire employment as unarmed, undocumented investigator. All information obtained to be released to the proper governmental agency concerned. Uncovered bookmaking operation, U.S. Post Office, Carmel, Indiana—no action taken!!

As this subject illustrates, there are a million crackpots out there. You must protect yourself and your department by identifying the crackpots and never use them. Always be prepared for this type of informant to go off. In this case, the informant shot himself in the head.

DEALING WITH INFORMANTS

When dealing with informants, there are several things you must do.

1. You must always ask the informants how they know the information they are providing is true. This question is asked to make sure that the information was obtained or witnessed by the informant and not just something the informant heard. The informant must have first hand knowledge as to the information provided.
2. You must always verify the information provided through a separate source. Do not believe informants. Try to verify information through other informants and through your background investigation.
3. You must determine the motivation behind the informant who is providing you the information. If the motivation is suspect, do not use the informant.
4. You must determine the reliability of informants before you use them. If you find that the informant is unreliable and a liar, you risk a major embarrassment to yourself and your department if you use them. Never use an informant who is listed as unreliable.
5. Before using the informant in your major case, give the informant a test run. You should give the informant an assignment and have another informant shadow the first, or use a police officer to verify the first informant's actions. If you let a new informant know what your major case is before you test them, you may lose the chance to continue. Remember: The bad guys will infiltrate law enforcement posing as an informant. *Always beware. Never trust.*
6. Never "lead" an informant. Try to structure your talk with a new informant in such a way as to draw out what the informant can do for you and not what you want the informant to do. Again, if you tell the informant what you want targeted you risk a major leak. Informants will often sell information to the bad guys, thereby placing you in jeopardy.
7. If an informant is a witness to or part of a deal, he must testify. Keep this in mind when you tell them whether or not they will be on the stand.
8. Informants should be required to do a post incident report and sign it. You need to do this to lock in their testimony for the future.
9. Before using an informant, always run a criminal check on them. Never let a wanted person work as an informant. If there is a warrant out for your informant, arrest them and then use them. Keep in mind also that

you need to check prior criminal histories on your informants. If they have bad prior histories, you need to decide now whether using them is worth the risk of embarrassment later in court.

10. It is better to get a person out of jail to do a deal and then return him than to get an informant out and let him disappear.
11. Never have an informant introduce you face to face, unless the informant has been used before and has proven himself.
12. If you intend to use informants who are on parole or probation, you need to get permission from their parole or probation officers. Keep in mind that what you are asking the informants to do is probably a violation of their probation or parole.
13. If you set a deal with an informant to drop charges, have an official authorize it in writing.
14. If an informant lies, *never* use him again.
15. Always explain exactly what you want the informant to do and rehearse it several times. This includes how to handle evidence, what to say, and what signals are to be used.

Safety Factors When Dealing With Informants

1. Never trust informants.
2. Use informants to gather information when it is too dangerous to use officers.
3. Expect informants to embarrass you and your department. Guard against this.
4. Expect informants to "double dip" with other agencies.
5. Expect informants to give you up to the criminals.
6. Expect the informant to try to trade you to another agency to get out of trouble.
7. Never give the informant large amounts of buy money.
8. Always cover all exits when the informant is making buys. They will run.
9. Never depend on an informant to give you accurate information about addresses or apartment numbers.
10. Expect informants to lie or drag out an investigation to get paid more.
11. Always ask the informants about booby traps. Is the target known to set them for safety?
12. Always ask about weapons at the scene. Is the target a "gun nut"?
13. Always ask the informant if the target is a drug user. What kind?
14. Always ask if the target is known for violence.
15. Always ask if the target has prior military service. What type?
16. Always ask if the target has special training such as martial arts, explosives, etc.

17. Always ask the informant what the normal procedures are. Will the target deal with a new face? Will the undercover officer be searched? Will the informant be taken aside and have to do the deal in private?

A warning about informants: On a regular basis we find ourselves looking bad on television because an error was made and we hit the wrong house with a search warrant. Some of the errors can be attributed to sloppy police work, but I have found that some criminals who expect to be hit off-and-on will provide the police with information that leads to errors. The following are two cases that I experienced where the bad guy tried to throw a monkey wrench into the system to mess up the police.

Case Example 1

This case involved a sports bookmaking operation. While conducting the investigation, I had occasion to drive by the location to obtain a property description for my search warrant. As I drove by the residence, I looked up the driveway and observed three numbers on the corner of the residence denoting the address. I continued to note the curved drive, satellite dish, and other identifying features of the residence. As I turned north on the road west of the residence, I observed four numbers on the corner of the building. I returned to the office and began my background to try to determine the true address. I found that the address which was viewed from the driveway did not exist. The suspect had intentionally placed it there to attempt to give his lawyer something to argue about in case a search warrant listed the fictitious address.

Case Example 2

While conducting an investigation on the west side, I had occasion to go by the target location to obtain a description for a search warrant. As I proceeded through the neighborhood, I noted the addresses progressing from low to high (6714, 6716, 6718). As I reached the target location, the address went from 6724 to 5728. The address was on the post that held the roof over the porch. I took down the description of the property and then proceeded to the 5700 block and discovered that the house at 5728 was the exact double of the house in the 6700 block. In this case, the bad guy had identified a residence in the area which was identical to his and he then painted and set up his property to look exactly like the other, in the hope that the police would hit the wrong house.

In both the above cases the bad guy attempted to trick law enforcement into making a mistake. When dealing with informants, never trust them to provide accurate information about addresses and numbers. Always check the targets to verify that they do not contain errors that will provide litigation in court. Never depend on an address alone for your search warrant. Always get an in-depth description of the target and verify that it exists.

VALIDATION OF INFORMATION

Never believe the information provided. Always verify it. Once you receive information that a person or business is involved in criminal activities, you can conduct a background search without leaving your office.

Phase I is designed to validate information and decide whether or not to continue the investigation into the covert area, or Phase II.

At the time you begin your background check, you should gather information with three purposes in mind:

1. Obtain information to prosecute under criminal statutes.
2. Obtain information to use in civil proceedings to forfeit assets.
3. Obtain information to assist the IRS in filing tax cases (state and federal).

By using these three purposes, you can effectively put criminal enterprises out of business.

Phase I

Within the Department

Look for information showing involvement in criminal activities. Key on prior arrests for the type of crime you are investigating. Run the target, be it a business or person, through the departmental sources.

Computer check: If your agency has access to a computer which is used to compile information on subjects and location, you need to run the following entries:

- *Name and AKA ("also known as").* If your computer has the sound-alike feature ("soundex"), you should just enter the last name of the subject and hit "sound alike"; this will make up for misspelled names. During this stage, you should also look for relatives and their addresses.
- *By co-defendants.* Check any persons that were arrested or associated with your subject in prior incidents.
- *By address.* When checking by address on the computer, get in the habit of running what I call the address cube. This is a two block check around your target address. Check two blocks along the street the target is on, then check two blocks on the next street west and the street east. You should look for addresses that show the same last names as your target; these could be relatives. You do not want to set up a surveillance in front of the target's mother's house. In addition to relatives in the area, you need to key on activities in the area of the target. If the area seems to have a large number of reported violent crimes or a lot of weapons violations are noted, you must consider the safety of your officers when setting up your activities. *Special note:* If gang activity

is noted in the area of your target or reference to satanistic activities, you must take this into consideration when you serve a search warrant.

- *By case status.* This entry provides you with patterns on specific types of crimes. Enter the code for burglaries and the time frame you want covered, and it will kick out all incidents that apply.
- *By Social Security number.* Use this type of check to determine vehicle plates and vehicles owned by, or listed to, your target.
- *By family members.* Identify family members, their AKAs and maiden names and conduct a background on them to identify co-conspirators.
- *By associates.* Track associates through the computer to identify other associates of the target. Each associate should be backgrounded.
- *Prior police reports.* Check the computer for prior incidents which identify vehicles, associates and locations where the target is mentioned. Keep in mind to check for the type of incident, especially if weapons were involved.
- *Property inquiry.* If you have access to this screen you need to identify property ownership if possible.
- *Follow-up reports.* Check detective follow-up reports to gain information specific to your target.
- *Probable cause inquiry.* If possible, get copies of probable causes on prior incidents involving your target. This information may give you patterns, tendencies, and information that show your target is predisposed to committing the crime you are investigating.
- *Pawn inquiry.* This inquire, if accessible, will list all items pawned by your target. It will also give you a way to track some stolen property.
- *Alarm permit inquiry.* If an alarm permit is required in your area in order to install an alarm, this information can be obtained through the computer or hand search. This can help establish ownership and residency at the target location.
- *Driver's license information check.* Conduct a computer check using driver's license information. This information can give you a wide range of information as to what was driven by the target and where.
- *Traffic ticket inquiry.* Through the computer, track traffic tickets received by the target or co-conspirators. This can assist in giving vehicles driven and locations frequented.
- *Suspect/witness inquiry.* Use this inquiry to determine if your target has been a suspect or witness in the recent past.

Your background investigation should provide you with all the answers necessary to conduct a safe and effective investigation. The following are some questions for which you will need answers.

- Is the target a gang member?
- Is there gang involvement?
- Where is the target employed?

- What vehicles are accessible to the target?
- Where are the target's normal hangouts?
- What assets are involved?
- Is the target a drug user? What types of drugs are used?
- Has the target prior military training? Type of training received?
- Are traps present at the target location? Is the suspect known for setting traps?
- How many people are normally present?
- Are weapons present? What types?

If you do not have enough information to conduct a safe entry, then you should consider delaying your case until it develops more.

Identification and records check: Check identification and records section for the following:

- *Check for prior arrest.* Key on arrests that would show that your target is predisposed to committing the crime you are investigating.
- *Check for nicknames and AKAs.* Check arrest records for nicknames and AKAs, then conduct a background on what you discover.
- *Photographs and description sheets.* Obtain these from the records section and determine if there are any key identifiable features. Identify if there are tattoos and if they are gang-related. Identify anything that demonstrates that your target is affiliated with any known radical or violent group. This information is necessary to conduct a safe and successful investigation.
- *Identify any gang affiliation.* Identify tattooing or affiliation through those arrested with the target on prior investigations.
- *Identify all tattoos and scars present.* Identify scars, tattoos, and birthmarks that will help identify the target. If possible, identify the location of the tattoos. This information could assist in identifying affiliations with gangs.
- *Identifiers.* Identify all other identifiers listed. This will include relatives, employment information, height, weight, and color of eyes.

Interviews: During the early stages of an investigation you should conduct interviews with the following subjects. *Note:* Always keep in mind that the more people who know who your target is, the better the chance that a leak will occur. You should ask yourself, "Is the value of the information I may receive from this step worth the risk of a leak?". If it is not, then do not take that step.

- *Interview arresting officers.* If the target has prior arrests, you may want to interview the officers to determine if the target has a tendency toward violence. Is the target predisposed to commit the crime you are investigating? Is there any other information that will help you conduct your investigation?
- *Interview the source of the original information.* If you received the information about your target through a complaint or informant, you may want to

interview this person. If there was a source in a previous investigation you may want to interview that source.

- *Interview district officers.* If your target is active in a given area you may want to interview the officers who work that area. The district officers have a vast amount of information available to you for the asking.
- *Interview detectives.* If prior cases are found, you may want to interview detectives assigned to those cases. Request any background information that they have.

Traffic Unit Records: Keep in mind that many people in society have had contact with a traffic unit. A vast amount of information is available in this area.

- *Accident reports.* Pull out incident reports involving accidents. Identify vehicles, persons involved, passengers, and insurance companies from the records.
- *Traffic tickets.* Search for traffic tickets and identify locations, vehicles, personal information, and patterns (such as day, date, and time of day).

Communications: Communications can provide a wealth of information. Each dispatcher knows the hot spots in a given area and can provide other information, such as:

- *Runs to a targeted address.* Again, key on what type of run was dispatched.
- *Complaints.* What types of complaints are received and who are the complainants? If you can identify who called, you may be able to create an informant to help in the investigation (Figure 2.2). Following is an example of a complaint for which the motivation is obviously a cry for help.

I am writing this letter to the gambling vice squad. My husband is losing all his money to this restaurant called XXXXXXXX where I understand the owners Rick and Evon and their son who is the front for these bookies are paying off the vice. I'm told this by my husband. I read about you arresting people for gambling, and I do know that people who run bars can lose their license for gambling, but you close your eyes to this one place. I hear every bookie and gambler in the city hangs in this place. The main office is in the home at XXXX N. Kessler. I never hear of that place being raided. Why not? Also, a Keystone XXXXX is in with bar XXXXX. They work back and forth out of these three places with this man, Bob, they say owns this deli.

Rick and Evon are the top bookies in this city, and will never be arrested because they pay off. Also, I hear the Vice hangs in there too and place bets. I want this letter to go to you, the Prosecuting Attorney, and ask you why don't you clean up the whole city, not just the small guys. Go after the top bookies. You can get all the big ones, bookies and gamblers, in one area. Then maybe my husband just might come home with some money instead of owing all his money and losing it at XXXXXXXX.

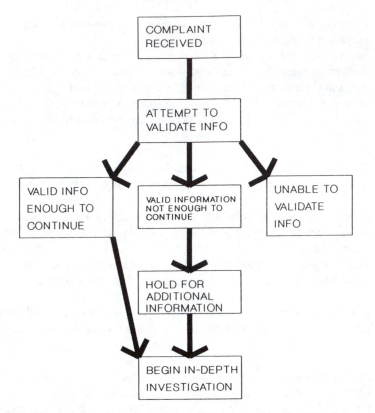

Figure 2.2. This chart demonstrates the process to follow to determine if a full scale investigation should be conducted.

You would sure do a lot of us at home who need this money to pay our bills and put food on the table for our children a great favor. I notice these people live very well on our money they take from my husband's heavy betting.

- *Crisscross location.* The crisscross is a book used to cross reference addresses and telephone numbers. If you have a telephone number, look up the number and it will list the address. If you have the address, look it up to find the telephone number. If the telephone number is unlisted, it will not be there. You will need a subpoena or court order to obtain it.

Vice Unit Records: Vice unit records can provide information as to personality problems identified as part of your target's profile. Look for:

- *Records of prior complaints.* Look for complaints by address and by name. Look for associates, vehicles, and locations involved. Attempt to identify the source of the complaint and see if this source can be used to assist you in your current investigation.

- *Identify any specific activities noted at the target location.* Information on activities may provide needed insight which can be used to infiltrate the group or provide the motivation for the crimes involved.
- *Prior investigations.* Identify prior investigations involving the target and/or location. Attempt to identify patterns, prior involvement, and predisposition to commit the crime you are investigating.

Outside the Department

Use of informants: Use informants to help validate information received. When using informants to validate, do it in such a way as to not reveal to the informant what your exact target is.

Information from other police agencies: You may be able to validate information by contacting another agency and asking if they have any information, past or present, which would lead you to believe that your information is true.

Information from court records: Identifying court records such as probable causes and court transcripts may validate the information received.

Information from probation: Information from probation officers may lend itself to the validation process.

Information from welfare: Welfare workers can be a good source of information. They see the target in a different light and may be able to assist you with your case.

City licensing: Local licensing boards can provide information that can help validate the original complaint.

Keep in mind that while you are conducting the initial background, you are looking for information that leads you to believe that your target is in fact involved in the illegal activity provided in the complaint.

Once this task is done, your next step is to enter the phase which will provide you with information for your probable cause and possible infiltration. If you decide to continue into Phase II, all the information you have obtained up to this point will be plugged into Phase II.

Phase II

The following are some steps you should take to show that the activities by the individual and/or business are indicative of an illegal operation.

Remember that you need the following: (1) information for criminal prosecution, (2) information for civil forfeiture (assets), and (3) information for IRS (state and federal).

Subpoena Telephone Records

- *Request subscriber information on phone number:* Subscriber information tells you to whom a telephone number is listed and the address. When you receive the subscriber information, you need to conduct a background on the name and address.

- *Request information on the number of telephones at the location.*
- *Request toll records:* Toll records list all long-distance calls from a specific number and all collect calls coming into it. When requesting toll records, request the ones for peak months which will give you the best information. For example, if you are looking at a bookmaker who works the telephones only during football season, you would not necessarily need tolls during baseball season. When you receive toll records, look for special features such as call forwarding. If they have this feature, you may need to verify where the target is when you have him on the telephone. You should check the amount of the bill and try to identify your target's contacts, both in-state and out-of-state. This information may come in very handy. *Note:* While you conduct your investigation, you should always be on the lookout for persons involved with your target who can be turned into witnesses against your target. The more witnesses you end up with the easier the case will be to bring to court.

Business Information

In most areas, the state will have a central location for corporation information. In most situations this is public record and you can get it over the telephone, in person, or by mail. When requesting information about corporations, request the following:

- *Ownership information:* Normally they will give the names and addresses of the officers of the company and any other ownership information.
- *Agent of record:* The agent of record is the person, normally a lawyer, who represents the corporation in that given area.
- *Subsidiaries:* Attempt to determine if the target corporation is a subsidiary of another corporation. If so, identify what other holdings are included in the parent corporation.
- *Financial statements:* Request a financial statement of the corporation and use it to assist in forfeiture in the case.

Assessor's Office

The assessor's office is an office at the local level which is responsible for assessing the tax value of property. Its name may vary, but the function will be similar.

- *Property ownership:* Request ownership information of the property which you have targeted. Request information as to length of ownership and previous owners.
- *Maps:* Request a map of the land description and other holdings of your targeted subject.
- *Other holdings:* Request a list of all land holdings in your given area which are listed to your target and his relatives.

Utilities

Request information as to who is billed for the address. Check to see if there are other names listed on the bill. Use the billing to establish residency. Keep in mind you want to bring about property forfeiture and assist the IRS, so you need to note assets which are listed to or paid for by your target.

Intelligence Branches

If you have an intelligence branch, use them to help your investigation. If you do not have one at your agency, you may be able to get help from a state-level law enforcement agency. An intelligence unit is charged with gathering intelligence and filing it in a retrievable fashion.

- *Suspect information:* Request information that would demonstrate that the target has had prior involvement in criminal activities. Key on prior cases which are similar to the case you are investigating.
- *Associates:* Request information as to associates known to be active with your targeted subject.
- *Prior informants:* Request information as to any informants who were used in the past. Under normal situations, they will not provide you with the names; instead, they will contact the officer who handled the informant in the past and ask that officer to contact you.
- *Other officers:* Request the names of other officers who may be able to give you information.
- *Link analysis:* Request assistance in the analysis of links between individuals, links between businesses, links between businesses and individuals, and links between telephone numbers.

County Recorder's Office

The recorder's office is where property deeds are recorded.

- *Deeds:* Request the deed for the property that you have targeted. Identify who the seller was and the purchaser.
- *Mortgages:* Request information as to who holds any mortgages on targeted property. Once you identify the bank that holds the mortgage you can then go to the bank and get further information.
- *Lead information:* When dealing with the above agencies, you are trying to gather information that will lead you to another source. Once you go through several sources you should have a complete understanding as to who your target is and what he is into.

U.S. Post Office

Federal policy as it pertains to *mail covers* includes the following:

- Information obtained from a mail cover is restricted and considered confidential.

- Mail cover information is to be used as an investigative tool only.
- Mail cover information cannot be used as evidence in court. It is provided as a source of lead information only.
- You should not refer to mail covers in court testimony.
- In order to obtain a mail cover you must submit a written request.
- In an emergency, a verbal request for a mail cover is acceptable, but it must be followed up by a written request (Figure 2.3).
- Mail covers can be issued only to law enforcement agencies.
- Mail covers should not be used as a sole or initial investigative tool.
- Target must be under investigation for a crime which has a penalty of 1 year or more in jail.
- Mail covers are restricted to uses which protect national security, locate a fugitive, or acquire evidence of a crime punishable by 1 year in jail.
- Mail covers record only the information found on the outside of the parcel of mail.

Mandatory information required to obtain a mail cover is as follows:

- *Mail cover justification.* To justify the use of a mail cover you must state your purpose for obtaining a mail cover. You must state what evidence you expect the mail cover to provide, and you must state reasonable grounds for the need for a mail cover. You need to state what information you have about the case (information from informant). Be specific.
- *Target identity.* Identify all subjects at the address in question and list all persons that should be covered by the mail cover.
- *Mail classification.* List all types of mail that you are requesting the mail cover to affect. The types of mail dealt with are (1) First Class (letters); (2) Second Class (magazines and newspapers); (3) Third Class (bulk mail); and (4) Fourth Class (books and parcels).
- *Time frame.* You need to list the time frame for which you want the mail cover to be in effect.
- *Criminal violation.* List the criminal violations you are investigating and list the specific code for the violation.
- *Legal representation.* If known, you must list the name of your target's lawyer. Mail between the target and his lawyer is exempt from the cover.
- *Daily documentation.* You need to specify how often you want receipt of the cover information.
- *Special instructions.* If there are any special instructions of request you should note them in this area.
- *Signature block.* In this area you should list your name, title, department, and telephone number and then sign above your typed name.

When dealing with mail covers you must remember that all forms are the property of the U.S. Post Office; any reproduction of the forms is prohibited.

Address all correspondence to:
Chief of Police,
   North Alabama Street
Indianapolis, Indiana 46204

POLICE DEPARTMENT
CITY OF

Mayor

```
January  XX, 19XX


Regional Chief Inspector
U.S. Postal Inspection Service
Main Post Office Bldg.
Chicago, IL  60607-5401

Attn: Management Operation Support Center


              Restricted Information

This  is  a  request  for  a  mail cover to acquire evidence of a
commission of a crime.   Through  the use  of an  informant and a
covert investigation, we have found that stolen property is being
purchased by the following person.   The property  is believed to
be  stored  at  his  address  and business and at another unknown
rented location.  Also,  we are  investigating the  laundering of
monies through various financial institutions and businesses.

The  subject  of  this  request has purchased stolen or purported
stolen property from our informant and this detective.   The cover
subject and the cover business are:


              (AND ALL OTHER NAMES)


              (AND ALL OTHER NAMES)


              (AND ALL OTHER NAMES)


All other  names should  be covered because recidivists often use
aliases  or  family  member names.   Mail  delivered  to  these
addresses  will  be  intended for XXXXXXXXXXXXXX,XXXXXXXXXXX(wife
and co-owner), or  to  the  XXXXXXXXXXXXXXXXXXXX.   No  one else
receives mail at these addresses.

First class  mail is  requested for  the cover  because bills and
business transactions are delivered in this category.

Cover is requested for 30 days, to begin immediately.
```

"Police and Community - Partners in Crime Prevention"

Figure 2.3. Examples of mail covers.

Any use of the forms in court is prohibited, and always avoid any reference to mail covers in court. The requesting official must maintain security of the forms.

Trash Searches

Since the Supreme Court has given law enforcement permission to use trash to gather documentation of illegal activities, you may find yourself digging

Address all correspondence to:
Chief of Police,
    North Alabama Street
Indianapolis, Indiana 46204

POLICE DEPARTMENT
CITY OF

Mayor

(page 2)

Our investigation concerns possible violation of I.C. 35-45-6,
Racketeer Influenced and Corrupt Organizations; violation of I.C.
35-43-4-2, Theft; receiving stolen property; violation of I.C.
35-43-2.3, "Dealer"; dealing in altered property. The penalty
for each is 8 years, 3 years, 3 years respectively. XXXXXXXXX has
not been indicted, but if he is formally charged during the 30
days requested, you will be promptly notified to terminate the
mail cover.

We are unaware of any legal representation for XXXXXXXXXXXXX.
However, if this information becomes available, the name of his
attorney will be relayed to you at once.

Forms 2009, INFORMATION CONCERNING MAIL MATTER, will be needed on
a weekly basis. We will not copy these forms. They will be
returned to you within 60 days of the mail cover completion date.

Respectfully submitted,

XXXXXXXXXXXXXX
CHIEF OF POLICE

Thomas I. Black, II
Detective
Property Recovery Unit

XXXXXXXXXXXX Police Department
Phone: (317) XXX-XXXX

"Police and Community - Partners in Crime Prevention"

Figure 2.3. (continued)

through refuse on a daily basis. You cannot imagine the vast amount of information that you can get from a person's trash. You should key on any information
that shows banking transactions, bills to be paid, assets, deliveries, and any item
that can be construed as indicative of an illegal operation.

You should take safety precautions when you begin to look through the trash.
You should have rubber gloves and some way to cover your nose and mouth to
prevent inhaling anything in the trash. Working up a trash case is a nasty job, but
the officer who does it will be more successful than the one who does not.

If you are working a residence, you should determine when the trash is set out for pickup. Go by and identify the type of bags used by your target, and then go through the area and find matching bags. Take the bags from this location and switch them with the ones that your target puts out. This technique will provide you with enough information to get a search warrant on your targets.

If you are working a bar, you want to be able to identify what trash came from which day. To accomplish this, place a piece of cardboard in the dumpster in such a way that when trash from a given day is placed in the dumpster, the new trash will be on top of the cardboard. With this you will be able to show what trash was dumped when.

Case Example: *Trash Search*

A 73-year-old woman was receiving handwritten notes dropped off at her house in the early morning hours. The notes consisted of sexual and threatening comments along with Polaroid pictures showing a white male naked from the waist down. The letters stated that he was watching her and he was going to break in and have sex with her. This case was passed through several units before we received it.

We observed the following in the photographs:

1. The interior of the room where the picture was taken had a sharp-peaked roof.
2. The picture showed three cartons of cigarettes, all the same brand, sitting on a table.
3. A unique type of wallpaper was on the wall of this room.

In the letters, the subject stated he had observed the victim through a specific window. We went outside and determined that only four houses in the area could see into that window. We proceeded to the alley at the rear of these residences and began looking in the dumpsters behind each residence. We found the following items in one of the dumpsters:

1. Three empty Polaroid film packages.
2. Two empty cartons of cigarettes of the same brand in the picture.
3. Handwritten notes similar to that of the letters in question.

We checked backgrounds on this location and found that a mother and son lived there. The son was 23 and worked nights. We approached the house and talked to the mother and asked to talk to the son. She refused to cooperate so we stated we would like to limit the embarrassment to her son by not having to get warrants. The son came out and agreed to talk. We told him we needed to talk so his mom would not hear the embarrassing parts of the investigation. The subject invited us up to his room. His room had a very sharp peak, the wallpaper was the same as in the photos, and the Polaroid camera was on the bed. In a small room off the bedroom was located a long telescope on a tripod. As I looked through the telescope, I realized it was pointing directly into the window of the victim. This subject was arrested and confessed. Without the trash, we had little if anything to tie up this case.

Initial Surveillance

Once you have gathered some information on your target's activities, you should be ready to conduct some surveillance to reinforce your probable cause. Initial surveillance should cover the target to identify his daily routine. Your first objective is to determine if he is in fact at the locations and involved in the activities you were informed of. Identify who the target meets and at what location. You should conduct a background on each.

If possible, insert an undercover officer at each location that a meeting is held. The officer should attempt to identify what activities occurred. Identify any vehicles used by your target and any and all vehicles used by subjects that are met. When conducting an initial surveillance, you should have a form designed to provide a simple way to make sure that the person keeping the surveillance notes will not inadvertently miss an item of importance.

This log should also contain the types of vehicles the plates were on, the vehicle the plate is registered to, and any other information or observation that is received (Figure 2.4). You never have too much information. Sometimes information that is gathered seems to be insignificant at the time, but proves to be important on the day of the warrant.

When conducting surveillance, a variety of things need to be done at the same time: license plate logs and description of vehicles, video and/or 35-mm of suspects and vehicles, and logs of observed activities.

With all this going on, it is easy to miss something. As a suggestion, you might want to use a tape recorder and record descriptions of people and vehicles as they appear. If you do this, make sure that whoever is responsible for recording this information writes it down as soon as possible. A minicassette recorder is a very valuable tool, especially when you need to get multiple license plate numbers at a given location. Remember that you want to identify witnesses against the target. You do not want it to be you against them.

City Controller's Office

The city controller's office is responsible for issuing licenses for everything from street vendors to house alarms. This office can be a valuable source, but you need to be aware of the possibility of information leaking out to your target. Remember that each time you seek information, you need to weigh the value of that information against the risk of a leak. If the risk is too great, do not seek the information.

Building Inspectors

Building inspectors are responsible for enforcement of codes in a given area. They may be able to provide blueprints of a building. They also issue construction

DATE: _____

TIME: _____

LOCATION: _____

CASE: _____

PLATE #: _____   VEHICLE: _____

                              REG: _____

                              SSN: _____

                              ADDRESS: _____

     D.L. CHECK BY SSN: _____

                        _____

     BACKGROUND PRIOR CASES: CASE # _____

                        _____

PLATE #: _____   VEHICLE: _____

                              REG: _____

                              SSN: _____

                              ADDRESS: _____

     D.L. CHECK BY SSN: _____

                        _____

     BACKGROUND PRIOR CASES: CASE # _____

                        _____

Figure 2.4. Vehicle plate log.

permits. You should build a relationship with them and identify what they can do to assist you in future investigations.

Welfare Office

Welfare workers can provide you with a large amount of information which could assist you in your background case. Information may be requested, but release is dictated by local policy.

Better Business Bureau

The Better Business Bureau provides information to the public at no cost. You can request information about a subject's involvement in congames and rackets, general information on subjects and businesses, and other information related to complaints filed against them.

State and Federal IRS

Federal IRS is able to assist in investigations where taxing information is involved. They can help track currency transaction reports (CTR), bank information, and other information if the law allows its release.

You may find that, due to federal limitations, you may be able to get more information from a state-level revenue office. If you have a state revenue office, I recommend that you start with them. The federal IRS investigates tax fraud relating to income tax, excise tax, and occupational tax.

Credit Card Accounts

When credit card accounts are located you may want to request the monthly statements. On the statement you will find payment due, date, account number, credit limit, date of transaction, reference number, locations where items were purchased, cash advances (may have a transaction photo), amounts of each purchase, and balances.

Example:

Trans.	Reference no.	Purchase	Amount ($)
6–23	123456J98765	PT Shoes, Tampa, FL	260.00
6–25	X17295F42173	Old Motel, Ft. Meyers, FL	75.00
6–25	123456789101	Ben's Bar & Grill, St. Petersburg, FL	27.50
6–26	76543T104010	Glen's Jewelry, Orlando, FL	5000.00
6–27	X01732198460	Gas Station, Montgomery, AL	28.25

With the information provided on the monthly statement, you can track your subject all over the country. This information can lead to other investigations. For example, you are investigating a narcotics dealer and you come across a telephone number which was called. During the conversation, negotiations for a purchase of narcotics were made. All you have is the phone number.

- Request subscriber information from the phone company. They provide you with a name and address.
- Work the address through surveillance, trash search, or mail cover and identify the bank the subject uses.
- Request records pertaining to credit card applications and brands of credit cards in the target's possession.
- Ask for monthly statements from nonspecific credit cards (ones that can be used anywhere for anything). You may receive statements which show the target stayed at a specific hotel in a specific town.

- Contact the hotel and request what ID was used to check in, who else was listed in party, what vehicle and plate were listed, and what telephone numbers were called from the target's room.

You are now in possession of telephone numbers of contacts in the area around where the target stayed. You also have numerous other bits of information which can lead you to needed information.

Hotel and Motels

Information which can be provided by hotels and motels is varied, depending on the quality of hotel or motel involved. Typical information that can be provided is

- Identification provided at check in. This may include copies of the identification.
- Other members of the party, each may have provided identification.
- Telephone records of calls to and from the rooms assigned to your target (these numbers may give you co-conspirators or other contacts involved in the illegal enterprise).
- Credit records on subject.
- How payment was made. (Keep in mind that legitimate businessmen want receipts. If everything is paid in cash, you need to look very closely at why.)
- How were reservations made and from where? Were there other reservations made? Check whether vehicles were reserved or rented.
- Vehicle descriptions and plates.

Voter Registration Office

Information found at the voter registration office can be used to get a sample of handwriting in a forgery case, and it can be used to establish residency. The registrar can provide the affidavit of registration with the signature of the affiant; name, age, and address; and occupation.

Federal Courts—U.S. District Courts

Every state has a U.S. District Court, and they have broad jurisdiction over law violations in the United States. They also have jurisdiction over bankruptcy. The files located in the District Court Clerk's office are easy to search, and most investigators concentrate on the case records, the minutes of the case, and the dockets. As you go through the files, you will find the docket sheet is a summary of what took place in the case, in the order it was presented. Use the docket as a quick reference source.

As you do your background remember the other courts that may provide information.

Securities Exchange

The Securities Exchange Commission provides information on corporate securities offered for sale to the public. Request information on financial statements of the company, officers of the company, ownership information, accountants' names, business history, and any violations noted.

Other Federal Agencies

The Department of Agriculture keeps records of food stamp serial numbers, which can be traced back to the issuing office. Request the name, address, and history of the person to whom the stamps were issued.

The Department of Defense can provide backgrounds on subjects, including their training and specialty.

The DEA enforces laws pertaining to narcotics violations and maintains records on users, dealers, and distributors of illegal narcotics.

The FBI can provide criminal records and fingerprints, national stolen property index, and national fraudulent check index.

The Post Office is a source for mail covers, photostats of postal money orders, and post office box subscribers.

ATF (Alcohol, Tobacco, and Firearms) offers a complete list of federal firearms license holders, a list of federal explosives license holders, the ability to track a firearm from manufacturer to dealer if made after 1968, and information on known bootleggers.

U.S. Customs provides information on import/export businesses and suspected violators.

The Secret Service maintains handwriting samples of known forgers and records on counterfeiting U.S. currency.

Source Contact List

A source contact list is nothing more than a list of the people and/or businesses you deal with during your investigation. Each time you contact a source of information, make note of who you deal with. This information should be kept on a source contact list so you can retrieve it quickly. Remember, if a person or business provides you with valuable assistance, you should have a letter of appreciation sent to them from your department head. This will assure their cooperation in the future.

BANK RECORDS

In 1976, the Supreme Court ruled that bank records were no longer privileged information. With this ruling and the passage of the RICO Act and the Money Laundering Act of 1986, bank records have become one of the most important ways to identify the assets of a criminal organization. Law enforcement is allowed to track illegal enterprises using banks to identify flows of currency. Banks generate a vast amount of paper for each transaction; for example, when a deposit is made the following documents are created: teller tape and proof sheet, original deposit slip, and microfilm copies of statement, deposit slip, cash in/out ticket, vault book entry, bank security film, and copy of the CTR. As you can see, there is a lot of value in knowing where to look and what to ask for.

To be an effective investigator, you must have a general idea of what can be obtained from bank records and how to use this information. In most situations, records can be obtained with a subpoena or a search warrant for the requested documents.

When requesting documents from a bank, be diplomatic in the way you request documents and keep in mind that the bank can charge for the service. Since this can be a major deterrent to how many items you request, you should request only the most important items. If you do not go overboard, you may not be billed, but if you are in doubt, you had better ask. For an in-depth look at what is offered from banking records, you should contact:

BJA Asset Forfeiture Project
Police Executive Research Forum
2300 M Street, Suite #910
Washington, D.C. 20037

Ask for their series on Asset Forfeiture, particularly no. 6: *Tracing Money Flows Through Financial Institution,* by Charles Morley.

What You Should Request

When requesting information from the bank, it will be easier to attach a list to the subpoena that denotes what you are requesting. My first request would include (1) a list of all accounts and the application for said accounts; (2) monthly statements for October, November, and December of 19___ ; and (3) signature cards on all accounts. With this information you can then determine what items of deposit and what checks you will need to see to conduct your investigation. Information from bank records provides you with sources of income to use in a financial analysis, leads to suspects and conspirators, and helps identify your target's assets for forfeiture.

Bank Statements (Checks and Deposits)

Once you have identified what account you want information for, you should request the name and address of the customer and the type of account. If you intend to freeze the account as part of your forfeiture procedure, you need to request the present balance in the account. Once you have this information, you can decide if a freeze is necessary.

Most checking accounts can provide the following: (1) account numbers, (2) monthly checking statements, (3) canceled checks, (4) specific dates of transactions, (5) past and present balances, and (6) all deposits and withdrawals. When requesting information, ask for checks front and back, and what made up the deposits noted. Also, you may want to request a copy of the application for checking.

Most savings accounts can provide (1) an application, (2) deposits and withdrawals, (3) monthly statement, (4) what made up the deposits, (5) signature cards, and (6) identification of all other accounts.

You should request copies of monthly checking and savings statements. These statements show transactions, deposits, and withdrawals that occur within the account. You may be able to establish patterns that will help track your target. If you can establish that your target picks up illegal money on Wednesday and a deposit is made on the same day, you can then forfeit anything purchased from this account.

As you look at the bank statement, you need to identify items that stand out; you can request copies of items which made up a deposit or a withdrawal on a date that is a key to your investigation, or an amount that is suspicious in nature. Once you obtain the checks, you need to chart them to identify patterns. Look for checks written to cash that show "for deposit only" on the back, or where your target uses two or more accounts on the same date and the checks total more than $10,000.00. You will need to identify into whose accounts checks were deposited to identify the checks recipients.

Other Information Banks Can Provide

You may be able to identify other sources of information from checking accounts, such as loans and credit cards. Loan records provide (1) the application, (2) amount borrowed, (3) amount of payments, (4) what collateral was secured, (5) co-signers, (6) references, (7) annual statements, (8) credit information, and (9) financial statements. The next time you are in a bank, request a copy of an application for a loan. You will see how much information is available from bank loan documents. A basic consumer loan application will ask for the following information:

Personal Information

Name	Previous Address
Date of Birth	Employer
Address	Employer's Address
Driver's License	Employer's Telephone Number
Social Security Number	W-2 Income Verification
Telephone Number	Occupation
How Long at Address	Supervisor's Name

Previous Employer and For How Long
Information on any Co-Applicant

Credit Information

Bank Name
Bank Address
Bank Account Number(s) for Checking and/or Savings
Name and Address of Landlord or Mortgage

    Property Titled Value
    Balance Owed
    Vehicles Owned and Descriptions
    Vehicles Financed by Whom
    Balance Owed
    List of Creditors (Present and Past)
    Collateral Description and Totals of All Outstanding Loans

With this information, you can take a substantial step forward in the gathering of background information on your target.

A mortgage application is also a valuable source of information. The following is an example of items required to complete a mortgage application:

1. Employer's address and name of supervisor (for husband and wife)
2. Banks' addresses and account numbers
3. Current mortgage company's name, address, and account number
4. All loans—names, addresses, and account numbers
5. Bond certification serial numbers and face or cash value
6. Stock certification—a copy of the stock statement from the broker
7. A statement from the insurance company regarding insurance cash value
8. Cost per month for child care
9. Divorce or separation documents
10. VA certificate of eligibility
11. Disposition of current real estate
12. Copy of canceled check for escrow deposit
13. Tax returns for the past 2 years

As you can see, with just the information provided in a mortgage application you can gather enough information to have a complete history of your target's finances.

Some other sources of information you may want to consider using are signature cards, safe deposit boxes, financial statements and credit reports, copies of promissory notes, certificates of deposit, records of purchases and payments, locations of ATMs where pictures are available, CTRs completed by the subject, bank films, copies of travelers' checks sales, assorted paperwork, other loans and investments, information on cashier checks, and wire transfers.

Signature cards are signed by the person who opens a specific account. This signature is used to authorize withdrawals and to cash checks. A signature card may provide information as to who introduced the customer, prior banking locations used by the customer, and where other accounts may be located.

Safe deposit box records provide (1) the application, (2) access records, such as the date and time entered, (3) signature cards, and (4) to whom the account is billed. If you get information about a safe deposit box, you should be prepared to secure it when you do your search warrant on your target.

What to Do With the Information

Once you have obtained bank records, be it from the bank or under a search warrant at the suspect's house, you need to identify what you have. The best way to accomplish this is to chart out those items that lend themselves to visual display.

Checking accounts are the easiest example to show (Figures 2.5A and B). You need to lay out checks by check number, date, amount, and from whom to whom. Example:

From: Doe	Check no.	1226	5–24–86	$1,600.00	*To: Apple*
		1227	7–10–86	$1,700.00	
		1228	5–24–86	$2,000.00	

As you can see, charting will provide you with questions to ask. In the above case, we asked why three checks in sequence were written to the same subject but the middle check was postdated 2 months. When dealing with several accounts, you need to show the flow of currency. See Figure 2.5C for an example.

One question generated by this chart is why a check from Smith to Doe on 8–14–86 for $4,000.00 was followed by a check on 8–18–86 from Doe to Smith for $26,000.00.

Keep in mind as you are charting checks that you want to develop enough information to prosecute the target and to identify those people who are involved whom you want to be witnesses. In the above case, T. Smith became a witness against J. Doe.

If you discover checks which have no endorsements and are for deposit only, you need to request the identity of the account in which the check was deposited. You then need to determine, "Is this person a co-conspirator and could he or she be a witness?".

Financial Crimes Enforcement Network (FinCin)

Financial Crimes Enforcement Network
3833 North Fairfax Drive
Arlington, VA 22203

When conducting a background, consideration should be given to requesting assistance from the FinCin system. This group was set up to assist law enforcement in developing intelligence relating to the financial side of criminal activity. Their purpose is to assist law enforcement in identifying potential criminal violations and locating fugitives.

They can provide information from databases both private and governmental, assist in analytical work, study financial crimes (such as money laundering), and provide information required under the Bank Secrecy Act.

Due to limited resources they have set up a prioritizing system.

1. Is the investigation a national or agency priority?

A. CHECKS FROM XXXXX ACCOUNT TO BETTORS 1986-1987

CHECK #:	DATE:	AMOUNT:	TO:
144	9-24-86	$3000	CASH
145	11-24-86	$5040	PAT
146	11-7-86	$2280	CASH
704	12-2-86	$1300	CASH
707	12-2-86	$6300	CASH
708	12-2-86	$6300	CASH
792	5-19-86	$6550	CASH
793	5-17-86	$1210	CASH
796	5-20-86	$1370	CASH
797	5-20-86	$1500	CASH
798	6-20-86	$1500	STAN
820	3-21-87	$1470	EARL
832	3-26-87	$830	CASH
838	3-26-87	$780	EARL
882	3-19-87	$2899	BOB
1226	5-24-86	$1600	ALVIN
1227	7-10-86	$1700	ALVIN
1228	5-24-86	$2000	ALVIN
1232	5-29-86	$160	FRED
1241	6-24-86	$520	STAN
1254	9-15-86	$2000	JIM
1265	8-6-86	$600	PERRY
1270	8-21-86	$2680	STAN
1282	11-24-86	$4990	PAT

B. CHECKS FROM ACCOUNT TO BETTORS: CHECKS FOR CASH AND ENDORSEMENT:

CHECK #:	AMOUNT:	ENDORSEMENT:
144	$3000	DEPOSIT ONLY
146	$2280	FOR DEPOSIT 8X9-71X-1
704	$1300	FOR DEPOSIT 8X9-71X-1
707	$6300	
708	$6300	
792	$6550	
793	$1210	
796	$1370	
797	$1500	
820	$1470	EARL
832	$830	DEPOSIT ONLY 8X9-71X-1
838	$780	EARL
1226	$1600	ALVIN 50594X1X
1227	$1700	. .
1228	$2000	. .
1254	$2000	JIM

Figure 2.5. Methods of charting checks.

C.

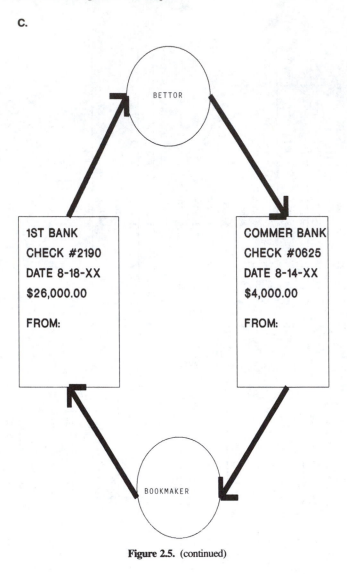

Figure 2.5. (continued)

2. Does it involve an organization or individual?
3. Is it national/international vs. local?
4. Is the target subject to forfeiture?

Each state is assigned a coordinator to assist in requests. The main contact telephone is (703) 516–0508. They should be able to provide you with a state contact and other information necessary to request assistance.

APPENDIX 1: BACKGROUND CHECKLIST
(PHASE I)

Computer Check
Name and AKA
Codefendants
By address
Case status inquiry
By SSN for vehicles
By family members
Associates
Check for prior police reports
Check property inquiry
Check for followup reports
Probable cause inquiry
Pawn inquiry
Alarm inquiry
Driver's license inquiry
Traffic ticket inquiry
Witness/suspect lists

Identification and Records Check
Check for prior arrests
Check nicknames or AKA
Obtain photographs and
    description sheets
Identify any gang affiliations
Identify any tattoos or scars
Identify any other identifiers

Interviews
Interview arresting officers
Interview source of original
    information
Interview district officers
Interview detectives

Traffic Records
Check accident records
Check traffic tickets

Communications
Check runs to targeted address
Check for complaints
Crisscross the address and
    telephone number

Vice Records
Check for prior complaints by
    address and person
Check activity in target area
Check investigations involving
    subject or address

Outside Sources
Informants
Other agencies
Court records
Probation
Welfare department
City licensing

Note: Look for information that leads you to believe that your target is involved in the illegal activity you are investigating.

APPENDIX 2: BACKGROUND CHECKLIST
(PHASE II)

Subpoena Telephone Records
   Request subscriber's information
   Request tolls
   Look for special features
   Identify out-of-state contacts
State Corporations Division
   Ownership information
   Names and addresses of officers
      of the corporation
   Agent of record
   Is the corporation a subsidiary of
      another?
   Request a copy of the financial
      statement
Assessor's Office
   Ownership of land, buildings, etc.
   Length of ownership
   Request maps
   Request locations of holdings
Utilities
   Who is billed?
   Where is bill sent?
   Establish ownership
Intelligence Branch
   Check files for prior involvement
   Prior associates
   Prior informants
   Link analysis
County Recorder's Office
   Deeds
   Mortgages
   Lead information
Post Office
   Mail covers
   Post office box information
Trash Search

Surveillance
   Cover peak activity time
   Identify vehicles
   Trips to the bank and other
      locations
   Meetings with co-conspirators
   Exchange of currency or other
      property
Bank Subpoenas
   Signature cards
   Applications for savings and
      checking
   Deposit slips
   Checks (front and back)
   Safe deposit box
   Loan information
   Credit cards
   Cashier's checks
   Wire transfers
   CTRs
City Controller's Office
   License information
Building Inspectors
   Permits for construction
   Blueprints
Welfare Office
   Case information
Better Business Bureau
   Congames and rackets
   Information on subjects
   Information on businesses
State and Federal IRS
   CTRs
   Bank information
   Subject information
   Business license information
   Tax information

APPENDIX 2: BACKGROUND CHECKLIST
(PHASE II, continued)

Credit Card Agencies
    Monthly statements
    Charge statements
    Application information
Hotel Information
    Identification provided at check-
        in
    Telephone calls made
    How bill was paid
    Vehicle description and plate
    Other members in the party
Voter Registration Office
    Affidavit of registration
    Name/age/address
    Occupation

Federal Court
    Case records
    Court docket
    Minutes of session
Securities Exchange
    Company financial statement
    Officers of company
    Ownership
    Accountants' names
    Business history
Federal Agencies
    FBI/DEA/ATF
    Secret Service
    Federal Aviation Administration
Your Source Contact List

3

Civil Forfeiture

Civil forfeiture began in 1970 when Congress enacted the Racketeer Influenced and Corrupt Organizations (RICO) and CCE statutes. In 1978, further expansion was achieved when Congress authorized civil forfeiture of any proceeds derived from narcotics trafficking in violation of federal law. State enactment of comparable provisions soon followed. However, although federal officials have pursued this remedy aggressively, its potential has not yet been realized by the states. Three factors may explain this phenomenon. First, federal forfeiture law is more favorable to prosecutors than most state statutes are. Second, federal resources exceed state levels. Third, there is the perception that forfeiture of profits is often impractical because with the absence of a monetary seizure concurrent with a narcotics transaction, the targeted asset must be traced to narcotics trafficking.

Although the exclusionary rule applies to forfeiture proceedings, untainted evidence may still be sufficient to meet the lower burden of proof. Indeed, civil forfeiture may be a viable option despite an acquittal on criminal charges.

The civil context provides other advantages as well. For example, prosecutors may resort to the discovery process to obtain information pertinent to tracing. The claimant may be deposed and disclosure of his records compelled. Perjury and contempt sanctions are potentially available against untruthful or recalcitrant witnesses. While the Fifth Amendment may still be asserted, a civil claimant risks an adverse factual finding by doing so. This possibility places the claimant in a particular bind if criminal charges against him are still pending. Involving the Fifth Amendment may result in an adverse factual determination, while answering questions may have incriminating consequences in the criminal proceedings. Regardless of whether criminal charges are pending, discovery is likely to provide useful information for impeachment if the claimant testifies at the forfeiture proceeding. Such testimony will often be necessary because, once the government's evidentiary burden has been sustained, failure to provide responsive proof will result in an adverse judgment.

WHY USE CIVIL FORFEITURE

There are many reasons to use civil forfeiture, however, the main one is to have a real impact on the criminal. We all know that the criminal with no prior arrests is not likely to serve time, let alone stop his criminal enterprise. The forfeiture of assets is the only way we can have a lasting impact.

ADVANTAGES OF CIVIL FORFEITURE

Standing: Before a subject can demand his property back, he must first establish standing. He must tell the court that the property in question is his and he wants it back. In many cases this can cause major problems for the criminal. If he claims standing, he also may be providing the IRS and other agencies with the evidence necessary to prosecute him. Whenever you do a case, be it a professional shoplifter or a fencing operation, you should attempt to get the subject to disclaim standing on tape. What we do is a walk-through with a video camera. As we walk through, we ask the subject, "Is that computer yours?". If he says no, we forfeit it. Ask additional questions, such as, "Where did the property come from?". You will be surprised how many will say they never saw it before.

In other situations where you have seized a large amount of property that you know is stolen but you cannot prove it, tell the subject he can identify the items he wants back. If he selects anything you find is stolen, you can place the charge on him. In most cases, the subject will only ask for those items back that he knows are not stolen.

Burden of proof: As you go through a civil case, you must keep in mind that the burden of proof is not beyond a reasonable doubt, but instead is the preponderance of the evidence (or slightly more than 50/50). This makes it much easier to make a forfeiture case than a criminal case.

Criminal prosecution: There is no requirement for filing a criminal case to make civil forfeiture. They are complete, separate cases and have no required tie to each other.

Deposition of defendant: One of the great aspects of civil forfeiture is the fact that you may depose the suspect and compel him to talk and/or produce records.

Fifth Amendment rights: You will find when you attempt to obtain a deposition from a subject he or she will raise the issue of self-incrimination. The beauty of the forfeiture statute is that a subject has the right to invoke the Fifth Amendment, but then risks an adverse finding by the court. If the subject decides to give a statement, it can be used against him in the criminal case. This also includes the situation where the subject gives evasive testimony; he again risks loss of assets.

Evidentiary burden of proof: Once the state's evidentiary burden has been sustained, the burden of proof shifts to the subject. The subject then must provide proof that the state's assertion is raised or there will be an adverse finding and he will lose the assets in question.

Areas in case law used in forfeitures include

- *Close proximity:* Items found in close proximity to narcotics are forfeitable.
- *Effort to conceal assets:* If you can demonstrate that the subject attempted to conceal assets, you can use this in the forfeiture.
- *Pretrial Statements:* Statements made to an undercover officer in reference to illegal assets may be used in the forfeiture process. If possible, try to have the undercover officer elicit information during the investigation which will assist in the forfeiture of assets.
- *Records of illegal activities.*
- *Evasive trial testimony.*
- *Net worth:* Demonstrate income vs. expenditures.

FEDERAL FORFEITURES

Property subject to forfeiture by the United States government includes the following:

- All controlled substances in violation of the federal statute
- All raw materials, products, and equipment of any kind that are used or intended for use in manufacturing, compounding, processing, delivering, importing, or exporting any controlled substance in violation of the federal statute
- All property that is used, or intended for use, as a container for property described in the federal statute
- All conveyances that are used or are intended for use to transport property described in the federal statute
- All books, records, and research, including formulas, microfilm, tapes, and data that are used or intended for use in violation of this statute
- All moneys, negotiable instruments, securities, or other things of value furnished or intended to be furnished in exchange for a controlled substance; all proceeds traceable to such an exchange
- All real property, including any right, title, and interest in any lot or tract of land and any appurtenances or improvements, which is used or intended to be used to commit or to facilitate the commission of a violation of this statute
- All controlled substances that have been possessed in violation of this statute

PLANNING FOR THE SEIZURE OF PROPERTY

When you enter an investigation where real property may be seized, be it through federal adoption or state level, you must make a determination as to whether you want to take possession of the property right away or allow the present owners to maintain it until the termination of the case. Issues that must be addressed are liability, upkeep, insurance, property sale, management of property, and possible contamination.

During the investigation, you need to research the ownership of the property to determine not only the value of the property, but also the equity the owner has in it. If there are several innocent mortgages and lien holders involved, you may want to just skip the forfeiture. Keep in mind that if you seize the property, not only do you have to maintain it (lawn mowing, repairs, insurance, etc.), but also you are liable for any injury and any damage that occurs during litigation. In addition if the target of the forfeiture is a business—such as a junkyard, service station, or chemical company—and you seize it, you may be required by the Environmental Protection Agency (EPA) to clean it up if contamination is discovered. This could be very expensive.

If the property is to be seized and renters are present, you may want to continue to allow them to occupy the premises. This will deter loss through vandalism. However, if you do so, you will need to address such issues as insurance coverage, maintenance, and payments by occupants. In most situations where we file forfeitures, we will have the court order the owner to maintain the premises in the same condition as when the forfeiture was filed. I recommend that you videotape the location and its condition so that you can show any violation of the court order to the judge. You should try to have a sale of the property timed so as to liquidate it as soon as possible after the forfeiture is upheld.

4

Shoplifting

One of the best sources of information about where and how stolen property is distributed is the professional shoplifter. In addition to fencing operations, the professional shoplifter will normally have a narcotic habit, thereby enabling you as the investigator to infiltrate both the fencing of stolen property and the narcotics trade in your area. In order to obtain the information necessary to conduct an investigation you must first be able to apprehend the shoplifter and then convince him or her to cooperate with you. Before you begin, you need to understand how shoplifters operate. The following is a short profile of shoplifting and what diversions are used.

HABITUAL SHOPLIFTERS

A person who steals for a living and has no other source of income or employment is a habitual shoplifter.

Characteristics of Habitual Shoplifters

Habitual shoplifters may attempt to steal large dollar amounts of merchandise; normally work in pairs or groups; have a long history for theft, drugs, and prostitution; talk about running returns; have no visible source of income; may be hard-core drug users and/or live out of cars or motels.

Information Possessed by Habitual Shoplifters

Habitual shoplifters know where the fencing operations are. They know members of other shoplifting rings. They also know persons involved in other crimes, such as drug dealers and credit card and check fraud artists.

Diversions Used by Habitual Shoplifters

There are several diversions used by habitual shoplifters:

- They attempt to confuse employees with nonsensical questions and requests such as, "Show me where the beer without yeast is." While the employee is distracted, the other members rip off the store.
- They will pretend to be ill and threaten employees with legal actions if employees do not assist.
- They will resort to any diversion to distract managers away from safes or registers, even exposing their body parts.
- They will pick up a homeless person at a shelter and offer him/her $50 to rip off specific items from a store and return them to the car.
- They will steal several items at each store, all being under $20 each. The lifter will then attempt to return items for cash.
- They will station one person in a vehicle outside the door of a store. The second will go in and grab an item and run out (*grab and dash*).
- Several subjects enter the store, with one person pulling the cigarettes and handing them off to a pusher whose job it is to hide them and leave the store (*puller pusher team*).
- They will use these items to hide stolen items: baby bags, baby strollers, large purses, and large coats.
- Several persons enter a store. All will pick up items and exit. Store personnel will be overwhelmed.
- They will make a small purchase with a large bill to see where the cash is kept.
- They will change bar codes on items.

STEPS TO BE TAKEN TO ATTACK THE PROBLEM

Two major steps may be taken to deal with shoplifting:

1. Obtain training in investigative techniques involving property crimes.
2. Make contact with businesses in your area and educate the security personnel involved in loss prevention. Training should include how to identify shoplifters, who to contact when a habitual shoplifter is caught, what processes are to be used in the infiltration of a fencing operation, what benefit is in it for the business, what dangers are involved, and what information is necessary to proceed.

If possible, involve loss prevention personnel in the investigation. This will greatly increase your success in the future. Whenever a person in security provides you with information, always write an appreciation note to him through his chain of command.

Tips for security include

- Watch for persons watching them.
- Check their clothing. Are they dressed for the weather?
- Check size of purse.
- Look for loose fitting clothes.
- Watch for nervous actions.
- Professionals conceal items right away.
- Check dressing rooms for items and loose tags.
- Know merchandise and prices.
- Identify areas in store suited for concealment.

One of the most important things for the investigator to do when looking at shoplifters as an information source is to get local businesses involved. Billions of dollars are lost each year through internal and external theft of merchandise (Figure 4.1). Businesses as a whole do not look to law enforcement authorities for help because they have never received any before. You as an investigator need to develop a coalition between law enforcement officials and the business community.

BENEFITS OF A COALITION FOR LAW ENFORCEMENT

Businesses are a political base and can assist investigators in clearing the way to conduct investigations. Millions of dollars each year are donated to law enforcement for investigative equipment by businesses. They can provide law enforcement officers with the information about suspects that is necessary to conduct a successful investigation. In addition, businesses can provide property to law enforcement authorities to conduct reverse stings. For example, in most retail businesses when an item is returned and it has been opened, the business will not repack it for sale. Instead they mark it as damaged and write it off at cost. If the same business donates it to law enforcement officials for use in a sting, they can write it off at the retail price.

Finally, businesses can apprehend professional shoplifters, notify law enforcement authorities, and allow us the opportunity to turn them into informants.

BENEFITS OF A COALITION FOR BUSINESSES

Businesses can receive training in the area of loss prevention and assistance in developing cases. They can receive tips from law enforcement officers as to how their store was targeted and what security changes are necessary to prevent future losses. Through an undercover investigation, businesses may be able to

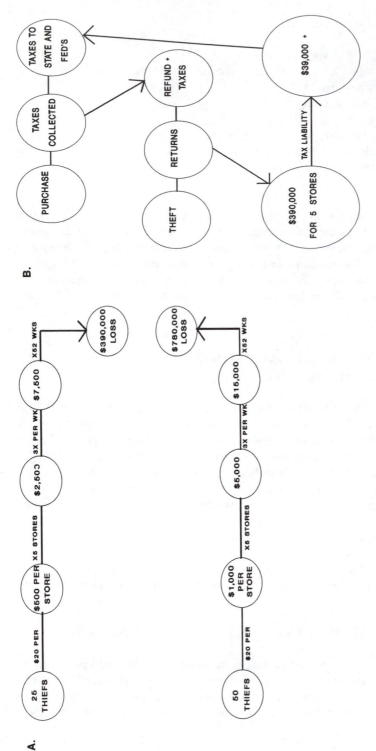

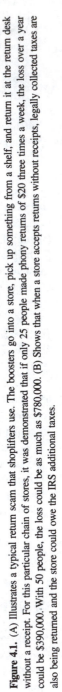

Figure 4.1. (A) Illustrates a typical return scam that shoplifters use. The boosters go into a store, pick up something from a shelf, and return it at the return desk without a receipt. For this particular chain of stores, it was demonstrated that if only 25 people made phony returns of $20 three times a week, the loss over a year could be $390,000. With 50 people, the loss could be as much as $780,000. (B) Shows that when a store accepts returns without receipts, legally collected taxes are also being returned and the store could owe the IRS additional taxes.

recover stolen property. They also can write off some current items and reduce future losses.

SECURITY AND LOSS PREVENTION SURVEYS

The purpose of these surveys is to identify and document areas of needed improvement to protect persons and property.

While conducting your investigations you will have a lot on your mind and each thing will have a different level of importance. If possible as you conduct your investigation, be ever vigilant for procedures that need to be changed to limit losses and increase security on property and personnel.

A security and loss prevention survey is documentation of observations and suggestions to prevent loss. Your observations throughout your investigation, such as areas where customers could become injured, are only part of the survey. The survey should also cover the following:

- Outside lighting, such as that at loading docks and parking areas
- Size of lunch containers, for example, one sandwich in a grocery sack
- Stocking procedures
- Dead spots in camera coverage
- Information from interrogations
- Information about techniques used in thefts
- Diversions used
- Packages that are used to hide items
- Identities of known thieves
- Recommended procedures to combat losses
- Recommended training

Surveys should contain anything that might have an effect on injury and or loss. When your case is completed, you should submit your observations and recommended changes to the affected organization.

Important: One of the most important sources of loss prevention information is the thief. Part of your case should be dedicated to drawing out the above information from him or her.

A FINAL WORD ABOUT SHOPLIFTING

Shoplifting terms include: boosting, rip, steal, lift, pinching, and hooking.

Remember that drug use is a major factor in professional shoplifting; because of this, safety is jeopardized. Always expect a violent confrontation. Prepare yourself and never take unnecessary risks.

Case Examples of Informants

CASE EXAMPLE 1: SHOPLIFTER

Complaint

A telephone call was made to Crime Stoppers on July 28, 19XX. The motivation was money. The complaint stated that John Doe (w/m/30), who lives at 123 W. 3rd, is actively involved in shoplifting in the area. Doe steals from drugstores and sells the stolen items to a fence on the east side of town.

Doe steals on weekends early in the morning and then delivers the items to the fence. The address of the fencing operation is unknown, but it is supposed to be a car lot with approximately 20 cars on it.

Background

Subject: His name is John Doe (w/m/30), who lives at 123 W. 3rd.

Computer check: This finds a prior arrest for shoplifting, no reports by address, and a negative area check.

Bureau of Motor Vehicles (BMV): A 1987 Chevrolet pickup (red) is listed to Doe at the address.

Assessor's Office: Doe is the owner of the property, with the mortgage company listed as Jones Mortgage Company. Doe has been owner of property for 7 years.

Intelligence branch: This organization has no record of John Doe by name or address.

Identification and records: We obtained a picture of Doe; no other information was present.

Tactical Plan

We planned to place Doe under surveillance on Saturday and then track him to the store to observe the theft. Next we would allow Doe to return to his vehicle and proceed to his home, where we would confront him and attempt to get him to cooperate. Our surveillance also should validate the complaint.

Priorities

Our goals were to confront Doe after the theft and attempt to get him to introduce us into the fencing operation. We also hoped to identify any other criminal entities with which he is associated.

Surveillance

July 28, 19XX

0850 hours	Doe leaves his residence
0910 hours	Doe arrives at parking lot at 246 W. 11th and enters the drugstore.
0911 hours	Detective follows and observes Doe steal several bottles of perfume.
0918 hours	Doe leaves the drugstore and is videotaped emptying his pockets into his pickup truck.
0920 hours	Doe leaves the parking lot and proceeds home.
0943 hours	Doe arrives at home and is confronted by detectives.

We recovered over $200 in perfume and began our interrogation. Doe decided to cooperate; he gave us information about the person who was buying the stolen property from him, and introduced us to him.

Information Received from Informant

Background

Subject: His name is John Smith; his residence is at 1111 Dee Street. A-1 Auto Sales is located at 1108 Dee Street.

Computer check: Smith has no prior arrests. He owns both addresses plus seven lots in the area that are listed on reports. An area check shows a large number of resident burglaries.

Bureau of Motor Vehicles: Five vehicles are registered to Smith, all at his residence address. He has an auto dealer license issued for the current year.

Assessor's Office: Smith is listed as the owner of the business and residence with no liens.

Intelligence branch: Intelligence had a prior complaint on Mr. Smith, stating that Smith was buying stolen property from burglars in the area.

Identification records: No photo is on file.

Traffic records: Two tickets have been written to Smith, with all identifiers entered.

Corporations' division: A-1 Auto Sales is not incorporated with the state.

Tactical Plan

We planned to get the police officer introduced to Mr. Smith. Then we would make five or more sales of purported stolen property to Smith, obtain a vehicle from the lot for purported stolen property, and make sales at the business and residence. The final goal was the forfeiture of Smith's assets.

Priorities

Our top priority was to always provide for the safety of undercover officer(s). Keeping that in mind, we would arrange to have the officer introduced to Smith, and would try to weed out informants. We also needed to identify co-conspirators and to obtain photographs of Smith.

Case Results

August 7, 19XX (1150 hours):

- Informant and detective arrived at A-1 Auto Sales with a large quantity of cigarettes.
- Smith was informed that the cigarettes were stolen. Smith offered $4.00 a carton.
- Detective asked what kind of stuff Smith wanted them to rip off. Smith stated he needed camera equipment, VCRs, and 35-mm film.
- Payment for the property came from a register in the business.

August 10, 19XX (0940 hours):

- Detective arrived and entered Smith's residence. He sold two VCRs and five rolls of 35-mm film.
- Detective stated it was easy to rip off the store because their security was at lunch when he arrived.
- Smith placed another order.
- Payment came from a small safe in the master bedroom of Smith's residence.

August 15, 19XX (1400 hours):

- Location is A-1 Auto Sales.
- Smith purchased 4 three-packs of 35-mm film, 6 bottles of perfume, and 50 cartons of cigarettes.
- Detective again informed Smith all the above items were stolen.
- Smith ordered 35-mm cameras.
- Payment came from the business register.

August 17, 19XX (1400 hours):

- Detective delivered three VCRs to Smith at A-1 Auto Sales.
- Detective stated he had walked out of a department store when no one was looking.
- Smith paid detective out of his left front pocket.

August 21, 19XX (1145 hours):

- Detective delivered 11 bottles of perfume to Mr. Smith and stated he had ripped them off from a drugstore on the east side.
- Smith stated he would take any more that he could get.
- Detective discussed the possibility of trading the stuff he brought to Smith for a car off the lot. Smith agreed.

August 25, 19XX (0900 hours):

- Detective arrived at Smith's residence with three VCRs purported to be stolen.
- Smith bought them and ordered more.
- Money came from Smith's pocket.

August 26, 19XX (1410 hours):

- Detective contacted Mr. Smith by phone and informed him that he had just ripped off $4,000 worth of 35-mm cameras.
- Smith told him to bring them over right away.

1450 hours:

- Detective arrived and informed Smith he had placed the cameras in a chest at a department store and then went through the line. The chest cost $19.95 and they never knew what he had inside.
- Smith traded him a car off the lot for the cameras.
- We then served the search warrants on him for the business and residence.

The end results of the case were

- Fencing operation forfeited 16 vehicles.
- Property worth $40,000 was seized.
- Defendant was convicted of multiple felonies.
- IRS filed a case on subject.

CASE EXAMPLE 2: SHOPLIFTERS AND NARCOTICS

A department store security person who had detained a shoplifter who wanted to cooperate called our department. We responded and determined that this subject was able to make a purchase of coke for us at 123 N. High Street. We conducted a preliminary background check and determined that the threat level at the location was low.

Next we wired the informant and sent her in to purchase coke, which she did. Over the next few days we continued to use the informant for purchases which resulted in the arrest of three dealers and the seizure of $10,000 in cash and property. All this was made possible because of an interview with a shoplifter.

CASE EXAMPLE 3: TAVERN FENCING

The information source was a professional shoplifter.

Information

This shoplifter stated that an east side tavern owner was involved in the purchase of stolen property from shoplifters and burglars in the central Indiana area. The owner, Mr. Jones, was known to buy from at least 50 people. The shoplifter agreed to assist us in the investigation.

Background

Computer check: We found that Jones had prior arrests for distribution of pornography and for gambling-related offenses. We also found reports referring to two taverns and two "dirty" bookstores, all owned by Jones.

Bureau of Motor Vehicles: We identified three vehicles registered to Mr. Jones.

Vice Branch: Records showed complaints against Mr. Jones for pornography, bookmaking, possession of illegal gambling devices, and fencing. From the records, it appeared the two taverns were used for fencing and gambling and the "dirty" bookstores were used to launder the illegal money.

Alcoholic Beverage Commission: We identified Mr. Jones as the owner of both taverns. Also, we obtained copies of the retailer's permit, the renewal form, and other pertinent information, in addition to copies of complaints from prior investigations.

Assessor's Office: An 11-year ownership of the property was listed to Jones with no liens. We also obtained information on other properties owned by Jones.

Intelligence branch: We found it was common knowledge that Mr. Jones was involved in illegal activities. We obtained names of two officers who had information about Jones.

Tactical plan: We planned to use an informant as an agent of the police and record sales of purported stolen property and to identify the size of Mr. Jones' operation.

Priorities: Our goals were to protect the informant; to provide for the safety of the officers; and to obtain enough information for issuing a search warrant and enough conversation for filing forfeiture. In addition, we would identify co-conspirators and other thieves, return property seized to the owners, and assist the IRS in their case.

Case Results (Time Frame 2 Weeks)

Monday (Sale No. 1): The informant was wired with a recorder and sent into the tavern with cigarettes and perfume. Conversation was obtained as to their prior transactions and requests. Mr. Jones was asked what he wanted the informant to steal. Jones requested telephone answering machines, one pair of denim blue jeans (size 38 × 32), and several other items such as cigarettes. Contact was made with a department store in the area which offered to donate the items needed to complete the case.

Tuesday (Sale No. 2): The informant contacted Jones by telephone and informed him that she had the stuff he wanted her to steal. Jones told her to bring it over. (Conversation on the telephone was recorded.) The informant, with body wire and minirecorder on, entered the tavern with the requested items. The transaction was recorded and Jones placed another order for stolen property.

Sale No. 3 through No. 5: These were conducted and a search warrant was obtained for the tavern. We recovered the following items: numerous handguns and rifles, 181 grams of marijuana, 9 televisions and cameras, plumbing equipment, 11 chain saws, depth finders and fishing equipment, 5 musical instruments, 7 microwaves, 3 generators, cordless telephones, and a large quantity of alcoholic beverages. The items seized were valued over $40,000.

End results: We returned approximately $25,000 worth of merchandise to local businesses, forfeiting all other items for use in stings. Jones was arrested for corrupt business influence and several other felonies. Forfeiture was filed. We received, in addition to items seized, Mr. Jones' Lincoln Town Car and $17,500 in cash. Mr. Jones also was charged by the IRS.

CASE EXAMPLE 4: EMPLOYEE THEFT

Complaint

We received a telephone call from a woman who offered to provide information about a subject who was ripping off furnaces from a business on the west side if we would promise that he would never know it was she who told. We agreed.

She provided the following information about the suspect: Bill Smith (w/m/ 30) lived at 876 East Hill (garage in rear), and drove a company truck.

Smith would drop off furnaces at his garage on a regular basis and then sell the furnaces for $150. The informant could introduce us to Smith if necessary.

Background

Computer check: No prior incidents were found by name or address.
Bureau of Motor Vehicles: Two vehicles were owned by Smith.
Identification and records: There was no listing for Smith.
Assessor's Office: The residence was rented by Smith but no other properties were listed.
Communications: No runs were listed to his address.
Intelligence branch: There was no listing for Smith.

Tactical Plan

Have the informant introduce an undercover officer to purchase a furnace. Videotape the transaction and verify that the furnace is stolen. Attempt to see whether suspect has additional items for sale.

Priorities

Protect the informant's anonymity and the safety of the officer. Obtain enough information for a search warrant. Interrogate and identify co-conspirators.

Case Results

- The informant was instructed to contact the suspect and to set up a purchase of a furnace by our detective.
- Surveillance was set up on the garage before the detective's arrival.
- Detective arrived in black pickup, paid the suspect $150, and assisted in loading the furnace in the truck.
- A second detective pulled up with the pretense of asking for directions. The second detective observed a 2 in. wide strip of paper on the side of furnace with a serial number on it.
- The detective observed other furnaces present.
- After the purchase, we checked the serial number and found that the furnace was stolen.
- We obtained a search warrant for the residence and garage, where we seized seven upflow furnaces, three heat pumps, and other items.
- We conducted an interrogation and obtained a confession. During the interrogation, we identified three other employees who also steal items from the business.

▬ ▬▬▬
US Attorney General
Federal Building
Indianapolis, INdiana 46204

Dear Mr. ▬▬▬,

I am wondering if you can tell me why the biggest bookmaker in town on
football games only is never bothered. Everyone know him and he is seen
mixing with Public Officals on a friendly basis quite often. If you are
really doing your job you will get a wire tap immediately on 783-▬▬,
although I believe a scrambler is used. If you raid his residence on any
Saturday or Sunday just before football kick-off you will find all the
necessary information to indict him. I can assure you he has plenty of
friends in high up places including many newspaper reporters and
policeman friends. Let's see how well you are at your job? It has to
be done before the end of football season because he then spends his
winter in Los Vegas and Florida. Let's see you get the big fish
instead of playing games with the little fish and letting the big ones
get away. The name is Dave ▬▬▬, ▬▬ ▬dison Avenue, Indianapolis,
Indiana 46227. Although he is pretty smart, if a a net worth check
was done on him by the IRS I am confident they could get him on
tax evasion charges too. I will be watching you for results.

Copies to:
Supt of State Police
State Office Bldg
Indianapolis, IN 46204

Chief of Police
Indianapolis Police Dept
100 N. Alabama Street
Indianapolis, IN 46204

Figure 5.1. Actual letter received in reference to a large bookmaker in the area.

- We then placed a body wire on the subject and had him return to work and
  engage in conversations with the other suspects. Three arrests were made as
  a result of this investigation.

In this case, we protected the informant by using the second detective's observations of the undercover buy. The second detective wrote the warrant from
personal observation of two white males loading a furnace with serial no. 123456
on it. The second detective then told how he had verified it was stolen through
the company.

CASE EXAMPLE 5: SPORTS
BOOKMAKING INVESTIGATION

The investigation began after the State Police submitted a complaint that had
been received in the form of a letter (Figure 5.1). The complaint noted that copies
were sent to the Superintendent of the State Police and the local police chief. The

complaint contained the following: (1) the name and address of the biggest book-maker (according to the writer); (2) the fact that the bookmaker had friends in high places, some of whom were reporters and police; (3) the telephone numbers used by the bookmaker and the fact that a scrambler was used; and (4) the suggestion that a net worth check be done on the bookmaker.

With the receipt of this complaint, Phase I of the investigative procedures began. As this case began, a second complaint was received from the local newspaper (Figure 5.2).

The second complaint cited the address and telephone number of the book-maker in the first complaint, that he had a membership in a big country club, and the fact that he takes bets up to $25,000 on a single game.

Phase I

After entering the bookmaker's name into the computer, this information was found. Over the last 40 years, John Doe had been arrested for gambling offenses several times. Interesting was the fact that all charges were listed as either no affidavit or judgment withheld. A close relative of John Doe was arrested for bookmaking 3 years prior. No complaints were found when a check by address was conducted, but John Doe had recently bought his location. In a check for license plates, none were found on file for Doe.

Pictures and files of Doe were obtained from the vice branch which covered the incidents involving the relative of Doe and Doe himself. Several paid inform-ants were contacted and asked whether they had any information on a subject bookmaking in the area of Doe's residence. Each informant we talked to identified Doe as having been involved in bookmaking for years. Several officers were contacted who had conducted investigations involving Doe in the past. They stated that it was common knowledge that Doe was an active bookmaker.

At this point and time, with the information obtained in Phase I, there was enough to conduct a full-scale investigation into the sports bookmaking operation of John Doe.

Phase II

The first step in Phase II was to obtain a subpoena and serve it on the telephone company, requesting both subscriber information for the telephone number that was in the complaints and toll records for the 3 months preceding the date the complaints were received. The 3 months requested were the end of football season and into basketball season.

From these subpoenas, several details were discovered. The telephone number that was provided was listed to John Doe at the address listed in both complaints (remember you are validating your complaint with the information you obtain). In addition, the toll records received showed calls to Las Vegas, NV; Louisville, KY; New York, NY; points in Florida; and Birmingham, MI. Along

January 18, 19

SPECIAL LETTER TO CITY EDITORS:

          AND SPORTS EDITOR

Dear People;

You have been the victims of a great big hype, a blowup and
inflated phony news about a big gambling bust and quote the
word "big". Many top officers in the dept. think those 2
eager beaver vice squad guys Kennie and Hudson are glory
happy and literally nuts . . . would give the death penalty
for jay walking . . .

They overheard a guy betting on a pay phone one day in a
bar, accidentally. They said they wanted to bet too so the
guy gave them Tony's phone #... Tony's operation was a
peanut small time operation with few big bettors if any
other than Schlictor---who probably never even paid them.
Tony was being financed by a prominent lawyer and this guy
Austin---I played golf a lot with Tony and worked there too
for a little while 'til I could see the handwriting on the
wall...There are at least 8 or 9 bookmakers in Indpls much
bigger and they are local people and have been doing
business here for 20 or 30 years. The biggest was even
invited to join a Golf   Club and joined it a few years
ago. He books bets as high as $25,0000 per game there and
frequently 5 grand or 10 grand per game...hell, they play
cards like gin rummy and poker every afternoon there for
thousands of dollars and on a Sat. afternoon thousands
change hands...

Those bettors Kinney had arrested are peanut bettors. They
could have all avoided arrest if they wold have told him

Figure 5.2. Complaint to local newspaper.

about other bookmakers. I never heard of little betters
getting arrested...Tony hasn't got any money he may tell
about others if they don't help him with his lawyers fees,
etc. One little guy lives with a diabetes diet, can't drink
or have se, and his only pleasure is betting a few football
and basketball games---so they arrest him and take that
pleasure away...he never hurt nobody his whole life...Please
tell Paul   , Joseph   and
especially Marc   to check on that phone stuff
about "Direct phone conections to Detroit and New
York"---what does that mean? They make it sound like mafia
and the best way to get Mafia in here is to get our local
books out of business...They made it sound to the reporters
like they had phones like the White House red phone to the
Kremlin..."direct phone connections"---A HUGE BUNCH OF BULL!
"And they also found narcotics"---MORE BULL...maybe one of
the helpers smoked pot but Ive never seen any bookmaker get
involved with dope...they hate it like you do and the police
filled you with bull to make their story sound bigger/...
Their figures are rdiculous too---they don t understand
betting and how numbers are arrived at...NOTE: they waited
to arrest these little people until they had an athlete's
name so they could draw your attention to this bull... Tell
Mr. Hall   about that guy Hanr   pleading guilty and
getting out with $10 fine and $50 court·costs...that makes
it a big headline deal, doesn't it? Vice Squad commander
ought to put Kennie and Hobson out stopping dope among our
school children instead of arresting legitimate citizens,
doctors, lawyers whose only fault is to bet on a football
game or basketball game to pleasure their TV interest in
sports.....this letter is just for your info...the big big
deal was a hype by police and a little deputy
prosecutor...and you fell for it.

Figure 5.2. (continued)

with the above calls were calls to sports line services, this being indicative of a sports bookmaking operation.

On contacting the county assessor's office, we discovered that the address listed in the complaints was listed to John Doe for the prior 6 months. The power and light companies were contacted; we were informed that a second address was listed to the same piece of property. The piece of property in the complaint was a corner lot with a street running on the north side of the property and another street on the east side of it. John Doe had intentionally placed an address on his house from both streets in an attempt to cause problems with anyone trying to write a search warrant. (This is not uncommon for a bookmaker to try to deceive you in this manner. In another incident, a bookmaker in the 2300 block of a street placed big incorrect numbers, 2127, on his house. Remember to always check and cross check your location.) In this particular situation, with two addresses, simply list both addresses on the search warrant.

We had no opportunity to infiltrate this organization, due to the fact that John Doe only took bets from regulars. An attempt was made to make a bet through an informant, but this was unsuccessful. This assured us that John Doe currently was and for years had been very active in sports bookmaking.

We conducted an initial surveillance on the residence to get a description of the property and to identify potential problems with any future entry. The residence had iron burglar doors on all doors and windows. On the corner of the house you could see numbers denoting an address on the north street, with another set of numbers on the opposite corner of the house denoting an address on the east side of the street. This was noted, and photos were taken of both addresses when the search warrant was served.

Additional information was needed to be able to obtain a search warrant for the location. A trash collection and search was attempted through the city of Indianapolis when trash was to be picked up in that area. (It so happened that the next day was when this occurred.) We went out early in the morning and observed John Doe placing two dark green trash bags at the curb. We went around the neighborhood and obtained bags of equal size and color and proceeded to Doe's residence. Using our vehicle as a screen, the bags were substituted.

A subsequent search of the bags turned up the following:

- Mail addressed to Doe's address (*very important to be able to demonstrate that the trash was in fact Doe's trash*)
- A sports schedule with the point spreads written in the spaces
- Telephone bills listing calls to a line service in Michigan under Doe's name
- Gas bill with the false address on it
- Lotto tickets (5) from out of state
- Several copies of *Gambling Times* addressed to Doe
- Mailings from "Sports On Satellite" to Doe
- Membership information for the country club listed in the complaint
- Information and pictures within one paper showing Doe with several people including politicians and police

We contacted several informants who did a little background search. They found that John Doe was still actively involved in sports bookmaking at his residence. They further stated that John Doe had a fairly elite clientele and was known to take bets as large as $25,000 on each game.

With all this information, we contacted the Prosecutor's Office and obtained a search warrant for John Doe's residence. The total length of time to take this case from a complaint to the search warrant was 10 days.

What Was Recovered in the Search

Among the items recovered in the search were six cashier's checks: four for $9,500.00 dated 1–16–87, one for $9,900.00 dated 2–13–87, and one for $900.00 dated 1–16–87. All but one of these checks were dated on the same day and signed by the same bank official; however, no CTR was done notifying the government of this transaction.

Also found were three legal-size pages of descriptions and limits on 40 bettors and other bookmakers. These varied, but the following are typical examples:

- Steve—$100–300, nice guy, honest, has awning company
- Fred Doe—Phones for home and office, $500–2,000, good customer
- Micky Doe—Too much trouble, small, not a very good customer
- Mike Doe—Fairly large book, very good customer, lays off and plays, has never been slow or late, any reasonable amount OK
- Wind Doe—Books honest, plays very little
- Tin Doe—Honest, bets moves-middles, $100–1,000, always has been good, but is a little irritating
- Jim Doe—Attorney, small but very good, home and office phone
- Bob Doe—Bad customer, pass him but he owes us if you got a chance collect, ex-Sheriff, home tx
- Chuck Doe—This guy will be a great customer in the future when he gets a hold of more of the family money, $500 player, has money
- Dr. Mike Doe—Has a lot of money, young and square
- Gary—$500–2,000, middles-moves, settle by mail
- Pat Doe—Fellow up by Chicago, he wants to be your buddy, will play whatever you will take

When you find a list like this, you should ask yourself why the bookmaker made this list. In most cases, he has to pass his book to a friend or a relative when he goes out of town and he wants them to know how to treat his customers. In each of the listings, the bookmaker cited a home and a business telephone. This makes it really easy for you to contact witnesses. Remember that you can offer them the opportunity to be a witness or a defendant. Note also that in some of the listings, they specify that the settle up is done by mail. This may be of interest to the postal authorities.

Other items found included numerous bettor total sheets listing how much each bettor owed, when and how much was paid, and any future settle up dates;

approximately 100 betting records ranging from $500.00 on a game to a doctor who lost $27,500.00 on a bet of Denver +10 for $25,000.00; numerous envelopes with bettors' return addresses on them; one legal-size sheet listing 40 bettors' home addresses; and a cashier's check receipt from the Bank of Nevada for $31,931.07. Finally, a large number of cancelled checks and statements were found. Among the cancelled checks, a larger number than normal were written for cash with even-numbered amounts. The reverse side of the check had been endorsed by people listed on the bettor description sheet. There were also several checks written by or to bettors which appeared to attempt to hide the total amount.

Analysis of Bank Records from Doe's Residence

How did Doe run his financial dealings through the banks? Figure 5.3 demonstrates that John Doe ran his illegal sports bookmaking operation by utilizing two separate banking facilities. One was on the north side and the other in the county south of his residence. By doing this, he felt that we were unlikely to identify both locations in our surveillance. As noted, the north side bank was the one that John Doe would send a runner to with personal checks from bettors to be exchanged for cashier's checks, these being hidden in the residence. This bank was "in his pocket" due to the fact that the manager was willing, for whatever purpose, to cover any transaction that Doe requested. The south bank location was the account that John Doe used to pay his bettors who were located outside of town. On checking, we found that personal checks from bettors would also be deposited into the second bank. This led us to believe that the first bank was used to hide income and the second bank was to pay gambling debts.

The U.S. Treasury Department was contacted in Indianapolis, and we provided the information about what was occurring. They began an investigation which paroled the case for the duration. Once this point was reached, a subpoena was obtained for both banks and the following documentation was requested:

- All checks over $200.00 written to cash for the last 3 months.
- All checks issued from this account over the last 6 months, either to or endorsed by any of the bettors on the list provided
- All monthly statements issued for the last year
- More specific deposit items shown on statements that were seized under the search warrant.

When dealing with bank records, you should have some idea as to how you can chart the information you receive and have it make sense. You will end up with volumes of information, but only a small portion will be of importance to you. The following charting methods can be used to assist you in identifying patterns of activity within the information you are provided.

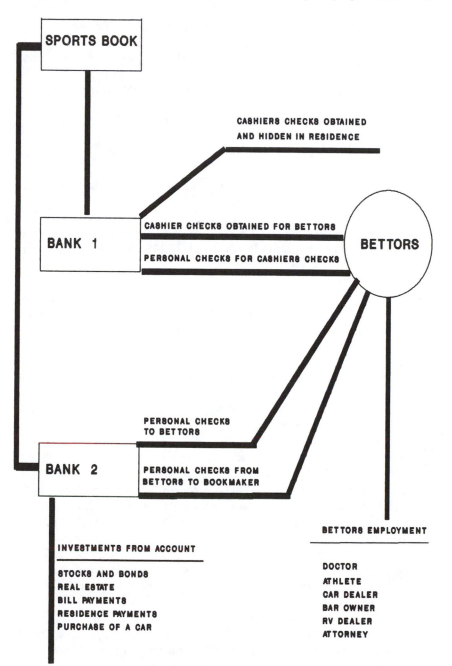

Figure 5.3. Sports bookmaking operation using two banks to launder illegal income.

Charting Checks by Check Number.   List data under these heads:

Check number   *Amount*   *Endorsement*   *Date*

This will give you patterns by check number, but you need to take it further.

Charting Checks by Date.   List data under these heads:

Date   *Check number*   *Amount*   *Endorsement*

This will give you pattern and evasion techniques where a bookmaker uses two or three different accounts or check pads.

Charting by Day of the Week.   This will sometimes give you information on settle up days and banking activities when you combine check information and deposits.

Charting by the Month.   This will give you the highest gambling times and possibly give you information on whether the bookmaker is involved year-round. Endorsements on checks may also tell you where the bookmaker is staying when he is out of town.

Once you have received the information you requested from the bank, you should attempt to chart out the banking activities and to identify any patterns that emerge. This particular case contained several patterns that resulted in the filing of criminal charges against one bank official involved. If you look at Figures 5.4 and 5.5 you can see several patterns emerge:

- Checks no. 704, 707, and 708 were written on the same day to cash and deposited in the same account but there is no sign of checks no. 705 and 706. Ask yourself why the total amount was not put on one check. You should request that the bank provide you with a copy of checks no. 705 and 706.
- Why were checks written from two different check pads, no. 1282 and no. 145 for a total of over $10,000 on the same date?
- Why were there three checks written to Alvin (checks no. 1226, 1227, and 1228)? Check no. 1227 was dated 2 months later than the other two.
- Why was Stan written three checks (no. 796, 797, and 798) on the same date? Two were to cash and one was to Stan.
- Why are checks no. 146, 704, and 832 written to cash with no endorsement on the back except for "deposit only" and an account number. You should request information on whose account that number goes to.

Once you have completed your bank charting, you are ready to call in the bettors and offer them the opportunity to be a witness or a defendant. This case resulted in the arrest and conviction of the bookmaker and the bank official. The bookmaker agreed to pay $400,000.00 in fines.

CHECKS FROM XXXXX ACCOUNT TO BETTORS 1986-1987

CHECK #:	DATE:	AMOUNT:	TO:
144	9-24-86	$3000	CASH
145	11-24-86	$5040	PAT
146	11-7-86	$2280	CASH
704	12-2-86	$1300	CASH
707	12-2-86	$6300	CASH
708	12-2-86	$6300	CASH
792	5-19-86	$6550	CASH
793	5-17-86	$1210	CASH
796	5-20-86	$1370	CASH
797	5-20-86	$1500	CASH
798	5-20-86	$1500	STAN
820	3-21-87	$1470	EARL
832	3-26-87	$830	CASH
838	3-26-87	$780	EARL
882	3-19-87	$2899	BOB
1226	5-24-86	$1600	ALVIN
1227	7-10-86	$1700	ALVIN
1228	5-24-86	$2000	ALVIN
1232	5-29-86	$150	FRED
1241	6-24-86	$520	STAN
1254	9-15-86	$2000	JIM
1265	8-6-86	$600	PERRY
1270	8-21-86	$2660	STAN
1282	11-24-86	$4990	PAT

Figure 5.4. A check chart showing the flow of money from the bookmaker's account to the bettor's. Note the questions generated by this chart, such as why two checks were written from different check books (#145 and #1282) to the same person on the same date. Look at the total of $10,030.

A civil Racketeer Influenced and Corrupt Organizations (RICO) action was filed by the prosecutor against this subject. This action was filed as part of the ongoing investigation into this subject's bookmaking activities. Three financial accounts were frozen immediately due to this action. Approximately $400,000 was frozen in place: Bank 1—$102,000, Bank 2—$266,000, and stock account—$22,000.

Summary of the Investigation

Two complaints were received. A computer check was conducted by name, address, and license plate numbers. Identification and Records obtained a picture and a criminal history. Several informants and officers from prior investigations were contacted. Telephone records and subscriber information were subpoenaed. Also, the County Assessor was contacted for ownership information and the utilities for billing information. Finally, surveillance was conducted to get a description of the residence, a trash search was conducted on two occasions, and a search warrant was obtained for the residence.

A.

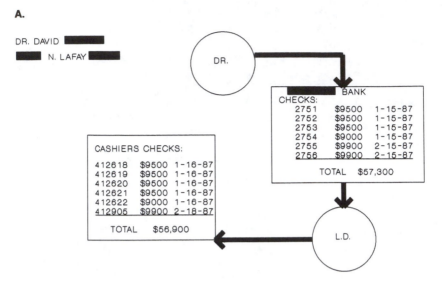

B.

CHECKS FROM ACCOUNT TO BETTORS: CHECKS FOR CASH AND ENDORSEMENT:

CHECK #:	AMOUNT:	ENDORSEMENT:
144	$3000	DEPOSIT ONLY
146	$2280	FOR DEPOSIT 8X9-71X-1
704	$1300	FOR DEPOSIT 8X9-71X-1
707	$6300	
708	$6300	
792	$6550	
793	$1210	
796	$1370	
797	$1500	
820	$1470	EARL
832	$830	DEPOSIT ONLY 8X9-71X-1
838	$780	EARL
1226	$1600	ALVIN 50594X1X
1227	$1700	" "
1228	$2000	" "
1254	$2000	JIM

Figure 5.5. Check charts showing a pattern of money laundering.

C.

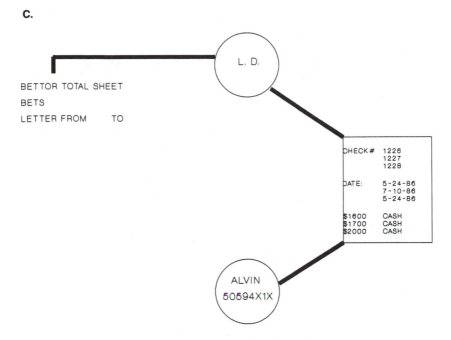

Figure 5.5. (continued)

CASE EXAMPLE 6: EMPLOYEE THEFT AND FENCING STOLEN PROPERTY

While we were working in the area of a shopping mall, Subject 1 approached and offered to sell a large quantity of current tapes and CDs. Subject 1 was asked how many he could get, and he stated his partner could get as many as we wanted. When we looked into the trunk of his car, we observed stickers on tapes from three different businesses. Two were in Indiana, but the third did business only in Michigan and Ohio.

We informed Subject 1 that we knew a buyer who might be interested in everything he could get. We asked for a telephone number where we could contact him and he stated that might be a problem. He gave us a telephone number but said that he would only be there for about 5 hours. He then provided us with five tapes.

We began conducting a background check and found the telephone number listed to a pay telephone in a tavern located near the shopping mall. We contacted the businesses listed on the price stickers and found that one tape came from Nebraska, three tapes were from the Indianapolis area, and one tape was from Ohio.

We asked the Ohio company whether these items could ever be found to-gether. They stated that this was possible only in a repacking plant. A repacking plant takes tapes from many different stores, pulls the stickers, and then resells them. We requested the location of any known repacking plants and found one located in Indianapolis.

We contacted Subject 1 by telephone and informed him we had a buyer for everything he had. We asked him when he would get more items, and he stated that his partner was to obtain a large quantity that night. We set up a meeting and met with Subject 1, where we attempted to identify his partner. We asked how hot the tapes were, and he stated that they were from all over but could not be traced. We then identified ourselves and asked whether he would be willing to cooperate. He agreed. He stated his partner worked at the repacking plant. He had talked to his partner that morning and was advised that the partner was going to rip off a large quantity of tapes before he got off work. Subject 1 further stated that he had been in his partner's house that morning and had observed approximately $10,000.00 in stolen tapes and CDs. Subject 1 stated that he was supposed to meet with his partner during his lunch break at the plant. We placed a body wire and recorder on Subject 1 and sent him to meet with his partner. We wanted the subject to find out how many other employees were stealing and whether his partner still intended to steal tapes that night. We obtained a search warrant for the partner's house based on the observations of Subject 1 while he was inside his partner's house that morning, and we waited for his partner to get off work. All in all, we recovered $15,000.00 worth of stolen tapes and CDs and forfeited the vehicle he used to transport the stolen property.

CASE EXAMPLE 7: NONSUFFICIENT FUNDS (NSF) CHECKS

Complaint

On January 2, 19XX, a subject entered an Indianapolis department store and purchased furniture, passing check no. 389 from Bank A. The subject requested delivery of the furniture between 8 A.M. and 12 P.M. the next day at 1234 N. Hills Drive. Taking the check, the clerk wrote down the following description of the subject: w/m, 6 ft., chunky build, short dark hair, name Joe Doe.

Background Investigation

This information was discovered during the background portion of this case: check no. 389 was from an account which was opened on July 31, 19XX, and was closed by the bank on December 20, 19XX, for insufficient funds. The name on the account was Joe Doe of 123 W. 4th Street. We obtained a Regiscope camera photo of the transaction involving check no. 389 and determined through the background check that a warrant for Joe Doe did exist for theft. We identified several more checks written to businesses where Doe had used the same account and several others, all of which were closed for NSF. Further, we obtained photos of other transactions where the same subject was involved. We conducted a photo lineup for the clerk who accepted check no. 389. She identified Joe Doe as the one who passed the check.

Tactical Plan

Our next step was to set up a tactical plan to deliver the items ordered to the address that Doe had listed. We arranged to borrow a company truck and have a list of items ordered. We then delivered the furniture and had Mr. Doe review the list and sign for them. The subject was arrested, and a search warrant was served on the residence for the items purchased by the other checks.

Probable Cause Affidavit

This detective, a police officer for the city, found the following information from his investigation, that on 01–02–XX, a person who identified himself as Joe Doe, 12345 Ross Drive, Indianapolis, Indiana, purchased merchandise from a department store in Marion County, Indiana; and for his payment for said merchandise, Joe Doe presented check #389 on Merchants National Bank Account #46799XXX, made payable for $483.00. Joe Doe requested that the merchandise be delivered to 1234 Hills Drive, Indianapolis, Indiana. According to the Bank, this checking account of which check #389 is a check was opened on 07–31–XX and closed by the bank on 12–20–XX due to insufficient funds to pay any checks.

The sales clerk who transacted this sale identified in front of IPD detectives a Regiscope photograph of a particular individual as the person who identified himself as Joe Doe. This Regiscope photograph is one of four that this affiant possesses. All four appeared to this affiant to be the photograph of the same person.

All four Regiscope photographs were related to incidents in which this individual passed checks that turned out to be either closed accounts or to have insufficient funds. These four incidents occurred in 19XX and all four incidents concerned checks on different bank accounts and or different ones used in the abovementioned incident. These four checks bear the name of either Charles J. Doe or Joe Doe.

On 01–11–XX this affiant along with other detectives went to 1234 N. Hills Drive and posed as deliverymen for the department store.

Upon arrival, undercover police officers were greeted by a person who identified himself as Joe Doe. Mr. Doe signed a delivery receipt and accepted delivery of the merchandise, to wit an entertainment center valued at $483.00.

Mr. Doe was then placed under arrest for theft on an outstanding warrant issued out of Municipal Court. He was advised of the Miranda warning and he admitted to opening the checking accounts at various financial institutions for the express purpose of defrauding said institutions and or retail merchants. He stated that he changed the account numbers on the magnetic strips located on the bottom of the checks in order to "confuse the banks" and in hopes "they would not catch on to me".

He further admitted to passing hundreds of checks knowing the same would not be honored due to the accounts having been closed or without sufficient funds to cover the draw and with the numbers having been altered in an attempt to hide the offense.

This affiant personally examined checks in the possession of Indianapolis police that had been written by Charles Joe Doe, several for which the account numbers were changed to make them appear to be that of a different account number.

Mr. Doe admitted purchasing the following merchandise with checks that he knew to be "bad": he admitted purchasing a portable compact disc player from a stereo company.

He further admitted obtaining a sleeping bag, a telephone, a set of luggage, and a 20-inch color television set from another department store.

Further he admitted purchasing a Minolta 3000I, 35-mm autocamera from ABC using a bad check.

He further admitted purchasing a pair of shoes from a store located in Chicago, Illinois, with a bad check.

He further admitted purchasing a pair of ice skates, ski goggles, ski gloves, ski pants from a sporting goods company with a bad check.

He further admitted to purchasing a wall mirror and wall hanging picture from a trading company with a bad check.

He further admitted purchasing linens, sheets and towels, and two floor speakers from the CDE Company with a bad check.

He further admitted to purchasing two men's shirts and an assortment of men's ties from the FGH Company using bad checks.

Further he admitted purchasing a dresser and shelves from the HIJ Store in Castletime using the above described checks.

He further admitted purchasing sweatshirts and a man's dress shirt from the KLM Company with the above described checks.

He further admitted to purchasing the above described entertainment center along with a watch, several pairs of expensive socks, two speakers, AM/FM stereo deck, a compact disc player, a component system and a VCR, and a large amount of cologne from a department store using the above described checks.

He also admitted to purchasing an expensive man's belt from a men's store using one of the above described checks.

Also, he admitted purchasing four men's polo shirts from a store located in Chicago, Illinois, using one of the above described checks. He also admitted purchasing two watches using one of the above described checks.

Further he admitted to purchasing a gold chain and two king size bed pillows from XYZ Company.

He also admitted purchasing ski socks and a ski bag from distributors.

Further he admitted purchasing an expensive queen size comforter from another store located in Chicago, Illinois, using one of the above described checks.

Also he admitted purchasing several assorted compact discs using the above described checks. He also admitted purchasing several sets of mini-blinds and smoke detectors from a department store using one of the above described checks.

He also admitted purchasing a brass bed, mattress, and box springs from liqui-
dators using one of the above described bad checks.

The value of the above mentioned merchandise is approximately $10,000.00.
These items were recovered from Doe's home after he admitted purchasing the
above items by the above stated means.

I hereby incorporate by reference the facts contained in the accompanying
information and swear and affirm that the facts contained herein are true and
accurate to the best of my knowledge.

Affidavit for Probable Cause—State of Indiana,
County of Marion, SS

This detective, a police officer for the city, swears, affirms, and has good
cause to believe from his investigation that he learned from a reliable person the
following facts and attending circumstances that:

On July 2, 19XX, a person identified as Charles Joe Doe, a white male, SSN
123–44–5678, DOB 01–02–67, of 1234 North Hills Drive, Indianapolis, Indiana,
appeared at XXXXX Department Store at 60 East 82nd Street and presented
check #3119, in the name of "Joe Doe" written on the Federal Savings and
Loan Bank in the amount of $50.00. This transaction was recorded on a Regi-
scope camera. On this check, the account number was altered to read
#98XXXXX91508, the correct account number being #58XXXXX91508.

On July 6, 19XX, Doe again appeared at the XXXXX Department Store, 60
East 82nd Street, Indianapolis, Indiana, and presented check #121 also written
on Federal Savings and Loan Bank, in the amount of $50.00. This transaction
was recorded on a Regiscope camera. On this check the account number was
altered to read #5869384XXXXX, the correct account number being
#5865384XXXXX.

On July 9, 19XX, Doe appeared back at XXXX Department Store at which
time he presented check #142 written on the Trial Savings Bank, Indianapolis,
Indiana, under account number 8679XXX, in the amount of $50.00. This trans-
action was also recorded on a Regiscope camera.

On July 27, 19XX, Doe returned to the XXXXX Department Store, and on
this visit he presented check #127 written on the Bank of Indiana, under account
number 53–03XXX, in the amount of $50.50. This transaction was recorded on
a Regiscope camera.

On September 18, 19XX, Doe traveled to XXXXX Department Store, located
at 102 East Washington Street, Indianapolis, Indiana, at which time he presented
check #127 written on the Bank of Indiana, under account number 5303XXX,
in the amount of $50.50. This transaction was recorded on a Regiscope camera.

All of the above checks were returned to XXXXX Department Store by the
various financial institutions due to insufficient funds and/or closed accounts.
The affiant personally compared the above Regiscope photographs with a pho-
tograph of Charles Doe obtained from the Police Department Identification
Branch. All of the photographs appear to be the same person, i.e., Charles Doe.
Further, all of the above checks were exchanged for United States currency.

On January 11, 19XX, this detective had an occasion to speak with Charles Joe Doe. After advising him of the Miranda warning, Doe admitted opening the checking accounts at various financial institutions for the express purpose of defrauding said institutions and/or retail merchants. Doe admitted changing the account number on the magnetic strips on the bottom of the checks in order to "confuse the banks" and in hopes "they would not catch me". He further admitted passing hundreds of checks knowing the same would not be honored by the banks due to the accounts having been closed or having insufficient funds to cover the draw, and the account numbers having been changed in an attempt to hide the offense.

6

How to Chart Investigations

As it progresses, each investigation should be charted.

You should chart associations of people and businesses involved. I have found that it is much easier to understand assorted information if it is in a pictorial format.

Once the investigation is completed, the assigned officer should provide charts for court presentation and charts which will be attached to case summaries (Figure 6.1, page 80).

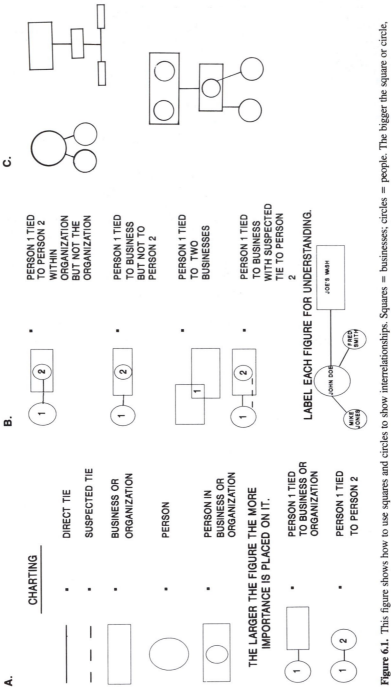

Figure 6.1. This figure shows how to use squares and circles to show interrelationships. Squares = businesses; circles = people. The bigger the square or circle, the bigger the business or person. A solid line from a person to a business indicates a direct tie; a dotted line would indicate a suspected tie.

Infiltration

QUALITIES OF AN INFILTRATION SPECIALIST

As you reach the stage where you intend to make entry into an illegal organization, consideration should be made as to who is the most appropriate infiltration specialist. The target and objectives of the investigation will have a major bearing on who is selected, but some general qualities which are necessary follow:

Adaptability: A good infiltration specialist must be able to react quickly to any situation that arises. You can train and practice for every foreseeable event to face the officer, but nothing can replace the officer who can react and think on his feet.

Good Actor: An infiltration specialist must be a good actor to be effective in the area of covert operations. It is easy to say that acting comes naturally, but in truth it is something that takes practice to be effective. In some situations, you are able to learn to act on the job and you learn by your mistakes; however, I feel that there is too much risk, both to the officer and to his self-confidence, to just say, "Go get them and good luck." The best way to get practice in acting is to assist your training branch when they have rookies in class. You need to send your people out to the academy and volunteer them to act out scenarios and assist in the critiques of the rookies' reactions to a given situation. Your investigators are more apt to learn because they are not under pressure to make an arrest, and it becomes fun for them.

Resourcefulness: Resourcefulness is similar to adaptability in that an investigator must be able to respond to questioning in a smooth and relaxed manner while at the same time closely monitor his conversation and attempt to anticipate the next line of questioning.

Good listener: Being a good listener runs hand in hand with being resourceful. An investigator must be able to carry on a conversation and hear what is being said around him. This may seem easy, but it is one of the most difficult things to learn.

Good memory: There is little value to information that is obtained during an investigation if that information cannot be remembered long enough to make notations. It is true that with modern body wires and recording devices you may always have someone monitoring and taking notes for the covert officer. The first time you depend solely on the body wire for information, though, you will find it is not working.

Confidence: Confidence is a key factor to the success of an investigator, and the best way for an investigator to obtain self-confidence is through training. You must stress that training is the most important thing that a department can provide. If the department limits the amount of training offered, then the investigations will be flawed and liability to the department will dramatically increase.

Good judgment: Good judgment cannot be taught. Either you have it or you do not. You can provide an investigator training in the area of planning and organization, which will help his judgment. If an officer can plan and organize an operation, he should be able to see the consequences of his decisions and his judgment will improve.

Creativity: As stated earlier in the book, creativity is the cornerstone to success. Seldom do you run across an investigation which plays out as planned. You need the ability to be creative in reacting to obstacles which come between you and your goals.

Covert photography techniques and equipment: Any undercover officer who is selected to infiltrate an organization should know or be taught how to operate and secrete camera equipment into an undercover setting. The purpose of covert photography is to get a visual description of the actual activity on film. With the major advances in 35-mm and video equipment today, this task is not as difficult as one might think. The major difficulty is convincing the department to purchase covert packaging for our equipment. Great pictures of gambling activities have been obtained in a bar setting by putting a 35-mm camera in a shoe box inside of a paper bag with a power wind and plunger-type activator to trigger the camera (Figure 7.1). You may not be able to use covert camera equipment in every situation, but you should know what is available. If your department does not have covert packaging, then you should meet with the major private investigation companies in your area. They will often rent or lend you the equipment necessary to conduct your investigation. Remember, the way to sell this equipment to your administrators is by demonstrating that money will be saved in court time, due to the fact that little or no testimony is necessary when you have all the evidence on tape.

Body wire and the use and operation of recording devices: It is most important that when using recording devices (such as minicassettes and microcassettes), you should first get a legal opinion on whether the recording of your conversation with another person is legal in your state. Always before you conduct any case, get a legal opinion on the techniques you intend to use. This goes for all techniques in all phases. Any covert investigator who is chosen should have training in how to put on a body wire and or recorder. The officer should be able to do simple trouble shooting on the equipment and make on-site repairs. Remember that the body wire is the lifeline to the troops when a line of sight surveillance is not available.

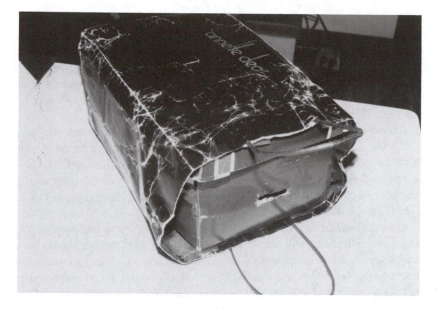

Figure 7.1. A shoe box inside a bag that was used to sneak a 35-mm camera into a tavern to take photographs of targets. The camera had a plunger firing mechanism and a power winder, and shot full frame pictures through the slit in the end of the box.

Willingness to alter appearance: An undercover person should be willing to dress up and at times dress down to fit a given situation. This may include getting grimy and living a role that is very offensive to most people. This area will be covered further in this chapter.

Ability to handle stress: A covert officer should be evaluated, be it formal or not, for the capacity to deal with stress. Covert situations, especially long-term exposure to stress, can not only destroy a family but also an officer. Someone within the unit should be assigned the responsibility of keeping a constant watch for signs that the covert officer is having difficulty dealing with his role assignment. If a change is observed, then the officer must be pulled from the case.

To summarize, a checklist for desirable qualities of an infiltration specialist includes (1) adaptability, (2) good actor, (3) resourcefulness, (4) good listener, (5) good memory, (6) confidence, (7) good judgment, (8) creativity, (9) covert photography techniques and equipment skills, (10) body wire use and operation of recording devices, (11) willingness to alter appearance, and (12) stress management.

COVER STORY

The establishment of a cover story is a very critical aspect of the investigation. An officer cover story must be able to stand up to scrutiny and yet be easy to assume by the covert officer. The extent to which you go to secure a cover from in-depth scrutiny will be dictated by the amount of time you intend the covert officer to be undercover. If he is doing a quick in and out, you may be able to improvise your way; however, if you intend to do a long-term investigation, you will need to lay a support network that will verify your cover if questions are asked. The following are some guidelines which will help to establish a cover story that will be comfortable for the covert officer:

Choose a cover story that is close to covert officer's real life: Once you have decided who is going to do the covert work, you should sit down with that person and identify skills and experiences that you can use to develop a cover. The best place to start is work experiences that may be used, such as experience as a plumber or electrician. You can build a cover as an employee of a business that conducts that kind of work.

Cover should be easy to assume: The cover chosen must feel comfortable to the covert officer or it will not work. The officer going undercover should have a major say in the development of his cover. Do not try to use a cover of a construction worker when your covert officer has soft hands with no calluses. The "bad guys" will know as soon as they shake hands with someone whether they have never lifted a hammer. Again, develop a cover that fits your officer.

Cover should be easy to remember: The cover selected should be second nature to your officer. You may need to put the covert officer through a questioning session to get him to respond effectively to inquiries. Things get very tense when you go in a telephone company shirt and someone inside your target works at the same location. The key to a confrontation with a person who questions you about your employment is for you to ask the questions first. For example, I once made an entry into a location as a telephone employee and was faced with another employee. He asked me if I worked for the telephone company and I said that I did. He then stated that he did, too. Immediately I asked him where he worked and he told me. I was able to demonstrate that I was from another office and things went well. If he had been allowed to ask me first where I worked, I would have risked a chance of naming the same place that he worked. Always be ready for confrontational questioning from both the targets and the citizens that frequent the location you intend to infiltrate. Again, putting your covert officers through a series of practice confrontations will help them dramatically when this situation arises.

Cover should be hard for the suspect to check on: Prior to providing your target with information on your cover story, someone in the unit should go over it to see how easy it will be to verify the information. If you use a business as a front, then you had better have someone there who will field any inquiries as to whether the officer does in fact work for them. Do not give so much information that they have an easy time. The "bad guys" should be forced to drag out the cover piece by piece so as to give the officer a longer time period to function under that cover. Limit what is volunteered in the way of cover information.

Use landmarks or cities only if familiar to cover officer: If you intend to use a city or a landmark as a location where you work or were born, you must be able to carry on a conversation about it. Every time a specific location is used, the "bad guy" or a patron will ask specifics about it. Be prepared.

The cover should provide the covert officer with flexibility: Never use a cover so limited that the covert officer cannot be flexible. For example, you may want to use the cover of being a construction worker vs. being an electrician. What will your response be when the "bad guy" wants you to wire his business? There may be a time when the officer wants to volunteer to help put in a telephone or do some other kind of labor to gain favor, but this should be done only if the covert officer possesses the skills. This is a good way to get other officers introduced into the organization. Once they help the bookmaker, they will be accepted.

A cover story that involves a job: The covert officer must be familiar with the type of work that is included in the cover story.

The cover story must be attractive to the bookmaker: This is where the background you have done on your target will help. Look for details such as where the target was born, where he went to school, what work experience he has, and what businesses he has, then try to build a cover that will incorporate them. It is like anything else . . . if you were born in the same state, like the same college football team, and drink the same beer, you will be friends for life.

The cover story must fit the location: If you intend to work a "hillbilly" bar, you do not choose a cover of being a professor at Harvard. You need to prepare a background on the location: identify what type of people live in the neighborhood, who frequents the location, which vehicles are driven, and what clothing is worn there. You should also study your target location during the time of day that you intend to frequent it. There is a major difference between the crowds at noon at a tavern and the crowds that frequent it at night. You want to select the dress and behavior that will be appropriate while you are actively involved at the location.

Cover Story Checklist

- Choose a cover story that is close to a covert officer's real life.
- The cover story should be easy to assume.
- The cover story should be easy to remember.
- The cover story should be difficult for the suspect to verify.
- Landmarks or cities used must be familiar to the covert officer.
- The cover story should provide flexibility to the covert officer.
- If a job is listed in the cover, the officer must be familiar with the work required.
- The cover story must be attractive to the suspect.
- The cover story must fit the location.

Supporting a Cover Story

Having a great cover story is never enough to get by. You must have supporting material to substantiate your role. This can be accomplished in two ways: false identification and role camouflage.

False Identification

False identification can be obtained from many sources, both official and unofficial. You can pick up any teen magazine and see advertisements for ordering a wide range of identifications. You submit the information you want on it with a photo and you can obtain a picture ID. Following are some pieces of identification that can be obtained.

Driver's license: In most states you can obtain a driver's license from the state if your administrator is willing to submit a request. You also can get one from underground sources or a teen magazine. Remember if you trust the state, you risk someone passing your information to the street.

Vehicle license plates: Vehicle license plates can be obtained in most states by submitting a request from your administrator. Some states are willing to give plates to law enforcement officers outside the state. Keep this in mind if you intend to use a cover that involves another state.

SSN card: For requests for Social Security Number (SSN) cards, contact the federal government for information.

Insurance cards: Most insurance companies will cooperate with a police agency and provide a card for covert work. Keep in mind that if you intend to show this card, you should have an agent whom you trust to verify that you are insured with the company under your false name.

Birth certificates: Birth certificates can be obtained through magazines and papers. They also can be obtained through the state on request.

Bank account information and documentation: Bank account documentation can be obtained by opening an account and depositing currency. This is especially good for situations where you are in a position to settle up with a bookmaker. If you can pay for gambling debts with a check, you can track it through whatever account it passes and possibly seize all items in and bought through that account.

Video clubs: Video clubs, in most cases, can be joined for free and they give you a membership card. Although it is the type of material that one would expect to find in someone's wallet, keep in mind at times you may have to give your wallet to the bookmaker on demand. This may make the bookmaker feel a little more comfortable with you. You should avoid having a sterile wallet which only contains formal identification. You should have pictures, receipts, and other miscellaneous items which are common to most people's wallets.

Check stubs: Having check stubs from the business that you supposedly work for is very valuable.

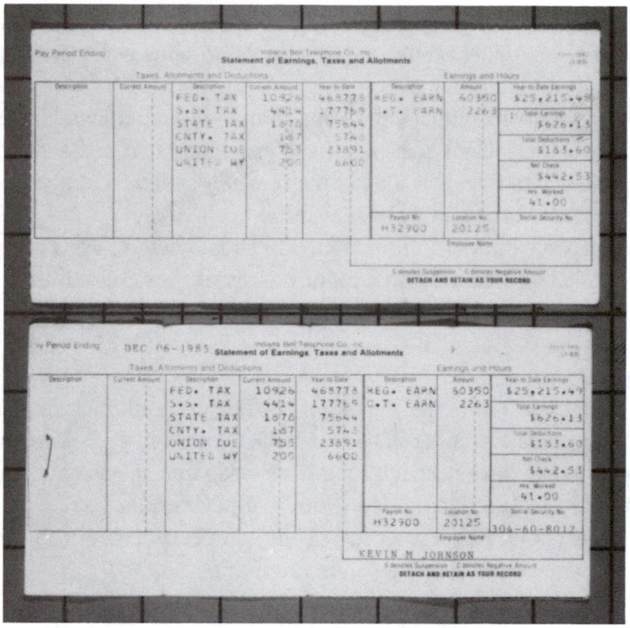

Figure 7.2. Example of a check stub remake.

Cover Story Documentation

How do you come up with documentation for a cover story when official sources are not available? The answer to this question is simple: *white out*. The check stub remake procedure (to be followed in securing false identification) will assist in making your cover story good (Figure 7.2):

1. The first thing to do is to obtain a check stub from the business that you want to show as your employer. You may contact the business directly or obtain a stub from an employee.
2. Write out the information that you intend to replace such as the name, SSN, and any other information that you want to delete.
3. Run off a copy of the original after you have used the white out.
4. Type in the information that you want in the areas that you deleted.
5. Run off another copy of it and cut it down to a check size.
6. Put a staple through one end to make it look as if it was attached to a pay envelope.
7. If you want it to look old, place a little baby oil on the back side of the stub and fold it up and put it in your wallet. After a few days it will look as if you have had it there forever.

This technique will work for most documents, such as discharge papers, medical records, and other nonpicture identification. Figure 7.3 shows false identification obtained by a criminal.

For other picture identification, such as employee identification, you can contact a variety of businesses that will have machines that can laminate picture identification for you. Plan ahead and obtain identification from a variety of businesses long before you begin an investigation.

No matter what kind of information, you should always use a name that you will react to. You will be tried on a regular basis. If they call out your name and you do not immediately react, then your cover is blown.

Where to Start

Birth certificate: Go to the Recorder's Office; look through the death certificates that were filed for children who were 10 years old or younger when they died and who would have been approximately the same age as you. For example, if you were born in 1952, look up a death that occurred in 1962 when the child was 8 to 10 years old. Request a copy of the birth certificate for the child listed. You can now build a false identification around it.

What other identification you need: Depending on the depth and duration of your undercover role, you will have to decide how much identification you will need. For a long-term case I recommend you obtain driver's license, fake employee identification, Social Security card, library card, military discharge papers, check stub with false information on it, and business cards and stationery. Join organizations such as the VFW and video rental clubs. Once you have a birth certificate you can obtain any of the above identifications, but you should first consult with your legal advisor.

ROLE CAMOUFLAGE

Background

The ability to blend into almost any location is what separates a good investigator from a great one. Role camouflage can be the way you talk, the way you carry yourself, and the vehicle you drive; however, more often it is the clothes you wear. Your physical appearance is the most important part of role playing. In order to be successful in role playing, you must have a good background check done on your target. You need to know what the area around your target is like: upperclass, middleclass, blue collar workers, or poor. You need to know the types of people who frequent the location, their clothing description, and the types of vehicles they drive. You may think that this is unnecessary, but the first time you frequent a bar where the clientele are all American auto workers and you pull up in a Japanese car, you will see what it is like to be treated like a leper. You must have a good background prepared to be successful.

A.

B.

Figure 7.3. Actual examples of false identification obtained by a criminal. This subject is still missing.

Physical Appearance

When consideration is given to altering the physical appearance of a person so that he is less likely to be identified as the police, one must begin with the *eyes.* The eyes are the hardest to train. After a few years of police work, you have a tendency to intimidate with your eyes; this tendency has to be corrected. When you conduct your investigation, you must concentrate on having a neutral or submissive look in your eyes for the initial contacts with your target. The first few times you are exposed to your target, he will try to gauge your threat level. If you stare a hole through him or if you look as if you would just as soon kill him as look at him, do not expect much interaction to occur. Try to concentrate on how to look just like one of the guys. You may want to stand in front of a mirror and change the opening of the eyes and raise and lower the eyebrows to see how you look for any situation you can envision. Again, practice makes perfect.

The second thing that must change is the habit of looking at every person who comes in or walks by you. This is a dead giveaway that you are the police. Once you have mastered your facial features, you also need to consider *body language.* Again, threat level can be gauged by the way you carry yourself. Go back to the mirror and practice moving your shoulders forward and back and see how it changes your threat level. For the first few contacts do not go in with your shoulders back and head up, and do not strut as if you are looking for a fight. You should go in looking meek, with shoulders forward in a timid pose, walking with your head slightly down. As I have mentioned, avoid eye contact for the first entry.

Clothing and Other Aids

Some effects can be achieved with clothing and accessories that will assist in the alteration of your outside appearance and can be very beneficial. Not only do you want to fit in, but also you want to lower your perceived threat level. The following are items that can assist you in assuming your role.

Glasses: When thinking of how to limit the effect of the eyes on the suspect, glasses that are not designed for you are most effective. Keep all of the old glasses that have been worn by your family and use them on a regular basis. When you put on a pair of glasses that were made for a young person, you really look like a goof. This has been one of the most effective items used. Remember, you are attempting to limit your threat level and to limit the effect of your eyes on the suspect. What better way to do that than to wear goofy glasses. If you do not have any glasses at home, you can pick up a pair for around a dollar at Goodwill, DAV, or the Salvation Army. It will cost you approximately $8.00 to change the lens to clear glass.

Hats: Hats are very effective in breaking up your facial appearance. They also can be used as a conversation piece or introduction. If you identify that your target is a Dodger fan, wear a Dodger hat and rave on about the Dodgers. If you

Figure 7.4. Examples of shirts that can be worn to assist in role camouflage.

want to have a jovial approach, have a hat with a funny saying on it and use that to start a conversation. Some locations may collect hats. This is a good way to get acquainted with them. Give them your hat for the collection. Hats can be part of your issued equipment. There are several sources for baseball caps with built-in voice transmitters. The hat is a regular baseball cap with a team logo on it, but it contains a state-of-the-art voice transmitter that will give you an operating time of approximately 3 hours.

Work clothing: Work clothing not only needs to fit the target location, but also it must fit the type of work you are supposed to do. The best work items found are shirts with a business logo on them (Figure 7.4). You can obtain shirts and other items from Goodwill, DAV, and Salvation Army for almost nothing. We also have a good working relationship with several businesses in our area who provide us with uniforms. The effectiveness of clothing can be seen in the results that you receive. We conducted a raid where we used gas company uniforms and made an arrest at a residence. When neighbors asked why the person was arrested, they were told that he had not paid his gas bill. The gas company informed us that for the next several days, there was a run at their office to pay back gas bills. Clothing can be like a chameleon's skin; if you select the right clothing, people will have a tendency to accept and ignore you. Once you reach this stage, infiltration is easy.

Shoes/Boots: Footwear should be selected to fit the area and the work you do. The main thing to avoid is to present yourself as a long-time construction worker while wearing tennis shoes or new boots. You must fit the part from head

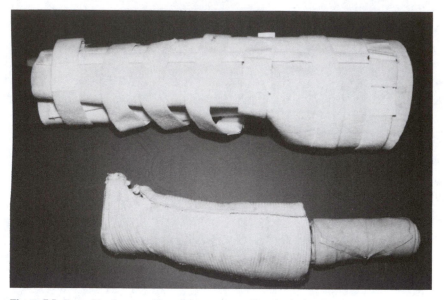

Figure 7.5. Examples of casts and braces that can be used in role playing. For even more convincing role-playing, go to a hospital to take pictures of actual injuries, such as knee surgeries.

to toe. Again, old boots and shoes can be obtained at Goodwill, DAV, and Salvation Army. You may want to request that your department maintain a stock of work shirts, pants, and other covert clothing to assist in this area of role camouflage. If this is not possible, then maintain a collection yourself.

Jewelry: Jewelry also can be used as a way to get an introduction, if you can identify that your target is in an organization which promotes jewelry. However, the most important thing to remember about jewelry is that you should keep a log as to when and where you wear it. The "bad guys" will know what you wear and use this as a way to identify you.

Casts: Everyone knows that no police officer is allowed to work with a broken limb, so the use of arm and leg casts is a very easy way to get accepted (Figure 7.5). You can contact any costume store and obtain a cast for an arm or a leg; however, in most cases, it is best to contact your local hospital and request that a member of its staff make one for you. The cast will be put on you and cut off when it dries. When you use it in a covert setting, you should cover it with an elastic bandage so that the target will never know the difference. The target may actually feel the cast to see if it is real. You can even let the target sign it if you want. With the new innovations in leg supports, you can obtain braces that have foam with strips of metal holding it straight. A way to be even more convincing is to carry pictures of a postoperative, swollen, stitched-up knee to show if you are asked what happened. Once this occurs, you are no longer a threat to your prospective target.

Tools: Tools should be job related, and the covert officer should have knowledge of how to use them. Major mistakes made when using a role where tools are required are that the covert officer's hands do not show the necessary calluses and that the tools are brand new. When tools are to be used, never use new ones; it is a dead giveaway that you are the police.

Vehicles: As stated before, the vehicle you drive to the target location must fit the role you intend to portray.

Props: Briefcases, coolers, and other support items may be necessary. When looking at props that will carry the covert officer's role, think of items that can be used to secrete a 35-mm camera or video into the location. If a prop can be used for covert photography, use it to dramatically increase the value of your court presentations.

Makeup and Scarring Techniques

The use of makeup and scars to alter a person's appearance has been used for years by moviemakers, but it is not common within the law enforcement community. These techniques could give an agency a much needed lift in the ability to infiltrate organizations that are conducting illegal enterprises in its area. You can go to the library to obtain copies of several books that will instruct you in the use and techniques of makeup and scarring materials. You may want to contact schools or stage companies that have acting departments and request that demonstrations be provided.

For the purpose of this book, a simple system is shown that has been employed for years and has been found to be very effective. A kit can be obtained that contains one small brush, one large blush brush, cotton balls, one bottle of rigid collodion, one container of brown makeup, and one container of blood-red makeup.

With these items, you can place a scar on your officer that will look and feel like a real scar (Figure 7.6). The procedures to follow are

- Lay out your two types of makeup, two brushes, the collodion, and the cotton balls on a work surface that allows you easy access.
- Select the area where the scar is to be located. This should be, if possible, on loose skin such as the cheek or neck, or any other area where you want a scar.
- Put a small amount of the brown makeup on the blush brush, and apply it to the area selected for application. Smooth the brown out so that it looks like a smudge over the whole area of the scar.
- Use the small brush to draw the desired scar design with the blood-red makeup over the brown makeup.
- Use the blush brush to go over the scar to break up its harsh appearance.
- Open the bottle of rigid collodion and use the brush inside it to trace over the scar that you have drawn. Cover only the scar itself, not the whole brown area. Let it set for a moment to dry. As collodion dries, it has a tendency to

A.

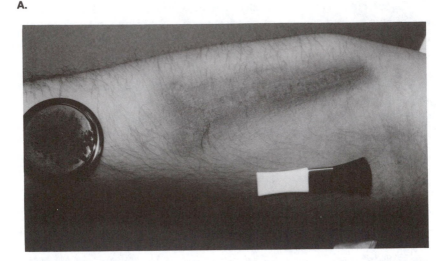

B.

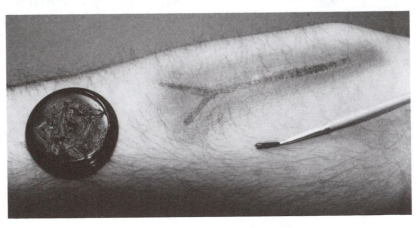

Figure 7.6. (A), (B), and (C) demonstrate the process used to put on fake scars.

draw the skin up into what appears to be scars. It has a strong smell, so if you intend to place it on the face of an officer, you should warn him to close his eyes and hold his breath.

- Once the first application of collodion has dried, then take the small brush and outline the scar with the brown makeup. Using the cotton balls, wipe off the excess brown by rubbing lightly. What you want left is a brown edge to the scar that will look like a scab.
- Now take the small brush and redefine the scar with the blood red makeup, and again buff it with the blush brush to make it blend in. You want the

C.

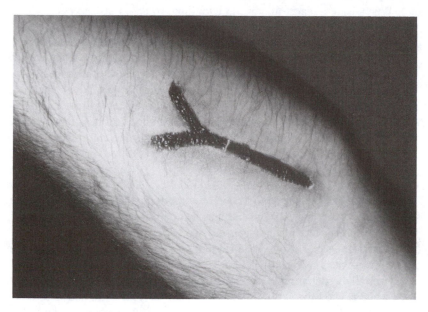

interior of the scar to appear red and the outside brown. Take the bottle of rigid collodion and again trace over the scar. Let it dry and observe the reaction.

- Repeat the use of the collodion two to three times until you have the look you want. When you reach this point, you will notice a slight shine to the area of the collodion. You need to brush a slight coat of brown on this to dull the shine.
- The last step is to take a rag or cotton ball and buff off the remaining brown makeup outside the scar.

This technique is very effective for scars, puncture wounds, needle marks, and bullet scars. You should use this kit in practice sessions and get comfortable with it. It is great for Halloween for the kids and has been used to trick a nurse at a hospital. If you are interested in buying this kit, the cost is approximately $20 and is available from:

Alsup & Associates
6100 N. Keystone Ave. No. 357
Indianapolis, IN 46220

The scars mentioned have worked on many occasions, both indoors and even out in the rain. Scars help prevent a person from being able to identify you after an entry is made due to the fact that it is human nature to see the scar, not the face. When using a scar, you must do two things to ensure its success:

1. Always take a picture of the scar before entry so that you can put the scar on the same location the next time. (It is tough to explain why the last time you were at a location the scar was on the other cheek.)
2. You must have a reason or story to explain the scar. We conducted an investigation where the target has had an accident on a motorcycle. We used a scar and a cover story involving an accident on a motorcycle to get close to the target. Try to identify background information such as this that you can use to make entries easier.

Example

Go to a used clothing store to purchase the following: a lime green leisure suit (the kind worn in the 1960s) and a brown pair of boots that zip up the side. Then obtain a pair of children's glasses, two paper sacks with handles attached (shopping bags), some assorted oddball junk to place in the bags, and a straw hat with a green-tinted visor attached to it.

Wear all these items into the target location. For a better effect, you need to place white tape on the glasses, tuck in only part of your shirt, and wear a bow tie. The subjects in the location will have nothing to do with you. You will be seen as a goof but not a threat. Your targets will continue to conduct business as usual. This type of deception makes the job fun and if the job is fun, you will get a lot more out of your team members.

INFILTRATION TECHNIQUES

The infiltration of an organization by an undercover officer is the most hazardous assignment in any operation. All other assignments must be made with the support and protection of the undercover officer in mind. The undercover officer should have a major say in how the operation should be set up. He or she should be provided the opportunity and authority to walk away from the covert side of the operation at any time. *It is better to walk away than to be carried away.* Techniques used to infiltrate operations can range from the very complex to the very simple. They normally require intelligence information to be effective. The following are some suggestions as to how to infiltrate an illegal organization.

Informant Introductions

Informant introductions are the most common way for police officers to infiltrate known illegal groups. Although it is the easiest, care must be taken to ensure that the informant is controlled every step of the way. Problems that must be considered when using informants are as follows:

Always expect that the informant will work both sides of the fence: He will provide you information while at the same time he will be asking questions and observing what you and your team are doing. He will provide this information to the highest bidder on the street. There are several ways you can control this and determine whether your informant is a leak. First is the use of disinformation. Provide the informant with information early in the investigation that you can track. You may want to give information about a location where you have another informant. Use that informant to see whether he is working both sides. Second, never identify all of the members of your team to the informant. Only expose the officers that have to work with the informant. This always gives you someone to work with who is unknown. Third, at times you may want to use several informants in the same location. Never let informants know who the others are. Have each informant check on the others. You may want to send in someone and have him or her do something that should be reported. If your informants fail to report what occurred, then you have a problem.

Double dipping: Informants will pass information to several agencies, collecting money from each. You should always be on guard for other agencies working cases that parallel your own. Once you identify that this is happening, you should make a notation that this informant is a double dipper and should be used with caution.

Drag out investigation: Always keep in mind that paid informants at times make a living by providing information for pay. There is no incentive for an informant to end an investigation early. You must always be on the lookout for your informant trying to control the investigation. Remember, every day that an informant drags out your investigation, you jeopardize the life of your undercover officer.

Informant crimes: Informants will commit crimes while under the disguise of being an agent of the police. You must always cover this in your discussion with the informant. You should inform the informant that any activity not cleared and approved by the control officer will not be tolerated. If the informant commits an illegal act, he will be prosecuted to the limits of the law. You should reinforce this on a regular basis to ensure compliance.

Never trust informants: They should be considered the lowest form of life. You should also make sure that the control officer does not become too friendly with the informant. If a relationship begins to evolve, the control officer should be replaced with another officer. Informants are very slick people. They will attempt to get you to like them and all the time they will use you to the limit. *Never trust an informant!*

Monitor, search, and control: When using an informant always search your informant before and after you send him or her to a location. This will eliminate many problems that you may face when the issue of entrapment or planting evidence arises. The only way you can control what is taken in is with a good search. Along with a good search, you should monitor your informant's entry and departure from the location to be safe. Never trust an informant to go to a location alone. Along with monitoring and searching, you also must always control the informant. You should always prep the informant before entry as to what you want to accomplish on each date. Reaffirm what can and cannot be done. You must control everything the informant does because he is acting as an agent of the police and you are liable for what happens.

Unknowing Accomplice Introductions

Friends of Suspect

Your background check should identify several friends of the suspect. You may want to work up a friendship with one of these individuals who can then introduce you into the organization that you have targeted. Attempt to identify hangouts of friends of the suspect and then try to approach them and engage them in conversation. Attempt to identify activities that the friends like to do and then mold your meeting around them. This meeting can be anywhere. It does not have to be at the target location. The end product is that you want to either be taken to the target by the friend or be able to use the friend's name as an introduction.

Employees of Suspect

Employees of a suspect are normally well aware of what is going on. You may be able to get an introduction through an employee if you work it right. If the employee is a waiter or waitress, you start by tipping well. You will never get a thing being cheap. You should show no interest in the activities that are occurring within the target location until you have been frequenting it for a while. By then, the employee is doing everything he can for you to get the tip. Ask a question every once in a while about what you observed and make sure you do not push. If the employee has accepted you as no threat, then he will gradually come around and assist you. If the location the person is working is only a drop off point, then he still can introduce you to the bookmaker. Work him slowly and carefully, maintain your role, and never be in a hurry.

Patrons

You can approach patrons if you select the right times. If the location you are working is a tavern, you need to identify when the most gamblers will be present. This normally is on weekends and on nights when the bar is promoting an evening game, Monday night football, for example. You need to frequent the location on these days and identify the people who you think can get you to the criminal. You want to make sure that you are cheering for the same teams that they do. Never be against them, for this can eliminate any chance you have. During the game, gradually move into their circle of friends. You may want to engage in conversations about how the team is doing or what needs to be done. At times like this, you need both an understanding of the game and the teams involved. You may want to bet a beer or a round of drinks during the game. You will discover that a drunk sports fan who finds someone to buy his drinks will be your friend forever. Use this to your benefit.

Intelligence Seeking Surveillance

When conducting intelligence seeking surveillance, you should look for patterns that will give you an edge to use in your infiltration. Patterns of activities will give you locations where your target hangs out, but may also give you additional targets and witnesses. A bookmaker example follows:

Settle up day (tavern): If your target is a tavern, you should set up a surveillance on the days that bettors and bookies settle their debts. During football season, this is normally Tuesday and Wednesday. You should position yourself to be able to photograph anyone entering and talking to anyone who you suspect to be involved. Normally bettors will spend very little time with the bookmaker. They will enter and pay or receive what is owed. You need to photograph, if possible, these activities. If you see people enter and spend a long time together and they have people come up to them, then there is a chance that they are bookmakers. You need to note this, remembering that bookmakers layoff bets to other bookmakers. Along with taking photos and videos, you need someone who is responsible to obtain the plate and vehicle descriptions from the persons you are observing. The best way to do this is by using a minirecorder. If you attempt to write down plates and descriptions, first you will be identified and second you cannot cover several vehicles in a hurry.

Settle up day with suspect: When all you have is a suspect and no known locations, you must set up an intelligence-seeking surveillance on the subject. Pick him up at his residence or location where you know him to be. Track him to every location he visits. Some will first go to the bank. This is very important, because if he has made a withdrawal to pay bettors, you can show that the account in question is being used for illegal activity. You need to photograph and take videos of all his activities and determine whether he meets with the bettors or drops off an envelope. The use of an aircraft is very important if one is available. You can let the chopper track while you hold off the perimeter. Once you identify the locations involved, you need to identify anyone else involved and determine whether the other locations and persons should be included in your main objective.

Use of a Gimmick

If no introduction is available, you may want to attempt to use a gimmick such as being a salesman, a telephone man, or even a doctor. All it takes is a shirt with a logo and half the battle is won. If you go in with a telephone company shirt on, more often than not you will be accepted as a telephone company employee. Go by your hospital and obtain some scrubs, pick up a stethoscope, and make a name tag so that you can go into the tavern as a nurse or doctor. If you do not feel comfortable filling these roles, then go in as a thief. You may laugh now, but this is one of the best ways to enter. Go into the tavern and ask whether you can trade a VCR or other items for lunch and a few drinks. The bartender or owner will never think that you are the police. Be creative and do not stick to the techniques that all police officers use.

Working Cases on Patrons

During your surveillance, you should be watchful for small-time hoods on probation or parole and other persons who cannot afford the publicity of being arrested. Observe these persons until you have enough to file a case on them, and then afford them the opportunity to cooperate. When doing this, you should have the consent of the prosecutor to make this person a witness and not a defendant. This means of gaining access to the illegal operation should be done in such a way that the person does not know what your real target is. Let him tell you what he has to offer in the way of targets. Do not ever tell him that you want to target a specific person or place.

Traffic Stops

Using a traffic stop to gain entrance to the operation is as "old as the hills," but like the good guy, the bad guy routine always seems to work. Everyone has been stopped by the police, and the patrons can relate to your feelings after you have been given a ticket. Have the uniformed officer stop you outside the tavern that you intend to enter and write you a ticket. When he leaves, park, go in, and sit alone at a table if possible. Order a drink, set the copy of your ticket down, and just stare at it. By the time you order a second drink, you will have everyone in the tavern feeling sorry for you. At this time, if a pay telephone is present, place a call to your fictitious wife. Get in an argument with her in such a way that it sounds as if once you tell her you received a ticket, she will not let you get a word in edgewise. Hang up and go to the bar and order another drink. From this point on, every man in the place will be your friend.

Work for Food or Odd Jobs for Money

Depending on how much time you have, you may want to offer to do odd jobs for money or food. You may want to apply for a job and fill out an application. There is normally an interview involved; if not, ask to see the owner. You can tell him that you would like some part-time work. If he asks you what your experiences are, you should attempt to demonstrate that you could be valuable in his illegal enterprise. Even if he does not bite, you have just gotten the introduction you needed. Just remember that the information you put on your application must not come back to haunt you.

COVERT EQUIPMENT

In this section we will cover covert equipment and function. This area is probably the most neglected area in law enforcement, and yet it can dramatically increase the conviction rate of your unit. In this section we will cover covert photography, covert packages, and covert equipment.

Photography

Covert photography may range from sitting in a van taking photos of license plates to sneaking a camera into a location with you so that you can have a pictorial display of what you have observed. It is of great value to your case when you can go into court and show a video, stating that it is a true and accurate description of what occurred. In order to be effective in an area of covert photography, you must first understand the function of the 35-mm camera. Before conducting an investigation where video and or 35-mm cameras will be used, you should take a course that will make you feel comfortable with their function. To increase your expertise with your agency's equipment, a policy needs to be established where officers can use the equipment for events which occur during their free time. The more a person uses the equipment, the better the chances are that he or she will be able to function with the camera in a covert setting.

There are many booklets that describe covert photography on the market today. The U.S. Department of Justice had one printed for the FBI titled, "Surveillance Photography Guides." Since its printing in January 1979, it has been used as a guide by many agencies. This booklet has since gone out of print, but you may be able to obtain copies from your local FBI office.

When you begin your work with the 35-mm camera, you not only need to understand the camera, but also understand the terms that are used to explain the camera and its function.

Some general hints that may be helpful in the successful use of your camera follow:

- *Sharpness of a picture:* This comes from a good focus and a steady hand. Try to shoot at 125th of a second or greater to avoid camera jiggle.
- *Bracket your shots:* To bracket a shot means that you take a picture at the recommended f-stop. Then you take an additional shot at one f-stop higher and one f-stop lower.
- *Panning a shot:* This is where you center your moving target in the viewer; then you move the camera with the subject as you take the picture.
- *Depth of field:* This is the area in front of the subject and behind the subject that is in focus. A small lens opening gives the greatest depth of field. Automatic modes will not take depth of field into account.
- *Control the amount of light:* This is accomplished by the film speed, shutter speed, lens opening, and light on the subject.
- *Flash:* A flash is only good for approximately 50 feet.
- *Prefocus:* Aim the camera on the place where the shot is to be taken.
- *Focus:* For a recognizable image, use a lens that has a focal length two times the distance from the camera to the subject in feet. For example, from the camera to the subject is 60 feet. You need a lens that is 120 mm.

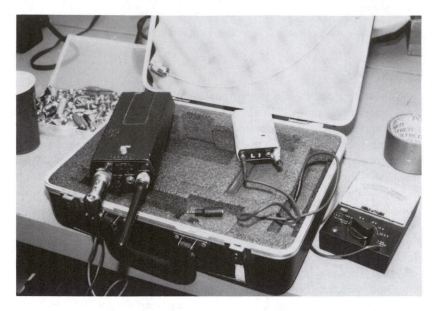

Figure 7.7. An example of a body wire and receiver.

- **Distances of over 500 feet:** You may encounter problems with heat waves and other atmospheric problems.
- **If possible, do not shoot through windows:** If you shoot at less than 1/30 of a second, use a tripod. Remember that pictures are used in court, so try not to photograph other officers involved in horseplay.

Other Equipment

Covert equipment is that used by a covert officer to document activities and or provide protection for the officers involved. Because most agencies do not have vast amounts of money to buy high tech equipment, they are forced to get by with the bare essentials.

The following are items that are on the market today or that can be manufactured by yourself:

Body Wire/Voice Transmitter

In the area of voice transmitters, creativity has been taken to the n'th degree (Figure 7.7). There are voice transmitters that are disguised as a functional handgun or are hidden in a briefcase, a cigarette pack, a Walkman, or any number of different packages. The only limitation to the way they are packaged is the person's ingenuity and ability. There are several points to keep in mind when using voice transmitters. They are

- Never base your whole operation on the transmitter working! If you do, I guarantee there will be a malfunction.
- Always double cover your undercover officer! Use the transmitter and a surveillance team, preferably having a direct line of sight on the officer.
- Consider having the undercover officer carry a tape recorder. This can make up for any lost transmissions from the wire.
- Consider using a repeater close by. A repeater is nothing more than a device that takes in a signal and sends it back out at a much greater wattage.
- Even if you use a wire that is taped to the body, keep in mind that some body wires can get very hot, so do not put it against the skin.
- A body wire against the body is often directional. Have your officer try to turn toward the receivers.
- Do not wear silk or nylon clothing over the wire, because movement will cause the transmission to be scratchy.
- If the body wire is located on your back, you should avoid sitting down and blocking the signal between your body and the chair.
- *Always put on the antenna before you insert batteries.*
- The transmitter should be at least 15 feet away from the receiver before you turn it on for a test. It can damage the transmitter.
- When removing the body wire from the officer, use caution that you do not damage the antenna or exterior mikes.

Tracking Devices

Tracking devices are nothing more than devices that can be attached to a vehicle or carried by an undercover officer which transmits a signal to a receiver. This signal can be followed, and in some cases the receiver will actually give you a readout of exactly where the transmitter is located in degrees (Figure 7.8).

Surveillance Vans

Normally the only surveillance vans that are set up the correct way are those owned by federal authorities or private investigation firms (Figure 7.9). Keep this in mind if you need to borrow one. A good surveillance van is extremely expensive; it will contain many of these items: several power outlets, air conditioning and heating system, portable toilet system, comfortable seating, carbon monoxide sensor and alarm, desk and shelves, insulation from cold and heat, video and audio capabilities with equipment, periscope system with camera mounts, window camera mounts, receivers and transmitters, recorders and digital time capabilities, and carpet and interior lighting. These are only a few items that are needed. As you can see, the expense of outfitting such a van is prohibitive for a local agency to possess one.

Low Light Photography Equipment

There are many different types of low light equipment. They can be attached to weapons, cameras, and videos; and many are handheld light intensifiers. The

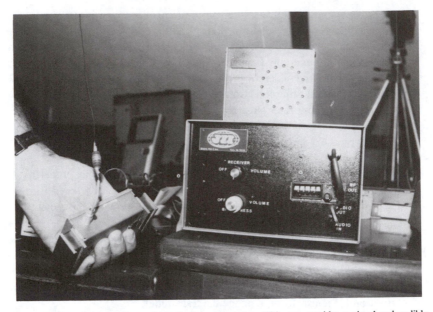

Figure 7.8. An example of a tracking device and receiver. This one provides a visual and audible signal indicating the location of the target.

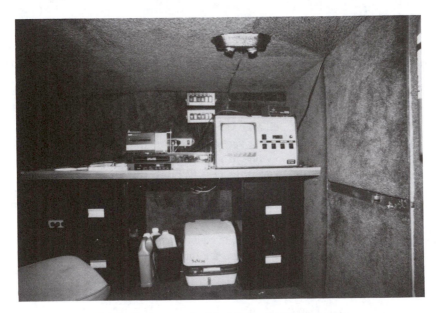

Figure 7.9. An example of the interior of a surveillance van.

key with this type of equipment is that it provides you with the opportunity to see and record activity in near to total darkness. The best equipment:

- Provides you with high quality black and white photos or videos
- Is designed to be easy to operate
- Can be used for long-distance observations

Covert Packages

Covert packages are photographic equipment (35-mm and video) concealed inside something to hide the true purpose. *This may be another area that you will want to clear with your prosecutor before you use any of the items mentioned.*

There are several companies in the United States that specialize in discreet surveillance systems. Most systems are completely portable and are very easy to operate. Some require an outside power source while others have their own power unit contained within the package. Your choice of the type of system will be determined by how and where you meet the suspect. In most cases you will need to use the systems that are completely portable and have a self-contained power source. Figures 7.10–7.17 show the types of items that large private investigation firms have in their surveillance inventory. Some of the items are purchased from a distributor, but many are manufactured by the private investigators themselves to accomplish a specific task. In most cases these items can be rented by your agency. International Investigators, located in Indianapolis, provided us with the items in Figures 7.10–7.17. As you can see, there is much creativity invested in the packages and equipment provided. If your agency is willing to provide you with the money to purchase covert surveillance systems, you should first go to one of the trade shows held for the private investigations industry and identify all the items that are on the market. Then you can make the best choice.

Other items on the market that are not mentioned above include a flight case with a self-contained video unit; radio and stereo speakers with a video unit inside; smoke alarm unit with a video; emergency overhead sprinkler video unit; assorted pictures, clocks, and other wall accessories with video units; and thermostats, plants, and potted trees with video units.

There is no limit to the types of packages that can be manufactured. You can go to the Goodwill and pick up a briefcase for $1.00 and insert a video camera. You can use a shoe box to conceal a 35-mm camera for taking photos inside a tavern. The key now is that you need to make the secretion of photographic equipment a part of every investigation you conduct. If your agency has none and you cannot borrow any, you need to challenge yourself and others in your unit to come up with ways to use photography to document all transactions.

SURVEILLANCE

The general definition of surveillance is the secretive observation of persons, place, and or things. The main purpose of surveillance is to gather information.

A.

B.

Figure 7.10. A video camera hidden in a book.

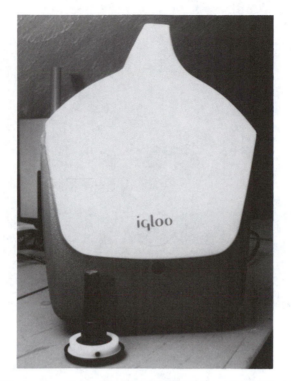

Figure 7.11. Video camera container. The video is hidden in the cooler and shoots through a hole using a pin hole lens.

Although the types of surveillance will vary from background surveillance to officer support, the objectives are generally the same. They are to:

- Gather information for your probable cause
- Identify co-conspirators
- Verify information received from sources
- Locate and record the possession of assets
- Identify patterns of activities
- Identify locations that are frequented by suspects
- Protect and support undercover officers
- Obtain verification that a crime is occurring
- Obtain evidence to be used in court
- Develop lead information

These objectives seem to be common sense and on the face appear to be easy to accomplish; however, one of the most difficult jobs is that of the surveillance specialist. When consideration is given to the selection of an officer to conduct surveillance, great care should be taken. The selection should be made only after conducting a review of the recommended abilities for a surveillance officer.

A.

B.

Figure 7.12. 16-mm camera hidden in a stereo speaker. The camera is fired when someone breaks the beam emitted by the device.

A.

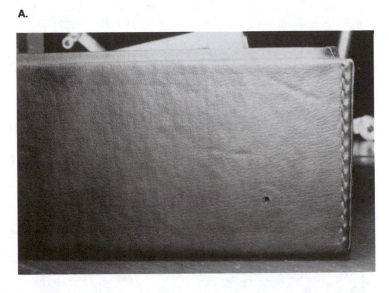

B.

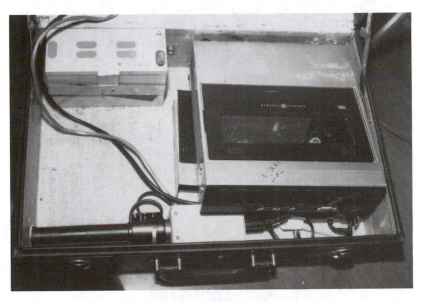

Figure 7.13. Briefcase video unit.

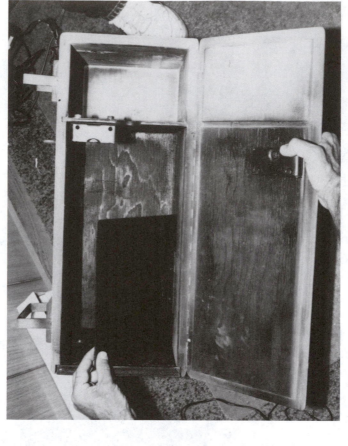

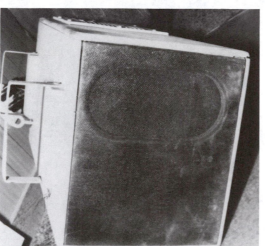

Figure 7.14. Covert package designed to contain a video camera while appearing to be duct work.

A.

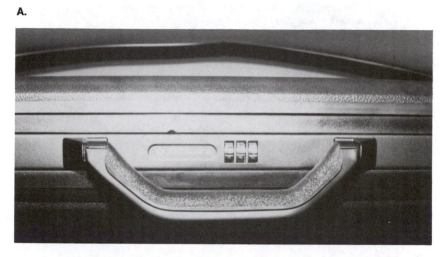

B.

Figure 7.15. Briefcase tape recorder. When the combination is set to zero, the recorder will record.

Figure 7.16. Microcassette recorder.

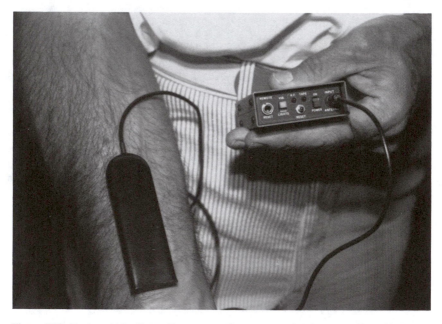

Figure 7.17. Device which vibrates if a tape recorder or a transmitter is present. Keep this item in mind when conducting infiltrations.

Surveillance Planning

To plan a safe and effective surveillance you must first have the following information:

- What type of operation are you conducting?
- What is your goal?
- Where is the target?
- Get criminal histories on all subjects.
- Identify co-conspirators and relatives in the area.
- Identify all vehicles used by the suspects in the area.
- Check for countersurveillance.
- Obtain undercover vehicles that match the neighborhood.
- Identify the technical equipment needs of the team.
- Get descriptions and pictures of all involved.
- Are there gang affiliations?
- Always have a Plan B.
- Make sure you have the time necessary to conduct the surveillance.
- Are the subjects known to have weapons? Do not be outgunned.
- Get a complete background check on subjects and locations if possible.

A *tactical plan sheet* is designed to make sure each person involved understands what the plan is and what he or she is required to do. *If you do not assign duties, they will not get done.* See Figure 7.18 for an example of a tactical plan.

Recommended Abilities of a Surveillance Officer

Observe and record: A surveillance specialist must have the ability to observe and accurately record what he has observed. This may seem easy but you may have only a split second to record a license plate, the physical description of the driver, and the make, model, and color of the vehicle. All this has to be retained while the car passes you at 30 miles per hour. There is a skill to the accurate retention of this type of information, and the worst thing you can do is to place an officer with the retention of a rock in this position.

The ability to blend in: The ability to set up a surveillance and not be detected is one of the most valuable skills that a surveillance specialist can possess. Some officers have a natural knack for this, but most need to be trained on how to hide in the open. This skill can be helped by access to a variety of vehicles and a variety of clothing and roles that can blend in with what is found in the target area.

Patience: Patience is a virtue when dealing with a surveillance situation. The surveillance specialist must endure excessive heat and cold, long periods of monotony, and long periods with no relief, not to mention the fact that personal necessities are limited. There are very few officers that can handle long-term

A.

TACTICAL ACTION LOG   CONTROL #:_____
SPECIAL TASK TEAM   CASE #:_____

A. TYPE OF OPERATION:

    _____ BUY BEST   __XXX___ SURVEILLANCE

    _____ SEARCH WARRANT   __XXX___ OTHER:_____

B. PRIORITIES:___Record Conversation between CI & Target_____

     Control Area of Surveillance

     CI'S Safety

C. SUSPECT(S): NAME, DESCRIPTION

1.___Matt_____ W/M 25   6'2"   210 lbs   Brown Hair   (armed)

2.___iz_____ W/F 26   5'5"   125 lbs   Blond Hair

3._____

4._____

D. LOCATIONS: (ADDRESS AND DESCRIPTION)

1.___Parking Lot of Berger Park   800N/5000 W

2._____

3._____

E. VEHICLES:

1.___49X1234   1980 Toyt Brown_____ 2._____

3._____ 4._____

F. ASSISTING PERSONNEL & TASK: (INCLUDING UNDERCOVER UNITS)

NAME	VEHICLE	UNIT #	TASK	UNDERCOVER UNIT YES / NO
1. T. Hall	On Foot	4321	Back-Up	Yes
2. A. Alford	Van	4322	Kell/Record	Yes
3. K. Kinnee	Linc	4323	Back-Up	Yes
4. M. Bates	Van	4324	Radio	Yes
5.				
6.				

G. BACKGROUND: (CRIMINAL HISTORY, OTHER CASES)

     Target #1 Has Prior DWI Known to carry a gun

     Target # 2 Has a prior DWI

H. SPECIAL PROBLEMS: (WEAPONS, VIOLENCE, COUNTER SURVEILLANCE)

     Target # 1 Set Time and Place for meeting (CAUTION)

Figure 7.18. Tactical action log to be used prior to any tactical actions. This assures that all officers are aware of and understand what they are supposed to do. If you do not assign tasks, they will not get done.

I. BUST SIGNAL: (PRIMARY, SECONDARY & RIP-OFF)

    If the CI says the word CHUMP undercover units will remove CI from location

    and take the target down.

J. CASE INSTRUCTIONS:

    CI is to meet the target and obtain details about who is to be killed at 2 PM

    Bates will be the only one on the radio except for emergencys

    All units in place by 1315 hrs.

K. CLOSEST HOSPITAL: Comm. East   1000 W East.

L. RADIO CHANNEL TO BE USED: Tack 2

M. DIAGRAMS: YES XXX   NO

B.

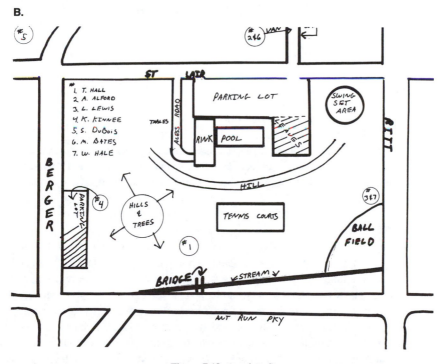

Figure 7.18. (continued)

assignments in a surveillance van without rebelling. Keep this in mind and rotate the duties on a frequent basis.

The ability to stay alert: It is very difficult to conduct any long-term surveillance and maintain a high state of alertness. You must guard against complacency because a surveillance can turn into a life and death struggle in a heartbeat if your operation is discovered.

The ability to operate equipment: Equipment, such as transmitters, receivers, recorders, 35-mm cameras, and videos, is a must in most surveillance situations. No matter how expensive your equipment is, it is of no value if the surveillance specialist fails to possess the ability to operate the equipment. Training and practice must be provided to the officer selected in order to obtain the best results. Consider having several qualified officers in your unit.

Memory: The surveillance specialist must have a good memory. This ability, along with the ability to detect specific items of interest, can be very important to an investigation.

The ability to keep accurate surveillance logs: The paperwork necessary to maintain an accurate, legible record of all events occurring while on a surveillance is very important. Remember this documentation will follow you to court and represent you and your department when you are not present.

TYPES OF SURVEILLANCE

Moving Surveillance

Moving surveillance is nothing more than shadowing the suspect to obtain information. This may be done in a variety of ways ranging from tracking on foot to utilizing an aircraft to follow a suspect. Over the years investigators have devised a variety of ways to track subjects. They may vary slightly from one situation to another, but the following are some general techniques used in moving surveillance.

Single-Vehicle Technique

When a situation arises that you are by yourself and you must follow someone, you must stay as close as possible. This type of surveillance is the most difficult, and the odds of you being successful are slim. You should always have items such as glasses, hat, and tie in your bag so that you can change your outward appearance as you proceed with the track. If you are in a vehicle, you are going to have to anticipate traffic conditions and move your vehicle, foreseeing what the target will do to counter any surveillance he may anticipate. In a situation such as this, you may just want to hang back and hope instead of spooking the target. Single-person surveillance, be it on foot or in a vehicle, should be avoided if at all possible.

Two-Vehicle Technique

This is very similar to one-vehicle tracking except you have a little more room for error. Always try to have a vehicle between you and the suspect vehicle. Alternate the lead surveillance vehicle on a regular basis. You should avoid trying to parallel the suspect. It is inevitable that if you try to parallel the target, he will backtrack and then you are down to a one-vehicle track. Again, when you are not in the lead vehicle, you should change your appearance, for example, by taking off your shirt or adding glasses and a hat; then when you take over the lead, you will look different to the suspect.

Three-Vehicle Technique

With three vehicles you can execute a variety of maneuvers such as parole and intercept the suspect at intersections, and you may be able to form a sandwich with the subject between two vehicles and the third in reserve or on a parallel track. By altering the lead vehicle, you should be able to track the suspect for a long distance. The key is to anticipate the suspect's moves and be there to pick him up.

Moving Surveillance on Foot

The success of a surveillance on foot at times is dependent on the number of officers involved. The more you have involved, the better chance you have of being successful. As with surveillance from a vehicle, if there is only one of you, all you can do is stay close and hope the suspect is not expecting a tail. Follow the suspect to where you feel that you cannot go any further without being burned; then walk away. If the routine of the suspect is consistent, you may be able to pick him up where you lost him on another day. If this is possible, then you can continue to track him to his destination.

Two Persons on Foot

If you have two officers involved in the track, one should lead and the other should either follow or cross over to the other side of the street and parole at a slight distance behind. The technique used should be dictated by the size of the crowd on the street. If it is crowded, then you can stay close on the same side of the street. When you are tracking a suspect, you should continually check behind to determine whether you are the object of a counter-surveillance team positioned by the suspect.

Three Persons on Foot

Having three persons is the ideal setup. The two lead officers track the suspect from opposite sides of the street while the third watches both officers from the rear and also tries to detect any countersurveillance. Remember, if you use a three-man team, the rear officer is hung out to dry if you do not cover him also.

Knowing When You Have Been Discovered

I can remember the first time I blew a vehicle surveillance. It was a one-vehicle track. The suspect drove me all over the place. Finally as I rounded the corner, there he was. He waved and laughed at me as I went by. This taught me a very valuable lesson; never depend on a track to make your case unless you intend to use an aircraft. It just will not work.

In order to be successful in the area of foot and vehicle surveillance, you must be able not only to anticipate what your suspect is going to do, but also to read your suspect's actions and determine whether he is looking for a track. A suspect may not want to let you know that he has identified you because if he knows where you are, he can manipulate you away from his actual destination. Look for the following actions.

Stopping to look in windows: As he is looking in the windows, see whether he is turning his upper body to look at the reflections from where he has just come. Normally, if he is looking for a track, he will pick a window that is angled to show where he has come from. If he does this, you must never alter your stride; just keep moving. If you anticipate this activity, you should never get caught.

Turning a corner: Look for turning a corner and stopping to lean against the building. Never do a hard turn around a corner when a suspect has preceded you. You may end up running into him and then he can better evaluate whether you are a police officer. Using this technique can also give the suspect the opportunity to put you down while apologizing for bumping into you. If he detects a gun, you could die right there.

Evasive Maneuvers: These include:

- Entering a business and leaving by another exit
- Entering a business and watching who enters after them
- Crossing the street back and forth
- Abruptly turning around and walking back the way he has just come
- Cutting through areas where the foot traffic is slight to see who follows
- Getting on elevators
- Walking up or down stairways in hotels
- Alternate running and walking

These are a few situations that you will encounter if you try to track a suspect. There is only one way to become effective in the art of tracking someone and that is to practice on a regular basis. Set up a scenario and have a team track a person to a meet and from it. You may want to use officers from other agencies as suspects so that they will not know your people before the tracking begins.

Stationary or Static Surveillance

Stationary or static surveillance is observing activities from a nonmobile location, such as an apartment building roof or a stand of trees. In most situations you will find that you need a combination of both moving and stationary surveillance to accomplish your goals.

Several problems are encountered when dealing with a stationary situation, such as how you set up and conduct a surveillance in a neighborhood without being detected. Think of all the equipment that must be moved into position. How do you cover this activity? You should automatically conduct a background investigation on the area and the people with whom you intend to deal. You cannot afford to rent an apartment from the suspect's sister, and you cannot identify whether the suspect has relatives in the area until you do your background check.

While conducting your background, you should also attempt to match your investigators with the community they intend to frequent. Their behavior, clothing, language, and total overall appearance must not draw any attention if they are to be effective. Once in place, the officers must keep an accurate log of all the events that occur.

Using a two-person team is very effective. One officer can keep the log as the other officer takes 35-mm photographs and backs them up with video. Using tape recorders to take down initial information is handy, especially when events begin to occur rapidly. In situations like this, officers should record the activities, descriptions, and directions of travel; then they should transcribe the details into the log when activity subsides. The worst thing you can do is observe important activities and not have the accurate information for your log. Figure 7.19 is an example of a surveillance log. When making notations for the log, attempt to identify persons who are photographed by description and number of photos on the roll.

AIR COVERAGE

Air coverage can provide ground officers with a constant eye on the target without the subject knowing it. In addition to being a great platform for photographing the target, air coverage can provide information about upcoming problems with the roadway, possible alternate routes, and any observable countersurveillance present. If you intend to use air coverage, you should consider having someone familiar with the case in the aircraft as an observer.

IMPORTANT SURVEILLANCE TIPS

The targets of your investigation will resort to countersurveillance measures to protect their illegal enterprise. You must take steps to protect your people. When you set up your surveillance team you need to do a drive through after the members are in place. Look for others watching you. Countersurveillance could be as simple as a young child on a bike riding around the block or as intricate as surveillance cameras and roof spotters.

SURVEILLANCE LOG

Day of the Week_____ Date_____ Month_____ Year_____

Surveillance Units: Undercover Units:

_____   _____

_____   _____

_____   _____

_____

_____

_____

_____

_____

_____

_____

_____

_____

_____

_____

_____

_____

_____

_____

_____

_____

_____

Tape No._____ Start_____ End_____

Incident No._____ Audio_____ Start_____ End_____

Figure 7.19. Surveillance log.

When you consider countersurveillance you need to also expect that the "bad guys" will try to infiltrate your operation. Lately we have noted that they will send a member into the police to pretend to be an informant. Their goal is: (1) to identify all the team members present, (2) to identify the techniques used by the team to conduct investigations, (3) to identify the types of equipment used and available to the team, (4) to identify what subjects the team has targeted, and (5) to obtain any other information available.

While working with an informant do not ever identify your whole team. Always have someone held back that can do a case on the informant if need be. When dealing with an informant do not let him wander around your office. Place him in a secure location and control what he sees. Do not let him be in a position to see desks, pictures of family members, charts, or graphs. He will use what he sees against you.

When conducting surveillance, do not use aluminum chairs on wood surfaces. They make too much noise. Do not lean back in a chair on a wood floor when you have $7.00 in change in your pocket. It will hit the floor. If you intend to urinate in a 3-pound coffee can, put a paper towel in the bottom or the whole town will hear.

PREPARATION FOR SURVEILLANCE: HOW TO BEGIN

The most important thing you can do to ensure the success of a surveillance is to be prepared. Your preparation must include each officer involved in the surveillance knowing not only what his responsibilities are, but also how to accomplish his task in an efficient and acceptable manner. Each person must be informed and trained as to what he is to do. There are a number of arrangements that should be made prior to conducting a surveillance. The following is a suggested checklist that may be used:

Surveillance Background Checklist

- Decide on the date and time the surveillance is to be conducted. Try to anticipate the length of time the surveillance will take.
- Determine where you intend to set up. Identify the best location for vehicles and cameras to be positioned and determine whether a stationary position is needed. Position vehicles to maximize your view of the target location. Try to cover all entrances and exits. Use equipment that will provide the quality you want in your pictures but still afford you the ability to be far enough from the target to avoid detection.
- If possible, have photographs taken from the air.
- Prepare backgrounds on the target and location.
- Prepare backgrounds on the suspect and co-conspirators.

- Identify the types of people in the area for role camouflage.
- Identify patterns of activities by suspects.
- Determine what type of communication equipment is necessary.
- Determine what security for personnel and equipment is necessary.
- Check on the availability of personal comforts. These include toilets, air conditioning, heating, water, and food.
- Review the number of officers available and who will be needed by you.
- Decide on the specialty groups necessary for surveillance.

After you have conducted the surveillance background check list and have obtained the information that you feel is necessary to adequately prepare the surveillance team, you must begin the actual preparation for the surveillance.

Surveillance Preparation Checklist

- Identify the team leader. Inform him of his duties.
- Review all information that has been obtained from background checks on the location and suspects.
- Review patterns of activities with team members.
- Identify all relatives and associates in the surveillance area to team members.
- Review the criminal history of suspects. Note any identifiers and, if possible, have photos of the suspects available for review.
- Identify, if possible, any tendencies toward violence.
- Review all known vehicles with team members.
- Use photos from the air. This will help you to identify the layout of the target area.
- Inform the team of the locations. Identify good observation points in the target area.
- Inform the team members as to what clothing and vehicles will be necessary for them to blend into the area.
- Review the law violations that you expect to observe. Explain what to look for, such as passing envelopes or currency.
- Review the statute that applies to the law violation. Understand what is necessary to make a case in court.
- Identify and inform all members as to the exact nature of their involvement.
- Conduct training if necessary.
- Review arrangements and make sure no questions are unanswered.

Presurveillance Equipment Checklist

The presurveillance equipment checklist is one of the final things that is done before the team enters the field. This is very important because if you fail to have the necessary equipment or the equipment is not functional, you may not only jeopardize your case, but also the lives of your team. It is recommended that a checklist be established and followed to the letter to ensure success of your mission. The list should include the following:

- *Transmitters and receivers:* Check the batteries and test both transmission and reception. Have extra batteries on site. Make a visual inspection of the equipment for any obvious problems.
- *Tape recorders:* Check power source and function of the equipment. If batteries are necessary, have extra present.
- *Communications:* Check communication equipment to be sure it is functional and will perform the task required.
- *Binoculars and scopes:* Check to make sure they are functional and that there are enough to go around.
- *35-mm camera:* Check batteries in the camera and make sure that there are extras. Check to make sure that film is available and the correct type of film is used.
- *Video equipment:* Check power source and function of the unit. Have extra batteries and videotapes present. It is recommended that backup units be present for both video and 35-mm cameras.
- *Assorted camera equipment:* Check for tripods, bipods, and camera mounts. Check for covert packages to be used for camera equipment, if the assignment calls for it. You should have repair tools, cleaners, and other items such as plunger-type shutter releases.
- *Vehicles:* Check the gas, oil, tires, defroster, heater, air conditioner, communication equipment with the vehicle, windshield wipers, license plates, battery, and general appearance of the vehicle (will it fit in).
- *Vans:* These should have comfortable seating with a place to write, portable toilet, cooler for drinks and food, and writing materials and logs.

During this stage, you should make sure everyone understands what they are to do. As a last step, you should:

- Review the use of the 35-mm camera.
- Review the use of video equipment and the types of activity you are interested in recording.
- Review any signals you may have provided your team for use in specific situations.
- Review the use of covert packages for camera equipment, if used.
- Recheck all communication equipment.
- Review the verbiage to be used for communications.
- Assign equipment and vehicles to assigned members of your team.

APPENDIX 1: CHECKLISTS

Undercover Officer Should

Be adaptable

Be resourceful

Be a good actor

Be confident

Have good judgment

Be creative

Be a good listener

Have a good memory

Be willing to alter appearance

Handle stress well

Be able to operate covert equipment

Cover Story Must

Stand up to scrutiny

Be easy for officer to assume

Be attractive to suspect

Be easy to remember

Be hard to check

Be flexible

Fit the location

False Identification Should Include

Driver's license

Birth certificate

License plates

Video club membership card

Check stub

Insurance card

Role Camouflage

Glasses

Jewelry

Work shirts

Casts and braces

Shoes/boots

Makeup

Vehicles

Tools

Infiltration Techniques

Informant introduction

Frequent the location

Surveillance for information

Associate with friends of target

Join clubs

Traffic stops

Flip small time criminal

Use a gimmick

Use a female as cover

Surveillance

Moving or stationary

Purpose: gather information on persons, places, and things for prosecution

Surveillance Specialist Should

Have patience

Be alert

Have knowledge of equipment

Be able to blend in

Be observant

Preparation for Surveillance

Review all information on suspect

Review all information on location

Check all equipment

Review use of 35-mm and video cameras

Review all signals

Check for required paperwork

APPENDIX 2: EQUIPMENT NEEDS

A good microcassette recorder

Body wire (1/4 watt), e.g., miniature voice transmitter, pager transmitter, baseball cap transmitter, wallet transmitter, and Walkman transmitter

Repeater (car mount or briefcase)

Regular cassette recorders

35-mm cameras with pinhole lens

Bipods and tripods

Night vision system with camera adapters

Mobile surveillance system

Video units with pinhole adaptability

Covert packages for 35-mm and video cameras, such as purse, briefcase, gym bag, or igloo cooler

Portable phones

Property for reverse strings

Receivers such as pocket receiver, handheld one, and briefcase for recorder

Covert vehicles

Covert disguises

Expense account

Informant fund

8

Search Warrants

PROBABLE CAUSE DEVELOPMENT

Probable cause development starts the first second that you begin your investigation. As you begin, you should have a firm grip on what your goals are and what is going to be required to accomplish those goals. Earlier in the book we stated that the four goals of an illegal sports bookmaking investigation were to:

1. Eliminate the illegal organization
2. Seize the assets of the organization
3. Assist the IRS in its investigation
4. Identify and investigate co-conspirators

In order to be effective in the area of asset forfeiture and to assist the IRS, you must have an understanding of what is required.

When it comes to your assisting the IRS in conducting an investigation, remember that the suspects are more afraid of the IRS than your criminal charges. Use this to your advantage. Normally, when dealing with the IRS, we attempt to identify the following information throughout our investigation which the IRS will need:

- Suspect's name, address, Social Security Number (SSN), aliases, sex, and race; and the name of the suspect's business
- Occupation
- Police record
- Police placed bets, dates of bets, amounts, other known bets, and records of betting taken during raids
- How long the suspect was in business, and the sources for this information
- Informants—reliability and can they be used
- Records, ascertaining whether the suspect kept records and whether they are available for review

- Banks used
- Property—real property, leased or owned; vehicles, leased or owned
- Amount of currency confiscated
- Any narcotics involved

Rewards from the IRS for Information

Under Section 7623 of the Internal Revenue Code, there is a procedure that allows the Internal Revenue Service to pay a reward to any person who provides information leading to the detection and punishment of anyone who violates Internal Revenue laws. The only stipulation is that you cannot be employed by the Department of the Treasury at the time you received or provided the information, or you are not a present or former employee of the federal government and received the information in the course of your official duties.

How This Can Help in the Investigation

The answer is simple. Most departments do not have a large amount of money to pay for information from informants, but if you can direct the informants to the Treasury Department and work with those authorities, you may be able to get your informant a reward.

How Much Can Be Rewarded

The District Director of the Internal Revenue Service will decide whether a reward is warranted for the person providing the information. As to the amount of the reward, he uses the following criteria:

- If the information is specific and it causes an investigation that results in a recovery, the reward may be 10% of the first $75,000.00 recovered, 5% of the next $25,000.00, and 1% of any additional money recovered (not to exceed $100,000.00).
- If the information provided caused an investigation and was of value in determining what taxes were due, or was a direct factor in the recovery of taxes owed, the reward would be: 5% of the first $75,000.00 recovered, 2½% of the next $25,000.00, and ½% of any additional amount recovered (not to exceed $100,000.00).
- If the information provided caused an investigation but was of no value in determining tax due, the reward would be 1% of the first $75,000.00 and ½% of anything else recovered (not to exceed $100,000.00).

The above information is provided by the Department of the Treasury, Internal Revenue Service, in Publication 733 (revised 5/84); also located in this publication are the procedures that must be followed for your informant to file a claim for a reward. If you are interested in having your informants provide information to the Internal Revenue Service, it is recommended that you contact a local criminal investigator for the IRS and attempt to work out a meaningful relationship for both investigative concerns.

Preparation and Critiques of Covert Officers

The Fourth Amendment mandates that any arrest or search conducted by the police must be based on probable cause and that the probable cause must exist at the time of the arrest or search. Each officer should be afforded the opportunity to update his or her training in this area to maintain the most current level of understanding of what is required to establish probable cause. No matter what your goals are, you should develop your probable cause day by day throughout the investigation. If for some reason your investigation is discovered, then you should be able to have the required paperwork for warrants completed in a much shorter time by possibly salvaging some of the evidence before it can be destroyed. It is recommended that after each covert entry, the information for the probable cause be typed in the format required by your judicial system.

Throughout your investigation you must keep your goals in mind and steer your investigation to best accomplish them.

When developing your probable cause, you must continually prepare and critique the actions of your covert officers. For example, each officer must understand what elements are required to arrest a subject for a specific violation of law. In Indiana, to charge a person with promoting professional gambling you must have the following elements: *a person who, before an event on which gambling may be conducted, transmits and or receives gambling information by any means.* Once you know and understand the required elements, you can direct your covert officers in what is necessary each time he or she makes a covert entry.

To prepare your covert officer in the area of probable cause development just sit down with the officer prior to entry and identify the questions and answers that you need to establish your probable cause. These questions and answers should confirm that the subject is, in fact, violating the criminal statute for which you are investigating him or her. Each time you send in a covert officer, you should sit down with him or her and discuss the best way to obtain the information necessary to arrest and convict your suspect. The more people involved in this meeting, the better the chance that you will come up with a successful format. Remember, rehearse the covert officer's cover with him or her and cover all areas for which you need information.

After each covert entry, someone should evaluate and critique the way the covert officer handled him- or herself. An evaluation of what information was obtained should be done, as well as noting any areas that the covert officer needs to improve. The sooner that this critique can be done, the better opportunity the covert officer has to correct any deficiencies.

Additional Information to Develop Probable Cause

The following is a list of areas to look at when developing your probable cause. Some are listed in earlier sections, but they bear repeating:

- *Prior arrests:* Look for prior charges similar in nature that can be used to demonstrate your target as predisposed to commit the crime you are investigating.
- *Prior case files:* Check for prior involvement in old case files. Check these files for possible informants who you may be able to use in this case. Also use old files to show a continuing illegal enterprise with similar techniques and locations.
- *Public records:* Look for ownership information of locations used.
- *Mail covers:* They provide leads to co-conspirators, both bettors and book-makers; bank accounts, which lead to co-conspirators; charge accounts; assets, land, and vehicles; and other illegal enterprises.
- *Surveillance:* Show patterns that are indicative of bookmaking activities and establish co-conspirators, bookmakers and bettors, vehicles of co-conspirators, and assets.
- *Informants:* The best way to make your probable cause stand up in court is to use informants on a limited basis. Have the informant introduce the covert officer, then use the officer to establish the probable cause.
- *Trash searches:* These will reveal records, telephone bills, bettor names and addresses, and assets.
- *Banking institutions:* Look for payments to co-conspirators and money laundering through cashier's checks; correlate dates, times, and amounts of deposits with known information and look for patterns; correlate dates, times, and amounts for patterns of withdrawals; and study loan information, assets, and co-conspirators.
- *Complaints*
- *Officers' expertise and experience*
- *Unit expertise*

How to Build Probable Cause

To build probable cause, you should list your information step by step as you gather it day by day. You should describe it in such a way that even the lay person will understand what was occurring. Never make the mistake of taking it for granted that the judge will understand. You must put everything into the probable cause that is necessary to substantiate the charges that you are making. The probable cause will be judged later on its face value only, so be sure to list everything you have. Following are examples of how you may record the steps that you may take in building your probable cause.

Case Example: Gambling

Complaints

Affiant for a Fact:
   On September 7, 19XX, I received a complaint which stated that John Doe was actively involved in sports bookmaking at 1234 Thelma Street using telephone number 234–5678. This complaint was received by phone in the vice branch office, and the information was provided by a person who declined to leave his name.
   On October 4, 19XX, I received a complaint which stated that John Doe was involved in sports gambling at 1234 E. Thelma Street, where he was known to threaten bettors who were late in paying their gambling debts. This complaint was in the form of a letter that was received through the U.S. mail and was signed only by the word "Help".

If you choose to shorten the above version, you may want to put the same information down as:

Affiant for a Fact:
   Since September 19XX, I have received several complaints, both oral and written, which stated that John Doe was actively involved in sports gambling at 1234 Thelma Street using telephone number 234–5678. In one complaint, Doe was accused of threatening bettors who were late in paying debts.

Background Information for Probable Cause: Records Check

Affiant for a Fact:
   I, Detective _____ , conducted a background investigation on John Doe and discovered that he had several prior arrests and convictions for gambling-related offenses. In addition to the above, I, Detective _____ , discovered that on April 2, 19XX, a search warrant was served at 1234 Thelma Street. The probable cause for the search indicated that Mr. John Doe was involved in sports bookmaking at that location, and during the search a large quantity of sports bookmaking records were seized under case number 123456A.

Information from the Telephone Company

Affiant for a Fact:
   On October 1, 19XX, I, Detective _____ , contacted Bell Telephone and requested information as to who was listed to the phone number that I provided in the complaints. I was informed that telephone number 234–5678 was a nonpublished number and the release of that information would require a subpoena. On October 2, 19XX, I obtained a subpoena for subscriber information and toll records for the preceding 3 months for telephone number 234–5678. I delivered this subpoena to Bell Telephone on this date.

Affiant for a Fact:

On October 8, 19XX, I, Detective _____ , received the toll records and subscriber information from the phone company which I had requested. Records showed that phone number 234–5678 was listed to John Doe with an address of 1234 Thelma Street. The toll records showed that there was a large number of calls placed to line information services, for example, 1–900–987–6543, which is listed to Jo's National Line Service. From my experience, I have found that numerous calls to services which provide up-to-date point spreads on events, such as football games, are indicative of a sports bookmaking operation.

Information from Surveillance

Affiant for a Fact:

On Tuesday, October 10, 19XX, I, Detective, _____ , conducted a surveillance of John Doe and his activities. The surveillance began at 0600 hours at his residence at 1234 Thelma Street. At approximately 0700 hours, Mr. Doe left his residence and was observed driving his 1989 red Corvette with license plate number XXXX. Mr. Doe arrived at Les Deli located at 0987 South 7th Street. This location has a history of catering to sports bookmakers and their bettors. In the 2 years prior to this date, there had been several arrests on the premises for gambling-related charges. Mr. Doe entered the deli and took a seat by the front door facing toward the parking lot. From 0730 until 0840 hours, I observed 21 subjects enter the deli. Of those, 16 were greeted by Doe and sat down at Doe's table. Of the 16, 11 spent only a very short time at the table and they either passed currency to Doe or Doe passed currency to them. Each time after the currency was passed, Doe would make a notation on a yellow piece of paper he carried in his left front shirt pocket. Once this was done, the person would leave. Of the five remaining subjects, all approached Doe and a transfer of U.S. currency between Doe and them occurred. Doe made a notation on the yellow sheet and the subjects then took seats at different tables.

Covert Officer Observations

Affiant for a Fact:

On Tuesday, October 10, 19XX, at approximately 0730 hours Detective _____ entered Les Deli located at 0987 South 7th Street. Detective _____ was present in the deli for approximately 1½ hours during which time he overheard conversations being held at the next table. The conversations were between a subject known to him as John Doe and several subjects who entered the deli. Each person passed or received U.S. currency and talked about different sporting events which he had bet on. Each time they requested their totals (how much they owed or were to receive), and Doe would refer to a yellow sheet that was located in his pocket. After payment was paid or received, Detective _____ would observe John Doe making a notation on the side of this yellow sheet. From my experience and training in the area of sports bookmaking investigations and my 15 years in law enforcement, I have found that the above observed activities are indicative of a sports bookmaking operation.

Ownership Information from Background Check

Affiant for a Fact:

    I, Detective _____ , checked with the County Assessor's Office on October 1, 19XX, and discovered that the residence located at 1234 Thelma Street had the owner listed as John Doe.

    I, Detective _____ , contacted the corporation division of the state of this date and discovered that Les Deli located at 0987 South 7th Street had a president of the corporation listed as J. Doe with the address of P.O. Box XYZ 722.

Trash Search Information

Affiant for a Fact:

    On October 15, 19XX and again on October 22, 19XX, I observed Mr. John Doe place trash bags from his residence on the street side in front of his residence located at 1234 Thelma Street. I recovered three bags of trash on each of the above dates for a total of six bags of trash. On each of the dates, I recovered assorted mail within the bags which was addressed to John Doe at 1234 Thelma Street. On October 15th, I also discovered [*list all items that are indicative of sports gambling*]. On October 22nd, I discovered _____ [*list items*] in the trash seized. From my experience [*repeat qualifications*], I have found that the above items are consistent with the operation of a sports bookmaking operation.

Placing Bets

You, not the informant, decide what the bet will be and you dial the telephone number to the suspect.

Affiant for a Fact:

    On October 23, 19XX, I, Detective _____ , dialed the telephone number 234–5678 and a bet was placed on an event that was scheduled for that date. The above phone number was the one provided in the complaints and was listed with the phone company to John Doe located at 1234 Thelma Street, Indianapolis, Marion County, Indiana. The above bet was placed with a person I recognized as John Doe.

or:

    On October 23, 19XX, I, Detective _____ , dialed telephone number 234–5678 at which time a wager of U.S. currency was placed on a sporting event with a person whose voice I recognized as that of John Doe.

You should stick with the same format and list all bets by date; however, unless required to do so, do not give the exact bet placed. This information could get your informant hurt.

Case Example: Fencing Stolen Property

Complaints

Affiant for a Fact:

Since May 19XX, I, Detective _____ , have received numerous complaints which stated that a black male named Chan was actively buying and selling stolen property at 1234 W. Sherman, Indianapolis, Marion County, Indiana.

Background Information

Affiant for a Fact:

I, Detective _____ , conducted a background investigation on Mr. Chan and the location at 1234 W. Sherman and found that on January 4, 19XX, a search warrant was served at 1234 W. Sherman, and investigators recovered a large quantity of stolen stereo equipment under case number 9876543A. I also discovered through court records that Mr. Chan was arrested and convicted for receiving stolen property under the same case number.

Surveillance

Affiant for a Fact:

I, Detective _____ , conducted a surveillance at the residence of Mr. Chan located at 1234 W. Sherman on June 24, 19XX. I observed seven subjects enter the residence in a 4-hour period. Subjects were carrying stereo equipment when they entered the residence and after a few minutes they were observed leaving the U.S. currency in their hands. I obtained license plate information from the vehicles that they drove and discovered that two of the subjects were listed as habitual shoplifters in our files. This activity is indicative of an operation which is fencing stolen property.

Infiltrations

Affiant for a Fact:

On June 27, 19XX, at approximately 1100 hours, I, Detective _____ , arrived at 1234 W. Sherman. I knocked on the front door and it was opened by a black male subject known to me to be Mr. Chan. I stated that I had been informed that he was interested in buying stereo equipment and tools and I stated that I had a bunch of stuff in my car if he was interested. Mr. Chan and I proceeded to my car where he looked at the items I had in my trunk. Mr. Chan asked me how hot the items were (hot is a street term which is used when referring to stolen property). I stated that the items were stolen from a warehouse on the south side but they couldn't be traced. Mr. Chan then paid me $70.00 U.S. currency for [*list each item*] seven items with a total value of $430.00.

Sales Made on Five Other Dates

Each sale included mention of the items being stolen and in several cases from where the item was stolen. After you infiltrate the operation, keep in mind that the conversation you get is the key to a conviction. Get as much conversation as to the target's activities as possible. Each item sold must be marked prior to sale and noted in the probable cause.

Identify the Specific Law Being Violated

Somewhere in the body of your probable cause, you need to specify the exact law violation that you are investigating. It is recommended that you use terminology similar to that which is used in your criminal statute. In Indiana, the statute states that a promoter of professional gambling is a person who before a race, game, contest, or event on which gambling may be conducted, knowingly or intentionally transmits or receives gambling information by any means. You would utilize this definition in a probable cause by stating that your subject on each occasion knowingly or intentionally before a race, game, contest, or event transmitted or received gambling information, this being in violation of Indiana State law. This type of information can be added after each betting transaction or at the end of your probable cause. It is recommended that you contact your legal advisor and prosecutor for help in the actual format to be used.

SEARCH WARRANTS

Depending on the type of investigation you are conducting, you may have a variety of ways to put your search warrant together. It is recommended that you always look at the use of financial elements within your warrant. The Bureau of Justice Assistance, located at 633 Indiana Avenue, N.W., in Washington, D.C. 20531, has published a series of booklets that cover a wide variety of asset forfeiture subjects. In February 1989, they produced one titled "Financial Search Warrants" by Richard S. Stolker. This series of booklets is free to law enforcement officers and can be very important in maintaining a current understanding of today's issues in forfeiture investigations.

Elements Necessary to Produce a Good Search Warrant

Person or Place

If the target of the search is a person, you need to be as descriptive as possible. Give all personal traits, hair color, height, weight, race, and eye color. If a picture is available, one can be added to the warrant. It is best to use an officer who is familiar with the subject to serve the warrant. This will ensure that the correct person is searched.

If your target is a place, you must provide a good enough description so that a person not familiar with the location will have sufficient information to search the correct location. Remember what was said earlier in the book: the criminal will change numbers on the house and make every attempt to discredit any warrant being served. Be sure that you not only use the address of the target, but also do an in-depth description of the buildings and area surrounding the target location. Remember to mention any outbuildings or other areas on the premises that may be used to conceal evidence. If you have the ability to take pictures from the air, they can be very valuable in your description of the target location.

Vehicles To Be Searched

When a vehicle is the target of the search warrant, it must be described in such a manner that it can be distinguished from all others of the same year and manufacturer. You need to mention the make, model, year, color, plate number, and any other characteristic that will make it easy for the officer who serves the warrant to identify the correct vehicle. Look for items, such as wheel description, bumper stickers, window decals, and any identifiable damage that can be used to quickly identify the target vehicle. Remember that if you base your warrant on the vehicle's make, color, and plate number, you may lose if the plate is changed or the vehicle is painted before you serve the warrant.

The Object of Your Search

Describe what you are searching for in such a manner that what you intend to seize and why will be apparent to anyone who is reading the warrant. Describe your training and experience as well as why and how the items you intend to seize are related to the targeted illegal criminal enterprise. Figure 8.1 shows an example of a description of property to be seized and a brief explanation of how it fits into a sports bookmaking network. Using the same format you can justify seizing items for most any case. For example, the affidavit in Figure 8.2 uses the same format but is for a fencing operation.

SPORTS BOOKMAKING

AFFIDAVIT
FOR PROBABLE CAUSE

_____

STATE OF INDIANA, COUNTY OF MARION. SS:

_____ swears or affirms that he believes and has good cause to believe from my investigation, I learned from reliable persons the following facts and attending circumstances that:

AFFIANT TO THE FACT THAT:

1. Books, records, receipts, notes, ledgers, and other papers relating to the transportation, ordering, purchase, and distribution of gambling materials -- in particular, gambling income -- payouts, and sports gambling records.

2. Books, records, invoices, receipts, records of real estate transactions, bank statements and related records, passbooks, money drafts, letters of credit, money orders, bank drafts, and cashier's checks, bank checks, safe deposit box keys, money wrappers, and other items evidencing the obtaining, secreting, transfer, and/or conceal-ment of assets and the obtaining, secreting, transfer, concealment, and/or expenditure of money.

3. Electronic equipment, such as computers, telephone answering machines, and related materials and manuals used to generate, transfer, count, record, and/or store the information in the above items of this exhibit. Additionally, computer software, tapes and discs, audio tapes, and the contents there-in, containing the information generated by the aforementioned electronic equipment.

4. United States currency, previous metals, jewelry, and financial instruments, including stocks and bonds.

5. Photographs, including still photos, negatives, videotapes, films, undeveloped film and the contents therein, slides, photographs of co-conspirators, and assets.

6. Address and/or telephone books, Rolodex, and any papers reflecting names, addresses, telephone numbers, pager numbers, fax numbers and/

Figure 8.1. Examples of items that may be seized under a financial search warrant.

or telex numbers of co-conspirators, sources of supply, customers, financial institutions, and other individuals or businesses with whom a financial relation exists.

7. Indication of occupancy, residency, rental and/or ownership of the premises described herein, including, but not limited to, utility and telephone bills, canceled envelopes, rental, purchase or lease agreements, and keys.

Based on his or her training, experience, and participation in other financial investigations involving gambling enterprises, the affiant has found that:

• Sports bookmakers often purchase and/or title their assets in fictitious names, aliases, or names of relatives, associates, or business entities to avoid detection of these assets by law enforcement authorities.

• Even though these assets are in the names other than that of the bookmaker, the bookmaker actually owns and continues to use these assets, exercising dominion and control over them.

• Sports bookmakers keep large amounts of U.S. currency on hand in order to maintain and finance their ongoing sports bookmaking enterprise.

• It is common for sports bookmakers to maintain books, records, notes, ledgers, and receipts relating to the purchase of financial instruments and/or the transportation, ordering, sale, and distribution of gambling materials. These books, records, receipts, notes, ledgers, etc. are kept where the sports bookmaker has ready access to them.

• Sports bookmakers keep proceeds of the gambling enterprise and records of said gambling in secure locations within their residences, their businesses, and/or other locations over which they have dominion and control, for ready access and for concealment of these items from law enforcement authorities.

• It is common for persons involved in sports bookmaking to maintain evidence about their obtaining, secreting, transferring, concealing, and/or spending gambling proceeds. This may include currency, financial instruments, precious metals and gem stones, jewelry, books, records, invoices, receipts, records of real estate transactions, bank

Figure 8.1. (continued)

statements and related records, passbooks, money drafts, letters of credit, money orders, bank drafts, cashier's checks, bank checks, safe deposit keys, and money wrappers. These items are maintained by the sports bookmaker within his residences, businesses, or other locations over which he has dominion and control.

• Sports bookmakers often utilize electronic equipment such as computers and telephone answering machines to generate, transfer, count, record, and/or store the information described in the items listed above.

• When sports bookmakers amass large proceeds from their gambling enterprise, they attempt to legitimize these profits through money laundering activities. To accomplish these goals, sports bookmakers use, but are not limited to, domestic banks and their attendant services, securities brokers, professionals such as attorneys and accountants, casinos, real estate, shell corporations and business fronts, and otherwise legitimate businesses which generate large quantities of currency.

• Sports bookmakers commonly maintain addresses or telephone numbers in books or papers providing names, addresses, and/or telephone numbers of their associates in the gambling enterprise.

• Sports bookmakers have photographs taken of themselves, their associates, their property, and their materials. The bookmakers usually keep these photographs in their possession.

Figure 8.1. (continued)

FENCING STOLEN PROPERTY

AFFIDAVIT

FOR PROBABLE CAUSE

_ _

STATE OF INDIANA, COUNTY OF MARION. SS:

_____ swears or affirms that he believes and has good cause to believe from my investigation, I learned from reliable persons the following facts and attending circumstances that:

AFFIANT TO THE FACT THAT:

1. Books, records, receipts, notes, ledgers, and other papers relating to the transportation, ordering, purchase, and distribution of stolen property -- in particular, [LIST THE TYPES OF ITEMS SOLD] records.

2. Books, records, invoices, receipts, records of real estate transactions, bank statements and related records, passbooks, money drafts, letters of credit, money orders, bank drafts, and cashier's checks, bank checks, safe deposit box keys, money wrappers, and other items evidencing the obtaining, secreting, transfer, and/or conceal- ment of assets and the obtaining, secreting, transfer, concealment, and/or expenditure of money.

3. Electronic equipment, such as computers, telephone answering machines, and related materials and manuals used to generate, transfer, count, record, and/or store the information in the above items of this exhibit. Additionally, computer software, tapes and discs, audio tapes, and the contents therein, containing the information generated by the aforementioned electronic equipment.

4. United States currency, previous metals, jewelry, and financial instruments, including stocks and bonds.

5. Photographs, including still photos, negatives, videotapes, films, undeveloped film and the contents therein, slides, photographs of co-conspirators, and assets.

6. Address and/or telephone books, Rolodex, and any papers reflecting names, addresses, telephone numbers, pager numbers, fax numbers and/

Figure 8.2. Example of an affidavit for probable cause for a fencing operation.

or telex numbers of co-conspirators, sources of supply, customers, financial institutions, and other individuals or businesses with whom a financial relation exists.

7. Indication of occupancy, residency, rental and/or ownership of the premises described herein, including, but not limited to, utility and telephone bills, canceled envelopes, rental, purchase or lease agreements, and keys.

Based on his or her training, experience, and participation in other financial investigations involving fencing operations, the affiant has found that:

• Fences often purchase and/or title their assets in fictitious names, aliases, or names of relatives, associates, or business entities to avoid detection of these assets by law enforcement authorities.

• Even though these assets are in the names other than that of the fence, the fence actually owns and continues to use these assets, exercising dominion and control over them.

• Fences keep large amounts of U.S. currency on hand in order to maintain and finance their ongoing illegal enterprise.

• It is common for fences to maintain books, records, notes, ledgers, and receipts relating to the purchase of financial instruments and/ or the transportation, ordering, sale, and distribution of stolen property. These books, records, receipts, notes, ledgers, etc. are kept where the fence has ready access to them.

• Fencing operations keep proceeds of the illegal enterprise and records of said operation in secure locations within their residences, their businesses, and/or other locations over which they have dominion and control, for ready access and for concealment of these items from law enforcement authorities.

• It is common for persons involved in fencing property to maintain evidence about their obtaining, secreting, transferring, concealing, and/or spending illegal proceeds. This may include currency, financial instruments, precious metals and gem stones, jewelry, books, records, invoices, receipts, records of real estate transactions, bank statements and related records, passbooks, money drafts, letters of credit, money orders, bank drafts, cashier's checks, bank checks, safe

Figure 8.2. (continued)

deposit keys, and money wrappers. These items are maintained by the fence within his residences, businesses, or other locations over which he has dominion and control.

• Fencing operations often utilize electronic equipment such as computers and telephone answering machines to generate, transfer, count, record, and/or store the information described in the items listed above.

[Note: As you can see from the above entries, all you have to do is take this format and select the items that fit your case and eliminate the ones you do not want to use. If you list an item to be seized, you should have a justification for it.]

• When fences amass large proceeds from their illegal enterprise, they attempt to legitimize these profits through money laundering activities. To accomplish these goals, fencing operations use, but are not limited to, domestic banks and their attendant services, securities brokers, professionals such as attorneys and accountants, casinos, real estate, shell corporations and business fronts, and otherwise legitimate businesses which generate large quantities of currency.

• Fences commonly maintain addresses or telephone numbers in books or papers providing names, addresses, and/or telephone numbers of their associates in the illegal enterprise.

• Fences have photographs taken of themselves, their associates, their property, and their materials. The fences usually keep these photographs in their possession.

Figure 8.2. (continued)

APPENDIX 1: CHAPTER SUMMARY
(PROBABLE CAUSE DEVELOPMENT)

Probable cause development begins the second you start your case.

Goals of the Investigation

- Eliminate the organization.
- Seize assets.
- Assist the IRS.
- Identify co-conspirators.

Need to Understand the Process of Civil Forfeiture

- The suspect must establish standing.
- The burden of proof is lower in civil cases.
- Criminal charges are not necessary to file civil forfeiture.
- The suspect may be deposed and compelled to produce records.
- The burden of proof shifts to the suspect.
- If the suspect is evasive, he may lose assets.

Need to Understand What the IRS Needs

- Provide as much background on the suspect as you can.
- The IRS has a reward system that can be used.

Preparation of Officers

- Officers need to understand the elements of the laws that are being violated.
- Officers should be informed as to what questions need answers prior to each entry.
- Officers should have input as to the best way to gather this information.

Critiques of Officers

- Each officer in a covert setting should be critiqued after each entry.

Other Sources of Information for the Probable Cause

- Background investigation
- Officer experience

How to Build a Probable Cause

- Build the probable cause day by day.
- Be sure to list as much information as possible.

Each year millions of automobiles worth billions of dollars are lost to thieves. This is elevating auto theft into a bracket where there are immense profits with little risk of incarceration. Law enforcement's response is to develop new programs to fight auto theft. However, until the profit is eliminated and punishment is reinstated, new programs will not work.

One critical area to examine once we catch a thief in a stolen vehicle is what the next step should be. In most cases, the subject is arrested and walks away with a smile on his face. This is wrong! Cases should always be taken two or three levels further. The next step should include identifying the following:

- Why the vehicle was stolen
- For whom it was stolen
- Where it was to be delivered
- How we can get into the operation

Responding to these issues can impact a large number of future vehicle theft incidents. Remember, if the buyer (fence, chop shop, retitler) is eliminated, then crime can be prevented in some cases.

WHAT IS AUTO THEFT?

Four basic categories of auto theft should be mentioned:

Joy riding: This category has little investigative value due to being spur of the moment and normally not done on order. Look for gang initiation and involvement.

Sale of parts (chop shops and fencing): In this situation, the vehicle is dismantled and parts are dispersed to area users. If a chop shop is involved, you will normally find only small parts of the vehicles left.

Retitling: In this case, vehicles are retitled and sold in other areas as legitimate resale vehicles.

Theft for facilitation of crime: In this situation, the vehicle is a means to an end. It is stolen so that the thief can accomplish his true goal of robbery, burglary, etc.

WHAT IS THE FIRST STEP?

Once you have determined that you want to impact auto thefts in a given area, you need to analyze all the information you have in your possession. As we mentioned in earlier chapters, you need to do some charting to determine whether there are any patterns that may help your investigation.

What Will Patterns Show?

- Where auto thefts are most likely to occur
- Where you are most likely to find/recover stolen vehicles
- What type of organizations are involved
- The most likely suspects
- Motives for the crimes
- Who benefits from the crime

What Should Be Charted?

- Day of the week when the auto theft occurs
- Day of the week when the recovery occurs
- Time of theft and recovery
- Date of the auto theft and recovery (day of month)
- Location of the auto theft (unique location)
- Items missing
- Items contained in original car
- Recovery of the auto
- Method of entry to auto
- Way vehicle was started
- Involvement of fire
- Other crimes in the area of the theft and recovery

TYPES OF AUTO THEFT INVESTIGATION

As you review reports, you need to try to identify what type of investigation you are going to employ.

Fencing Parts

If all your stolen vehicles are recovered with tires and stereos missing, you are looking at a fencing operation. The thief strips the vehicle and sells the parts to a storefront location. In this case, your attack would be to identify patterns involved and set up a surveillance to catch the thief. Once this is accomplished, ask these four questions:

1. Why was the vehicle stolen?
2. Was it stolen for someone?
3. Where do the parts go?
4. Will you help us infiltrate the operation?

From this point on, you need to:

- Conduct your background check of the target.
- Identify sales to the targets where they know the items are stolen.
- Get them to order high dollar items.
- Identify whether the money paid for the stolen property comes from the business (register).
- Purchase property back and determine whether the money paid goes into the business (register or safe).

Retitling—Salvage—Replating (most profit)

In this case, there is much more work to be done. You need to verify that you are losing vehicles and no recoveries are being made. Identify patterns from the day of week when the theft occurred, time of day, location of theft (parking lot, car dealership, etc.), type of vehicle (condition, components), and other crimes in the area. Try to gather enough information to target a location or person.

You also need to research individuals in your area who have prior arrests for this type of activity. Check the newspapers for listings of mechanic liens and cross check ownership of businesses with prior criminal involvement. Check suspected junkyards/owners for sale and use of salvage titles. Cross check suspected vehicle identification numbers (VINs) with the Bureau of Motor Vehicles. Look for salvage title indications.

Car Jacking

Car jacking is not new, but in the past several years it has been given new life through national news coverage of specific incidences where people have been killed. Car jacking can take many forms, but in most cases the vehicle is the prize. The attack may vary greatly, but usually one of the following situations will occur.

Fake Accident

The criminal will bump the victim's car and get out to check the damage. When the victim gets out of the car, there is an altercation with the criminal, armed or unarmed, forcing the victim to give up the vehicle.

Unattended Vehicle

This occurs when the owner/operator of the vehicle leaves the vehicle running for whatever reason and the criminal commandeers it.

Situational

This occurs when the criminal stakes out a location such as a grocery store and waits for the victim to return to the vehicle after shopping. Then the criminal will confront the owner and take the vehicle (armed or unarmed).

Retitle Case Example

An informant contacted law enforcement officials stating that John Doe was stealing cars and then getting clean titles through his business, ABC Auto Repair. A background was conducted on John Doe, and it was found that he was wanted on a felony warrant for battery. The warrant was served on the subject while in a suspected stolen vehicle. The subject was arrested and transported but not informed as to the true nature of the investigation. The vehicle was inspected and found to be stolen. The VIN plate was from a salvage title from a wrecked car of the same year and type as the stolen one. Research was done and it was found that a few months after the salvage title and VIN plates were obtained, dummy work receipts were written through the auto repair place for work which was supposedly done to the car. As required by law, a registered letter was sent to the last known owner of the salvage vehicle showing what was owed and ads were placed in the newspaper as a public notice. Once this was accomplished, Doe and his co-conspirators would petition the state for a new title due to the mechanic's lien. The state would issue a clean, clear title to Mr. Doe. Doe would have the VIN plates from the salvage vehicle placed on the stolen vehicle.

A grand jury subpoena for records of the local newspaper uncovered 77 ads over a 6-month period listing mechanic liens on vehicles by Doe. Each of the vehicles listed had to be researched to identify whether it had started as a salvage item, and then a search to locate the stolen vehicles was conducted. Keep in mind, when you conduct a case like this, you need to look for the records of the repairs on the questioned vehicles. In many cases, when you go to the parts supplier, you will find no existing orders for parts.

Car Jacking Case Example

November 18, 19XX: We received a list of associates of a suspected purse grabber named John Doe. Information provided showed that Doe would hang out in parking lots of banks that had drive-up windows or ATMs. Doe would focus on older females making withdrawals. He would then follow them to their next stop, confront them, and take their valuables but not their cars. No home address was known.

January 4, 19XX (2102 hours): We obtained a surveillance camera photo from bank X showing Doe making a withdrawal from an ATM using a victim's card and password.

January 13, 19XX: We received information that John Doe and John Jones had paired up and were committing robberies throughout the county. One subject had a prior arrest for murder on 11–26–XX and was out on bond. No valid address was known.

January 15, 19XX: This information was distributed throughout the department: within the last several months, numerous robberies, larcenies, and vehicle thefts have occurred. The crimes appear to be cluster-type crimes where once a vehicle is stolen numerous larcenies and robberies will occur. The method of operation (MO) is as follows:

- A GM-type vehicle is stolen.
- A victim is selected by the criminal as he or she leaves a bank or ATM.
- The criminal will be wearing a hooded sweatshirt tied down tight around the face.
- The criminal either will wait for the victim to go to his or her next stop or in some cases the criminal will bump into the victim's vehicle.
- The targeted victim normally will be a female, 40 to 70 years old.
- When the victim stops to check the damage, the criminal will slam the victim and steal their purse and other valuables.
- The criminal will flee in the previously stolen vehicle.
- There will be one or two other incidents in a 40-minute period, then the criminal will dump the stolen vehicle and be picked up by his partner in an older, rusty, primer-coated van.

A request was made that when a GM-type vehicle was stolen, and a theft occurred which involved the stolen vehicle, then an all-jurisdiction broadcast be made.

January 19, 19XX: This background information was obtained:

12–14–XX	Car is stolen at 3300 North
12–15–XX	Bump and grab occurs at 7000 East; purse is recovered 10th and Arlington; car is recovered 10th and Post
12–18–XX	Van is stolen at 5300 North; van is used for a bump and grab after the victim had left a bank at 2800 South and in another bump and grab at 3800 South after a woman had left the bank
12–19–XX	Van is recovered with three empty purses at 1600 North
12–19–XX	Car is stolen at 1600 North, used in a bump and grab at 700 North; car is recovered at 400 North
12–28–XX	Car is stolen at 1500 North
12–29–XX	Stolen car is used at 5700 West for a purse grab at a gas station, victim had just left ATM; stolen car is used in a bump and grab at 3000 West and in a purse grab at a convenience store at 2000 West; stolen car is stopped by law enforcement; subject flees, five purses are recovered (empty)

1–8–XX	Car is stolen, is used in three crimes, and then is abandoned
1–9–XX	Car is stolen, is used in one bump and grab, and then is abandoned
1–12–XX	Car is stolen, is used in three crimes, and then is abandoned
1–13–XX	Car is stolen, used in a bump and grab, and then is abandoned
1–14–XX	Car is stolen, used in a crime, and is abandoned; suspect is seen getting into an old, rusty van with second suspect driving
1–15–XX	Purse is grabbed at 7100 East; stolen car is involved
1–16–XX	Car is stolen; a bump and grab occurs; car is abandoned
1–17–XX	Car is stolen at 7300 North; a bump and grab occurs at 4600 North
1–18–XX	Same vehicle is used in three bump and grabs; vehicle is abandoned

The breakdown on the victims showed 88% white females, 73% over 40 years old, seven had just left financial institutions, seven had just left grocery stores, and two had just left drug stores.

The day and time study revealed:

Sun.	Mon.	Tues.	Weds.	Thurs.	Fri.	Sat.
1	1	4	1	1	5	3

with 80% of the crimes occurring between 0930 and 1645 hours.

January 29, 19XX: We set up a county-wide surveillance on likely locations for targets. Suspect information was provided.

January 30, 19XX: Three subjects were arrested for robbery, vehicle theft, and violation of the firearms act. The subjects had confronted a victim at a grocery store. They took her purse and groceries and then fled in a stolen vehicle. All three subjects were under 18 years old. Over the next week, several other arrests were made because of surveillance and background information.

February 4, 19XX: An article appeared in the newspaper about the rash of bump and grab crimes. A picture accompanied the article of one suspect using an ATM. This article generated several calls identifying the subject and his activities. Callers identified where the suspect lived and what vehicle he was driving. A surveillance was placed on the suspects and arrests were made.

Vehicle Theft Ring Case Example

Complaint

An informant called and stated that he had been approached by three subjects who had several stolen vehicles for sale. They requested that the informant look for buyers. The only information that could be provided about the subjects was their nicknames and that they lived on the south side.

Background

We debriefed the informant and then located two of the vehicles which were for sale, both of which were in fact stolen. We asked the informant to set up a meeting where we could buy the vehicles.

Intelligence Branch

We found no reference to the subjects involved by nickname or area of residence.

Tactical Plan

We used the informant to get an introduction to the car thieves. Also, we attempted to get into a conversation so that we could determine who had stolen the cars, where from, and how many vehicles they had stolen. We also tried to identify other locations where they had sold cars.

Priorities

Our priorities included officer safety, obtaining enough conversation on tape to arrest and convict the subjects, and identification of all persons involved and of all outlets for stolen vehicles.

Case Results

The informant set up a meeting on the south side where we could look at the vehicles. We arrived and were introduced to the three car thieves. The informant then left the location. These vehicles were present: 1989 Blazer, 1990 Chevy pickup, and 1985 Chevy Z28.

The three subjects informed us that they had ripped off the vehicles, and they wanted $400 for all three. We requested delivery of the vehicles to be made at a department store parking lot on the south side. This lot was fenced in and we would have good control. They agreed. We left and met them 30 minutes later.

We paid them $400 in cash and then took them down. Two of the subjects ran as the uniformed officers approached, but due to the selection of the delivery site we caught them with no problems.

We discovered that all three subjects were 17 years old and had several prior arrests for vehicle theft. One of the three cooperated, and we were able to locate several other vehicles which were stolen. These subjects stole an average of at least one vehicle a night.

Vehicle Theft Case Example

On March 11, 19XX, at approximately 0800 hr, we were notified by a detective from Hamilton County that a 1986 red Cavalier convertible with a black convertible top, VIN XXXXXXXXXXX, under a Hamilton County case number, had been stolen from the hospital parking lot on March 9, 19XX. He further advised that the vehicle contained a mobile telephone with a serial number

AXXXXXX. He also advised that there had been several calls made from the telephone after the robbery.

The telephone calls were made to 1234 East Avenue, 543 West Ham Avenue, and 246 North Stone Avenue. We researched the three locations and found the address of 246 North Stone Avenue to be the address given by Bert Vey, who has a prior arrest for vehicle theft on February 14, 19XX. We then drove by the address on Stone Avenue where we observed the vehicle that was reported stolen in front of the residence.

Then we observed a black male, later identified as Bert Vey, exit the residence at 246 North Stone Avenue, remove an item from the vehicle, and take it back into the residence. Mr. Vey later came back out of the residence accompanied by a female who was later identified as Gina Carn. They left in the stolen vehicle southbound on Stone. Mr. Vey then fled from the officer. Mr. Vey crashed the vehicle into a residence at 123 East Mont Street.

At this time, both suspects were arrested. After an inventory search incidental to arrest, it was determined that the telephone was not located in the vehicle. The original license plate from the vehicle, XXXX, was also missing. At that time we requested a search for the license plate described above and for the telephone mentioned above.

On March 11, 19XX, at about 1650 hours, we served a search warrant at 246 North Stone to search for the above items. During the search, we recovered two magazines from a .380 automatic handgun, a pouch with 36 rounds of ammunition, and one police badge.

10

Bad Checks

In today's society, it is second nature for people to write checks; in fact, each year over 45 billion checks are passed for goods and services. Of this total 1 out of every 100 checks will be returned for nonsufficient funds (NSF). This is over 450 million bad checks.

The volume of NSF checks is so great that law enforcement authorities cannot come close to handling them. In response to this, businesses have turned to companies which offer programs that will guarantee no losses on approved checks. These companies offer check approval and databases that offer businesses a way to minimize losses.

You, as a law enforcement officer, may be able to access information from these businesses to assist in tracking your check fraud suspects. I recommend that you contact your local banking institutions and request information on bank scams such as check kiting, manager approval scams, and confidence schemes. In most cases, banks will have case examples and video training that may be available to you.

In addition, you should try to hold monthly meetings with bank employees to discuss such topics as new trends in bank scams, latest lists of suspects involved in fraud, and any other information that may help in future case preparation.

CASE EXAMPLE 1: CHECK FRAUD

In September of 19XX, members of the Retail Merchant's Council complained to the County Prosecutor that merchants in the Indianapolis area were sustaining substantial monetary losses in the form of bad checks. The council complained that these checks were insufficient fund checks, but they felt there was more to the story than just a typical consumer overdrafting an account.

The basic information provided by the complainants (which consisted of large groups of names) was then given to Sergeant Tim Viles, who was asked by the prosecutor to determine whether law enforcement could be of some further assistance to these merchants.

Sergeant Viles immediately started meeting with merchants from the community. He collected a number of sample NSF checks from these merchants to start his analysis of the names that were presented to him. His analysis soon indicated that a group of persons were operating in our community to defraud not only the merchants that were complaining, but also other merchants and a number of area financial institutions. The size of this operation appeared to be of major significance.

Sergeant Viles, having identified what he believed was a major financial crime, requested to open a criminal case targeting one specific group of individuals (who became known as the "Anigans"). This group of eight individuals were determined by Sergeant Viles, on his initial evaluation, to be using approximately 50 different names on various checking accounts. This investigation started in December of 19XX.

Sergeant Viles was able to identify a number of means by which these suspects were able to perpetrate these offenses on unsuspecting merchants and financial institutions. One such method was that these suspects, after having established false identities would go to financial institutions and open checking accounts with minimal deposits. There they would obtain a supply of checks for these accounts. They would then very quickly (perhaps all in a day) flood merchants with these bad checks.

Sergeant Viles coordinated information from over 20 law enforcement agencies from all across the United States regarding the suspected individuals. He additionally requested that the prosecutor subpoena records on approximately 113 different checking accounts that had been fraudulently obtained by the suspects.

In May of 19XX, Sergeant Viles presented a probable cause affidavit to the prosecutor for the purpose of requesting that eight search warrants be issued to further collect physical evidence relating to this unfolding criminal enterprise. Search warrants were issued and allowed investigators to seize numerous pieces of false identification and a large number of unissued checks. Property which had been purchased from unsuspecting merchants with these forged checks was also seized at this time.

Sergeant Viles was constantly reviewing, for evidentiary purposes, documents received from subpoenas that had been issued, evidence that was supplied from merchants, and those items seized in the search warrants. From his evaluations, he then utilized resources available through the U.S. Postal Service Forensic Laboratory in Chicago, IL (for the recovery of fingerprints from passed checks), as well as the resources of the county forensic laboratory (to identify individual suspect's handwriting). His efforts met with great results, and large amounts of physical evidence were recovered from the submitted items.

During December 19XX, about a year after he started this investigation, Sergeant Viles submitted a request to the County Prosecutor for charges to be filed on the eight suspected individuals. As a result of this investigation all eight suspects were charged with 120 different felony charges ranging from defrauding financial institutions to forgery. In addition to these charges, over 100 outstanding misdemeanor warrants were served are cleared up based on information provided by Sergeant Viles' investigation. Also as a result of this investigation, and recommendations made in part by Sergeant Viles, legislation was introduced to the state legislature recommending changes to the current check deception statute to provide additional relief to merchants in our community.

Affidavit for Probable Cause—State of Indiana, County of Marion, SS

I, Timothy C. Viles, an officer of the Police Department swear or affirm that I believe and have good cause to believe from my investigation and information from reliable persons, the following facts and attending circumstances:

That I have been involved in an investigation, since November of 19XX, concerning a ring (family) of individuals involved in the crime of check deception, forgery, fraud, fraud on financial institutions, and theft.

That this investigation was initiated as a result of a complaint from the Retail Merchants Association to the County Prosecutor's Office concerning possible commonality among a group of approximately seventy (70) persons whose names were listed on checks that had been reported to the County Prosecutor's Office as being invalid checks.

That during this investigation, I have determined that approximately fifty (50) of the listed names are believed to be aliases used by eight (8) specific individuals. All eight of these individuals appear to make use of certain common information in the furtherance of their criminal activities.

That this investigation has identified eight members of this criminal organization as:

1. Joyce L. Anigan
2. Betty J. Anigan-More
3. Sharon Anigan Dunk
4. Deborah D. Anigan-Homas
5. Renita G. Anigan
6. Lisa Anigan
7. Janet Rotter Anigan
8. Carmen Kenn

That information has been obtained from various law enforcement agencies, in regard to the identification of the eight named individuals. Other agencies providing information leading to the true identities of the eight named persons are Federal Bureau of Investigation, U.S. Postal Inspection Service, County Department of Public Welfare, U.S. Department of Health and Human Services, and Employment Security Division.

That this investigation, utilizing documents obtained from the above named agencies and other public agency records, has determined that these eight (8) individuals are related to each other through birth and marriage. Criminal histories were obtained from the Police Department, for the named eight (8) individuals. A review of those criminal histories shows in excess of 100 arrests for the charge of check deception.

That security personnel representing retail merchants in Indiana, Ohio, Kentucky, Missouri, and Illinois have been contacted and/or interviewed regarding this criminal organization. They have reported instances where the stores they represent have been victims of check schemes involving the above named persons. The information contained on the checks, and the manner of the presentation of the checks, conform to the *modus operandi* of the members of this criminal organization. Interviews and merchants' surveillance films show that members of this criminal organization are in groups of two (2) or more when they pass these checks.

That the subpoenas were issued to the following fourteen (14) financial institutions requesting documentation for approximately one hundred (100) checking accounts, utilizing information obtained from checks passed by the eight persons listed above.

All of the above financial institutions are federally insured, in accordance with IC 35–43–5–8(b).

A review of the subpoenaed document has identified at least one method of obtaining checks by this criminal organization. By opening a checking account, with a minimal amount of cash, the individuals are able to obtain a large (250 to 500) supply of checks. This investigation has shown that the information on the applications for checking accounts provided to the financial institution is false or the applicant made fraudulent representations.

That the members of this group use these checks to obtain goods and services. In order to successfully issue these checks for goods and services, the members of this group utilize false or fictitious articles of identification. The investigation has determined generally, that after obtaining merchandise, members of this group participate in returning the merchandise to the merchants and request refunds. This practice has been repeated as late as May 3, 19XX, at the Ko Department Store, Speedway, Marion County, Indiana.

That on May 17, 19XX, search warrants were lawfully issued and served at 8 locations.

That this affiant has reason to believe that:

(RE: *JOYCE LOUISE ANIGAN*)
AKA: Joyce L. Ree
Mary Elisa Par
Teresa J. Cann
Linda M. Coll

Information received from the U.S. Department of Health and Human Services shows Joyce Louise Anigan's true Social Security number to be 309–46–XXXX and date of birth 01–25–19XX.

1. On January 6, 19XX, a person identifying herself as Joyce L. Ree, opened checking account #89467XXX with Bank and Trust Company, Lawrence Branch, located at 909 E. 38th Street, Indianapolis, Marion County, Indiana, with a deposit of $85.00. Bank records show this account was closed (approximately 20 days after opening) on January 26, 19XX, with a negative balance of $220.82 due to overdrafts of this account. Information submitted to the bank at the time of opening by Joyce L. Ree included her address: 413 N. Keny, Indianapolis, Indiana; her telephone number: 545–1XXX; occupation: Purn Tire Service, telephone number 926–9XXX; and Social Security number 551–65–XXXX. Numerous checks were written on this account until at least March 24, 19XX. The signature on the information card and the signature on the check appear to be the same.

a. On March 14, 19XX, after this account had been closed for insufficient funds, a person identifying herself as Joyce L. Ree wrote check #559, drawn on bank account #8967XXX to Ko Department Store, Castleton branch, 602 E. 82nd Street, Indianapolis, Marion County, Indiana, in the amount of $78.73, as payment for merchandise. Joyce L. Ree presented Indiana identification card #8950–13–XXXX as a picture identification. This information was recorded on check #559, by the Ko store clerk. This check was dishonored and returned to Ko marked "Not on File".

On February 20, 19XX, latent fingerprints were taken and developed from check #559, by the U.S. Postal Service, Chicago Crime Laboratory. Comparisons made by the Chicago Crime Laboratory, with known fingerprints of Joyce L. Anigan, show the prints to belong to Joyce L. Anigan.

b. On January 26, 19XX, after this account had been closed for insufficient funds, a person identifying herself as Joyce L. Ree wrote check #515, drawn on the same Bank and Trust Company account #8946XXXX to Zar Department Store, 202 E. Washington Street, Indianapolis, Marion County, Indiana, in the amount of $103.95. The same Indiana identification card #8950–13–XXXX was used by Joyce L. Ree as picture identification. This information was recorded on check #515 by the Zar store clerk. This check was dishonored and returned to Zar marked "Account Closed".

On May 17, 19XX, evidence was obtained through the service of a search warrant at 454 Edward Court, which included one Indiana identification card #8950–13–XXXX which was issued on 04–04–XX in the name of Joyce L. Ree; date of birth: 01–25–XX; address: 213 E. Leigh Drive, Indianapolis, Indiana; with a photograph of Joyce L. Anigan; Indiana driver's license #8950–13–XXXX in the name of Joyce L. Ree issued 11–16–XX; address: 3314 N. Chest Avenue, Indianapolis, Indiana; and a check carbon copy from bank account #896XXXX.

2. On March 14, 19XX, a person identifying herself as Joyce L. Ree Anigan opened checking account #53 8XXXX with Bank O, Indianapolis, Marion County, Indiana, Branch #67, located at 215 Arlington Avenue, Indianapolis, Marion County, Indiana, with a deposit of $35.00. Bank records show this account was closed (approximately 43 days after opening) on May 3, 19XX, with a negative balance of $363.25 due to overdrafts of this account. Information submitted to the bank at the time of opening by Joyce L. Ree Anigan shows Joyce L. Ree Anigan's address to be 164 Kitly, Indianapolis, Indiana; telephone number 351–XXXX; and Social Security #432–11–XXXX. Joyce L. Ree Anigan presented the same Indiana identification card #8950–13–XXXX as picture identification. Numerous checks were written on this account until at least September 15, 19XX. The signature on the information card and the signature on the checks appear to be the same.

a. June 21, 19XX after this account was closed for insufficient funds, a person identifying herself as Joyce L. Ree Anigan wrote check #368, drawn on Bank O account #53 8XXXX to Max Department Store, 733 Commer Drive, Marion County, Indianapolis, Indiana, in the amount of $136.47.

This check was presented with altered magnetic bank encoded information. Joyce L. Ree Anigan used Indiana identification card #Y240–08–XXXX as picture identification. This information was recorded on check #368 by Max Store clerk. This check was dishonored and returned to Max marked "Unable to Locate".

On February 20, 19XX, latent fingerprints were taken and developed from check #368, by the U.S. Postal Service, Chicago Crime Laboratory. Comparisons made by the Chicago Crime Laboratory, with known fingerprints of Joyce L. Anigan, show the prints to belong to Joyce L. Anigan. Further examination showed that the magnetic account #53 XXXX was altered to read 59 XXX1.

On May 17, 19XX, evidence was obtained through the service of a search warrant at 602 Terrace, which included one checkbook containing blank checks in the name of Joyce L. Anigan, under the account #53 XXXX (the same account as listed above).

3. On August 9, 19XX, a person identifying herself as Mary Elisa Par, opened checking account #8948XXXX with The Bank and Trust Company, located at 909 E. 38th Street, Indianapolis, Marion County, Indiana, with a deposit of $80.00. Bank records show this account was closed (approximately 29 days after opening) on September 7, 19XX with a negative balance of $273.69 due to overdrafts of this account. Information submitted to The Bank and Trust Company by Mary Elisa Par at the time of opening show her address to be 204 Stouff and her Social Security number 432–18–XXXX. Numerous checks were written on this account until at least November 25, 19XX.

On April 11, 19XX, latent fingerprints were taken and developed from check #139, account #8948XXXX by the U.S. Postal Service, Chicago Crime Laboratory. Comparisons made by the Chicago Crime Laboratory with known fingerprints of Joyce L. Anigan show the prints to belong to Joyce L. Anigan.

a. On October 14, 19XX, after this account was closed for insufficient funds, a person identifying herself as Mary Elisa Par wrote check #274, drawn on the same bank account #8948XXXX to Zar Department Store, 101 N. Keystone Avenue, Indianapolis, Marion County, Indiana, in the amount of $183.75. This check was presented with magnetic bank encode information altered by adding a pen stroke, causing the number to read 8948XXX1. Mary Elisa Par used Indiana identification card #1560–02–XXXY and Social Security number 409–56–XXXY. This information was recorded on check #274 by the Zar Store clerk. The bank dishonored the check and returned it to Zar marked "Account Closed".

b. On October 14, 19XX, after this account was closed for insufficient funds, a person identifying herself as Mary Elisa Par, wrote check #275, drawn on the same bank account #8948XXXY to Zar Department Store, 101 N. Keystone Avenue, Indianapolis, Marion County, Indiana, in the amount of $149.21. This check was presented with magnetic bank encode information altered by adding a pen stroke, causing the number to read #8948XXX1. Mary Elisa Par used Indiana identification card #1560–02–XXXX and Social Security number 409–56–XXXX. This information was recorded on check #275, by the Zar Store clerk. The Bank dishonored and returned this check to Zar marked "Account Closed".

On July 27, 19XX, checks 139, 274, and 275 were examined by a Forensic Scientist of the Indianapolis Marion County Forensic Services Agency. He reported that both checks #274 and #275 were altered by adding a pen stroke to the fifth numeral (6) in the magnetic encode number 8948XXXY causing the magnetic encode number to read 8948XXX1. He noted handwriting similarities in the checks numbered 274 and 275 with check #139.

Records from the Bureau of Motor Vehicles show that on July 13, 19XX, Maryelisa A. Par applied for and received an Indiana identification card #1560–02–XXXX; address shown was 204 Stouff Lane, Indianapolis, Indiana.

On May 17, 19XX, evidence was obtained through the service of a search warrant at Joyce Anigan's sister's residence, located at 602 Terrace, including one Indiana driver's identification card #1560–05–XXXX bearing the name of Mary Par, 545 Edward Court, displaying a photograph of Joyce L. Anigan, and blank checks from bank account #8948XXXX.

4. On November 1, 19XX, a person identifying herself as Teresa J. Cann, opened a checking account #43811XXXY, with Credit Union, located at 75 N. Pennsylvania, Indianapolis, Marion County, Indiana, with a deposit of $50.00. Credit Union records show this account was closed (approximately 69 days after opening) on January 8, 19XX, with a negative balance of $1,255.00 due to overdrafts of this account. Information submitted to the Credit Union by Teresa J. Cann at the time of opening show Teresa J. Cann's address to be 605 Bals, Indianapolis, Indiana, and the Social Security number 438–11–XXXX. Numerous checks were written on this account until at least August 25, 19XX.

On August 10, 19XX, latent fingerprints were taken and developed from the Credit Union signature card account #43811XXXX by the U.S. Postal Service,

Chicago Crime Laboratory. Comparisons made by the Chicago Crime Laboratory with the known fingerprints of Joyce L. Anigan show that the developed prints from the signature card account #43811XXXX belong to Joyce L. Anigan.

a. On January 5, 19XX, a person identifying herself as Teresa J. Cann wrote check #486 on the same Credit Union account #443811XXXY to Targ Department Store located at 250 W. 38th Street, Indianapolis, Marion County, Indiana, in the amount of $91.33. Teresa J. Cann used Indiana driver's identification card #2400–01–XXXX as picture identification. This information was recorded on check #486 by the Targ clerk. The Credit Union dishonored this check and returned it to Targ marked "Account Closed".

b. On January 5, 19XX, (19 minutes after writing check #486) a person identifying herself as Teresa J. Cann, wrote check #487, drawn on the same Credit Union account #43811XXXX to Targ Department Store, located at 250 W. 38th Street, Indianapolis, Marion County, Indiana, in the amount of $90.77. Teresa J. Cann used Indiana identification card #2400–01–XXXX as picture identification. This information was recorded on check #487, by the Targ store clerk. Credit Union dishonored this check and returned it to Targ marked "Account Closed".

c. On April 27, 19XX, after this account was closed for insufficient funds, a person identifying herself as Teresa J. Cann, wrote check #569, on the same Credit Union account #438119XXXX to B Square, located at 695 Commercial Drive, Indianapolis, Marion County, Indiana, in the amount of $122.45. Teresa J. Cann used the same Indiana identification card listed above, which was altered to read #2430–01–XXXX. This information was recorded on check #569, by the B Square clerk. The Credit Union dishonored this check and returned it to B Square marked "Account Closed".

On May 17, 19XX, evidence was obtained through the service of a search warrant at 54 Edward Court, Indianapolis, Indiana, which included one Indiana driver's identification card #2400–01–XXXX, altered by scratching out the third digit (0), with a photograph of Joyce L. Anigan, and checkbooks with blank checks in the name of Teresa J. Cann and the same account number listed above (#43811XXXX), including a carbon copy of check #570 written on April 27, 19XX, to B Square.

5. On April 24, 19XX, a person identifying herself as Linda Coll opened a checking account #55001XXXX with the Credit Union, located at 101 E. 56th Street, Indianapolis, Marion County, Indiana, with a deposit of $10.00. The Credit Union records show this account was closed (approximately 63 days after opening) on June 27, 19XX, with a negative balance of $384.00, due to overdrafts of this account. Information submitted to the Credit Union by Linda Coll (account #55001XXXX) at the time of opening, show Linda Coll's address to be 753 Station Street, Indianapolis, Indiana, and a Social Security number of 550–01–XXXX. Numerous checks were written on this account until at least May 16, 19XX.

a. On May 9, 19XX, a person identifying herself as Linda Coll wrote check #203 on the same Credit Union account #1550019XXXX to L. S. Store #07 located at 101 N. Stone Avenue, Indianapolis, Marion County, Indiana, in the amount of $183.75. Linda Coll used Indiana driver's identification card #1980–04–XXXX and other identification with the Social Security #550–01–XXXX as picture identification. This information was recorded on check #203 by the L. S. clerk. The Credit Union dishonored and returned this check to L. S. marked ''Non-Sufficient Funds''.

b. On May 10, 19XX, a person identifying herself as Linda Coll wrote check #207 drawn on Credit Union account #1550019XXXX to L. S. Store #11, located at 919 N. Lafayette Road, Indianapolis, Marion County, Indiana, in the amount of $199.21. Linda Coll used Indiana driver's identification card #1980–04–XXXX and other identification with Social Security number 550–01–XXXX as picture identification. This information was recorded on check #207 by the L. S. clerk. The Credit Union dishonored this check and returned it to L. S. marked ''Non-Sufficient Funds''.

c. On May 16, 19XX, a person identifying herself as Linda Coll wrote check #213, on Credit Union account #1550019XXXX to L. S. Store #11, located at 919 N. Lafayette Road, Indianapolis, Indiana, in the amount of $157.50. Linda Coll used Indiana identification card #1980–04–XXXX and other identification with Social Security number 550–04–XXXX as picture identification. This information was recorded on check #213, by the L. S. clerk. The Credit Union dishonored and returned to L. S. marked ''Non-Sufficient Funds''.

d. On May 16, 19XX, a person identifying herself as Linda Coll wrote check #214, on Credit Union account #1550019XXXX to Targ Department Store located at 250 W. 38th Street, Indianapolis, Marion County, Indiana, in the amount of $94.94. Linda Coll used Indiana identification card 1980–04–XXXX and Social Security number 550–01–XXXX. This information was recorded on check #214 by the Targ clerk. The Credit Union dishonored this check and returned it to Targ marked ''Non-Sufficient Funds''.

On May 17, 19XX, evidence was obtained through the service of a search warrant at 602 Terrace and 454 Edward Court, which included: (1) an Indiana identification card #1980–04–XXXX in the name of Linda M. Coll, listing an address of 954 Wix Court, Indianapolis, Indiana, with a picture of Joyce L. Anigan; (2) Amer Health identification #621XX with Social Security number 550–01–XXXX in the name of Linda Coll with a picture of Joyce L. Anigan; (3) sales receipts from L. S., one dated 5–9–XX totaling $183.75, one dated 5–10–XX totaling $199.21, and one dated 5–16–XX totaling $157.50, all listing account #198004XXXX, and one sales receipt from Targ issued on May 16, 19XX, for the purchase of a man's watch (model #267 378), totaling $94.49, and one man's watch with Targ price tag $89.99 (model #267 378).

(RE: *BETTY JEAN MORE*)
AKA: Betty J. Anigan
Betty J. Vea
Betty E. Anigan
Betty Jean Will
Betty Jo Will

Information received from the United States Department of Health and Human Services show Betty J. Anigan Vea Burt More's true Social Security number to be 312–48–26XX.

1. On January 14, 19XX, a person identifying herself as Betty Anigan opened checking account #3107896 with Finance Center Deral Credit Union, Branch #1, located at 710 E. 5th Street, Indianapolis, Marion County, Indiana, with a deposit of $200.00. Deral Credit Union records show this account was closed (approximately 31 days after opening) on February 24, 19XX, with a negative balance of $590.71. Information submitted to the Credit Union at the time of opening the account by Betty Anigan show her address to be 341 N. Payt, Indianapolis, Indiana, and her Social Security number as 310–78–96XX. Numerous checks were written on this account until at least June 14, 19XX.

a. On February 28, 19XX, after this account was closed due to insufficient funds, a person identifying herself as Betty Anigan wrote check #2034 drawn on Finance Center Deral Credit Union account #3107896 to Ks Department Store #135, located at 730 N. Stone Avenue, Indianapolis, Marion County, Indiana, in the amount of $63.79. Betty Anigan used Indiana driver's license #S312–48–26 and V charge card #4302 3801 5981 67 as identification. This information was recorded on check #2034, by Ks store clerk. The Deral Credit Union dishonored this check and returned it to Ks marked "Account Closed".

b. On April 27, 19XX, a person identifying herself as Betty Anigan wrote check #2080 drawn on Finance Center Deral Credit Union account #3107896 to B Square #1480, located at 60 N. Short Road, Indianapolis, Marion County, Indiana, in the amount of $218.79. Betty Anigan used altered Indiana driver's license #312–98–20XX as picture identification. This information was recorded on check #2080 by the B Square store clerk. The Deral Credit Union dishonored this check and returned it to B Square marked "Account Closed".

On May 17, 19XX, evidence was obtained through the service of a search warrant at 365 Park (Betty More's residence), including one Credit Union V card #4302 3801 59 6787 in the name of Betty Anigan. Evidence obtained from 985 Court (Carmen Kenn's residence) on May 17, 19XX, included one Indiana driver's license #312–48–26XX, in the name of Betty More Anigan, displaying the photograph of Betty J. More.

On March 21, 19XX, the forensic scientist for the Indianapolis-Marion County Forensic Services Agency, compared the handwriting on checks #2034 and #2080 with known handwriting of Betty J. More. He identified Betty J. More as the writer of checks #2034 and #2080.

2. On October 12, 19XX, after the Deral Credit Union account #3124826 had been closed for approximately five months due to overdrafts, a person identifying herself as Betty J. More wrote check #294 drawn on this account to Zar Department Store, 102 E. Washington Street, Indianapolis, Marion County, Indiana, in the amount of $241.98. This check was presented with altered magnetic bank encoded information. Betty J. More used Indiana driver's license #8939–19–77 as picture ID and V charge card #4302 3801 5981 67 as ID. This information was recorded on check #294, by the Zar Store clerk. The Deral Credit Union dishonored this check and returned it to Zar marked "Account Closed." Numerous checks were written on this account until at least October 19XX.

On May 17, 19XX, evidence was obtained through the service of a search warrant at 365 Park (Betty Anigan's residence), which included one Indiana driver's license #8939–19–77 in the name of Betty More Anigan (altered by burning the last numeral "2"). Evidence was obtained on May 17, 19XX, through the service of a search warrant at 985 Court (Carmen Kenn's residence) which included one Credit Union V card #4302 3801 5981 67.

On March 21, 19XX, a forensic scientist for the Indianapolis-Marion County Forensic Services Agency compared the handwriting on check #294 with known handwriting of Betty J. More/Anigan. He identified Betty J. More/Anigan as the writer of check #294. He also noted the magnetic encoded number was altered to read 8124826.

3. On July 21, 19XX, a person identifying herself as Betty E. Anigan opened checking account #894387, with The Bank and Trust Company, located at 69 E. 39th Street, Indianapolis, Marion County, Indiana, with a deposit of $50.00 cash. Bank records show this account was closed (approximately 20 days after opening) on August 11, 19XX, with a negative balance of $361.83 due to overdrafts. Information submitted to the bank by Betty E. Anigan at the time of opening, shows Betty E. Anigan's address to be 341 N. Payt, Indianapolis, Indiana; Social Security number to be 318–48–05XX; employer: Indiana School; and home telephone number 547–448X. Numerous checks were written on this account until at least August 19XX.

a. On August 11, 19XX, after this account was closed for insufficient funds, a person identifying herself as Betty E. Anigan wrote check #242 drawn from the bank on account #894387 to Zar Department Store #82, located at 102 S. Washington Street, Indianapolis, Marion County, Indiana, in the amount of $188.89. Betty E. Anigan used Indiana driver's license #8939–19–77XX and V charge card #4302 3801 5981 67 as identification. This information was recorded on check #242 by the Zar Store clerk. The Bank dishonored this check and returned it to Zar marked "Account Closed".

On May 17, 19XX, evidence was obtained through the service of a search warrant at 985 Court (Carmen Kenn's residence) which included V charge card #4302 3801 5981 67 and Indiana driver's identification #8939–19–77XX.

On March 21, 19XX, the forensic scientist for the Indianapolis-Marion County Forensic Services Agency compared check #242, drawn on Bank account

#894387, with known handwriting of Betty J. More/Anigan. He identified Betty J. More/Anigan as the writer of check #242.

On September 13, 19XX, a person identifying herself as Betty E. Anigan opened account #52 271XX, with Bank O, located at 420 N. Franklin Road, Indianapolis, Indiana, with a deposit of $65.00 cash. Bank O records show this account was closed (approximately 31 days after opening) on October 14, 19XX, with a negative balance of $73.47 due to overdrafts. Information submitted to Bank O by Betty E. Anigan show her address to be 341 N. Payt Avenue, V charge card #4673 601 926 6, and Social Security number 318–76–91XX. Numerous checks were written on this account until at least July 19XX.

b. On October 12, 19XX, a person identifying herself as Betty E. Anigan wrote check #125 drawn on Bank O account #52 271XX to Zar Department Store #82, located at 102 E. Washington Street, Indianapolis, Marion County, Indiana, in the amount of $180.08. Betty E. Anigan used Indiana driver's license #8939–19–77 and V charge card #4302 3801 5981 67 as identification. This information was recorded on check #125 by the Zar Store clerk. Bank O dishonored this check and returned it to Zar marked "Account Closed".

On May 17, 19XX, evidence was obtained through the service of a search warrant at 985 Court, which included one Indiana driver's license #8939–19–77XX, one Credit Union V charge card #4302 3801 5981 67, and one V charge card #4673 601 926 6.

On March 21, 19XX, the forensic scientist for the Indianapolis-Marion County Forensic Service Agency examined check #125 and noted the magnetic encoded number was altered to read 82 2712. He compared the handwriting on check #125 with known handwriting of Betty J. More/Anigan and identified her as the writer of check #125.

c. On June 30, 19XX, after this account was closed for overdrafts, a person identifying herself as Betty E. Anigan wrote check #130 drawn on Bank O account #52 2712 to Cobs Department Store, Indianapolis, Marion County, Indiana, in the amount of $200.00. The memo section on check #130 notes "Payment" toward Cobs charge account #636 229 06. On the back of check #130 is noted, "Customer number 63622906".

Cobs Department Store credit application #636–229–06 shows the applicant was Betty Anigan; address: 3417 N. Payt; telephone number 547–448X; Social Security number 304–48–06XX; employer: Indiana School; and driver's license #8939–19–77XX. The date of this application was September 8, 19XX.

d. On June 29, 19XX, after this account was closed for approximately 19 months, a person identifying herself as Betty Anigan wrote check #149 drawn on Bank O account #52–2712 to Rogers, located at 255 Circle, Indianapolis, Marion County, Indiana, in the amount of $163.44. Betty Anigan used Indiana driver's license #8939–19–77XX as picture identification and listed her telephone number as 898–480X. This information was recorded on check #149, by the Rogers store clerk. Bank O dishonored this check and returned it to Rogers marked "Unable to Locate".

e. On July 4, 19XX, after this account was closed for approximately 20 months, a person identifying herself as Betty E. Anigan wrote check #147 drawn on the same Bank O account #52–2712 to Rogers, located at 255 Circle, Indianapolis, Marion County, Indiana, in the amount of $84.77. Betty Anigan used Indiana driver's license #8939–19–77XX as picture identification and listed her telephone number as 898–480X. This information was recorded on check #147, by a Rogers store clerk. Bank O dishonored this check and returned it to Rogers marked "Unable to Locate".

Information obtained from the Indiana Bureau of Motor Vehicles shows Betty More/Anigan requested and received a duplicate driver's license on June 11, 19XX, after driver's license #8939–19–77XX was confiscated on May 17, 19XX, utilizing the address of 365 Park Drive. The signatures on the checks listed above appear to be the same as the signature on the information card signed by Betty J. More.

5. On November 17, 19XX, a person identifying herself as Betty J. Will opened checking account #42430 036 with Bank Branch 243, located at 1 Market, Indianapolis, Marion County, Indiana, with a deposit of $100.00. Bank records show this account was closed (approximately 26 days after opening) on December 13, 19XX, with a negative balance of $265.59. Information submitted to the bank by Betty J. Will included an address of 52 Crest; date of birth: 08–05–19XX; employer: 01 Services; telephone number 634–66XX; Indiana identification card #2400–02–62XX; and Social Security number 415–76–98XX. Numerous checks were written on this account until at least December 19XX.

a. On December 15, 19XX, after this account was closed for overdrafts, a person identifying herself as Betty J. Will wrote check #460 drawn on bank account #42430 03 to Zar Department Store #80, located at 60 E. 82nd Street, Indianapolis, Marion County, Indiana, in the amount of $171.14. Betty J. Will used Indiana identification card #2400–02–62XX and Mont charge card #391 870 62 as identification. This information was recorded on check #460 by the Zar Store clerk. The bank returned this check to Zar marked "Account Closed".

On May 17, 19XX, evidence was obtained through the service of a search warrant at 365 Park (Betty More's residence), including one Indiana identification card #2400–02–62XX issued to Betty J. Will, 527 N. Crest, Indianapolis, Indiana, with the photograph of Betty J. Anigan. Evidence confiscated from 985 Court (Carmen Kenn's residence) included one Mont charge card #391 870 62 in the name of Betty J. Anigan.

6. On January 24, 19XX, a person identifying herself as Betty J. Will opened checking account #262013 with Cap Credit Union, located in the Office Building, 10 Senate Avenue, Indianapolis, Marion County, Indiana, with a deposit of

$15.00 into a savings account; no deposit was made in the checking account. Cap Credit Union records show this account was closed (approximately 31 days after opening) on February 23, 19XX, due to overdrafts with a negative balance of $19.30. Information submitted to the Credit Union at the time of opening show Betty J. Will's address to be 527 Crest, Indianapolis, Indiana; telephone number: 895–040X; and Social Security number 310–44–62XX. Numerous checks were written on this account until at least March 19XX.

a. On August 12, 19XX, after this account was closed for insufficient funds, a person identifying herself as Betty J. Will wrote check #1118 drawn on Cap account #862018 to L. S. Department Store #7, located at 61 Keystone Avenue, Indianapolis, Marion County, Indiana, in the amount of $195.30. Betty J. Will used Indiana identification card #2400–02–62XX and work identification #417–55–09XX as picture identification and listed her telephone number as 542–944X.

b. On August 19, 19XX, after this account was closed for insufficient funds, a person identifying herself as Betty J. Will wrote check #1124 drawn on Cap account #862018 to L. S. Department Store #7, located at 61 N. Keystone Avenue, Indianapolis, Marion County, Indiana, in the amount of $206.83. Betty J. Will used Indiana identification card #2400–02–62XX and Zar charge card #86 7027 284 as identification.

On May 17, 19XX, evidence was obtained through the service of a search warrant at 365 Park (Betty More's residence) which included one Indiana identification card #2400–02–62XX in the name of Betty J. Will, address: 527 N. Crest, Indianapolis, Indiana, with a picture of Betty J. More/Anigan; one Norr Services employee identification listing the name of Betty J. Will, address: 527 N. Crest, Indianapolis, Indiana; and Social Security number 417–55–09XX, with a picture of Betty J. More/Anigan.

On May 17, 19XX, evidence was obtained through the service of a search warrant at 985 Court (Carmen Kenn's residence), which included one Zar Department charge card #86 7027 284, in the name of Betty J. Anigan.

On March 21, 19XX, a forensic scientist for the Indianapolis-Marion County Forensic Services Agency examined checks #1118 and #1124 drawn on Cap Credit Union account #262013, and noted the magnetic encoded numbers were altered to read 862018.

CASE EXAMPLE 2: STOLEN CASHIER'S CHECKS

October 11, 19XX: We received information from an informant that a subject named John Doe, who was in jail, contacted the informant and offered to trade him ten stolen cashier's checks for enough money to bond himself out of jail. Doe stated that if the informant fronted up enough money for the bond, Doe would work up the checks with teller numbers and authorized signatures for him.

The informant was directed to go to 1800 N.W. 10th and meet with a female named Joyce. She would show him the checks.

October 11, 19XX (1800 hours): The informant met with Joyce at the above address and she stated she was out of checks but she would get more in a week.

October 12, 19XX: The informant was contacted by John Doe, who was informed as to what occurred at 1800 N.W. 10th in reference to the cashier's checks. Doe states that he would straighten it out.

October 14, 19XX: The informant received a call from John Doe instructing him to again contact Joyce at 1800 N.W. 10th and tell her that Doe had sent him. Doe stated that she would give the informant ten blank checks. Doe further stated that when he got out of jail, he could provide 3,000 to 4,000 additional checks, but the price would be much greater.

October 14, 19XX (1756 hours): The informant met with Joyce at 1800 N.W. 10th as directed. Joyce searched the informant for a body wire before she would talk to him and then stated she was afraid he was a cop. Joyce refused to give the informant ten checks but instead gave him three. The checks were from Sun Bank, 1234 W. Arlington. The numbers on the checks were 101123, 10124, and 101125. Upon checking, we found the checks were stolen on August 3, 19XX under case no. 123456FA.

October 15, 19XX: We found through our background check that since the checks had been stolen several had been passed, and pictures were taken of the persons cashing them. We obtained copies of the pictures and verified that the person depicted was the female known to us as Joyce. It was also determined that there were four bank bags full of blank cashier's checks stolen from a courier when the original loss was reported.

Case Results: With the above information, we secured search warrants for the address at N.W. 10th and recovered a large quantity of blank cashier's checks and a machine used to put cash totals on checks. Both subjects were charged and others were implicated by them when they were interviewed.

11

Counterfeit Clothing: A Case Example

The case began with the traffic stop of two illegal aliens who were transporting counterfeit jackets from Chicago to Indianapolis. The jackets were headed for K, one of the locations that we targeted. Knowing that Karl Mand, a private investigator, represented trademark holders and that he has some expertise in counterfeit clothing, we asked for his assistance. Karl identified the jackets as being counterfeit.

Taking interest in making a case of this, we asked Mr. Mand to check out K to see whether they were selling counterfeit merchandise. Mr. Mand not only identified K as selling the counterfeit merchandise but also five other locations. We collected this information from Mand along with the names of individuals from the companies that hold the trademarks. We also enlisted the cooperation of these people and then began utilizing detectives from our office to make covert transactions from the target locations. The monies used were made available from Karl Mand. The idea was to make six purchases from each of the target locations. Each purchase would include both counterfeit and legitimate merchandise. We would watch for money paid for the purchase to be kept together and identify where the money went (cash drawer).

After collecting the merchandise that we believed to be counterfeit, we sent the merchandise to the respective trademark holders to be identified as counterfeit. We did find that all the suspected items were in fact counterfeit. The victim businesses returned the items along with an affidavit identifying the items as counterfeit.

Armed with this knowledge, search warrants were obtained for each location. With the search warrants in hand, a plan was formed for a synchronized execution of five search warrants. Utilized were 20 detectives, 20 uniformed officers, 3 sergeants, 1 lieutenant, 1 captain, 2 people from our forfeiture unit, 3 private investigators, and 1 representative of the Collegiate Licensing Company. The civilians who assisted us were representatives of the various victim businesses who were authorized to verify the validity of the various merchandise.

The instructions given for execution of the search warrants were to take pictures and videos of the entire store and the employees prior to search, take inventory of the merchandise as it was placed in boxes, videotape the files and paperwork as they were confiscated, and limit the handling of merchandise to the detectives in charge.

A Ryder truck was rented to transport confiscated material to the property room. With the aid of the search warrants, counterfeit materials, business records, and money were taken; bank information was identified; and civil forfeiture proceedings were initiated against the five businesses. An opportunity was given to the business owners to cooperate and inform us as to their business dealings and the suppliers of counterfeit merchandise.

Affiant: Detective Thomas I. Black, II

In October of 19XX, Mr. Karl Mand, an investigator with Investigators of Armel, approached Detective Thomas I. Black, II, of the Police Department's organized crime unit with information concerning counterfeit clothing. Mr. Mand stated that he and his associates had identified five retail stores that were selling counterfeit clothing and other items. Mr. Mand stated that he and investigators represent Levi, the National Basketball Association, the National Football League, Major League Baseball, Collegiate Licensing Company, Fendi, National Hockey League, Walt Disney, and NIKE; and, as representatives of the above companies, they investigate the sale and/or manufacture of counterfeit goods of the above trademark holders.

Investigators identified the following retail businesses as selling counterfeit clothing and material:

Indiana G & B   ABC, Inc.
231 N. 30th Street   735 N. 30th Street
Indianapolis, IN 46218   Indianapolis, IN 46218

A B S   K M E
509 N. 30th Street   505 E. 30th Street
Indianapolis, IN 46218   Indianapolis, IN 46218

AIR US
504 E. 30th Street
Indianapolis, IN 46218

It is this affiant's belief that the sale of counterfeit items is a violation of trademark protection and further believes that the utterance of such a written instrument is a violation of the Indiana code, namely: forgery. Forgery, IC 35–43–5–2, states that "a person who, with intent to defraud, makes or utters a written instrument in such a manner that it purports to have been made . . . (4) by authority of one who did not give authority commits forgery, a class C felony." IC 35–43–5–1 "Definitions" states, "A written instrument means a paper, document, or other instrument containing written matter and includes money, coins, tokens, stamps, seals, credit cards, badges, trademarks, medals; or other objects or symbols of value, right, privilege, or identifications.''

With this information in mind, officers of the Police Department began purchasing from the targeted locations both suspected counterfeit items and legitimate items. The intent of the investigation was to show that the retail stores were in fact selling counterfeit material along with rightful products and that monies from said sales were combined and laundered through the business as legitimate.

Between 10/26/XX and 02/03/XX, seven separate purchases of suspected counterfeit label merchandise were made from ABC, 735 N. 30th Street, Indianapolis, Marion County, Indiana.

On 10/26/XX at approximately 1420 hours, investigators entered ABC at 735 N. 30th Street, Indianapolis, Marion County, Indiana. We purchased a black "Gucci" t-shirt for $8.99. The total paid was $9.44 and the money was placed in the cash register. The label on the t-shirt was not a "Gucci" label, the lettering on the t-shirt was backed with paper to make it appear stiffer, and the price was less than those found on the retail market for a designer label "Gucci" t-shirt. For these reasons, we believed the t-shirt to be counterfeit.

On 11/02/XX at approximately 1239 hours, investigators entered ABC at 735 N. 30th Street, Indianapolis, Marion County, Indiana. We purchased a "Fendi" purse for $39.99 and a jewelry box for $.99. The total of $43.03 was placed in the cash register. The purse appeared to be made of vinyl and the price was much less than what is found on the retail market for a "Fendi" purse. For these reasons, we believed the purse to be a counterfeit article. The purse was sent to a representative of the Fendi Corporation who found that the purse was counterfeit and was not manufactured by Fendi S.A.S. Di Paola Fendi E. Sorelle.

On 11/09/XX at approximately 1200 hours, investigators entered ABC at 735 N. 30th Street, Indianapolis, Marion County, Indiana. We purchased a "Hornets" hat for $12.00 and a bottle of Bumpoff for $2.89. The total of $16.67 was placed in the cash register. The hat had no tag or any other marker identifying it as being an officially licensed product of the NBA. Therefore, we believed it to be a counterfeit item. The NBA is the trademark owner of the Charlotte Hornets, and the hat was sent to the Assistant General Counsel for NBA properties who found the hat was in fact a counterfeit article as it was not produced by a licensed vendor.

On 12/08/XX at approximately 1155 hours, investigators entered ABC at 735 N. 30th Street, Indianapolis, Marion County, Indiana. We purchased a "Fendi" purse for $39.99, a curling iron for $3.99, and a beaded purse for $21.99. The total of $69.27 was placed in the cash register. The purse appeared to be made of vinyl and the price was much less than is found on the retail market for a "Fendi" purse. For these reasons, we believed the purse to be a counterfeit article. The purse was sent to a representative of the Fendi Corporation who found that the purse was counterfeit and was not manufactured by Fendi S.A.S. Di Paola Fendi E. Sorelle.

On 12/28/XX at approximately 1230 hours, an investigator entered ABC at 735 N. 30th Street, Indianapolis, Marion County, Indiana. He purchased a Raiders shirt and shorts set for $29.99 and a Raiders hat for $7.99. The total of $39.88 was placed in the cash register. The hat had attached to it a tag that identified it as an "officially licensed product" of the NFL. The shorts and shirt had no identifying tags or marks indicating that they were officially licensed products of the NFL. For these reasons, we believed them to be counterfeit. The NFL is the trademark owner of the Los Angeles Raiders, and the shirt and shorts were sent to the Director, Licensing Division, of NFL Properties, who found the shirt and shorts set was in fact a counterfeit article as it was not produced by a licensed vendor.

On 12/29/XX at approximately 1347 hours, investigators entered ABC at 735 N. 30th Street, Indianapolis, Marion County, Indiana. We purchased a Los Angeles Lakers jacket and pants set for $20.99 and a bottle of nail polish for $2.39. The total paid was $25.00 and the money was placed in the cash register. The jacket and pants set did not bear any tag or label identifying it as a licensed product of the NBA and the price was less than is found on the retail market. For these reasons, we believed them to be counterfeit. The NBA is the trademark owner of the Los Angeles Lakers, and the shirt and shorts set was sent to the Assistant General Counsel for NBA properties who found the shirt and shorts set was in fact a counterfeit article as it was not produced by a licensed vendor.

On 02/03/XX at approximately 1130 hours, Detective Tom Black entered ABC at 735 N. 30th Street, Indianapolis, Marion County, Indiana. He purchased a pair of black bibbed overalls with white stripes with "Raiders" and the Raiders logo on them for $17.49 and a pair of gloves for $2.99. The total of $21.88 was placed in the cash register. The overalls did not have any tag or label identifying them as a licensed product of the NFL and the price was less than is found on the retail market. For these reasons, Detective Black believed them to be counterfeit.

Items To Be Seized

1. Books, records, receipts, notes, ledgers, and other papers relative to the translation, ordering, purchase and distribution of stolen or counterfeit property.
2. Papers, tickets, notes, receipts, and other items relating to domestic travel.
3. Books, records, invoices, receipts, records of real estate transactions, bank statements and related records, passbooks, money drafts, letters of credit, money orders, bank drafts, and cashier's checks, bank checks, safe deposit box keys, money wrappers and other items evidencing the obtaining, secreting, transfer, and/or concealment of assets and obtaining, secreting, transfer, concealment, and/or expenditure of money.
4. United States currency, precious metals, jewelry, and financial instruments, including stocks and bonds.

5. Photographs including still photos, negatives, videotapes, films, undeveloped film and the contents therein, slides, in particular photographs of co-conspirators and/or of assets.
6. Address and/or telephone books, Rolodex indices and any papers reflecting names, addresses, telephone numbers, fax numbers and/or telex numbers of co-conspirators, sources of stolen property, customers, and existing financial relationships.
7. Indications of occupancy, residency, rental, and/or ownership of the premises herein, including but not limited to utility and telephone bills, cancelled envelopes, rental, purchase, or lease agreements, and keys.
8. Firearms and ammunition, including but not limited to handguns, pistols, revolvers, rifles, shotguns, machine guns and other weapons, and any records or receipts pertaining to firearms and ammunition.

Detective Black swears or affirms that he believes and has good cause to believe from his investigation he learned from reliable persons the following facts and attending circumstances that the source of the affiant's information and the grounds for his/her belief are as follows:

Based on the affiant's training, experience, and participation in other financial investigations involving the buying and selling of stolen or counterfeit property he/she knows:

A. That persons who deal in stolen or counterfeit property often purchase and/or title their assets in fictitious names, aliases or the names of relatives, associates, or business entities, to avoid detection of these assets by government agencies.

B. That even though these assets are in names other than the persons who deal in stolen or counterfeit property that they actually own and continue to use these assets and exercise dominion and control over them.

C. That persons buying stolen or counterfeit property must maintain on hand large amounts of U.S. currency in order to maintain and finance their ongoing organization dealing in stolen or counterfeit property.

D. That it is common for fencing organizations or organizations dealing in counterfeit properties to maintain books, records, receipts, notes, ledgers, airline tickets, receipts relating to the purchase of financial instruments, and/or the transportation, ordering, sale and distribution of stolen or counterfeit property and that the aforementioned books, records, receipts, notes, ledgers, etc., are maintained where the fences have ready access to them.

E. That it is common for operators of the above type of organization to secrete proceeds of stolen or counterfeit property and records of sales in secure locations within their residences, their businesses and/or other locations over which they maintain dominion and control for ready access and to conceal these items from law enforcement authorities.

F. That it is common for persons involved in selling and buying stolen or counterfeit property to maintain evidence pertaining to their obtaining, secreting, transfer, concealment, and/or expenditure of stolen or counterfeit property proceeds, such as currency, financial instruments, precious metals, and gem stones, jewelry, books, records, invoices, receipts, records of real estate transactions, bank statements and related records, passbooks, money drafts, letters of credit, money orders, bank drafts, cashier's checks, bank checks, safe deposit keys, and money wrappers. These items are maintained by the operators within their residences, businesses, and other locations over which they maintain dominion and control.

G. That when the above amass large proceeds from stolen or counterfeit property, they attempt to legitimize these profits through money laundering activities. To accomplish these goals, they utilize, including but not limited to, domestic banks and their attendant services, securities brokers, professionals (such as attorneys and accountants), casinos, real estate, shell corporations and business fronts, and otherwise legitimate businesses which generate large quantities of currency.

H. That persons who buy and sell stolen or counterfeit property common maintain addresses or telephone numbers in books or papers which reflect names, addresses and/or telephone numbers of their associates in the above organizations.

I. That persons who buy and sell stolen or counterfeit property take or cause to be taken photographs of themselves, their associates, their property, and their product. That these persons usually maintain these photographs in their possession.

Therefore, your affiant respectfully requests the court to issue a search warrant directing the search for and seizure of the following described property.

12

Credit Cards

CASE EXAMPLE 1: EMPLOYEE THEFT

On April 16, 19XX, a police detective received information from Mr. Ant of Lane, Inc., in reference to a credit card fraud investigation. Lane, Inc., is located at 23 Eastern Avenue, Indianapolis, Marion County, Indiana. According to Mr. Ant, on April 14, 19XX, an order was placed for merchandise through Lane in the amount of $471.17. The order was placed over the telephone using Discover credit card no. XXXXXXXXX and was to be sent to a Nancy Son at 38 S. 31st Street, Indianapolis, Indiana. According to Lane records, the actual owner of the above credit card was a Rita Doe, R.R. 2 Box 10, Lake City, TN 3776X. On April 16, 19XX, Mr. Ant contacted Rita Doe in reference to her Discover credit card. According to Rita Doe, she did not place an order for merchandise through Lane on April 14, 19XX, and did not give anyone permission to use her credit card number. On May 6, 19XX, the detective contacted Rita Doe in regard to the above investigation. At that time, she reiterated the fact that she had not used or given anyone permission to use her credit card through Lane, Inc., on April 14, 19XX.

On April 17, 19XX, the detective went to 38 S. 31st Street to make a controlled delivery of the Lane merchandise, acting in the capacity of a deliveryman. A black female answered the door. At that time, the detective stated to the woman that he had a delivery for a Nancy Son and asked if she was Nancy Son. The black female then replied she was Nancy Son. The detective then asked the female to look over the order invoice to double check her order for all the items. To this request, the female replied that yes, the order looked proper. At that point, the detective observed the black female sign the name Nancy Son to the invoice sheet. Upon seeing the signed invoice sheet, the detective asked the black female if she was Nancy Son, to which she again replied yes. After identifying himself as a police officer, he identified the black female as Tracy Buck (b/f/27, DOB 4–17–65); she agreed to cooperate by talking with the detective. Tracy Buck was then advised of her Miranda rights and stated an understanding of these rights. At that time, Tracy Buck stated that approximately 1 week prior to this incident she was told by her sister, Kelly Whit, to expect a package to be delivered at her house and to accept the package. The detective advised Tracy Buck to come to police headquarters on April 20, 19XX, to give a statement as to her involvement in this investigation. Tracy Buck was also advised to bring her sister Kelly Whit.

On April 20, 19XX, Tracy Buck and her sister Kelly Whit went to headquarters and agreed to give voluntary statements. After both subjects were cited their Miranda rights, Tracy Buck reiterated what she had previously told the detective: 1 week prior to the delivery her sister (Kelly) had called her (Tracy) and told her to expect a package in the next 10 days. She was then supposed to accept the package and sign for it. According to Tracy Buck, she did not know the contents of the package but only that she was to accept and sign for the package. Tracy further stated that after the delivery incident she contacted the number given to her by one of her friends.

Kelly Whit stated that on April 13, 19XX, she placed an order for clothing items through Lane, Inc., and requested the items be sent to her sister's residence at 38 S. 31st Street. Kelly further stated that she used the name Nancy Son as the person ordering the merchandise. According to Kelly Whit, she placed the order using a Discover credit card number that had been provided to her by one of her friends. Kelly stated that on two separate occasions, the last being approximately 6 weeks ago, she was provided credit card numbers by her friend, Mellondie Bens (b/f/22) who was employed at Lane, Inc. Kelly stated that on the last occasion she received a credit card number from Mellondie Bens, it was written down on a piece of tissue paper. At the time Kelly stated she received the credit card numbers, she was told by Mellondie Bens that you could order items over the telephone by using the credit card numbers and further that if anyone such as the police came to your door to just play dumb. According to Kelly, she was told by Mellondie that she had obtained the card numbers through her employment at Lane. On April 21, 19XX, the detective made contact with Mellondie Bens via the telephone. At that time, Mellondie Bens denied any involvement and was uncooperative in the above investigation. Mellondie Bens was asked several times by the detective to come to IPD headquarters to explain her side of the story; however, she failed to show up for a scheduled interview.

According to Mr. Ant of Lane, Inc., Mellondie Bens was employed at Lane from May 21, 19XX until February 22, 19XX. While employed at Lane she worked as a fashion consultant, which consisted of taking telephone orders from customers for merchandise. Mr. Ant stated that on February 20, 19XX, Mellondie Bens was terminated for unsatisfactory performance. According to Mr. Ant, each fashion consultant uses a computer and is assigned an operator identification number when taking telephone orders. Mellondie Bens' operator ID number was 3410. Lane records show that on January 3, 19XX, while Mellondie Bens was working, she received a telephone order from Rita Doe, R.R. 2 Box 10, Lake City, TN 3776X using a Discover credit card number XXXXXXXXX in the amount of $67.45. The operator ID number on this order was 3410, indicating to Mr. Ant that this was the same Discover credit card number used to order merchandise on April 14, 19XX, and set up delivery to 38 S. 31st Street.

CASE EXAMPLE 2: STOLEN CREDIT CARD DELIVERY

On October 4, 19XX, a call was received from Mike Ant of Lane, Inc., at 23 Eastern Avenue, Indianapolis, Marion County, Indiana, in reference to a clothing order that was placed over the telephone using an AE card with the account no. XXXXXXX. According to Mr. Ant, AE had the card number listed as stolen. The owner's name was Loren Shell from Park, Michigan. The order was placed under the name of Michelle Hards.

On October 5, 19XX, a detective went to 28 W. Priscilla Avenue, the address where the order was to be delivered. On arrival, we were greeted by a black female subject; when told the order was for Michelle Hards, she identified herself as Michelle Hards and said she had been waiting for the order to be delivered. The black female was asked to sign the invoice to show she had received the merchandise. The black female then signed the invoice with the name "Michelle Hards." The detective then asked the black female to check over the invoice to make sure the prices and the total amount was right. She stated the amounts were correct. At this point, the detective identified himself. The black female was then identified as Crystal C. Hard (DOB 5–08–70). He asked Crystal Hard if she would agree to be interviewed at police headquarters. She agreed. Crystal C. Hard was read her Miranda rights at police headquarters; she stated that she understood her rights and gave a statement. Crystal C. Hard then admitted to forging the name Michelle Hards, attempting to take possession of property that was not going to be paid for, and conspiring to fraudulently use a credit card that was not hers to attain goods.

On October 8, 19XX, the detective talked to the rightful owner of the credit card, a Loren Shell from Park, Michigan. Mr. Shell said that he did not know a Crystal C. Hard and she did not have permission to use his AE card to buy merchandise.

CASE EXAMPLE 3: CREDIT CARD FRAUD (I)

On Tuesday, August 4, 19XX, a call was received from Mike Ant of Lane, Inc., at 23 Eastern Avenue, Indianapolis, Marion County, Indiana, in reference to a clothing order that was placed over the telephone using a V credit card with account no. XXXXXXXX. According to Mr. Ant, after checking with the actual owner of the V card, Martin Della of 70 Pk. Dr. E. #1, Flushing, New York 1136X, it was determined that she did not place an order for the merchandise listed on the order in question. Ms. Della stated that she had not given anyone permission to use her V card.

On Wednesday, August 15, 19XX, a detective went to 42 N. Hill Circle, Indianapolis, Marion County, Indiana, the address where the order was to be delivered. Upon arrival, he was greeted by a black female subject, who when told the order was for Regin Aurie identified herself as Regin Aurie. The black female was asked to sign the invoice to show she had received the merchandise. The black female then signed the invoice with the name "Regin Aurie." The detective then asked her to check the invoice for price and to see if it was the right amount. She stated the amount was correct.

At this point, the detective identified himself. The black female was then identified as Hope Turn (b/f/18, DOB 8–25–71). The detective asked Hope Turn if she would be willing to give a statement. She agreed and then was transported to police headquarters. Hope Turn was read her Miranda rights; she stated she understood and gave a statement. Hope Turn then admitted to forging the name of Regin Aurie, attempting to take possession of property that was not going to be paid for, and fraudulently using a credit card that was not hers to attain goods. Hope Turn was then arrested for forgery and fraud.

CASE EXAMPLE 4: CREDIT CARD FRAUD (II)

During the month of May 19XX, the loss prevention personnel of XXX Stores, Inc., in Indianapolis, Indiana, noticed a high usage rate on a credit card at the store located at 302 S. Stone Avenue in Marion County, Indiana. The credit card was an AE card and belonged to a Jack Doe. The card number was XXXXXXXX. The loss prevention personnel of XXX then contacted Robert Son of AE and asked whether the account of Jack Doe had any fraudulent usage. Robert Son contacted Jack Doe, who stated that all charges from the XXX Store in Indiana should be considered fraudulent because he had never been to the store. Jack Doe lives in New York State.

AE then checked all recent charges on Jack Doe's account and found eight charges at the XXX Store located at 302 S. Stone Avenue, Indianapolis, Indiana. The XXX loss prevention personnel then checked the register rolls; they showed that every time Jack Doe's AE account was used, Caesar Smith (DOB 3–15–73) was the register operator. This was confirmed by checking Caesar Smith's identification number with the one used during the fraudulent transactions. XXX loss prevention personnel from that point on videotaped Caesar Smith every time he came to work. The XXX loss prevention personnel also contacted Detective DuBois to have him start on the investigation.

During the months of June and July 19XX, the XXX loss prevention personnel videotaped two suspicious credit card transactions for which Caesar Smith was the cash register operator. One transaction was an AE card account and one was an SA card account. Detective DuBois contacted Robert Son of AE and asked him to check several AE accounts to see whether there had been any fraudulent charges against the accounts. The account numbers were ones for which Caesar Smith had been the clerk of the transaction. All the transactions had happened at the XXX Store at 302 S. Stone Avenue, Indianapolis, Indiana.

Robert Son of AE security forwarded information to Detective DuBois about three account numbers for which there had been fraudulent charges. The cardholders' names were Jack Doe, W. R. Jones, and James E. Jones, M.D. All the fraudulent charges had occurred at the XXX Store, 302 S. Stone Avenue, Indianapolis. XXX loss prevention personnel took this information and found that Caesar Smith had been the cash register operator on all the fraudulent transactions.

On August 12, 19XX, Detective Steven DuBois went to the XXX Store at 302 S. Stone, Indianapolis, Indiana, and confronted Caesar Smith. Smith was transported to the roll call site and interviewed. Smith was given his Miranda warnings and agreed to give a statement. Smith stated that he had been helping in fraudulent credit card transactions at the XXX Store on S. Stone Avenue. Smith said that he was helping a black male with the first name of Derick. Smith stated that he did not know where Derick lived, but could get a message to him. Smith said that Derick had been giving him credit card numbers to use in the fraudulent credit card transactions. Smith said that normally the transactions would occur when Derick came into the XXX Store at 302 S. Stone Avenue. Derick would then pick out several items from the electronics department where Smith was working. Derick would then go to the counter and give Smith a stolen credit card number. Smith would manually input the number into his cash register because he did not have the actual credit card. Derick would then sign the charge slip with a false name and leave the store with the merchandise.

Caesar Smith admitted to being involved in several fraudulent credit card transactions. He stated that he had used several stolen AE account numbers to get merchandise for himself and the black male named Derick. Caesar Smith then stated he would help Detective DuBois find out what Derick's last name was and where he was getting the AE numbers.

Caesar Smith agreed to make a telephone call to a Craig Edsoe to try to find out Derick's last name and address. Craig Edsoe was the person who had introduced Smith to Derick. Smith made the telephone call and talked to Craig Edsoe. Edsoe stated that Derick lived in Kentucky and his last name was Good. Caesar Smith then told Craig Edsoe to have Derick Good call him because he needed more of the credit card numbers. Craig Edsoe stated that if Derick Good called him he would give him the message.

Detective DuBois then contacted Robert Son of AE Security and asked whether he could find out if any of the affected card holders had been in Kentucky recently. Robert Son later reported that all three affected card holders had been in Louisville, Kentucky, and had stayed at a hotel called the Brown Berley. Detective DuBois then called Louisville and requested that authorities find out whether a Derick Good worked at the hotel in question. The Police Department confirmed that a black male by the name of Derick Good (DOB of 4–28–68) worked at the hotel.

During the next 2 weeks during different telephone conversations between Caesar Smith and Derick Good, Derick Good gave Smith two more AE account numbers. Detective DuBois instructed Smith to ask Good what he wanted for the numbers. Good stated that he would like to have more merchandise from the electronics department at XXX. Caesar Smith stated that he could no longer do the transactions with Good, but he could do them himself; then he and Good could meet and divide the merchandise. Good and Smith set up a date of August 25,

19XX, to meet and divide the merchandise Smith obtained from XXX with the credit card number Good had given him. Good agreed that they would meet at the parking lot of UPU on 1200 East Street, Indianapolis, Marion County, Indiana.

On August 25, 19XX, at 11:50 A.M., several undercover detectives set up a surveillance of the parking lot at 1200 East Street. A detective acting in an undercover capacity drove Caesar Smith to the parking lot. Derick Good and Craig Edsoe arrived just after 12 o'clock noon. Derick Good was in a brown Toyota with a Kentucky plate. Craig Edsoe was in a blue truck with an Indiana plate. Craig Edsoe approached the officer and Caesar Smith as they sat in the parking lot. Craig Edsoe said, "You kinda picked a wide open spot, didn't you?" Derick Good then pulled up. Craig Edsoe and Derick Good both wanted to move farther south in the lot because of the appearance of a police car. When the police car followed both Edsoe and Good to the south area of the parking lot, they left. Several minutes later both reappeared and wanted to move the meeting because of the police car. The meeting was moved to the back parking lot of the Grounds Inn at 502 38th Street.

The officer, Caesar Smith, Craig Edsoe, and Derick Good all met and parked their cars in the back lot. Smith and Good talked about the merchandise. Good believed that Smith had gotten the merchandise with the stolen credit card number he had given to Smith the night before. The merchandise was the property of the police department and was packaged to look as if it came from XXX Store. Three VCRs and a TV were in the officer's van. Derick Good opened the hatchback to his car and VCRs were then loaded into his car. Craig Edsoe was present during the whole event. Undercover detectives then moved in and detained all the subjects involved.

Both Edsoe and Good were transported to Police Headquarters. Good was read his Miranda rights and agreed to give a statement. Good said that he had been stealing credit card account numbers from his place of employment in Louisville, Kentucky. He admitted that on April 29, 19XX, he went to 302 S. Stone Avenue, Indianapolis, Indiana, and used a credit card account number of XXXXXXXX to buy three cameras and a roll of film worth $845.45. He stated that he had stolen this number from his place of employment. He also stated that James E. Jones, the cardholder, had not given him permission to use the card. Good stated that he signed an unreadable name to the charge slip. Good stated that Caesar Smith was the clerk during the transaction and knew the credit card account number was stolen because he had to manually input the number into the cash register. XXX personnel are not allowed to use only a credit card number during a transaction; they must have a valid credit card.

Good admitted that on May 7, 19XX, he went to the same XXX Store and used the AE account number of XXXXXXXX. Good stated that he had stolen this number from his place of employment; that he did not have the permission to use the card from Jack Doe, the cardholder; that he bought a camera worth $272.99; and that he again signed an unreadable name to the charge slip. He also stated that he was again assisted by Caesar Smith, who knew the credit card number was stolen.

Good admitted that he had made plans to meet with Caesar Smith on August 25, 19XX, to pick up merchandise that he believed Smith had bought from XXX with a stolen credit card number. Derick Good stated that he believed Smith would use the credit card account number he had given him the day before. Good further admitted that he showed up at the parking lot with the intention of picking up the merchandise he believed to be stolen. The credit card account number that Good believed was used for this transaction was XXXXXXXX. He stated that he had stolen this number from his place of employment and then called Caesar Smith and gave the number to him over the telephone.

On August 26, 19XX, Detective DuBois called Dr. James Jones who was the cardholder of the AE account number XXXXXXXX. Detective DuBois reached Dr. Jones' wife, Sue Jones. Mrs. Jones stated that she had been given permission to use Dr. Jones' AE. She stated that she did not know a Caesar Smith or a Derick Good, and they did not have permission to use Dr. Jones' AE account.

On August 26, 19XX, Detective DuBois called Jack Doe, the cardholder of AE account number XXXXXXXX. Jack Doe stated that he had given no one permission to use his AE account number. Jack Doe also stated that he did not know a Derick Good or a Caesar Smith.

On August 31, 19XX, Caesar Smith was again interviewed by Detectives DuBois and Bates at police headquarters. Smith waived his Miranda rights and agreed to talk about the fraudulent use of several credit card account numbers. Smith stated that twice he had helped Derick Good use stolen AE account numbers to buy merchandise from the XXX Store where he worked. Smith stated that on April 29, 19XX, Derick Good came into the XXX Store where he worked at 302 S. Stone Avenue and used the stolen AE account number of XXXXXXXX to buy three cameras and a roll of film. The account number belonged to James E. Jones of Broadview Heights, Ohio. Smith stated that the next time Derick Good came into the store was May 7, 19XX. Smith stated that he helped Good use stolen AE account number XXXXXXXX to buy one camera. The account number belonged to Jack Doe of New York City. Caesar Smith stated that these were the only two times that Derick Good came into the XXX Store himself to obtain merchandise with a stolen credit card account number. Smith admitted that he continued to use several credit card account numbers to obtain merchandise from XXX, but that Derick Good was not present during the transactions. (Both Caesar Smith and Derick Good were charged with the above incidents on August 26, 19XX.)

Detective DuBois asked Caesar Smith about several other fraudulent charges on Jack Doe's AE account. Smith stated that on May 9, 19XX, an unidentified subject came to the XXX Store at 302 S. Stone Avenue and used Jack Doe's account number to obtain a VCR worth $304.49. Smith stated that he was working in the electronics department of the store, and the unidentified subject came to his cash register to check out. Smith stated that he manually input the credit card number of Jack Doe into the cash register and then had the unidentified subject sign the charge slip. The charge slip was signed with the name "Fred John." Smith stated that the unidentified subject then left the store with the VCR. Smith stated that both the unidentified subject and he knew that they did not have permission to use the AE account of Jack Doe.

Smith stated that the same thing happened on May 14, 19XX, when Jack Doe's account number was used fraudulently. Smith stated that the unidentified subject came to the XXX Store when Smith was working and picked out a TV and a VCR worth $440.98. Smith manually input the credit card account number of Jack Doe's account into the cash register and gave the charge slip to the unidentified subject to sign. The unidentified subject signed the name of "Fred Johns". The unidentified subject then left the store with the merchandise.

Smith stated that Jack Doe's account number was again used on May 21, 19XX. Smith stated that the unidentified subject came into the XXX Store when Smith was working and picked out a television and car stereo worth $383.24. Smith stated that he then manually input the account number of Jack Doe into the cash register and obtained a charge slip. The unidentified subject then signed the charge slip with the name of "John Young". The unidentified subject then left the store with the merchandise.

Smith stated that Jack Doe's account number was used again on May 28, 19XX. Smith stated that the unidentified subject came into the XXX Store when Smith was working and picked out a VCR worth $188.99. Smith then manually input the account number of Jack Doe into the cash register and obtained a charge slip. The unidentified subject then signed the charge slip with an unreadable signature. The unidentified subject then left the store with the merchandise.

The subject in the incidents described above remains unidentified because Caesar Smith has not helped to identify him.

Smith stated that Jack Doe's account number was again used on June 16, 19XX. Smith stated that Ronald Smith came into the XXX Store when Smith was working and picked out a television and a "boom box" worth $367.48. Smith stated that he then manually input the credit card account number of Jack Doe into the cash register and obtained a charge slip. Ronald Smith then signed the name of "Willy Johnson" to the charge slip. Ronald Smith left the store with the merchandise. Jack Doe's account number was again used on June 25, 19XX. Smith stated that Ronald Smith came into the XXX Store when Smith was working and picked out a VCR and a television. Smith stated that he then manually input the account number of Jack Doe into the cash register and obtained a charge slip. Ronald Smith signed the name of "Johnny Young" to the charge slip and left the store with the merchandise.

During the first and second interview with Caesar Smith, an incident of July 2, 19XX, was discussed. Dr. Char was in the XXX Store on July 2, 19XX. She used her credit card to pay for some film she had developed. Her account number was XXXXXXXX. The doctor was waited on by Caesar Smith. Smith admitted that after the doctor left his counter, he punched a code into his cash register to make a copy of her charge receipt. This receipt had the doctor's account number. Caesar Smith stated that he then called Ronald Smith and gave him Dr. Char's account number over the telephone. Smith stated that he told him to come to the

XXX Store where he was working to get more merchandise. One hour later, Ronald Smith came into the store located at 302 S. Stone Avenue and picked out a VCR and a telephone worth $251.98. Caesar Smith manually input the account number of Dr. Char into his cash register and obtained a charge slip. Ronald Smith signed "Ray Smith" to the charge slip and then left the store with the merchandise. During this time, XXX loss prevention personnel were videotaping all transactions in which Smith was the cash register operator. Detective DuBois has videotapes of both transactions involving this credit card account.

Detective DuBois asked Smith about a transaction on August 3, 19XX, using a W. R. Jones AE account number XXXXXXXX. Smith stated that he had gotten this number from Derick Good. Smith admitted that the first time the pair tried to use the account number it was rejected by his cash register. Smith stated that he later dropped the last number off the account number and found that the number would work. Smith stated that on August 3, 19XX, Ronald Smith came to the XXX Store at 302 S. Stone Avenue and went to the electronics department where Smith was working. He then picked out a television and a cord worth $277.18. Smith manually input the credit card account number of W. R. Jones into his cash register and obtained a charge slip. Ronald Smith signed the name of "Johnny Young" to the charge slip and then left the store with the merchandise. Loss prevention personnel of XXX also had this transaction on videotape.

During the interview with Caesar Smith, he stated that Ronald Smith was a black male whose sister lived next to him. Caesar Smith lived at 128 E. Broad Street, Indianapolis, Indiana. Detective DuBois checked Indianapolis computer files and found a Ronald L. Smith (DOB 7–24–68). Detective DuBois also viewed the video that XXX loss prevention personnel had provided and a police photograph of Ronald L. Smith. The video and the photo matched. Ronald Smith was living at 17 W. Capitol Street. Smith was contacted and agreed to come in for an interview. On September 8, 19XX, Ronald Smith came to police headquarters and was interviewed by Detective DuBois. Smith signed a rights waiver and gave a statement to Detective DuBois. Smith stated that he had helped Caesar Smith with fraudulent credit card transactions at the XXX Store located at 302 S. Stone Avenue. Smith admitted that he signed the charge slips for merchandise on the following dates: May 9, 14, 21, and 28 of 19XX. Smith further stated he did not have the cardholders' permission to use the account numbers and never intended to pay for the merchandise.

Smith stated that he knew he was not allowed to use any of the credit card accounts and that in doing so he was breaking the law. Smith also stated that Ronald Smith knew the credit card account numbers were stolen and that he was breaking the law.

Detective DuBois has three unauthorized uses of account number statements, one each from victims James E. Jones, Jack Doe, and W. R. Jones. The statements say that the cardholders were the only persons authorized to use the accounts. The total loss of merchandise from the XXX Store was $4,138.70.

Fencing Stolen Property

The buying and selling of stolen property is an illegal activity that receives too little attention in law enforcement today. Administrators have to divide limited resources among unlimited demands for service. Because of this, you as an investigator must demonstrate why your administrator should commit manpower and money to your project.

In order to do this, you need to demonstrate that: (1) fencing operations create a major percentage of crime in your area; and (2) if provided support, you can eliminate a portion of reported crime.

Most fences deal with thieves and burglars in a given area. If a fence deals with five burglars and each averages two burglaries a week, the fence buying from them promotes 520 burglaries in each year. He is in business. Using information such as this can go a long way toward convincing your administrators that investigations must be done.

GOALS

When you set out to investigate fencing operations you need to establish the goals that you intend to attain. The following are some examples:

- Aggressively go after subjects who buy and sell stolen goods.
- Attack the subjects in a three-prong system which includes: criminal prosecution; civil Racketeer Influenced and Corrupt Organizations (RICO) charges; seizing of money and assets; and assisting the state and federal IRS.
- Identify subjects known to be thieves and the techniques they use, and pass this information on to all agencies.
- Use all available laws to close down fencing operations. This includes both criminal and civil law.
- Your team should become a conduit for the dissemination of information to all agencies.

- Build and maintain contacts with agencies all over your area and help identify common criminal activities.
- Conduct in-depth property crime investigations.
- File forfeiture actions and track forfeited items.
- Recommend changes in the system which will benefit law enforcement in the attack on fencing operations.

Now that you have your goals to present, you need to identify what will be required of the personnel who are assigned to this task. You may want to consider the following:

JOB DESCRIPTION

- Conduct surveillances, review existing files, check background, and conduct photographic and electronic surveillance.
- Receive case assignments regarding property crimes and conduct a preliminary review of the case to determine elements and to identify a course of action.
- Prepare and serve search and arrest warrants, obtain search and arrest warrants, and conduct searches.
- Prepare for interviewing suspects.
- Prepare reports relating to investigations and maintain case file of investigative activities.
- Conduct undercover criminal investigation, establish cover identity, and identify prospective witnesses and informants.
- Maintain liaison with other law enforcement representatives.
- Participate in establishment and maintenance of a relationship between police and public sectors.
- Report to crime scene when requested to, assist officers with identification of stolen property, and conduct immediate interviews of arrested suspects.
- Conduct analysis of criminal activity information, prepare reports on analysis of data, and discuss trends.
- Maintain record of monies spent.
- Testify in court.
- Maintain personal appearance and equipment.
- Attend training sessions.
- Perform other duties as directed.

HOW TO ATTACK THE PROBLEM

The next step you must take is to decide how to best attack the illegal organization. Two answers come to mind: (1) stings, and (2) reverses.

Stings

If the time and money are available, a sting is a very effective way to have a major impact on crime in a given area. A sting operation can

- clear present and prior cases
- recover stolen property
- identify large numbers of criminals
- forfeit assets of targets
- deter future crimes

The major drawback is funding. Funding for sting operations must cover a wide variety of issues. For example, there should be funding for a store front or mobile operation; upkeep and renovation; the purchase of stolen property; manpower; transportation, storage, and security of purchased property; and equipment needs, such as video equipment, 35-mm cameras, safety features, weapons, transmitters, and vehicles.

Because most agencies will not make the commitment to go all out on a first case situation, I recommend that you begin with reverses, which are short term and impact specific target locations.

What Is a Reverse?

A reverse simply is selling instead of buying. Law enforcement officials have had to devise ways to have an impact on criminal activities in a cheap and effective manner. Reverses seem to fill the bill.

Reverses can cover any number of crimes in almost any area of the country. The only limitations we find are the creativity of us in law enforcement and our ability to convince administrators that we can conduct reverses effectively.

These are a few reverses with which we have had success: (1) trading purported stolen VCRs for dope, (2) sale of purported stolen property to fences, (3) vacation giveaways to identify wanted subjects, (4) street corner drugstores, (5) patronizing prostitution, (6) trading purported stolen property for guns, (7) trading guns for dope, (8) delivery of items obtained through credit card and check fraud, and (9) murder for hires.

The number and type of reverses you can come up with are unlimited; however, always remember that before you conduct any reverse or sting, you must contact your legal advisor or prosecutor to make sure you are on solid, acceptable ground.

CASE EXAMPLE 1: BUYING STOLEN PROPERTY (I)

We received information from an informant who knew from his personal knowledge that on numerous occasions the owner of Bon Motors at 45 North

Shadeland Avenue, a Mr. Rold Kei, had purchased stolen goods and that Mr. Kei had specifically asked the informant to steal designer blue jeans for him and his son, Rold Kei, Jr.

On February 21, 19XX, in the presence of a detective and while being tape recorded, the confidential informant placed a call to Bon Motors and spoke to the owner's son, Rold Kei, who placed an order specifically for designer blue jeans. The detective then contacted Julie Rell, Director of Security for Feder Department Stores. Miss Rell provided three pairs of designer blue jeans valued at $159.50. The confidential informant was searched for contraband and money by the detective. He was then given the jeans, and he went to Bon Motors where he represented the jeans as stolen to Rold Kei, (w/m/25) and his father, Rold Kei, Sr. (w/m/46). The senior Mr. Kei gave his son $40.00 in U.S. currency, and the son then gave the money to the confidential informant.

Before leaving, the Keis engaged in a conversation, ordered a video camera, and told the informant to "be sure all the attachments were included when he brought it back". The confidential informant then went to 21st and Shadeland Avenue, as he was directed to do, where he met with the detective. The detective then recovered the $40.00 U.S. currency.

A short time later, the detective procured a video camera and a video cassette recorder valued at approximately $1,500 from Rian Hots, a security officer for the Mart. The detective then searched the confidential informant and provided him with the video equipment. The confidential informant went back to Bon Motors where he represented the video equipment as stolen to the owner, Rold L. Kei, Sr. The owner told him that his son would take care of him. The senior Mr. Kei then left for a tavern for a meeting.

Mr. Kei, Jr., then discussed the price with the confidential informant. After the informant had told him how difficult it was to get the merchandise out of the store (even going into detail about how he did it), Rold Kei then offered him $400.00 for the equipment, but told him he would have to wait until his father returned because he did not have the money. He then sent the lot boy next door with a note for the senior Mr. Kei. He returned a short time later and stated that the senior Mr. Kei said that he would give $300.00 for the camera and the VCR and that he would be back in about a half an hour. Shortly thereafter the meeting broke up and the owner's son went over to the tavern to get the $300.00 from his father. He returned to the car dealership and gave it to the confidential informant.

At approximately 6:00 P.M., the detective, along with several assisting units, served a search warrant at Bon Motors and found one of the above pairs of blue jeans, the video cassette recorder, and the video camera in the owner's office inside the car dealership. Also in the back room area of the business, the other two pair of blue jeans were found on a golf cart. Shortly thereafter, the detective met with the confidential informant at 21st and Shadeland Avenue again and recovered the $300.00 U.S. currency.

CASE EXAMPLE 2: FENCING OPERATION

On November 10, 19XX, two employees of Universal Construction were working at a job site, 690 East 30th Street, Indianapolis, Marion County, Indiana. The two employees stated that while they were working, a black male (late 30s, 5 ft. 6 in., 150–155 lb. curly black hair, moustache, and goatee) approached them about buying some tools, which they refused. Then, sometime over the next 2-day weekend, without permission someone removed a rigid pipe cutter/threader that was on this site which was painted purple and yellow and belonged to Universal. All tools belonging to Universal are painted purple and yellow for identification by the company. Another employee, John Doe, stated that he had been reading a trade paper when he found the same make of pipe cutter/threader for sale that had been stolen. He contacted and then went to see the seller, Roy Jones, 87 North Street, Indianapolis, Marion County, Indiana, on January 9, 19XX, about the item. Mr. Doe stated that he saw two places on the tool with purple paint and one place inside the threads with yellow paint; he believed this to be his tool, which was taken from the job site on 30th Street. Mr. Doe made arrangements to buy the tool for $800.00 from Roy Jones, stating that the original value was $3,200.00 and that a good used cutter/threader would cost $2,000.00.

The next day, John Doe picked up the tool and returned it to Universal at 672 East Street, Indianapolis, Indiana. Detectives went to the business address and examined the tool, observing remnants of the purple paint on the casing and the disassembled tripod leg. It was also noted that the serial number plate had been removed from the same area where it was located on a second exact model still at the Universal business. Mr. Doe stated both pipe cutter/threaders were originally purchased at the same time. Mr. Doe stated that the purple and yellow paint scheme on tools is unique to their company.

Between August 22, 19XX, and August 29, 19XX, two thefts occurred. One took place at Valpar Court, Indianapolis, Marion County, Indiana. Stolen was a Carrier Corporation air conditioning exterior condensing unit, model no. 38EN036500, serial no. T410181, valued at $1,984.00. The other theft occurred at 567 Valpar Court. Stolen was a Carrier Corporation air conditioning exterior condensing unit, model no. 38EN0605105M, serial no. U428197, valued at $2,228.00.

On February 5, 19XX, detectives had occasion to visit 87 North Street, Indianapolis, Marion County, Indiana; they were answering an ad in a trade newspaper in response to an investigation initiated by Detective Sergeant Smith, whereby he had learned that Roy Jones (b/m/38, DOB 11–25–50) had sold a rigid pipe threader/cutter to Mike Doe, a representative of Universal Construction. The pipe threader/cutter had been stolen from Universal. Detectives spoke with Roy Jones and inquired about the ad in the trade paper. Mr. Jones stated that the item detectives were interested in was stored at his warehouse on Washington Street and that his partner had the key. Detectives asked to go to the warehouse and Jones stated that he could not get hold of his partner until the next day. The detectives then identified themselves as police officers and advised Mr. Jones he was under arrest for theft on a warrant. The detective then advised Roy Jones of the Miranda warning. Mr. Jones stated that he needed to go back inside of his residence and turn off heaters and retrieve his coat. A detective advised him that he would have to accompany him, as he was under arrest. Mr. Jones agreed and allowed the detective inside his residence. In plain view in the residence were several items such as construction equipment and building materials; racks of new clothes; and a red Fuji Club bicycle, serial no. FK303043, which was reported as stolen to the police department under their case no. 123456. The bicycle was stolen from 354 North Corner Drive on April 1, 19XX.

Detective Sergeant Smith then asked Mr. Jones to sign a standard Consent to Search form for his house and garage, which he did. Detectives then asked Mr. Jones where he had gotten the items. Mr. Jones stated, "Some of these things might be stolen, but I don't want you to think I stole them; my friends bring them over and leave them."

Detectives asked Mr. Jones who the friends were and Mr. Jones replied that he could not remember. Detectives then asked Mr. Jones about his warehouse. Mr. Jones stated it was at LaSalle Street and East Street, Indianapolis, Marion County, Indiana. Detectives asked Mr. Jones whether there were any stolen goods in the warehouse. Mr. Jones stated that there were stolen tools and building supplies in his warehouse, but he had not stolen them.

Mr. Jones then escorted the detective to his garage, unlocked the door, and allowed them in to search. Inside of the garage, detectives found thousands of dollars worth of stolen goods: there were five truckloads of goods removed from the garage. Detective Smith asked Mr. Jones what was stolen and what was not. Mr. Jones began pointing to several items and saying, "That's stolen, that's stolen," etc. He continued to say that he did not steal the items, but again that friends had left them there.

On February 7, 19XX, detectives went to the warehouse at 337 East Street, Indianapolis, Marion County, Indiana, and spoke with the manager and determined that Mr. Jones rented units no. J-10 and no. T-12. Detectives obtained search warrants and recovered, among other things, the previously mentioned two Carrier air conditioning condensing units and a total of three large truckloads of goods. There was a total of approximately 30 different victims who received their stolen property back as a result of the raid on Mr. Jones' garage, house, and storage warehouse.

CASE EXAMPLE 3: BUYING STOLEN PROPERTY (II)

Over the past several months, this unit of the police department received information that the social club also known as the Har-Ma Social located at 136 S. Dian Street, Indianapolis, Marion County, Indiana, has been buying stolen property. The owner of the bar and the person identified as buying the stolen property is a white male named Carl Roff. A background investigation showed a police report being made on December 5, 19XX, at which time the owner was identified as Carl Roff (DOB 6–13–31). In addition, on April 14, 19XX, a check through the township assessor's office showed that the property located at 136 S. Dian Street is owned by Clara Roff with a mailing address of 25 Nion Street, Indianapolis, Marion County, Indiana.

On February 11, 19XX, at approximately 9:30 P.M., this detective went to the club located at 136 S. Dian Street, Indianapolis, Marion County, Indiana. While at the above location, this detective made contact with a white male known by the first name of Carl. Background investigation revealed the white male known as Carl to be Carl Roff. During conversation with Carl, he gave $21.00 in U.S. currency for two cartons of Winston cigarettes and one carton of Camel cigarettes, all of which had been purported to him to be stolen.

On March 7, 19XX, at approximately 2:40 P.M., this detective went to the club located at 136 S. Dian Street, Indianapolis, Marion County, Indiana. While at the club, this detective made contact with a white male known as Carl Roff. During conversation with Carl, he gave $15.00 in U.S. currency for three 750 ml bottles of Jack Daniels whiskey, all of which had been purported to Carl as being stolen from Dosco Drugs. During the transaction, Carl removed the price tags and placed the bottles behind the bar. The $15.00 in U.S. currency Carl paid for the Jack Daniels had been taken from his pants pocket.

On March 11, 19XX, at approximately 2:45 P.M., this detective went to the club located at 136 S. Dian Street, Indianapolis, Marion County, Indiana. Upon entering the club, this detective made contact with a white male known to be Carl Roff. During their conversation, Carl agreed to give $38.00 in U.S. currency for four cartons of Marlboro cigarettes and two 750 ml bottles of Jack Daniels whiskey. All of the above items had been purported to Carl as stolen. During the transaction, Carl went to the bar and squatted down behind the bar in close proximity to a safe and retrieved U.S. currency. Carl then stood up and took additional currency from the cash register and gave $28.00 to this detective. Prior to leaving the club, Carl stated that he had shorted this detective $10.00 and that he would give him the additional $10.00 as agreed. At that time, Carl opened the cash register and gave this detective $10.00 in U.S. currency.

On March 18, 19XX, at approximately 1:45 P.M., this detective went to the club located at 136 S. Dian Street, Indianapolis, Marion County, Indiana. While at the above location, this detective made contact with a white male known to be Carl Roff. On entering the location, Carl was observed behind the bar. He asked what this detective had. At that time, Carl motioned for this detective to meet him in the back room of the bar. While in the back room, this detective showed Carl several items, specifically: one Zebco tackle tote with rod and reel, model no. 4298; one Daiwa reel (gold), model no. GS-10X; two Garcia Ambassadeur reels (red), serial no. 090902 and no. 810300; two cartons of Marlboro cigarettes; and two cartons of Marlboro Light cigarettes. All the above items had been purported to Carl as "ripped off" and "copped". (Ripped off and copped are street terminology for stolen.) During their conversation, Carl agreed to pay $43.00 in U.S. currency for the above purported stolen items. Prior to completing the transaction,

Carl went behind the bar and squatted down in close proximity to a safe and retrieved U.S. currency. Carl then returned to the detective and gave him the $43.00 which was agreed on for the above purported items.

On March 19, 19XX, at approximately 1:50 P.M., this detective went to the club located at 136 S. Dian Street, Indianapolis, Marion County, Indiana. On entering the club, this detective made contact with a white male known to be Carl Roff. While in the bar, this detective showed Carl two 750 ml bottles of Jack Daniels. Carl walked behind the bar and obtained $10.00 in U.S. currency from the cash register and then gave the money to this detective.

On March 20, 19XX, at approximately 3:00 P.M., this detective went to the club located at 136 S. Dian Street, Indianapolis, Marion County, Indiana. On entering the above location, this detective made contact with a white male known to be Carl Roff, who was standing behind the bar. This detective then followed Carl to the back room of the bar. At that time, this detective showed Carl one case of 12 750-ml bottles of Lord Calvert Canadian whiskey which was purported as ''ripped off''. During their conversation, Carl agreed to pay $60.00 in currency. Carl then gave the $60.00 to this detective. After the whiskey was given to Carl, he placed the case in a white-colored basket and then covered the top with a white towel.

After the transaction had occurred, assisting officers entered the above location and a search warrant was served. After identifying himself as a police officer, this detective performed a pat down on Carl Roff. Two handguns were located on his person. At that time, the above location was secured and a search warrant as well as Miranda warnings were read to Carl Roff. During the search, a safe was found behind the bar in the same proximity of where Carl on several occasions (including that day's transaction) had squatted down and obtained U.S. currency. This same currency was then paid to this detective for purported stolen property. Also found in the safe was U.S. currency in excess of $12,000.00 which was confiscated. Located in the safe along with the U.S. currency were six prescription bottles of suspected controlled substances. Five of the six prescription bottles had no patient information as required by federal law, indicating that he had no legitimate reason or right for possession. The sixth bottle had a loose prescription label stuck inside the bottle. The suspected controlled substances were confiscated and sent to the property room to be tested. Preliminary lab test results on the substances sent to the property room showed them to be positive, specifically:

        72   tablets of Phentermine, a Schedule IV controlled substance
        57   tablets of Alprazalam, a Schedule IV controlled substance
        14   tablets of Methylphenidate, a Schedule II controlled substance
         2   tablets of Propoxyphene, a Schedule IV controlled substance
         2   capsules of Chloryl Hydrate, a Schedule IV controlled substance

Due to the large amount of controlled substances found in two of the five unlabeled prescription bottles (specifically, 72 tablets of Phentermine and 57 tablets of Alprazalam), coupled with the fact that U.S. currency in excess of $12,000 was also found, this detective asked for charges of possession of a controlled substance as well as possession with intent to deal. Also confiscated during the search warrant was a total of 22 firearms, specifically: 11 loaded handguns, 8 shotguns, 2 rifles, and 1 fully automatic machine gun. All events occurred in Marion County, Indiana.

CASE EXAMPLE 4: FENCING STOLEN PROPERTY

Detective Michael G. Bates swears (affirms) that over the past several months, the Police Department Special Task Team has received numerous complaints about subjects buying and selling stolen property. The subjects identified as being involved as Bert Ham (w/m/44, DOB 2–17–49, SSN: 306–50–XXXX) and his wife, Kie D. Ham (w/f/38, DOB 03–12–54, SSN: 306–58–XXXX). According to the complaints, Bert and Kie Ham were purchasing stolen property from several well-known shoplifters, at their residence, 321 Nix Drive, Indianapolis, Marion County, Indiana. All the above items purchased by Bert and Kie Ham were stolen from area retail stores.

On 2–21–XX, this detective received information from a confidential and reliable informant that a large amount of stolen property was being stored at the Self Storage, located at 374 Kentucky Avenue, Indianapolis, Marion County, Indiana. The informant further stated that the stolen property was being stored in storage unit Q-9. According to the informant, over the last several months the stolen property was taken from area retail stores by shoplifters and then sold to Bert and Kie Ham at their residence, 321 Nix Drive. The informant stated that after purchasing the stolen property, the normal procedures would be for Kie Ham to place the stolen items into a vehicle in her possession and transport the items to Self Storage at 374 Kentucky Avenue in storage unit Q-9. The informant stated that all the stolen property items in storage were new and consisted of VCRs, VHS movies, Super Nintendo games and game cartridges, chainsaws, and portable generators. According to the informant, on 2–25–XX all of the stolen property in storage unit Q-9 was to be loaded into a vehicle owned by or in the possession of Bert and Kie Ham.

On 2–26–XX, the informant stated that Kie Ham and at least two other subjects would leave Indianapolis with the stolen property in their possession and proceed to Toledo, Ohio, in an attempt to sell the stolen property.

On 2–21–XX, a confidential and reliable informant agreed to make a controlled sale of purported stolen property to Bert and Kie Ham at their residence, 321 Nix Drive, Indianapolis, Marion County, Indiana. On the above date, the informant went to 321 Nix Drive and met and had conversation with a white male and white female known to the informant as Bert and Kie Ham. While at the residence, the informant showed Bert Ham a new Homelite chainsaw, serial no. HNO420162. During conversation with both subjects, the informant stated the above chainsaw was "hot" and taken from Wmart. (Hot is street terminology for stolen.) Bert Ham agreed to purchase the Homelite chainsaw for $25.00. Bert then handed the informant $25.00 which he had retrieved from his pants pocket. Prior to leaving the residence, both Bert and Kie Ham advised the informant they would take all the new TVs, VCRs, and Super Nintendo game cartridges the informant could get. Following the transaction, the informant left the residence and met with this detective. At that time, the informant turned over $25.00 in U.S. currency obtained from Bert Ham. The chainsaw sold to Bert Ham was property of the Police Department.

On 2–23–XX, a confidential and reliable informant agreed to make a controlled sale of purported stolen property to Bert and Kie Ham at their residence, 321 Nix Drive. On 02–23–XX, the informant proceeded to the above address and had occasion to meet with two subjects known as Bert and Kie Ham. While at the location, the informant showed Bert a new Homelite chainsaw serial no. HN2680054. At that time, Bert Ham stated to the informant that he had just gotten 10 chainsaws from Ada. Ada was believed to be Ada C. Mill, a well-known habitual shoplifter who has been previously arrested for theft by this detective. Also stated by Bert Ham was that Ada had gotten the chainsaws from Wmart. According to the informant, this subject was going to steal several more items from Wmart prior to quitting, specifically, VCRs and TVs. At that point, Bert Ham told the informant that he would take all the TVs and 4-head VCRs that the subject at Wmart could get. Bert Ham further advised the informant that he would pay $75.00 per VCR. Bert Ham agreed to purchase the purported stolen chainsaw from the informant for $40.00. Bert Ham then retrieved $40.00 in U.S. currency from his wallet and handed the money to the informant. The informant then left the residence and met with this detective, at which time the informant turned over $40.00 in U.S. currency. The item sold to Bert Ham was property of the Police Department.

On 2–25–XX, a confidential and reliable informant agreed to make a controlled sale of purported stolen property to Bert and Kie Ham. On the above date, the informant went to 321 Nix Drive and had occasion to meet with Bert Ham. During conversation with Ham, the informant showed him four VCRs. The informant advised Bert Ham that all the VCRs were ripped off from Wmart. At that time, Bert Ham agreed to purchase the stolen items for $280.00, or $70.00 for each VCR. Bert Ham then provided three $100 bills to the informant and advised he would need $20.00 change. The money paid to the informant by Bert Ham was retrieved from his wallet. During conversation with Bert Ham, the informant advised that the subject stealing items from Wmart was going to steal Super Nintendo cartridges. At that point, Bert advised that he would purchase all the nine- and thirteen-inch TV/VCR combinations he could get. Bert Ham further stated he would purchase Nintendo game systems and cartridges. After the transaction, the informant left the residence and met with this detective, at which time the informant turned over three $100 bills. This detective then took control of the money and gave the informant a $20 bill in change as requested by Bert Ham. The items sold to Bert Ham were property of the Police Department.

On 2–26–XX, a search warrant was executed at 321 Nix Drive. Bert Ham was located at the Bell Flea Market, 64 W. Washington Street, and brought to the residence. Kie Ham was located at the Self Storage, 374 Kentucky Avenue. When located, Kie Ham and another white male identified as Brad Barg were loading items from storage unit Q-9 and placing the items into a 1982 Ford van, license no. 49L84 registered to Kie Ham. A number of items that the informant had previously stated were stolen were observed on the van and in the open storage unit. Also observed on the floor of the storage unit were numerous price tags identified as Wmart tags that had been removed from new pre-recorded movies. It is common procedure among shoplifters and fences to tear price tags off of stolen merchandise, thereby making the merchandise difficult to trace. Some of the items located in both the van and storage unit included VHS prerecorded movies, Super Nintendo games and game cartridges, chainsaws, TV/VCR combinations, a Coleman PowerMate generator, car stereos, cordless telephones, and clothing. Kie Ham was then transported from the storage unit to the residence, at which time the search warrant was initiated at 321 Nix Drive. At the residence, numerous suspected stolen items were located and confiscated. Items confiscated included VHS pre-recorded movies, Super Nintendo game cartridges, chainsaws, VCRs, numerous power and hand tools, and assorted clothing items. Several electric drills, car stereos, and stereo speakers were located in the attic of the residence.

Located and confiscated at the residence were several prescription bottles containing pills and tablets. None of the prescription bottles that contained pills or tablets were in the name of either Bert or Kie Ham. Also found in Bert and Kie Ham's bedroom was a small purple Crown Royal bag that contained a green leafy substance suspected of being marijuana. All of the suspected stolen property was confiscated and transported to the Police Department. The prescription drugs and suspected marijuana were confiscated and turned over to the Property Room for testing by the Forensic Services Agency. On 03–01–XX, preliminary lab tests on the substances sent to the property room showed them to be positive for

30	pills of Darvin-N, a Propoxyphene
20	capsules of Darvin, a Propoxyphene
12.5	tablets of Diazepam
42	capsules of Flurazepam

All of the above are a Schedule IV controlled substance. The preliminary lab test on the marijuana tested positive for 12.20 grams of a Schedule I controlled substance.

Following the search warrant, both Bert and Kie Ham agreed to cooperate and give a statement to police. Both subjects were transported to headquarters and after receiving their Miranda warnings and signing their rights waiver agreed to talk with police. Both subjects admitted to purchasing stolen property from habitual shoplifters. All these subjects were well-known shoplifters and included Ada C. Mill, Jes J. Ricks, Penny Brow, Bert S. Carr, and Steve E. Clay. According to Bert and Kie Ham, these shoplifters would steal merchandise from area retail stores and then bring the merchandise to the Hams' residence to sell. Both subjects further admitted to giving their vehicles to Ada Mill and Jes Ricks knowing that the vehicles would be used to facilitate the theft and transportation of stolen merchandise. According to Kie Ham, after purchasing stolen merchandise at her residence, she would sometimes load the merchandise in a vehicle under her control and then transport it to the Self Storage at 374 Kentucky Avenue and place the stolen items in storage. Some of the stolen items purchased by Bert and Kie Ham consisted of VHS pre-recorded movies, Super Nintendo games and game cartridges, chainsaws, VCRs, cartons of cigarettes, and clothing items.

According to Kie Ham, when she was stopped by police she was in the process of removing items from the storage unit to take to the residence. From the residence, she stated she was leaving for Toledo, Ohio, to attend a large flea market or garage sale. During the interview, Kie Ham stated that for VHS pre-recorded movies they would pay $3.00 each and then sell them for $5.00 each. They would pay $10.00 per Super Nintendo cartridge and then sell them for $20.00 each. They would pay $7.00 per carton of cigarettes and then sell them for $10.00 each. They would pay from $75.00 to $100.00 for VCRs, depending on whether it was a 2-head or 4-head VCR. They would then sell the VCRs for $90.00 to $125.00 apiece.

The following items were seized:

		Value
		Value
928	VHS movies	$13,920.00
126	Nintendo game accessories	$ 8,750.00
102	cartons of cigarettes	$ 1,530.00
10	chainsaws	$ 1,250.00
	assorted tools	$ 2,000.00
	telephone/answering machines	$ 1,000.00
	assorted new clothing	$ 1,500.00
	car stereos	$ 1,000.00
	other assorted items	$ 3,860.00
	Total	$34,810.00

The charges obtained included

Count I	Corrupt business influence
Counts II & III & IV	Attempting to receive stolen property
Counts V & VI & VII	Possession of controlled substances
Count VIII	Possession of marijuana

CASE EXAMPLE 5: EMPLOYEE THEFT

On June 5, 19XX, Detective Smith spoke with Mr. Hal Ambel, owner of Batt Syst, Inc., located at 122 N. Washington Street. Mr. Ambel related that he had received information that some of his employees were involved in stealing expensive items from his company. On June 7, 19XX, at approximately 5:00 P.M. Detective Smith, while working undercover, met with John Doe (b/m, DOB 7–22–57), an employee of Batt Syst, Inc. The meeting took place at Mr. Doe's residence at 2416 Beckwith Drive. During the meeting, Mr. Doe formulated a plan by which he offered to steal a $300.00 battery charger and sell it to Detective Smith for $100.00 U.S. currency. Detective Smith was to call Mr. Doe the next day to arrange to pick up the charger.

On June 8, 19XX, at approximately 12:15 P.M., Detective Smith spoke on the telephone with a Howard Jones (b/m/41, DOB 11–03–47), also an employee of Batt Syst, Inc. Mr. Jones told Detective Smith that he and Mr. Doe had already taken the battery charger out of the warehouse and for Detective Smith to come to the back lot of the milk company at 120 E. South Avenue, directly adjacent to Batt Syst property. He became confused as to the directions and put Mr. Doe on the telephone to clarify where the meeting was to take place. Doe clarified the directions and verified the price for the stolen battery charger. He further told Detective Smith to arrive around 1:00 P.M..

At approximately 1:00 P.M., Detective Smith went to the parking lot as directed, where he first met with John Doe. Doe motioned for Detective Smith to pull to the back corner of the lot. Mr. Jones then pulled a Solar Model 480 6/12 volt battery charger, serial no. C683586, from a pile of trash and carried it to Detective Smith's car and placed it in the trunk. During this time, Mr. Doe was standing on a pile of wood acting as a lookout. Detective Smith asked Jones if there was any chance of getting caught stealing the battery charger, to which Mr. Jones replied "no". Detective Smith then gave him a $100 bill in U.S. currency. They then returned to the battery systems property, where Detective Smith identified himself as a police officer and placed Jones and Doe under arrest.

Mr. Ambel, the owner, was summoned to the back lot were he positively identified the solar battery charger as the property of his company. This was verified by inventory records. Mr. Ambel further stated that at no time did he give Jones or Doe permission to steal the battery charger, nor did they have permission to sell it to Detective Smith.

Subsequent to their arrest, both Jones and Doe gave tape recorded statements to Detective Smith admitting their involvement in the above theft and conspiracy.

14

Murder for Hire

CASE EXAMPLE 1: WIFE FILING FOR DIVORCE AS INTENDED VICTIM

November 11, 19XX. We received information regarding a possible murder for hire investigation identifying the alleged suspect as a Gary Mone (w/m/30). The person who provided us with the information was willing to introduce us to the subject. He was advised to contact the suspect (Mone) and set up a meeting.

November 12, 19XX. We received a call from the informant, who stated that the meeting was to take place at the Tain Tavern on Johns Street at 1300 hours. The suspect had chosen the time and the location for the meeting. We conducted a quick background and then proceeded to the tavern.

November 12, 19XX (1300 hours). We met the suspect, Gary Mone, at the tavern. Mr. Mone stated he wanted to make sure everyone was "cool" before he proceeded. The suspect looked around, then requested that we go to 1234 Cott to continue the meeting. We agreed and left the tavern.

1345 hours. We arrived at 1234 Cott, which we knew through our background was owned by the suspect. We met with the suspect, who again stated he wanted to make sure we were cool. He then requested that we meet him at the mart located on Madison Street. We agreed, but added that we had no more time for games. He agreed.

1415 hours. We arrived at the mart and the following conversation occurred. The suspect (Mone) advised us that the job to be done had to look like an accident because he would be the primary suspect. Mone stated no force was to be used to gain entry to the residence. It must look like an accident. Mone further stated that there were two other individuals who needed to be out of the way. Mone stated that he did not care how they were taken care of as long as they could not testify against him. Mone stated he had to appear in court on November 13, 19XX; however, he was trying to get a continuance. Mone further stated that if he could not get a continuance, he might end up in jail. If the continuance failed, he might need the job done that night. Mone stated he wanted everything including equipment for the job and valuables to go through a third party. This was to isolate himself from the incident. The suspect (Mone) was very concerned that our conversation was being recorded. On two occasions everyone involved was checked for listening devices. Both officers had to drop their pants. We left this meeting with orders to wait for further instructions.

November 16, 19XX. We met with deputy prosecutors, and they felt we did not have a strong enough case.

November 19, 19XX. We contacted the wife of the suspect and found that the suspect had an insurance policy for $500,000.00 on her. The court case was continued, and no further information was obtained from the suspect.

CASE EXAMPLE 2: SON AS INTENDED VICTIM

July 2, 19XX. Detective Steven DuBois received information from a concerned citizen about a possible murder for hire. Detective DuBois was told by the concerned citizen that a Cris Hens, a white female, was looking to hire someone to murder her alleged son. Cris Hens related to the concerned citizen that she wanted to find someone to kill Bobby, her son. Cris Hens said that she had a $25,000.00 life insurance policy on her son Bobby. She stated that she would give $12,000.00 of that to have her son Bobby killed. Cris Hens said that she could get money to pay travel expenses for the person she would hire to kill her son. Detective DuBois received information in handwritten form about Cris Hens' home and work telephone numbers and the hours she would be at both locations. Information Detective DuBois also received the address of 81 S. Wood Avenue, a location in Marion County, Indianapolis, Indiana, in handwritten form. Detective DuBois used the police computer reporting system to locate a Cecelia Hens (w/f, DOB 10–16–38) with a home address of 81 S. Wood Avenue. Detective DuBois also found a registration for a vehicle on file with the Bureau of Motor Vehicles (BMV) that showed a Cecelia Hens (DOB 10–16–38) with a home address of 81 S. Wood Avenue, Indianapolis, Indiana. Detective DuBois also found a driver's license on file with the BMV that gave the same information and address. Detective DuBois also checked the telephone number on the written note and found that number 543–1234 was assigned to 81 S. Wood Avenue.

1510 hours. Detective DuBois called the telephone number 234–5678, which came from the handwritten information Detective DuBois had received that had the name "Cris" written on it along with times to call. A male subject answered the telephone. Detective DuBois asked for Cris. A female voice then answered the telephone. Detective DuBois then identified himself as "Mike" and asked about a job Cris wanted to have done. Detective DuBois and Cris agreed to meet on July 3, 19XX, at 8:30 P.M. at the Twin Shopping Center located at 302 South Avenue, Marion County, Indiana, to talk about the job. Cris stated she would drive a red 1986 Ford LTD. This matched the BMV description of the car registered to Cecelia Hens who lived at 81 S. Wood Avenue. Detective DuBois asked Cris to bring what he needed to do the job. Cris replied, "You mean the piece." (Piece is a common street term for a gun.)

July 3, 19XX (2000 hours). Detective DuBois went to the Twin Shopping Center at 302 South Avenue to meet Cris. Detective DuBois was approached by a white female who had gotten out of a red Ford LTD. The white female identified herself as Cris. Cris stated that she had been looking for somebody for 2 months and did not want to be set up by an undercover cop. Detective DuBois then asked Cris what she wanted him to do. Cris stated that she wanted someone to kill her 23-year-old son who lived in Clarks, Tennessee. Cris stated she would give $10,000 to have her son killed. She said, "I think that is a good price." Detective DuBois and Cris then agreed to $10,000.00 for the killing of Bobby Goy of Clarks, Tennessee, the alleged son of Cris. Cris stated that she was going to pay Detective DuBois after a $25,000.00 life insurance policy paid off for the death of Bobby Goy. Detective DuBois and Cris agreed to $200.00 as expense money for the trip to Clarks, Tennessee. Detective DuBois was to leave as soon as he received the money.

July 8, 19XX. At approximately 1120 hours, Detective DuBois again placed a call to Cris by dialing telephone number 234–5678. Detective DuBois asked for Cris and the person who answered the telephone said, "This is she." Cris stated that she had the money Detective DuBois needed to get to Clarks, Tennessee. Cris said that she would meet him at 8:30 P.M. at the Twin Shopping Center with the money and more information about the subject to be killed. The detective received information that Bobby Goy did exist and lived in Clarks, Tennessee. Detective DuBois met with Cris, received the money for the trip. When he asked how she wanted it done, she stated "quickly". She also explained that DuBois should steal a Tennessee license plate when he entered that state and put it on his vehicle. After the murders he was to replace the Tennessee plate with his Indiana one. With the above information, Detective DuBois was able to obtain warrants for the arrest of Cris Hens.

15

Robbery and Extortion: A Case Example

July 10, 19XX (0958 hours). Officers were dispatched to N. 4th Street and Molle Road on an armed robbery call. When officers arrived, the victim William More stated that he was at 34 W. Lison Avenue, Indianapolis, Marion County, Indiana, to pick up his Mercury Merkur, which he had given to Willie Johns (b/f) to sell on consignment. The victim stated that while in the residence he was enticed by Willie Johns into the bedroom. More advised the officers that a second subject (b/m/24, 5 ft. 9 in., 190 to 200 lb.) displayed a sawed-off shotgun and pointed it at him after he protested picture-taking. Mr. More stated the black male, at gun point, took his stainless steel 22 caliber revolver, two gold rings, and $360.00 in cash. The victim's 1987 red Mercury Merkur was also taken. On the same day, William More spoke to robbery detectives. During the interview, Mr. More stated that while the black male held the sawed-off shotgun on him, the subjects laughed and told him that they would be able to blackmail him for whatever they wanted.

July 13, 19XX. This detective received information regarding this case. At 1400 hours, detectives spoke with Mr. More by telephone and were advised that he had spoken with the suspects at 12:00 P.M. and they wanted $10,000.00 in exchange for the pictures, money, car, and two rings.

July 14, 19XX. Detectives met with Mr. More at his office for an interview. During the meeting, a tape player was placed on Mr. More's business telephone to record conversations with the suspects. For several days, conversations were taped of Willie Johns and the black male suspect.

July 15, 19XX (1535 hours). The detective listened in on a conference call between Mr. More and the suspects while they were being tape recorded from Mr. More's office. Both admitted to involvement and stated that $10,000.00 was required before Mr. More could receive his property and photos.

July 16, 19XX (1430 hours). Mr. More was contacted by the black male suspect who advised that he would contact Mr. More on July 20, 19XX, to let him know when and where to meet to exchange $10,000.00 for the pictures and property owned by Mr. More.

July 20, 19XX (0910 hours). A search warrant was issued for 34 W. Lison Avenue to search for the victim's stainless steel 22 caliber revolver; $360.00 in U.S. currency; gold 1967 University J. D. men's ring with a red stone and white gold wedding band; 1987 red Mercury Merkur three-door and all paperwork pertaining to the vehicle; one sawed-off pump 12-gauge shotgun; and any photographs, negatives or documentation involving Mr. More. The search warrant was for Willie Johns, any outbuildings, and an unidentified black male believed to have the first name of "Jimmy."

1400 hours. A meeting between Mr. More and the unidentified black male known only as "Jimmy" took place at Fayette Square Mall. Mr. More met with this detective along with several assisting units to plan for the apprehension of the suspects involved. A Kel-set was placed on Mr. More's person to record the conversation between Mr. More and the suspects. The suspects had spoken with Mr. More at 10:00 A.M. and arranged to exchange the photographs for $10,000.00. Surveillance was set up at the meeting place at 391 W. Fayette Road. After several minutes, the detective observed a black male dressed in a reddish colored baseball cap, black shirt, and green colored jeans approach the victim and attempt to make a transaction. The victim, however, would not agree to exchange $10,000.00 for the photographs until he spoke with the main suspect, known as "Jimmy." The detective observed this suspect approach a second suspect who was driving a gray 1983 Oldsmobile 98. The two suspects then went into a department store and talked inside the double doors. The two suspects were observed exiting the building; they entered the gray Olds 98 and slowly drove through the parking lot. At that time, we stopped the vehicle and arrested the two suspects. The first suspect was later identified as Rey Bat and was found to have the photographs in his right rear pants pocket. The other suspect was identified as Jim Whit. Both suspects were transported to the homicide office for interviews. The detective then proceeded to 34 W. Lison Avenue for the search warrant. After arriving at the residence, entry was gained. Willie Johns, who was on the scene, was then arrested. The 1987 Mercury Merkur was found at the residence, along with the vehicle's title. Observed on the back of the title was the forged signature of "Mrs. Ellen More."

Case Results. Willie Johns was then transported to police headquarters for an interview. After talking with Mr. Jim Whit, he stated that he did photograph Mr. More and Mrs. Johns and that he did demand $10,000.00 for the photographs. He also stated that Mrs. Johns did take the weapon from Mr. More and give it to him. Mr. Whit stated that he did have the 22-caliber weapon at his residence and that he would make arrangements to turn in the gun. Mr. Whit further stated that he offered the second suspect, Rey Bat, half of the money to assist him with the exchange at Fayette Square. Willie Johns stated that she made the initial contact with Mr. Whit and advised him that she wanted to take photos of Mr. More and her while they were in the bedroom so that she could blackmail him and possibly get him in trouble with the Bar Association. Willie Johns further admitted that she had the victim's vehicle and that she had paid an unknown female $5.00 to sign the name ''Mrs. Ellen More'' to the back of the vehicle's title. This enabled her to place the vehicle in her name. During taped conversations between the suspects and William More, the suspects stated that in the event they did not receive what they were demanding, they would attempt to get him disbarred, would alert the media, and then would tape the pictures to his vehicle windows and leave the vehicle parked in his driveway so that his wife could see them. William More stated that he was uncertain as to the exact date he had given his vehicle to Willie Johns to sell on consignment; however, he believed it was either May 21 or 22, 19XX. According to William More, the title of the 1987 Mercury Merkur is in his wife's name (Ellen More).

July 23, 19XX. This detective talked with Ellen More. According to Mrs. More, she did not sell or sign the title of the above vehicle over to Willie Johns. The title was signed on July 15, 19XX, with the signature of Mrs. Ellen More, and it was signed over to Fannie Dun with a residence of 90 E. Stuart Avenue.

Chapter

16

Homicide Investigations*

Identifying and apprehending criminals has never been an easy task. In homicide cases this task is further complicated by the fact that the complainant, your main witness, is deceased and therefore will never be able to "point the finger" at the accused. Instead, the investigator not

only will have to rely on eyewitnesses or circumstantial evidence obtained from the crime scene, but also endeavor to elicit from the suspect an account of what actually took place. The officer in charge must then make a determination of whether this account is consistent with the other facts he or she has accumulated.

Higher crime rates and increases of violence put a strain on the resources and capabilities of law enforcement agencies. Many criminals today are more sophisticated and in many cases are "graduates of the penal system." They have been duly schooled by the "jailhouse lawyer" according to constitutional law as to just what the police can and cannot do. In addition, as our cities grow larger and more impersonal, many people become reluctant to get involved. Add to these factors some of the restrictive court decisions that have been forced on law enforcement agencies, and one can readily understand that the investigation of homicide and the initial actions by the police at the homicide crime scene may eventually determine whether the crime is ever solved or the guilty person brought to justice.

The homicide detective, in order to be successful, must have an eye for details and the ability to recognize and evaluate evidence. He or she must have an above average intelligence in order to absorb the many details that arise during a case and an ability to effectively interview and interrogate, not to mention relate with many different types and personalities of persons with whom he or she may come into contact. Actually, the secrets of an effective homicide investigation are flexibility and common sense.

The investigation of murder necessitates a certain tenacity and perseverance that transcends the ordinary investigative pursuit. Homicide investigation is an

*Material in this chapter is adapted from Geberth, V. J., *Practical Homicide Investigation: Tactics, Procedures, and Forensic Techniques*, 2nd ed., CRC Press, Baca Raton, FL, 1990, 442–478. With permission.

aggressive business. You must be prepared to use tactics and strategy for any given situation. "Good-guy" or "bad-guy", it never grows old. However, any number of tactics might be employed. The limit is only set by the imagination and initiative of the homicide detective, acting of course within the boundaries of constitutional law.

One fact is certain: homicide is a tricky and devious business. Whenever you deal with people, even under ordinary circumstances, they are at best unpredictable. It has been my experience that if you add murder to this obscurity, human behavior becomes a series of contradictory manuevers involving all the ramifications of the human mind. There are many factors that will complicate effective investigation. Whether it be the apathy and indifference of society, human behavior patterns, or a ridiculous overconcern for the defendant's rights by the courts, the homicide officer in charge must be able to overcome these obstacles, concentrate on what results he can obtain from the scene, and then through dedication and perseverance pursue the case.

THE CHANGING SEQUENCE OF COMMAND

All officers should be aware of the changing sequence of command at homicide crime scenes. The first officer on the scene is in command until a uniformed officer of higher rank or an investigator arrives on the scene. The ranking uniformed man will be in charge until the arrival of his superiors or an investigator. As soon as the investigator arrives, he will assume command from that point forward. He in turn will be superseded by an investigator of superior rank. Department regulations should provide for such shifts of command in these situations so as to avoid conflict and maintain a professional investigation.

PATROL OFFICER'S CHECKLIST

As a practical matter, the first officer's responsibilities in the preliminary investigation of homicide are divided into three specific duties:

1. Preserve life
2. Arrest the suspect
3. Protect the scene

The officer should record all homicide information in his memo book or notebook as soon as possible, preferably as it is obtained. This book should be retained for later court purposes and shown to the investigator when he arrives at the scene. All dead-body calls should be handled as homicides in this preliminary stage.

I have provided the following checklist of first-officer duties in order to assist the officer at the scene in refreshing his memory as to what vital information he should secure.

Initial Call/Receipt of Information

Record the exact time and type of call the patrol unit received. (In systems using modern computerized and recorded radio transmissions, the unit can check with police communications.) If first notification is received in person, detain this person for investigators. If you are unable to detain the person for some reason, obtain sufficient identification and information for a followup investigator.

Arrival at the Homicide Crime Scene

- Record the exact time of your arrival and/or notify police communications that you are on the scene.
- Enter the immediate crime scene area to view the victim. Only one officer should enter the scene, using only one path of entry and exit.
- Determine whether the victim is alive or dead.
- Arrest the perpetrator if present.
- If there is a possibility of life, summon an ambulance and apply appropriate first-aid procedures.
- If circumstances indicate the victim is near death or dying, attempt to obtain a dying declaration.
- If an ambulance crew is present before your arrival, determine whether the crew or anyone else moved the body or any items within the crime scene. If there were any items moved, record

    - What alterations were made
    - When the alterations were made
    - Purpose of the movement
    - Person who made the alteration

- Record the names, serial numbers, and hospital of the ambulance crew present at the scene.
- If the victim is dead, record the official time of pronouncement by the ambulance attendant.
- *If the suspect has just fled the scene, initiate a wanted alarm.*
- Record any alterations to the crime scene that were made as a matter of investigative necessity, for example:

    - Lights turned on or off
    - Door opened, closed, locked, or unlocked
    - Body moved or cut down

- Windows opened, closed, locked, or unlocked
- Furniture moved; anything touched
- Gas turned off, appliances turned off, motor of vehicle on or off

Protection of the Crime Scene

- Attempt to assess the entire crime scene, including paths of entry and exit and any areas that may include evidence. (*Remember, there is the possibility of a multiple crime scene.*)
- Establish a perimeter; secure and protect the scene by isolation and physical barriers such as ropes, cones, and other equipment as necessary.
- Record names, addresses, dates of birth, and telephone numbers, etc. of all persons present at the crime scene.
- Remove all persons from the immediate area. (*Be careful not to chase off witnesses or the perpetrator, who may still be present.*)
- If the victim is removed from the scene by ambulance, an officer should accompany the victim to the hospital riding in the rear of the vehicle with the victim (for a possible dying declaration).
- An officer should remain at the scene to provide for its security.
- If the victim's clothes are removed at the hospital, an officer should maintain control (victim's clothes are evidence).
- Request additional units as needed to protect the scene.
- If it is necessary that a clergyman or doctor enter the scene, have an officer accompany him through the designated path of entry and caution this person about contamination and/or alteration.

Notifications

- Make notifications by telephone if possible (police radios are often monitored by the press).
- *Never,* unless absolutely necessary, use a telephone inside the crime scene. Such a necessity would involve a life or death situation, the need for immediate transmission of alarms, etc.
- Notify the investigators or homicide division.
- Record the time of notification and who was notified.
- Establish a temporary headquarters outside of the central crime scene (preferably a location with two telephones, one for incoming and one for outgoing calls).
- Broadcast any alarms for suspects or descriptions of perpetrators from the command post to guarantee uniformity and to improve the possibility of verification.
- Notify police communications of the telephone numbers of the command post to facilitate communications between the various units.

Preliminary Investigation

- Initiate and maintain a chronological log recording the names, shield numbers, and commands of any police officers entering the crime scene. In addition, record the names, addresses, etc. of any civilians who may have to enter as well as names, titles, and serial numbers of any ambulance personnel. This log should reflect the entry and exit of any person who enters the crime scene.
- Isolate and separate witnesses or suspects. Do not permit any conversations relative to the crime. Hold witnesses and suspects for the investigators.
- Establish a path of entry and exit based on observation of the scene.
- For any civilian at the scene, record identifying information and his or her knowledge of the crime.
- Do not touch, move, or alter anything in the scene. If you do, record it.
- Refer all newspaper and media inquiries to the investigators.
- Stand by for investigators and assist them as required.
- Advise and inform investigators of all that has transpired since arrival of the first officer.

Suspect in Custody

- Determine whether the suspect is armed (search for weapons). If a weapon is recovered, record the description and location. Maintain custody pending arrival of investigators who will instruct as to vouchering and disposition.
- Handcuff the suspect and isolate him or her from any witnesses and/or associates. (Use rear handcuff method.)
- If the suspect is arrested outside the crime scene, do not return him or her to scene.
- If the suspect is arrested inside the crime scene, remove him/her immediately (remember scene contamination).
- Note and preserve any evidence found on the suspect and advise investigators.
- Do not permit the suspect to wash hands or use the toilet (you may lose evidence).
- Do not permit any conversation between the suspect and any other parties.
- Do not initiate any interrogation (wait for the investigators). However, in certain types of homicides the first officer will take statements. Make sure, though, that the suspect has been warned of his rights before taking any statement. As a general rule, no interrogation should be conducted.
- Carefully record all spontaneous statements (*res gestae* rule).
- Observe and record behavior of the suspect (e.g., nervous, erratic, emotional, unemotional, drunk, under influence of drugs, any unusual behavior, etc.).

Suicide and Accidental Deaths

- If death appears to be suicidal or accidental, handle it as homicide, pending arrival of investigators.
- Secure the immediate scene and detain witnesses.

- Preserve all evidence, e.g., notes, weapons, pills, vials, drugs, etc., in their original positions.
- Notify investigators.
- If vehicles are involved, do not allow their removal until photos have been taken by crime-scene technicians.
- If the suicide is by hanging and death is evident, do not cut the body down.
- If the body is cut down because death is not evident, make the cut above the knot.
- If relatives are present, get any background information which may assist investigators.

THE INVESTIGATIVE CHECKLIST

The homicide detective faces a monumental task at the crime scene. There are a multitude of duties to perform, and each event needs to be documented according to a routine procedure. This routine procedure is necessary so that valuable information or observations are not overlooked. Although each homicide is distinctive and unique, there are certain basic steps to be pursued at all crime scenes. The following investigative checklist is provided for investigators to use at the scene to refresh their memory and serve as an investigative guide. *Remember, the fundamental rule in homicide investigation is the documentation of events in the investigator's notebook.*

Initial Receipt and Documentation of Information

Record the date and time; method of transmission; name, rank, shield number, etc. of persons making notifications; and details of information.

Arrival at the Homicide Crime Scene

Record the exact time of arrival and the exact address of the scene. Also record outside weather/temperature conditions and outside lighting conditions.

Interview the first officer and other police personnel at the scene in order to determine the sequence of events that have occurred since their arrival. Record the persons present at the scene, such as officers, ambulance personnel, family or relatives, and witnesses. Ensure that the witnesses are kept separated, and provide for witness availability.

Record the location of the victim. Have an officer escort you through the scene using the same path used by responding police. Determine and verify death, noting the condition of the body.

Ascertain whether there are any suspect(s) in custody (if so, see the section on "The Suspect in Custody" that follows). Also determine whether there are any additional victims. If this is a multiple murder, establish separate case numbers.

Finally, transmit any alarms for suspect(s), and the present extent of the crime scene.

Implement a Crime Scene Control Procedure

Take preliminary photos with an Instamatic or Polaroid camera (preferably Polaroid so that the scene may be immediately reviewed by investigators). Stabilize the crime scene by identifying the perimeter, by determining the scope of the general scene, and establishing a perimeter. Assign patrol officers as needed. Update and expand the crime scene protection as necessary. (Is this a multiple crime scene?) Implement procedures to safeguard all evidence found at the scene.

Initiate a Crime Scene Log

Assign an officer to record the names of all personnel and citizens involved in the investigation at the crime scene to limit entry into the scene. Allow no entry to the scene except to authorized personnel. Record arrival/departure times of all officials. Establish a single path of entry into the crime scene area.

Record any alterations to the crime scene that were made as a matter of investigative necessity, such as lights turned on or off; door opened, closed, locked, or unlocked; body moved or cut down; and windows opened, closed, locked, or unlocked.

Also record the names of all parties who moved the dead prior to and during police presence at the scene. Ascertain whether any furniture was moved or anything touched; gas was turned off or on; or appliances were turned off or on. If a vehicle was involved, note whether the engine is off or on.

Ambulance Personnel

If ambulance personnel were present before the investigator's arrival, determine whether the crew or anyone else moved the body or any other items within the crime scene. If any movement occurred, record the following: time the alterations were made, purpose of the movement, persons who made the alteration, and time of death as pronounced by the ambulance crew.

Establish a Command Post or Temporary Headquarters

Select a location out of the central crime scene, preferably a location with two telephones, one for outgoing and one for incoming calls. Notify police communications and/or the station house of the telephone numbers of the command post to facilitate communications between the various units concerned. Make notifications as necessary from this location to the crime scene technicians, coroner/medical examiner, additional investigators, and prosecutor/district attorney.

Establish a Policy for Crime Scene Integrity

Do not touch, move, or alter anything at the scene until full documentation has been completed. Do not use any telephone(s) located inside the crime scene. Coordinate activities at the scene and direct investigators by fixing responsibility for the performance of certain duties. Implement procedures to protect evidence from damage by weather or exposure and the presence of investigators. Do not allow smoking by anyone at the crime scene. Also, do not turn water on or off, do not flush toilets, and do not use any facility at the scene. Finally, record the condition of lights, lamps, and electric appliances such as TVs, radios, clocks, etc.

Initiate a Canvass

Initiate a canvass of the immediate area by additional personnel to locate any witnesses or persons who may have information about the homicide. Make sure that the canvassers are provided with all information from the investigation and scene so that they may properly solicit information from prospective witnesses. Have investigators check vehicles and registration numbers of autos in the immediate area.

Require official reports from the canvassers indicating negative locations (locations with no results); locations that have been canvassed, indicating number of persons residing therein; positive locations for possible follow-up and reinterview; and information relating to the event being canvassed.

The Suspect in Custody

If the suspect is arrested and present at the scene, make sure that he or she is immediately removed from the crime scene and is not returned to the scene under any circumstances. This procedure is necessary to prevent scene contamination. Safeguard all evidence found on the suspect, including blood, weapons, debris, soil, proceeds of crime, etc. Ensure that the suspect does not wash his or her hands or engage in any conduct which may alter or destroy any evidence. Record any spontaneous statements made by the suspect, and do not permit any conversation between the suspect and any parties present.

Weapons

If a weapon is discovered, do not attempt to unload it if the weapon is a firearm. Record where the weapon is located and safeguard it for forensic examination. Be sure to have the weapon photographed before further examination.

If the weapon was a firearm, consider an examination of the suspect's hands for residue analysis. Determine whether the weapon is from the premises. Also, ascertain whether there is any blood or trace of evidence on the weapon.

Suspect in Custody: Interrogation at the Scene

If the suspect is in custody at the scene and circumstances indicate that immediate interrogation of the subject would be beneficial to the investigation, the following steps should be taken:

- Advise the suspect of his or her rights under the Miranda ruling prior to any custodial interrogation (preferably from a rights card).
- Determine whether the suspect fully understands his or her rights.
- Obtain an intelligent waiver of these rights from the suspect prior to any questioning.
- Document this procedure in the investigative notebook.
- Allow the suspect to make a full statement.
- Reduce this statement to writing and have the suspect sign it.
- Keep the suspect isolated at all times from other suspects, witnesses, prisoners, and any personnel not connected with the investigation.
- Advise any officers transporting the suspect not to engage the suspect in any conversation or questioning. However, if during transport the suspect makes any statement, the officers should document this information.
- If the suspect is brought to the police station, he or she should be placed in a separate holding cell.
- Alibi statements should be documented and recorded in the investigator's notebook.
- Any self-serving statements should also be recorded and documented, in the event the suspect later changes his or her story.

Crime Scene Processing

The crime scene search should not be undertaken until all crime scene photographs, sketches, measurements, dusting for prints, and written documentation have been completed.

Crime Scene Photographs

Photographs should be taken of:

- The entire location where the homicide took place
- Contiguous areas and sites
- Witnesses, if applicable
- Suspect(s), including clothing and shoes and any injuries (body, face, hands, etc.)

Do not add any chalk marks or markers prior to taking the original crime scene photographs. Markers can be added later on for close-up shots. Take photos from the general to the specific.

Documentation of Crime Scene Photographs

Documentation should be made of the date and time photographs are taken, the exact location of the photographs, descriptions of items photographed, compass direction (north, south, east, or west), focus distance, type of film and camera utilized, lights and weather conditions, and number of exposures. Also, record the identification of the photographer.

Eliminate extraneous objects including any police equipment before taking photographs at the crime scene. Show the relationship of the scene to its surroundings. For outdoor scenes, photograph fixed objects as they relate to the scene from eye level. Finally, for indoor scenes, photograph objects in the room such as doors, windows, etc. to "fix" the body to the scene.

Recommended Crime Scene Photographs

These crime scene photographs are recommended: front entrance of the building, entrance to the room or apartment where the deceased is found, two full-body views, a general view of the body and crime scene, and close-up shots of the body and any visible wounds. If the body has been removed, photos should be taken of the body's original location.

Also, photograph: possible entrance or escape routes used; areas where any force was used for entry or exit; and area and close-up views of any physical evidence such as bloodstains, weapons, shell casings, hairs, fibers, etc. Fingerprints—plastic, bloodstained, and latents, as well as any lifts—should be photographed before removal. After the body has been moved, additional photos should be taken of areas beneath the body and any additional evidence found beneath the body.

The Crime Scene Sketch

Make a simple line drawing of the crime scene, either in the investigative notebook or on a separate piece of paper. Include information about measurements and distance.

Also document a title block consisting of: name and title of sketcher, date and time sketch was made, classification of crime, identification of victim(s), agency's case number, names of any persons assisting in taking measurements, and precise address of the location sketched and compass north.

Prepare a legend to identify any objects or articles at the crime scene, and a scale to depict measurements used.

The Crime Scene Search

Establish the perimeters of the crime scene and document this location by photographs and sketches, including written documentation. Reconstruct aspects of the crime in formulating the search. Ascertain the legal basis for the search prior to any seizure of evidence. Visibly locate any physical evidence and determine which evidence should be gathered before any destruction or any alteration takes place. Establish a method of search based on your investigative theory, size of the area to be searched, and any other pertinent factors.

Areas that should be processed include the point of entry; the escape route; the suspect and his or her clothing, including injuries; the location where any physical evidence or weapons may be located; a vehicle used in the crime; the suspect's residence; the location where the actual assault leading to death took place; and the location from where the body was moved.

Dust for Fingerprints

These areas should be processed for "latent prints": areas of entry and exit, weapons or objects which were apparently handled, door handles, telephone instruments, windows, glasses, light switches, newly damaged areas, objects that may have caused death, and objects missing from their original location.

Description of the Deceased

A complete description of the body should be documented in the investigator's notes, including position of the body, sex, race, appearance, age, build, and hair color. Describe the clothing, the presence or absence of any jewelry, and evidence of any injuries (bruises, bite marks, wounds, etc.).

Note the condition of the body, including livor (leaden or bluish color) mortis, rigor mortis, decomposition, blood (wet or dry), insect activity, and putrefaction. Determine whether the condition of the body is consistent with the known facts.

Note and record the condition of the victim's hands for signs of evidence (defense marks, hairs, fibers, etc.). Also, note and record any creases and folds on the victim's clothing, and the condition of the pockets. Examine the immediate area surrounding the body for evidence, recording the direction and size of any bloodstains. Check the clothing and shoes for any trace evidence.

Preliminary Medical Examination at the Scene

Record the time of arrival of the coroner/medical examiner. Obtain a preliminary estimate on the time of death. Document the apparent cause of death in shootings and stabbings. Determine whether injuries are consistent with the suspected weapon involved.

Before release of the body, wrap it in a new or laundered sheet and bag the hands of the victim with paper bags to preserve any evidence under fingernails.

Evidence Process and Control

Ensure that all evidence is properly marked and packaged. Then establish a "chain of custody", designating a "searching officer" to take charge of all evidence. Record the name and unit designation of all persons participating in the homicide crime scene search.

Photograph all evidence in its original position (*in situ*). Record the position and location of all evidence on the crime scene sketch and in the investigative notebook. Record the name of any officer or person discovering any physical evidence and the location where it was recovered. Measure the location of any evidence found from two separate fixed points of reference.

Examine the weapon(s) involved. If the weapon is a firearm, check for the presence of shell casings, bullet holes, or spent rounds. Determine how many shots were fired. Note the position of bullets in a revolver. Is the safety on or off, is there a bullet in the chamber, and is the firearm unloaded or loaded? In addition, are the wounds consistent with the weapon suspected, and is there any trace evidence on the weapon?

Release of the Homicide Crime Scene

Note the telephone number of any phones at the scene. Have the mailbox of the deceased searched and note the date of any mail found therein. Do not release the scene prior to the completion of the canvass and any interrogation of witness(es) and suspect(s). Before leaving the scene, look over the entire area from the perspective of the defense counsel to make sure you have "covered all the bases".

If the scene is to be abandoned during certain investigatory procedures, implement procedures for the continued protection of the scene during the absence of investigators. Gather all materials used in the crime scene processing such as film cartridges, Polaroid negatives, flash bulbs, notes, etc. Have these materials removed from the scene for destruction at another location. (It is important to note that the extent of the crime scene search can be ascertained by examination of these materials if they are left behind at the homicide crime scene.)

Money Laundering

Over $100 billion of illegal money is laundered in the United States each year. To understand the process, one must understand the meaning of the term *money laundering*. The U.S. Justice Department definition is, "The process by which one conceals the existence, illegal source or illegal application of income, and then disguises the source of that income to make it appear legitimate."

In order to launder money effectively, one must convert cash to other assets and mask the identity of the persons involved. For this, you need the help of lawyers, accountants, and other professionals such as stock brokers. If a person cannot conceal both his possession of the "dirty" money and his involvement with the crime that produced it, he is very likely to go to jail.

Money laundering can be very simple or very complex. A typical three-step money laundering scheme is as follows:

1. Conversion of cash to cashier's checks, money orders, or other bearer instruments
2. Use of bearer instruments to acquire one or more types of assets such as stocks, bonds, land, and other items which support long-term investment objectives
3. Liquidation of laundered assets by reconverting them back to cash

Once the above steps are completed, there is little or no traceable documentation.

BUSINESSES THAT LEND THEMSELVES TO MONEY LAUNDERING

The best businesses to launder money through are those that deal in cash. The following businesses are prime examples: video arcades (difficult to tell how many quarters are dropped in), car dealerships (also a good place to look for bookmaking), taverns/restaurants (also gambling and fencing stolen property), "dirty" bookstores, vending companies, churches, car washes (particularly ones that leave the lights and water on all night long because they need to show large utility bills), parking lots, loan companies, limousine services, produce companies, fast-food establishments, and wholesale distribution.

For an in-depth guide to illegal money laundering, contact the following:

Bureau of Justice Assistance
Police Executive Research Forum
2300 "M" Street, N.W., Suite No. 910
Washington, D.C. 20037

HOW MONEY IS LAUNDERED

Traditionally, when one hears about money laundering, it is in the context of a narcotics operation. Probably the largest money launderers are involved in the narcotics trade, but anyone who makes money illegally must have a way to make it appear legitimate. Illegal money must be concealed or camouflaged in such a way as to prevent authorities from making the link from illegal currency to assets.

Laundering Services

Here professional persons such as attorneys arrange trusts, open foreign and domestic bank accounts, and hide the true owner. These services are expensive, but the layers of paperwork involved help to discourage authorities from following up on leads.

Legitimate Businesses

The laundering of money through legitimate businesses is the oldest method used. Businesses provide legitimate sources of income, sources of reported income for taxes, and locations to disguise the illegal operation.

Real Estate Investments

Investment in real estate facilitates money laundering. Real estate provides tax avoidance benefits, and down payments provide direct money-laundering vehicles. Keep in mind that the subjects may invest in precious metals and gem stones as a way to accumulate wealth through undocumented and untraceable sources.

Smurfs

Smurfs are people who are hired to launder money through banks. A typical scheme used by a smurf is as follows:

- Illegal currency is delivered to the smurf.
- The smurf will go out and buy hundreds of money orders, cashier's checks, and other bearer instruments.
- The smurf will deposit them in specific accounts over time, eventually ending in one account which may be a business account.
- Currency in this account is then transferred by wire to a Panamanian account or offshore account.

MONEY LAUNDERING SCHEMES

When you are investigating a criminal organization, look for a business tied to the suspects which deals in cash. If your background check shows involvement, for example, of a tavern, look for money from the illegal activity being laundered through it. Identify who controls the tavern, what illegal activities are involved, and whether money is laundered through it. Look at the business and determine whether the amount of products going into the business (beer, liquor, etc.) is equivalent to the sales that they report. If the tavern only buys 10 cases of beer a month but reports $80,000 in sales, you know you have a source where illegal money is being laundered (see Figures 17.1, 17.2, and 17.3).

Note: While you are conducting your background searches on businesses, you should key on businesses acquired under suspicious circumstances such as the sale of a piece of property for $1.00. Investigate whether the business may have been taken over by an outside party.

MONEY LAUNDERING EXAMPLE

We received information that a tavern on the west side was actively involved in the buying and selling of stolen property. We were introduced to the owners and began selling them property which was purportedly stolen from area stores. During the infiltration phase, we identified two video gambling devices that were present. The owners of the tavern informed us as to their function and how to get paid off on them. We continued our investigation, and when search warrants were served, we located notations that showed the laundering of several hundred dollars per week from the illegal gambling devices through the business account.

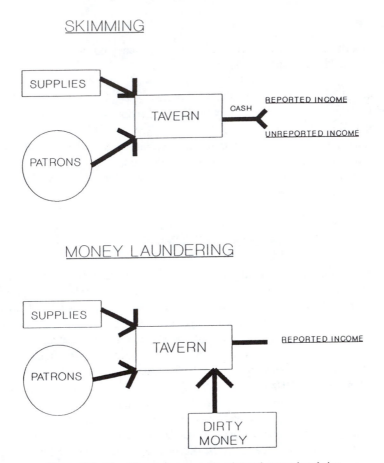

Figure 17.1. The difference between skimming and money laundering.

Receipts showing a 50/50 split from the video gambling devices were found, and when the 50% figure received by the tavern was compared to the business books, we found the exact figure was listed as commissions. In addition to the above, the owners underreported their income by $500,000 in 2 years (see Figures 17.4 and 17.5).

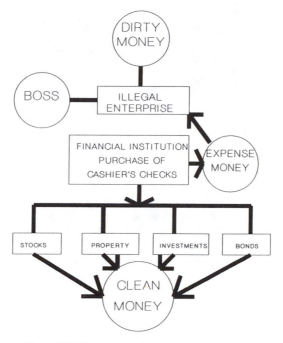

Figure 17.2. The process of laundering "dirty" money.

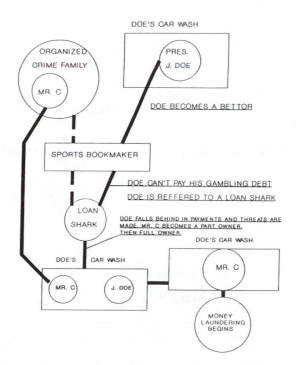

Figure 17.3. How a legitimate business can be taken over by using gambling and a loan shark.

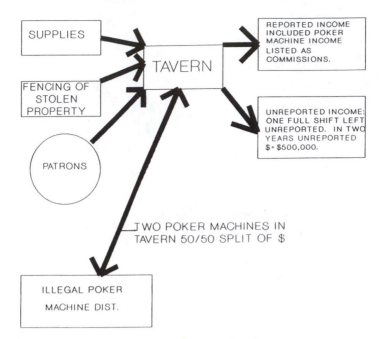

Figure 17.4. Money laundering through a tavern.

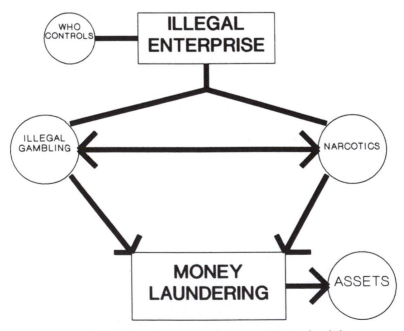

Figure 17.5. Charting illegal enterprises and money laundering.

Illegal Gambling

ORGANIZED CRIME AND ITS INFLUENCE ON ILLEGAL GAMBLING

When talking about organized crime, one must realize that a variety of organized crime groups are active in the United States today.

Organized crime units such as the Jamaican Posse's, Columbians, Asians, and Sicilians seem to show less interest in vice activities and gear their systems to the narcotics trade. For our purpose, the American Mafia and local organized groups will be the units we refer to when we talk about the influence of organized crime on sports gambling.

The Mafia has evolved in the United States since the late 1800s when it was involved in extortion. Even in its infancy corruption of public officials was a way of life and a way to protect its interests. Today the Mafia is active in murder, extortion, loan sharking, gambling, and many other crimes which have gained such a public awareness that the government has placed a high priority on the arrest and conviction of mob leaders. The federal government was the first to spearhead the use of the Racketeer Influenced and Corrupt Organizations (RICO) Act as a way to take the profit out of crime. The states have followed, but at a much slower rate.

Nearly every state has a resident mob family; some of the major states are New York, California, Arizona, Illinois, Ohio, and Florida. Mob business today ranges from transportation and construction to bars and restaurants all over the United States. The mob continues to absorb legitimate businesses into its crime unit through the use of intimidation, extortion, and loan sharking.

In 1986, the President's Commission on Organized Crime estimated that organized criminal enterprises had a total yearly income of more than $100 billion. On April 11, 1988, FBI Director William S. Sessions spoke before the United States Senate Permanent Subcommittee of Governmental Affairs. His topic was organized crime. Director Sessions gave a historical account of organized crime from 1920 through 1987. During his talk, he stated that history revealed that labor racketeering, narcotics trafficking, gambling, loan sharking, murder, kidnapping, extortion, prostitution, and smuggling are the Mafia's stock-in-trade. He further stated that money generated by the Mafia is often run through elaborate money laundering schemes. To establish his point he said, ''In a very real sense, organized crime touches every citizen in America.''

The Kefauver Committee and the McClellan Committee were investigative panels in the U.S. Senate; their task included looking into additional aspects of organized crime. They came to the conclusion that gambling bankrolled the rest of the underworld's empire and that legislative, judicial, and police corruption were inevitable consequences of allowing illegal gambling to operate unchecked for any length of time. As a result of these investigative bodies, three pieces of legislation were passed which gave the FBI the power to attack gambling.

The first legislative bill banned interstate transportation in aid of racketeering; the second legislative bill banned interstate transmission of wagering information; and the third legislative bill banned the interstate transportation of wagering paraphernalia. From 1961 until 1970, the FBI attacked organized crime with gambling as a major priority. In 1970, the RICO Act was passed. RICO statutes have provided the most effective weapon to date against organized crime and began the shift away from the FBI's use of gambling statutes. RICO statutes look at an organization and all its criminal activities instead of attacking one crime at a time. In 1977, the FBI began what it called a program management approach to organized crime investigations. This resulted in the setting of national priorities for the FBI, which had placed gambling very low on its list of priorities:

1. Labor racketeering
2. Corruption
3. Infiltration of legitimate business
4. Loan sharking
5. Gambling
6. Major impact crimes

Thinking back to 1961, the Kefauver and McClellan Committees stated that the lack of enforcement of gambling laws resulted in corruption and left local and state law enforcement officers in the position of having to assume the investigations.*

This chapter has been written to assist local and state law enforcement officers in understanding and the investigation of illegal sports bookmaking organizations.

---

*Copies of the Senate hearing used as a reference may be obtained by contacting: U.S. Government Printing Office, U.S. Government Bookstore, (614) 469–6956; request: "Organized Crime; 25 Years after Valachi," April 1988.

HOW TO GET THE GREEN LIGHT TO CONDUCT YOUR INVESTIGATION

Today's sports bookmaking is no longer a "Mom and Pop" type of enterprise. It always has been the mainstay of organized crime which has resulted in loan sharking, political corruption, narcotics trafficking, money laundering, and the takeover of legitimate businesses. Diversification is the American way, and organized crime intends to promote the American way.

Society as a whole, when thinking of organized crime, sees the pizza connection in New York and the control of unions and political corruption as evidence that organized crime exists in the United States. What society fails to see is the major impact that organized crime has on communities through illegal gambling. There is no community, no matter how small, that is not affected by illegal gambling.

This lack of concern by the general public, as well as the low priority assigned to gambling investigations by most administrators, is something you as an investigator must overcome. There are three ways that I have found to increase your ability to conduct an investigation of illegal sports bookmaking:

1. Demonstrate that the bookmaking operation is tied in any way to the trafficking of narcotics.
2. Demonstrate that the bookmaking operation is actively involved in laundering money in or outside your community.
3. Demonstrate that the bookmaking operation is influenced by outside sources, especially if you can show a connection to a mob city.

BEGINNING YOUR INVESTIGATION

Step 1

When trying to increase the awareness within your agency of the importance of maintaining pressure on organized units that are involved in illegal gambling activities, you must begin with the historical connection that gambling has had with organized crime. The best sources of information may be obtained from your library. Your search for information should include the last few years of newspaper and magazine articles that will assist you in documenting your case.

Excellent sources of information may include:

- *U.S. News and World Report,* February 3, 1986, "Busting the mob: hundreds of millions of dollars are derived from mob run sports gambling conducted from coast to coast."

- *Fortune,* November 10, 1986, ''50 biggest Mafia bosses: of the top 50 bosses, 34 are listed as being involved in gambling and or loan sharking'' and ''Chicago mob imposes a street tax on all illegal activities. Included in the tax are bookmakers.''
- *New York Times,* June 1, 1990, ''New approach to Mafia seen in recent charges''. This lists the traditional crimes as illegal gambling, loan sharking, hijacking, and narcotics.
- *Chicago Tribune,* February 8, 1990, ''20 linked to mob indicted''. Twenty alleged mobsters were charged with using money, muscle, and murder to run and protect the ''Chicago Outfit's'' lucrative gambling, extortion, and juice loan operation. Among the allegations were the murders of three gambling figures including the February 7, 1985, torture slaying of independent bookmaker, Hal Smith.

Step 2

Conduct a preliminary investigation into the background of your target. If your targeted investigation is of a property address, you first want to identify the ownership of the property and whether there have been any prior complaints at that location. You will then want to conduct a records check of the targeted subject and all associates you can identify with the subject for prior arrest records. The records check may provide the needed information to connect your targeted investigation of the subjects to narcotics.

Step 3

Attempt to locate information on income sources and co-conspirators. Attempt to determine whether there is an outside connection. If possible, request copies of telephone bills; this may document outside connections.

WHERE YOU GO WITH THIS INFORMATION

After you have obtained this information, you will have to package it for a presentation to your administrator(s) showing that this case has merit and there is a need to

- Investigate sports bookmaking
- Determine the extent of control organized groups have in your community
- Determine the method(s) of attacking the problem

WHAT YOU ASK FOR TO CONDUCT
THIS INVESTIGATION

You as an investigator need to determine what is necessary to infiltrate the sports bookmaking operation in your area. You will need to request:

- The manpower needed to conduct a covert investigation
- Training in the area of sports bookmaking and illegal gambling devices
- Equipment necessary to conduct the investigation

Some facts to keep in mind when conducting sports bookmaking cases are

- Sports bookmakers target key types of people as their bettors. They may be lawyers, firemen, police officers, and doctors.
- Many bookmakers own bars and give special service to these types of people.
- Bookmakers are on the lookout for coaches and players they can corrupt. With players, this may start in high school. Once a player takes money, the bookmaker owns him for life.
- Bookmakers prey on the fear of exposure to control and manipulate certain bettors to extract what they need, which may include point shaving, representation in court, and at times assistance in the laundering of money through a business or banks.

Sports bookmaking investigations should be viewed as a way not only to gauge the strength of organized crime in a given area, but also to serve as a very important tool to gather additional intelligence on a variety of criminal activities which go hand in hand with sports bookmaking.

Once you have started your investigation of a sports bookmaking operation, you must be aware of several important factors:

1. Who controls the organization and at what level?
2. Are there other illegal activities involved in the organization such as narcotics?
3. Where does the "dirty" money go? How do they launder it?
4. What assets are traceable to the organization?

Remember, the easiest way to launder money is to obtain a business which deals in cash. By inflating the sales on paper, this business can clean illegal money at will.

HORSE RACE WAGERING

Although horse race betting is not as big as sports wagering, you may encounter it on a regular basis. The following is intended to at least make you familiar with what occurs and the terms that are used by the bookmakers involved. Figure 18.1 shows typical examples of horse race bets.

Racing Forms

The racing form is one of many information sources that lists the different races at the various tracks around the country. This is where the bookmakers get their information for bets.

Racing forms list: the tracks by name, the horses by numerical order, the time and date of each race, and other information about the horse. In most cases, if you find betting material, you can identify the date of the race by looking up the track, the race number, and the horse listed on the bet.

Horse Race Terms

Win: This is a bet on a specific horse to win or come in first. It will only pay off if the horse is first.

Example:
9th No. 12 . . . Snow Chief . . . 5-X-X for $5.00

or

Latonia . . . 3–1–90 . . . 8th Race . . . 2 . . .
The Messengers . . . 6-X-X

In the first bet, you know that it is the 9th race and horse No. 12 named Snow Chief for $5.00 to win, but you do not know the track or date of the race. In the second bet, Latonia is the track; 3–1–90 is the date; in the 8th race on that date the second horse listed in the racing form is named Messenger and the bet is $6.00 to win.

Place: This is a bet that the horse in question will finish second or first.

Example:
Ky 6th . . . No. 3 . . . X-5X

Show: This is a bet that the horse will finish first, second or third.

Example:
Chi. . . . 1st . . . No. 2 . . . XX5

Across the board: This is a bet that places equal amounts across the board to win, to place, and to show.

Example:
7th . . . Ky . . . No. 10 . . . 2–2–2

A.

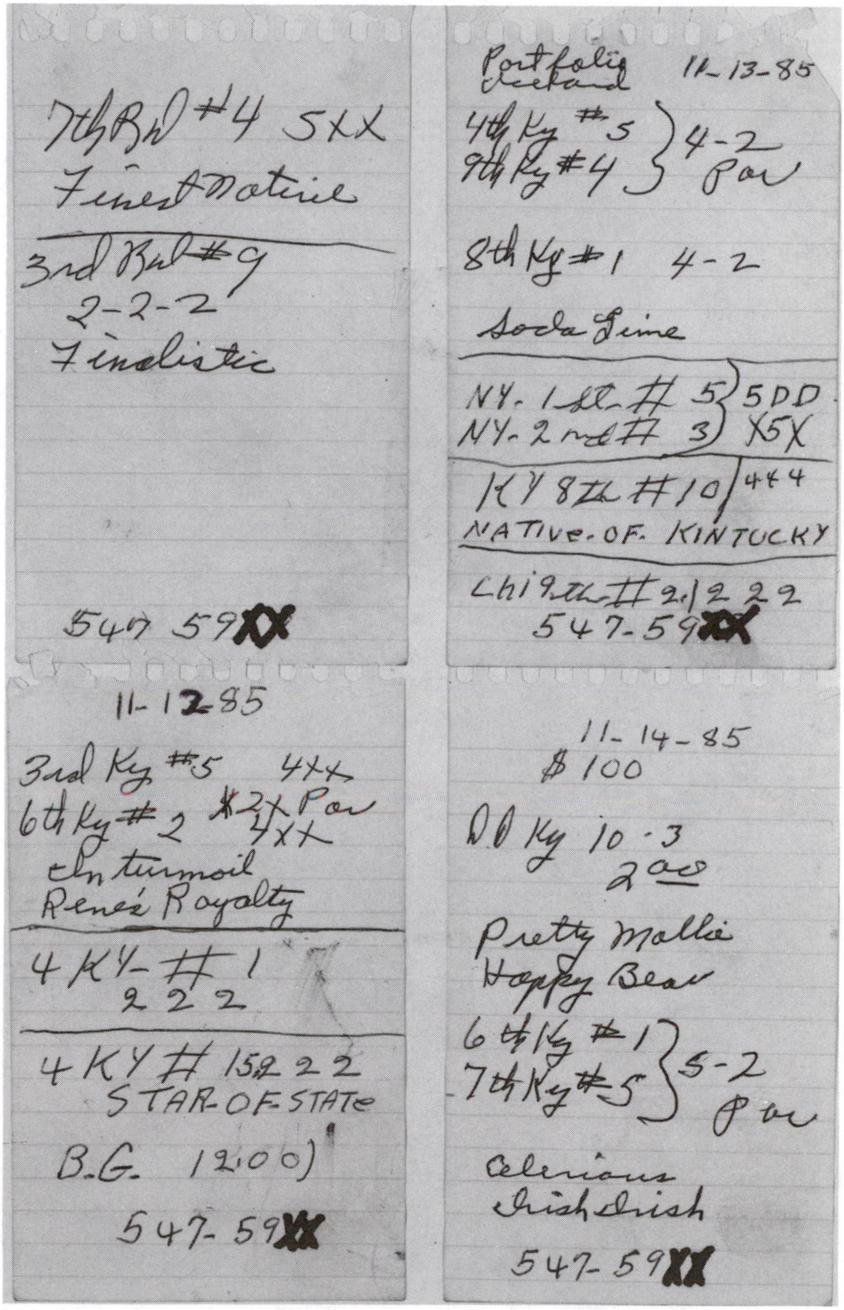

Figure 18.1. Examples of horse bets.

B.

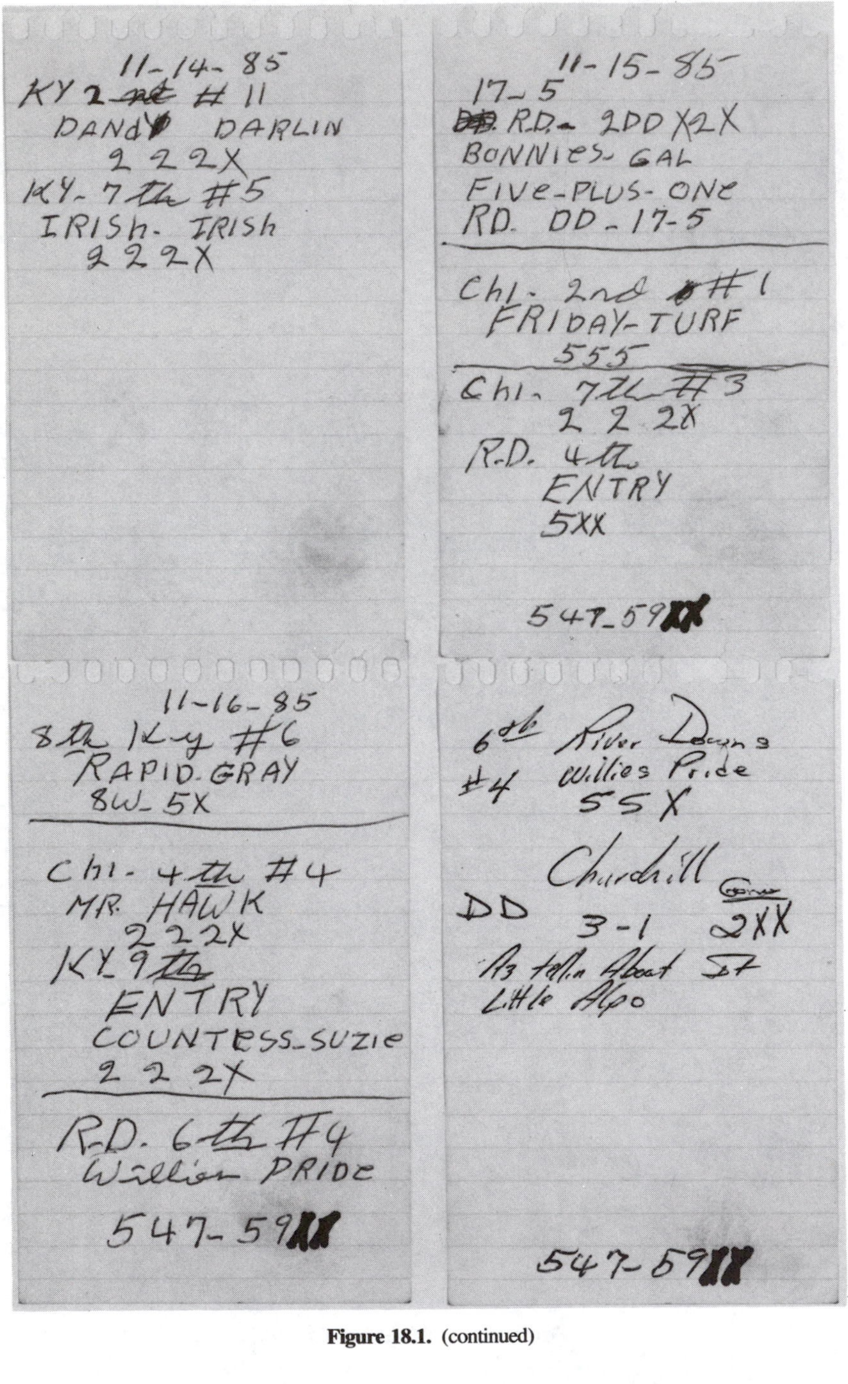

11-14-85
KY 2nd #11
DANDY DARLIN
2 2 2X
KY- 7th #5
IRISh- IRISH
2 2 2X

11-15-85
17-5
RD- 2DD X2X
BONNIES- GAL
FIVE-PLUS- ONE
RD. DD- 17-5

Chi- 2nd #1
FRIDAY- TURF
555
Chi- 7th #3
2 2 2X
R.D. 4th
ENTRY
5XX

547-59XX

11-16-85
8th Ky #6
RAPID- GRAY
8W- 5X

Chi- 4th #4
MR. HAWK
2 2 2X
KY 9th
ENTRY
COUNTESS-SUZie
2 2 2X

R.D. 6th #4
Willie PRIDE
547-59XX

6th River Downs
#4   Willies Pride
5 5 X

Churchill
DD   3-1   2XX
Po tella About Set
Little Ago

547-59XX

Figure 18.1. (continued)

Daily double: This is a bet where you choose the winners of the first and second race.

Example:
Chi. 1st . . . No. 4 . . . 5DD
　　2nd . . . No. 3

Quintella: This is a bet where you name the horse that will finish first and second in a single race. You need not name which will be first and which will be second.

Exacta: This is the same as the quintella except you must specify the name of the horse to finish first and the horse that will be second.

Trifecta: You must name the exact horses that will finish first, second, and third in a given race.

UNDERSTANDING BOOKMAKING TERMS

When you begin an investigation you must have a general understanding of the terms that are used by the bookmaker in his day-to-day work. This knowledge will get you through the investigation and the testimony that will be necessary to obtain a conviction. As you conduct your investigation, you will find yourself becoming more and more comfortable with these terms. There are many federal publications that explain and define bookmaking terms. The following are recommended:

"FBI Gambling Technology"
FBI Laboratory Technical Supplement, 1981
By Kier Boyd, Special Agent FBI

"Analyzing Sports Betting Records"
FBI Law Enforcement Bulletin, January 1979
By R. Phillip Harker

The use of federal publications as reference material, both during your investigation and for court testimony, will increase the perceived value of your testimony.

Sports Bookmaker

A sports bookmaker is like a stockbroker; for a fee (vigorish) he brings bettors together for the purpose of wagering on a wide variety of events. The bookmaker makes money on losing bets, for which he normally charges 10%. The ideal situation for a bookmaker is when he has equal bets for and against a given team. The bookmaker takes the losers' money, pays the winners, and keeps the vigorish as his profit.

Betting Line

The sports betting line used by bookmakers originates in Las Vegas, NV. This line provides a starting point for local bookmakers. Once the Vegas line is obtained, the local bookmaker must adjust up or down to compensate for betting trends on local or regional teams. The betting line has nothing to do with the strengths or weaknesses of a given team. The betting line actually is the number of points added to an underdog's score or subtracted from a favorite's score which the bookmaker feels will attract equal bets for and against the team. The bookmaker will often use national line services which are offered throughout the country to obtain the Vegas line, and then call several bookmakers in his area to obtain the line adjustments they are using. With this information, he will set his own line.

Nonwagering Line

The nonwagering line is the line that appears in the newspaper. It is based on the strengths and weaknesses of the two teams in a given event and how they match up. Injuries and illnesses are taken into account and then the line is set. The nonwagering line is the number of points added to an underdog's score or subtracted from a favorite's score which will make them even. The nonwagering line has nothing to do with betting, even though at times the lines are very similar.

Vigorish

Vigorish is the percentage charged on a losing bet by a bookmaker. It is normally 10%, but may vary. The vigorish is how a bookmaker makes his profit. For example, you have two bettors who want to bet $100.00 each. One bets for a team and the other bets against the same team. When the game is over, the loser pays the bookmaker $110.00 ($100.00 bet + $10.00 vigorish). The bookmaker takes the $100.00 and gives it to the winner, and he keeps the $10.00.

Push or Tie

A push or tie occurs when a wager placed on an event is even after adding or subtracting the point spread from the total. When a push or tie occurs, no money is won or lost. A push or tie can be eliminated by using point spreads with half numbers. An example would be a point spread of 12½ (Figure 18.2).

Figure 18.2. Recorded straight bet that ended in a push or tie. Note that there are carbon copies.

Balanced Book

When a sports bookmaker has equal bets for and against the teams he is carrying, he has a balanced book. A balanced book will always make a profit, regardless of the outcome of the number of bets that have been placed. The problem with a balanced book is that it almost never happens. The bookmaker must have a way to offset or eliminate his potential losses. This is accomplished by layoffs to other bookmakers or changing the betting lines.

Layoffs

A layoff is any bet made from one bookmaker to another with the intent of offsetting or eliminating the size of the potential loss caused by a book that is out of balance. Most bookmakers have a limit as to how much they are willing to risk; once they have reached their maximum risk, an attempt is made to locate another bookmaker to lay off additional bets. Two facts to remember about a layoff is that it is at the other bookmaker's point spread and there is no profit made on wagers that are laid off. When dealing with local or regional teams, some bookmakers will attempt to anticipate the betting trends of his bettors and lay off in advance of game day. This is called an anticipated layoff. (See Figure 18.3 for examples of a layoff bet.)

Scratch Game

When a game is scratched, it means that no further betting will be taken on this event. Scratching a game could be due to a player's injury or fixing of the event.

Circling a Game

When a game is circled, it means that caution should be taken when accepting bets. Sometimes wagers will be taken on circled games based on a specific player being able to play. If the player does not, the bet is off.

Printed Sports Schedule

Printed sports schedules are nothing more than preprinted lists of events on a given date. They list the teams, times they play, home teams, and any scheduled television broadcasts. Printed schedules make it easier for the bookmaker to give lines over the telephone. The schedule lists each game with a number next to it, in ascending order; instead of the bookmaker saying L.A. is −3 and Detroit is +5, he can say number 1 is −3 and number 3 is +5.

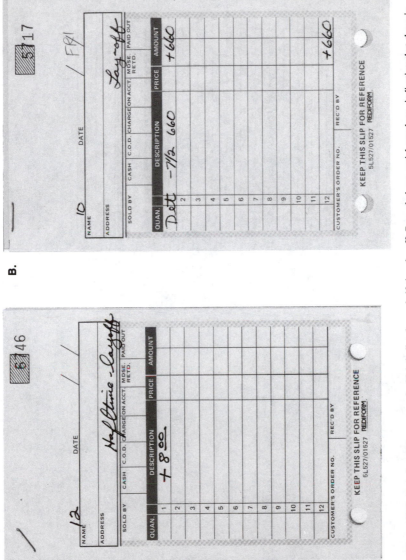

Figure 18.3. Two layoff bets, one of which is listed as a half time layoff. Records have serial numbers, indicating that there is someone else over the bookmaker.

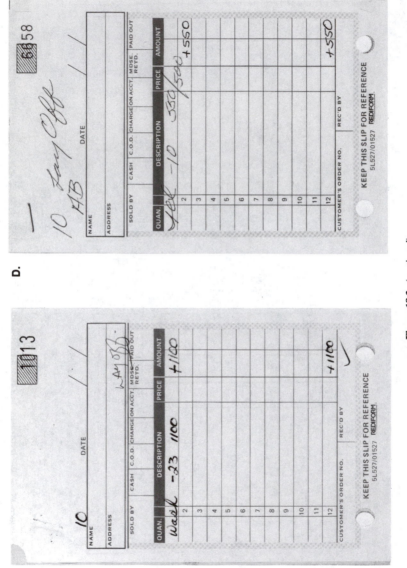

Figure 18.3. (continued)

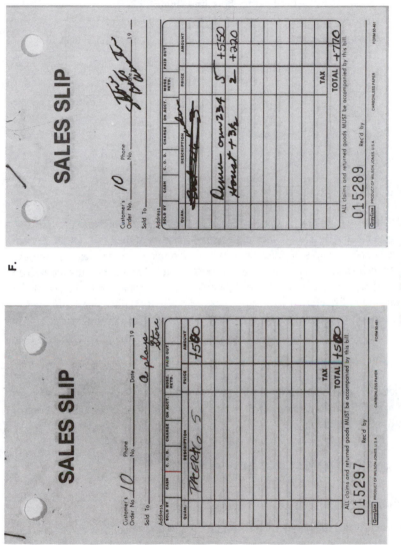

Figure 18.3. (continued)

A Pick

When a team is listed as a pick, it means that there is no point spread. A winning bet is either team that wins by any score. Normally, records will show a pick by the letter "P" being next to the game (Figure 18.4).

Wager Amount Terms

Amount	Term Used
$25.00	1 Quarter
$50.00	1/2 Dollar
$100.00	1 Dollar
$200.00	2 Dollars
$500.00	1 Nickel
$1000.00	1 Dime

DEVICES TO PREVENT DETECTION

Bookmakers will employ many ways to avoid detection. They use call forwarding to make it difficult to locate the actual location of the book. Other devices used are beepers, telephone message services, and telephone extensions. Beepers make it much more difficult to locate the bookmaker. The bettor calls the bookie on his beeper, leaves a number and the bookie calls from a telephone booth. To track this kind of operation will take a larger number of officers and many additional hours of investigation.

BETTING ON CREDIT

Illegal sports bookmaking is almost always done on credit and is never reported to the IRS. Because of this, it is an ideal way to hook a person and control him and or his business.

ORGANIZATIONAL STRUCTURE

Telephone Man or Office Worker

Normally, if a telephone man is used he is hired as a salaried employee. His job is to take bets over the telephone, give the lines, and keep records of who bets and how much is wagered.

Sub-Bookie or Street Agent

A sub-bookie normally works on his own. He has his own bettors and works his own route. He may be a bartender, car salesman, or real estate salesman, but

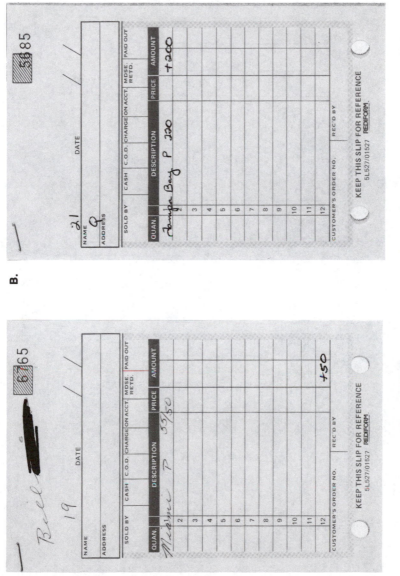

Figure 18.4. Demonstrates how a bet involving a pick is written.

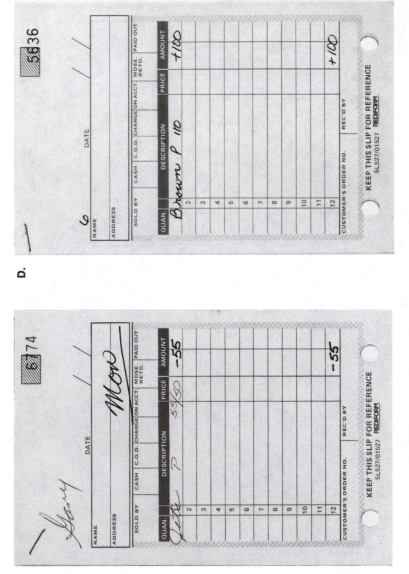

Figure 18.4. (continued)

a common element of each is his contact with the public. A sub-bookie will collect his bets and pass them to the bookmaker for a fee or percentage of the profits. The volume of bets turned in may vary from just a few to a large number of bets, based on the number of people with whom the sub-bookie has contact. In most cases, the sub-bookie will receive 25% of the profits made on the bets he turns in.

Beards

A beard is a person who places a bet for a bookmaker without letting the person know for whom the bet actually is. A bookmaker may use a beard to place bets that he could not place himself because either he is in bad standing with other bookmakers or he has inside information and he does not want others to know from where the bet is coming. Normally, a beard gets no compensation for his activities, but he can use the information provided to place his own bets. This is especially true when the beard placing the bet for the bookmaker is trying to obtain inside information for the bookmaker.

SETTLING UP

Bookmakers collect or pay out debts on betting activities on specific days of the week. During football season when there is a Monday night game, the normal settle up days are Tuesday and Wednesday. During basketball season, it may change to Monday and Tuesday. The bookmaker may meet the bettor at a restaurant or bar, or he may have a person designated to be the pickup man. They may drop off envelopes containing money and pick up the same way.

BOOKMAKING RECORDS

Betting Records

Betting records which show the actual recorded wagers are the best evidence to prove that illegal sports bookmaking did, in fact, occur. With a large enough volume of wagers, you can project income and meet your burden of proof for court. If you raid the location at the time when the telephones are open, you will be able to obtain wagers over the telephone. When doing this, you should attempt to identify the bettor by getting his identifiers and telephone number. One of the key facts you must prove is that the target is a bookmaker and not just a bettor. This can be done by demonstrating that the betting records you obtained show a vigorish is charged, a large number of bets will be repeated, and the records contain self-defeating bets (bets both for and against the same team). Recorded

		NAME	1	2 PREVIOUS DAY	3	4 ACCOUNT BALANCE
	1	BOB D.				
	2	JOHN L.				
	3	C. S.				
	4	JOHN G.				
	5	CANDY MAN				
	6	TOM B.				
	7	THE "DOC"				
	8	BILLY A.				
	9	CROME				
	10	A. B.				
	11	BIG JOHN				
	12	#12				
	13	A. S.				
	14	TONY G.				
	15	G. W.				
	16	CANA▬				
	17	DAN M.				
	18	L.				
	19	MILL▬				
	20	MAC				
	21	Q-MAN				
	22	HOWARD				
	23	TOM ▬▬				
	24	D - MAC				
	25	BOBBY C.				
	26	HARVEY				
	27	MIKE S.				
	28	MARVIN				
	29	E. B.				
	30	JERRY B.				
	31					

DATE _____   STORE   WEEK TO DATE TOTAL _____

EFFICIENCY LINE® 22-208

Figure 18.5. This shows a bettor list. In this case, the bookmaker not only used it for totals, but also as code identifiers. When the bettor called in and stated his identifier number (''17''), the bookmaker could refer to the list to determine that ''17'' was Dan M.

wagers will show the bettor identifiers (may be his name or code number), team wagered on, and the amount (at times the amount will include the vigorish).

Bettor Lists

Bettor lists are used by the bookmaker to identify bettors (Figure 18.5). These lists may contain the bettor's name, code number, and telephone number. They also show who introduced the bettor, how much he can bet, and when he will settle up.

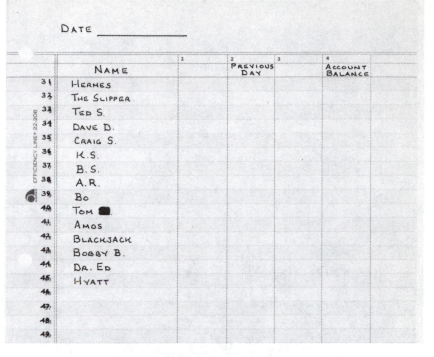

DATE _____

	NAME	1	2 PREVIOUS DAY	3	4 ACCOUNT BALANCE	
31	Hermes					
32	The Slipper					
33	Ted S.					
34	Dave D.					
35	Craig S.					
36	K.S.					
37	B.S.					
38	A.R.					
39	Bo					
40	Tom ▮.					
41	Amos					
42	Blackjack					
43	Bobby B.					
44	Dr. Ed					
45	Hyatt					
46						
47						
48						
49						

EFFICIENCY LINE® 22-208

Figure 18.5. (continued)

The bookmaker may have a list on the wall next to the telephones with just the bettor's code number and name. When the bettor calls in and gives his code number, the bookmaker looks at the list and calls the bettor by name.

Bettor Total Sheets/Balance Figures

Bettor total sheets are used by the bookmaker to keep a running total of what each bettor owes (Figures 18.6 and 18.7). When a bettor calls and asks for his totals, the bookmaker refers to this sheet. You will find that when bookmakers meet to settle up with bettors, there will be a notation of paid, carryover, or partial payment on the total sheet. Total sheets by themselves are only indicative of illegal gambling operations.

Bookmaker Total Sheet

Bookmaker total sheets list the bookmaker's total profit or loss. They may show the totals by the day, week, or year to date. Some sheets may list expenses incurred in the day-to-day running of the sports book.

Line Sheets

Line sheets, like sports schedules, list games by number and times played and provide space for the current lines on the games listed to be written. At times

A.

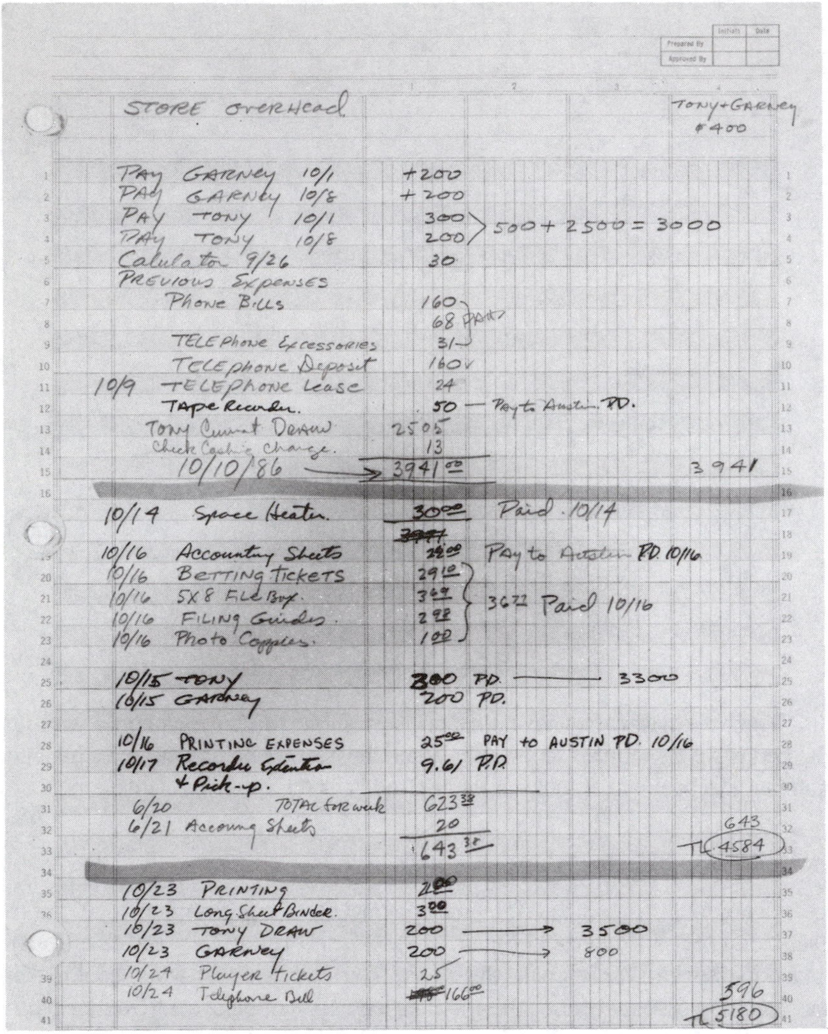

Figure 18.6. Total sheets for the bookmaking operation.

you will find several lines listed with initials over them. Normally when this occurs, it denotes the lines of other bookmakers contacted. Keep this in mind when you interrogate your target and you ask with what other bookmakers he has dealings (Figure 18.8).

Serial Numbers on Wager

When you encounter wager sheets with serial numbers on them, you should automatically consider the chance that your target is not the top dog. The presence

B.

The STORE BALANCES	DAY	WEEK	YEAR
	– 0 –	– 0 –	–1754
10/7/86 TUESDAY	+2415	+2415	+2415
		+2415	661
10/8/86 WEDNESDAY	+ 382	+382	+382
		+2797	+1043
10/9/86 THURSDAY	–30	–30	–30
		+2767	+1013
10/10/86 FRIDAY	–350	–350	–350
		+2417	+663
10/11/86 SAT	+2740	+2735	+2735
		+5152	+3398
10/12/86 SUN	+4603	+4603	+4603
		10770	9016
10/13/86 MON	–2000	–1960	1960
		7760	+6006

C.

STore Cash Summary
Thru 10/13/86

Capital – DM/AB   + 10253

Expenses
  Gorney   400
  Tony   3000
  Phones   443
  Tape Recorder 50
  Check Cashing   13
  Adding Machine 30
  Office Supplies   5
        TOTAL   – 3941

Players Position Thru 10/6   – 1754
Cash on Hand
Players Carry Over – Credit To Players – 3582
Other Adjustment

        TOTAL minus   10253

            TOTAL   0

Figure 18.6. (continued)

A.

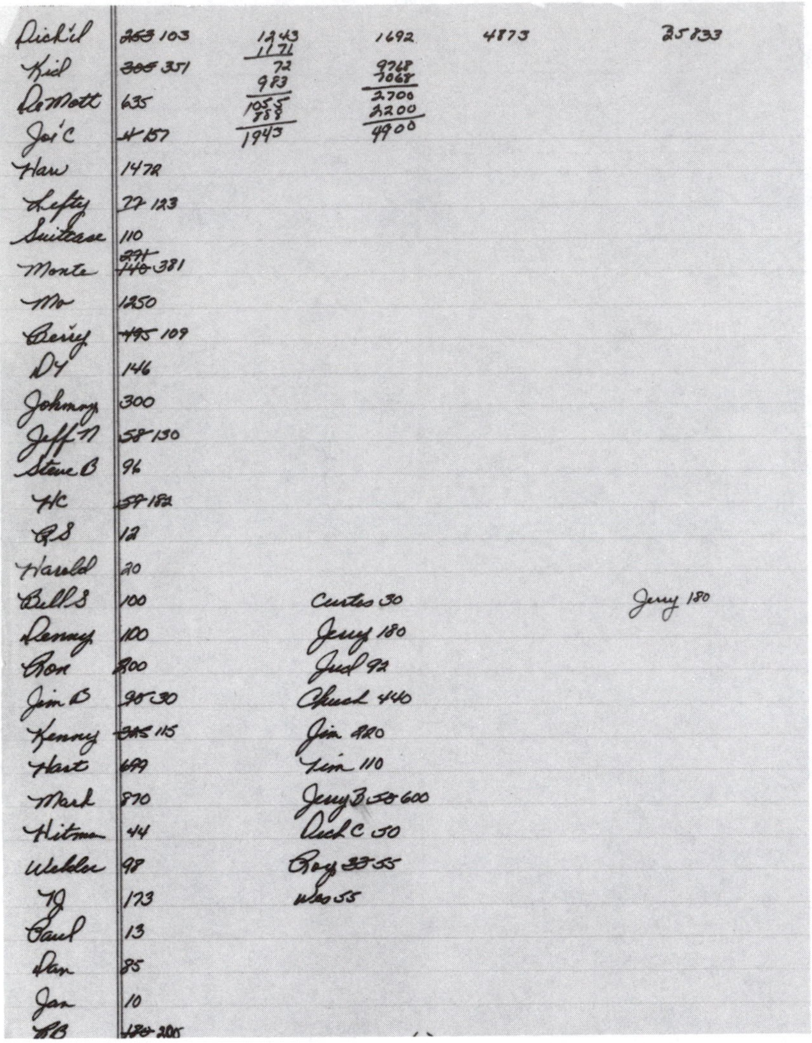

Figure 18.7. Bettor total sheets.

of serial numbers denotes accountability to someone. This someone may be the person who is the money behind the book or the partner of your target. It is imperative to determine this as soon as possible if there is any hope of arresting the other person (Figure 18.9).

Voided Wagers

If your investigation reveals serial number sheets with **void** on them, look for another person in the organization to whom your target is accountable.

B.

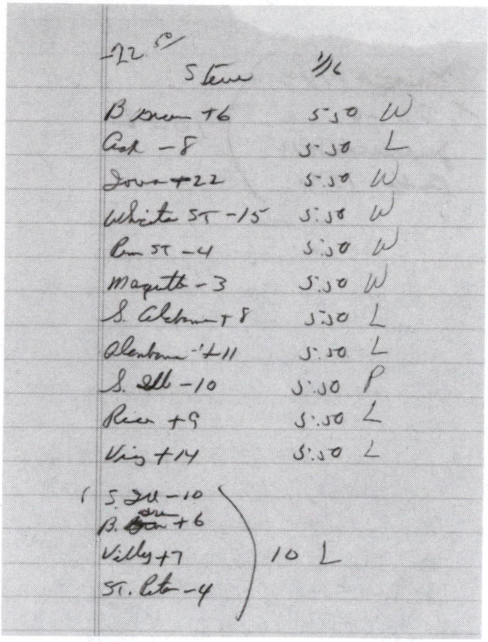
72 5/
Steve 1/6
Brown +6 5-50 W
Cal -8 5-50 L
Iowa +22 5-50 W
White St -15 5-50 W
Penn St -4 5-50 W
Marquette -3 5-50 W
S. Alabama +8 5-50 L
[illegible] +11 5-50 L
S. [illegible] -10 5-50 P
Rice +9 5-50 L
Virg +14 5-50 L
S. Ill -10
B. ~~Brown~~ +6
Villy +7
St. [illegible] -4
10 L

C.

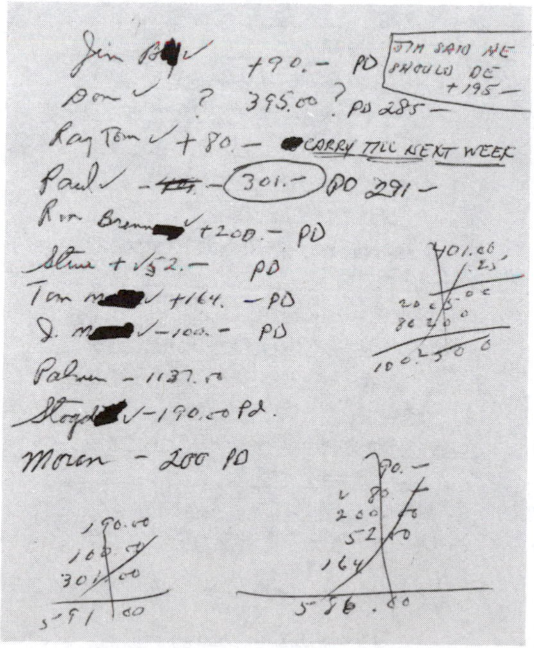
Jim B[redacted] ✓ +90.– PD
JIM SAID HE SHOULD BE +195–
Don ✓ ? 395.00 ? PD 285–
Ray Tom ✓ + 80.– [redacted] CARRY TILL NEXT WEEK
Paul ✓ – ~~[illegible]~~ – (301.–) PD 291–
Ron Bren[redacted] ✓ +200.– PD
Steve + ✓52.– PD
Tom M[redacted] ✓ +164. – PD
J. M[redacted] ✓ –100.– PD
Palmer – 1137.50
Stoyd[redacted] ✓ –190.00 Pd.
Moran – 200 PD

Figure 18.7. (continued)

D.

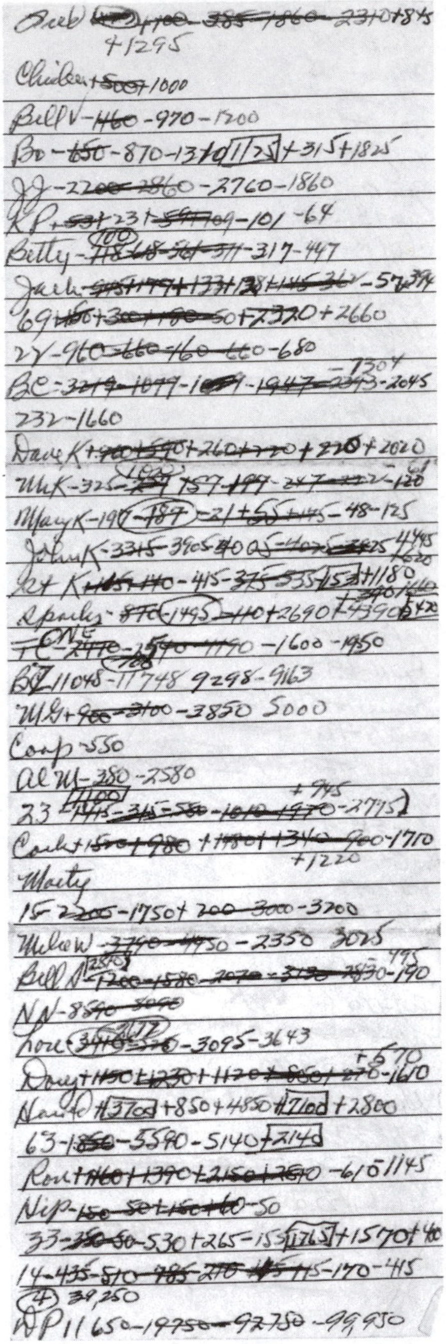

Figure 18.7. (continued)

E.

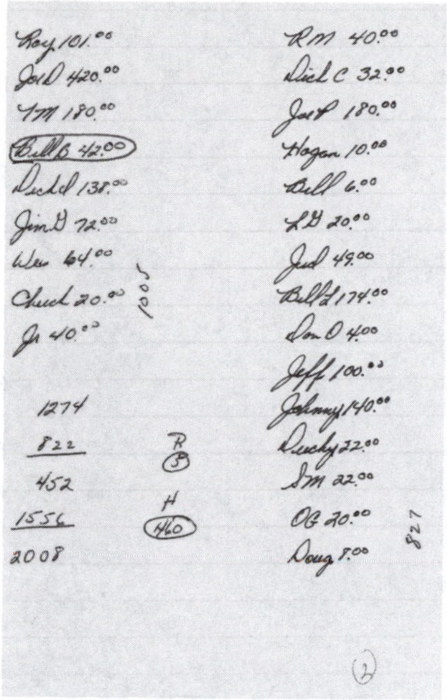

F.

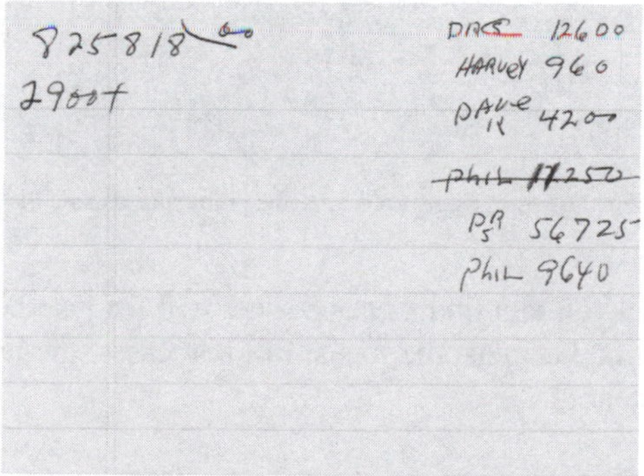

Figure 18.7. (continued)

Duplicate Wager Records

You may discover wagering sheets which have duplicate carbon copies. As above, these indicate that a partner or boss is involved. One thing you should look for is the presence of different notations on one of the sheets. Normally, when

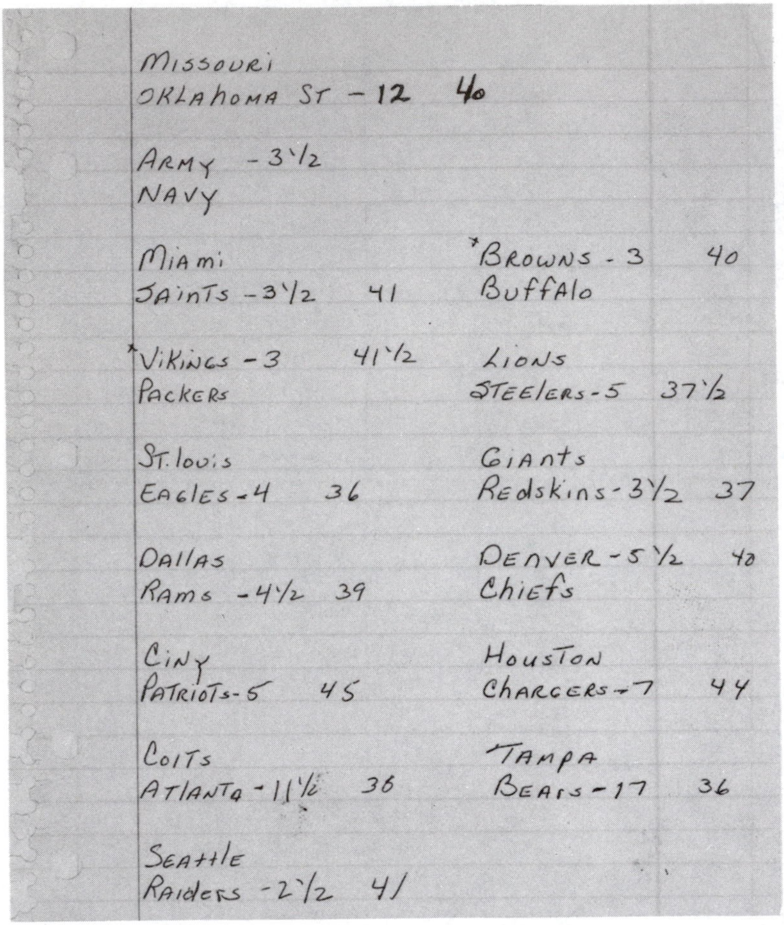

MISSOURI
OKLAhOMA ST — 12   40

ARMY — 3½
NAVY

MiAmi   *BROWNS - 3   40
JAinTS —3½   41   BuffAlo

*ViKiNGS — 3   41½   LioNS
PAcKERs   STEE/eRs-5   37½

ST. louis   GiAnts
EAGLES—4   36   RedsKins-3½   37

Dallas   DENVER—5½   40
RAms —4½   39   Chiefs

CiNy   HousToN
PATRioTs-5   45   CHARGeRs—7   44

CoiTs   TAmpA
ATlANTa—11½   36   BEArs—17   36

SeA+tle
RAideRs —2½   41

Figure 18.8. Handwritten line sheet listing the teams, the point spreads, and the over and under scores.

duplicates are used you will find that one sheet will list just the bet, whereas the second will have the bets plus the totals. In most cases, the handwriting on the total will be different.

TYPES OF BETS

Straight Bets

A straight bet is when a bettor bets on one team including the point spread. Normally the bettor risks $110.00 to win $100.00; for example, Pacers +7 for 110 (Figure 18.10).

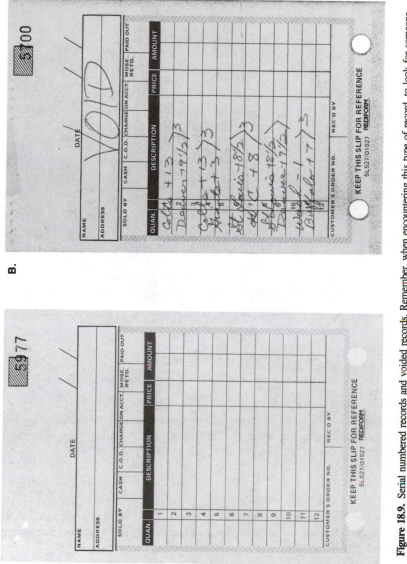

Figure 18.9. Serial numbered records and voided records. Remember, when encountering this type of record, to look for someone over your target in the organization.

C.

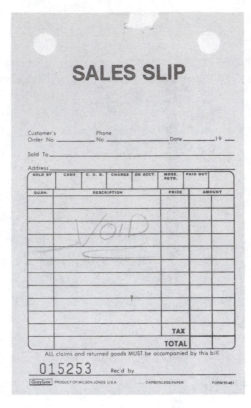

Figure 18.9. (continued)

Parlay Bet

A parlay bet is a single wager on two or more teams where each team must win by the point spreads in order to receive a payoff. A parlay bet is normally identified by the use of brackets; for example, Ind. +7] or Port. −3].

If Bets

A bettor places a bet on a single event and if the bet is a winner, all or a portion of the winnings are to be bet on a second event. If the first bet is a loser, the second is null and void.

Over and Under Bets

A bettor bets that after adding the final score of the two teams in an event together, the total will be above or below a certain number set by the bookmaker. For example, the over and under listed by the bookmaker on the Pacers vs. L.A.

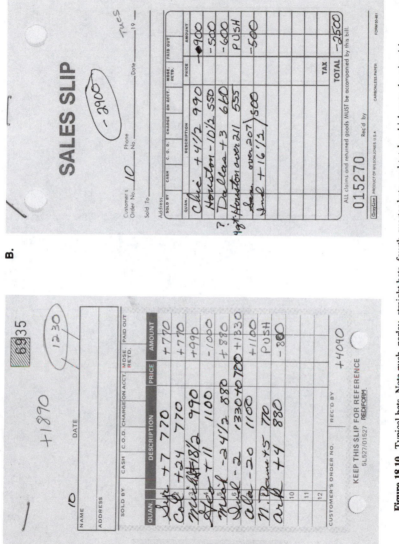

Figure 18.10. Typical bets. Note push, parlay, straight bets, fourth quarter bets, and totals which note the vigorish.

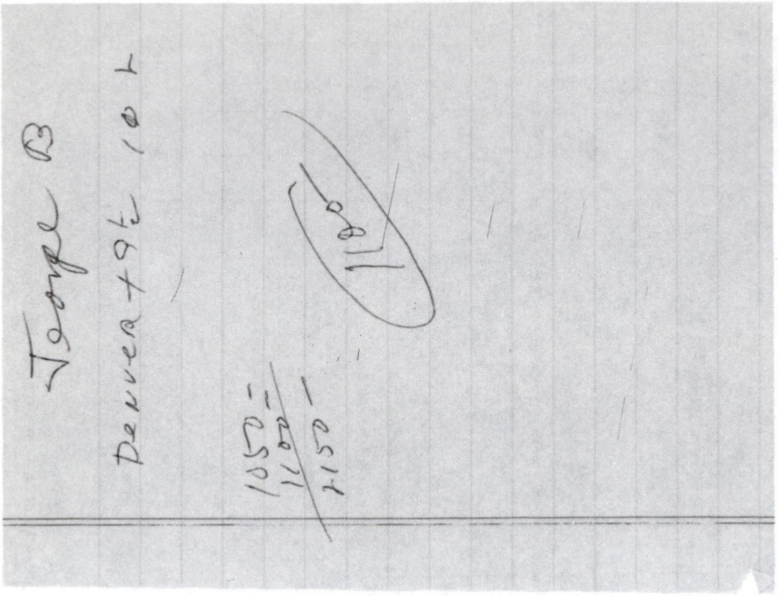

Figure 18.10. (continued)

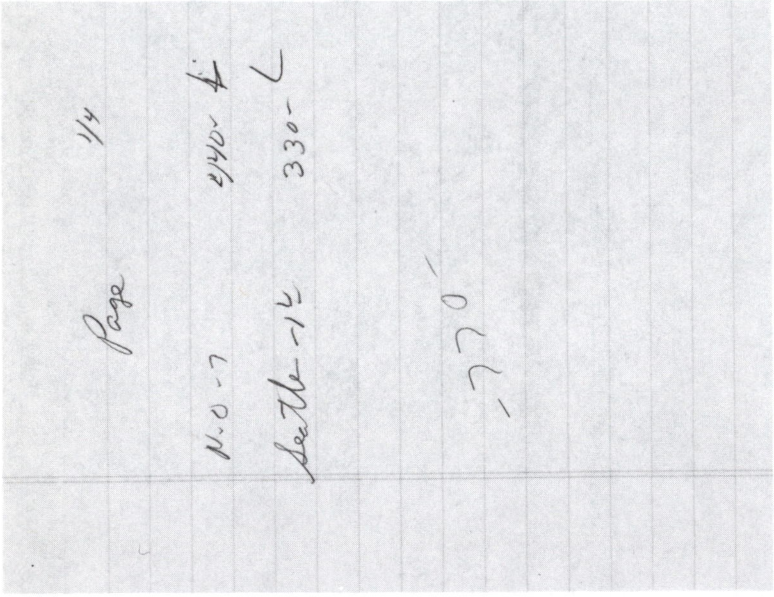

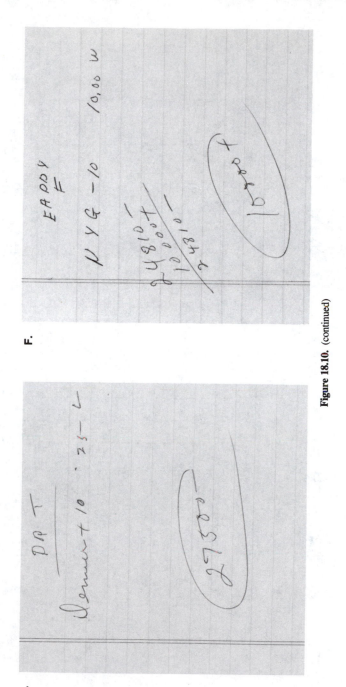

Figure 18.10. (continued)

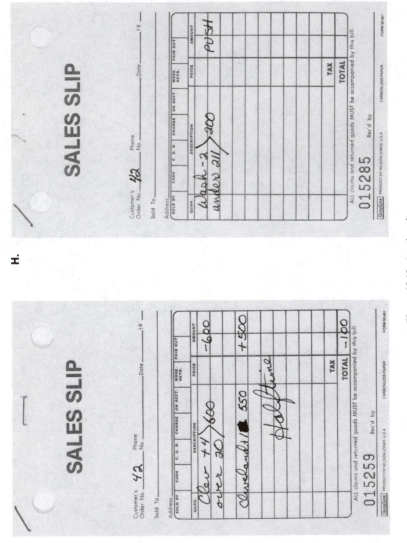

Figure 18.10. (continued)

game is 214. The bettor bet $100.00 that it will be over 214. The final score is Pacers 100 and L.A. 112. Adding the two scores together shows that the bet was a loser (Figure 18.11).

Teaser Bets

A teaser is a parlay bet where the bettor obtains additional points added or subtracted from the line which give him a better chance to win. For additional points, the bettor will obtain a smaller amount of money on a winning bet (Figures 18.12 and 18.13).

Half-Time Wagers

Some bookmakers offer half-time bets. They involve nothing more than at half time setting a new line and placing bets as if the games were just starting.

Round Robin

Round robins are parlay bets using three or more teams taking all the possible two team parlays.

SPORTS BOOKMAKING OPERATION

Where to Begin

Sports bookmaking can be found in many forms. It may be some little old man in a barbershop or an executive in a major corporation. No matter where they are, there is one thing they have in common: a base of operations. A bookmaker base may be an apartment, his residence, an office, or just a bar where he hangs out. The bookmaker may take bets hand to hand, through runners or subs, or over the telephone. For the purpose of this section, we will consider the situation where a bookmaker rents or leases a location to conduct his bookmaking activities (Figures 18.14 through 18.17).

The sports bookmaking operation process begins with the establishment of a base of operations. Normally the operation involves the use of the telephone. There are many ways to establish a bookmaking operation, but each will provide you with valuable intelligence.

The bookmaker begins his operation by renting an apartment or office. In most situations he will use false information on his lease agreement. Once this is completed, the bookmaker will contact the telephone company and request two or more lines to be run into his location. The reason for the two lines is that one is for bettors to call bets in on and the other is to be used as an open line for laying off bets. Once this is accomplished, the bookmaker must identify sources

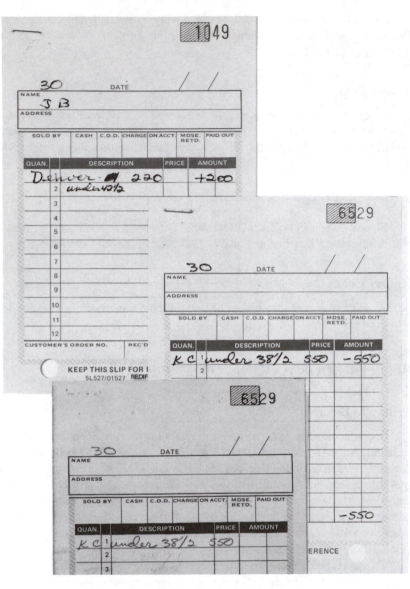

Figure 18.11. Over and under bets.

for the national line and layoffs. Normally, the source of the national line comes from line services which are offered all over the country. In order to obtain the local lines, the bookmaker must build a rapport with other bookmakers in the area. Remember that bookmakers are in competition with, but interdependent on, other bookmakers in a given area.

The bookmaker must identify sources for layoffs. They need to be local and outside the given area. An example of a need for an outside layoff source is when

```
                        FOOTBALL
*..OVERS/UNDERS.FINAL.SCORE**********************************************
  •  PARLEYS

       TEAMS      LAY WIN
         2         5   13
         3         1    6
         4         1   11
         5         1   22
         6         1   45

     •  ALL WINS AND ONE PUSH, WILL DROP PAYOFF ONE LOWER
        Example: 4 TEAM - THREE WINS ONE PUSH = 6 TIMES LAY.
        Example: 2 TEAM - ONE WIN ONE PUSH = 90% OF LAY.
**********************************************************************
  •  6,6½ or 7POINT TEASERS
      TEAMS    6POINTS      6½POINTS       7POINTS
               LAY WIN      LAY WIN        LAY WIN
        2       1   1       11   10         6    5
        3       5   9        5    8         2    3
        4       1   3        2    5         1    2
        5       2   9        1    4         2    7
        6       1   7        1    6         1    5
  •  ANY LOSS: LOSES
  •  ALL WINS WITH PUSH: NO ACTION
***.OVERS/UNDERS.IN.6.6½.OR.7.POINT.TEASERS.4.POINT.MOVE***********

  •  SPECIAL TEASERS
     •  9 POINT TEASERS THREE TEAMS LAY 11 WIN 10
     •  12POINT TEASERS FOUR TEAMS LAY 6 WIN 5
     •ANY LOSS:LOSES
     •ALL WINS WITH PUSH: NO ACTION
     •OVERS/UNDERS IN 9POINT TEASERS MOVE 6POINTS;
                    IN12POINT TEASERS MOVE 8POINTS;
**********************************************************************
LAY 6 to 5
  •  48 POINT SCRAMBLE
     •  SAME AS 12 POINT TEASER,BUT USE POINTS IN ANY COMBINATION (TOTAL 48PT?
        NOTE: SINCE OVERS/UNDERS ARE ONLY ALLOWED 8 POINTS, SUBTRACT
        FOUR POINTS FROM THE 48 FOR EACH OVER/UNDER USED.
**********************************************************************
  •  HOURS
     •  FRIDAY 5:00-07:00
     •  SATURDAY 10:00-03:00
              5:00-07:00
     •  SUNDAY   10:30-03:00 • MONDAY 6:00-09:00
     •  SPECIAL DATES-TWO HOURS BEFORE GAME TIME
  •  PHONES
     222-3333
     222-3334
```

Figure 18.12. Sheet that this particular bookmaker handed out as advertising. Note the descriptions of teasers, parlays, and 48 point scrambles. Note also the hours listed and the phone numbers.

an area has a local team. When betting is done on a local team, most bookmakers in the area will find themselves way out of balance and will have to resort at times to calling thousands of miles away to find a bookmaker who will take their layoff. Keep in mind these layoffs outside your area are important for intelligence purposes. They may identify a gradual infiltration of organized crime into the illegal gambling in your community. Another point to keep in mind is that when layoffs are made over long distances, the bookmakers must find a way to settle up. Look for mail services and/or the U.S. mail being used to pass illegal gambling income.

How They Recruit Bettors

Once the bookmaker has accomplished his basic setup procedures, he is ready to begin recruiting bettors. Bettors are recruited in a variety of ways which range from word of mouth to advertising.

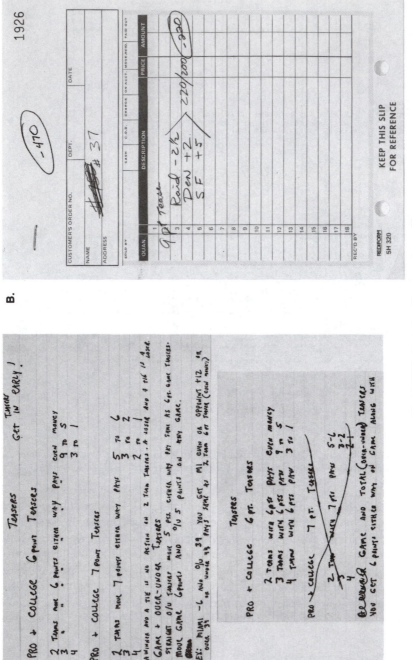

Figure 18.13. Examples of teasers and scrambles.

c.

Figure 18.13. (continued)

D.

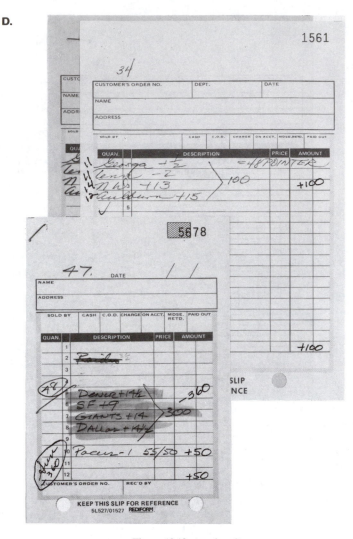

Figure 18.13. (continued)

How Bookmakers Advertise

Bookmakers advertise by contacting a printer. A bookmaker will approach a printer and request a variety of items, the first usually being the bookmaker's business card. This card will have the betting telephone numbers on it. Some cards will have pictures of footballs, basketballs, and other symbols which denote what sports they take bets on. Some cards will have the first name of the bookmaker. Other requested items are parlay cards and flyers that describe what the bookmaker will offer if you will join his clientele. Each of the above items are indicative or typical of a bookmaking operation, and it seems that police officers ignore or just overlook printers as a valuable source of information for their cases.

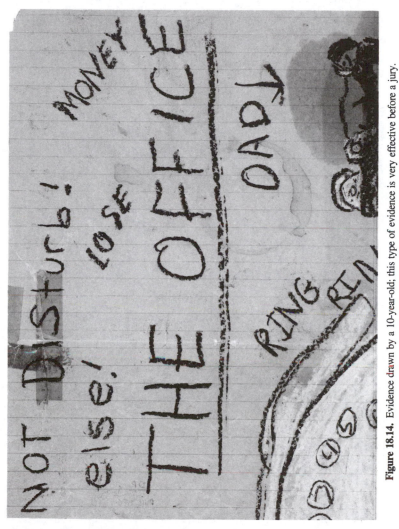

Figure 18.14. Evidence drawn by a 10-year-old; this type of evidence is very effective before a jury.

B.

C.

Figure 18.14. (continued)

A.

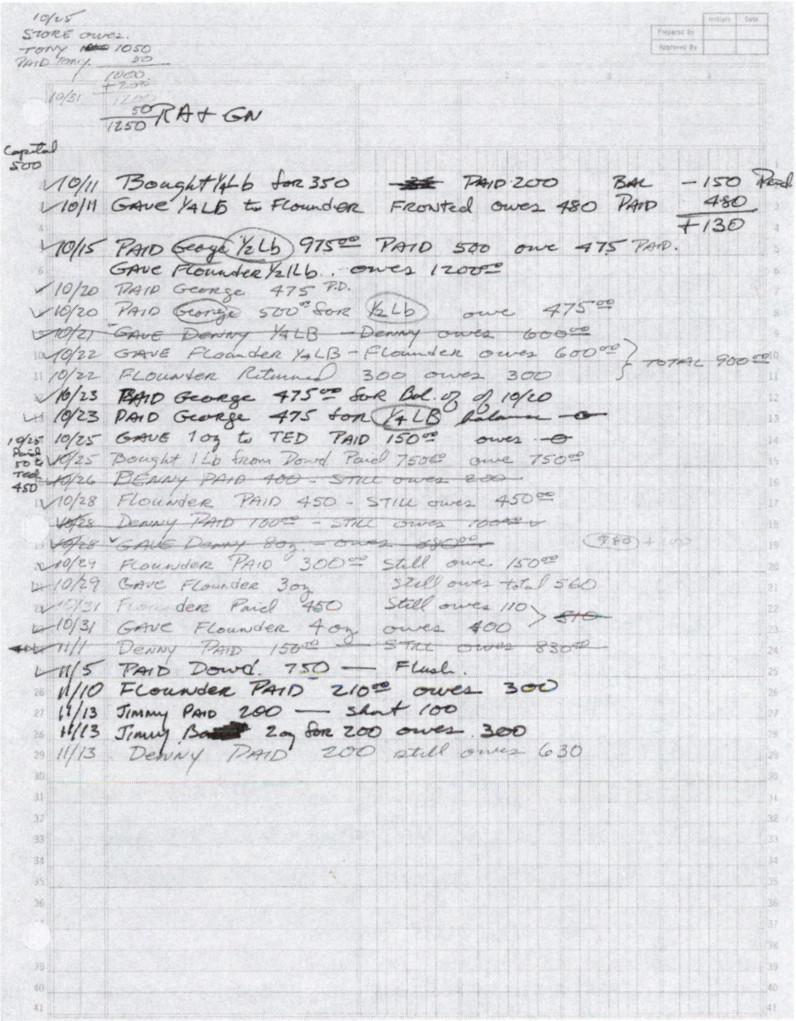

Figure 18.15. Records seized in raids. (A) notes how much marijuana was being fronted to people for distribution.

All You Have Is a Telephone Number . . . What Now?

When you receive any information on a bookmaking operation, you should attempt to expand on it to the point where you have enough to make the decision whether the target is one you want to pursue.

The first step is to check your crisscross listing for the address which coincides with the number. If there is none, then there is a chance the telephone number

B.

Started on Monday Dec. 11th

		MADE	RECIEVED	
week ending Dec. 15th		800	Dec. 19th 800	
week ending Dec 22nd		400	Dec. 26th 400	
week ending Dec. 29th		400 (700)	Jan. 2nd 300	—
week ending Jan. 5th		830	Jan. 9th 0	
week ending Jan. 12th		550	Jan 16th 500	(+830)
week ending Jan. 19th		900?	Jan 23rd 100	
week ending Jan. 26th	Thru Thursday		Jan. 30th 300	
week ending Feb. 2nd		0	Feb. 6th	
week ending Feb. 9th		0	Feb. 13th	
week ending Feb. 16th			Feb. 20th	
week ending Feb. 23rd			Feb. 27th	
week ending March 2nd			March 6th	
week ending march 9th			march 13th	

need 400 minimum
need 1200 minimum
need 600 minimum
need 500 minimum

GOALS : Must have two new bookies by week ending Jan. 12th
Have angelo on program by week ending Jan. 19th

This would produce a baseball program and
leave me with 8 to 10 M to begin florida program
This would also let me have 3 months of 1700 per mo. with the

15K Silver with Black Valoure
19 450 SE 44 to 53 M miles auto Sun Roof loaded
Show room car
in Jacksonville

Figure 18.15. (continued)

is nonpublished. Obtain a subpoena through the prosecutor or grand jury and serve it on the telephone company to secure the subscriber information. With this information, you can identify the subject(s) involved. Check the name(s) for prior arrests and check the address for prior incidents. This may give you other subjects who are involved. Then check the address and see what it is. Is it a residence, apartment, or business? Also check for vehicles and get any license plate numbers that you can. Sources that you can use to find information about your target include the following:

Apartment or Business Lease Information
Most lease agreements have lengthy forms which ask for employment (both present and past) and addresses in the last 10 years, and some request references.

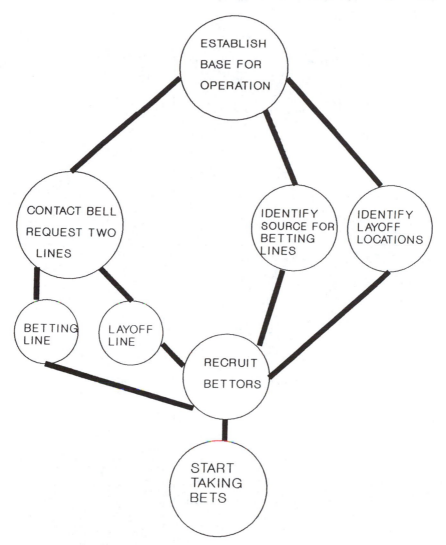

Figure 18.16. Example of how a sports bookmaking operation is set up.

Be cautious as to whom you approach for information. The person you ask may be a gambler.

Public Utilities

Water, sewer, and electric applications must be filled out to get services in most areas. Obtain the name on the bill sent to or for that address. Find out how long the service has been listed in that name and whether that subject is listed as a user anywhere else in the area.

A.

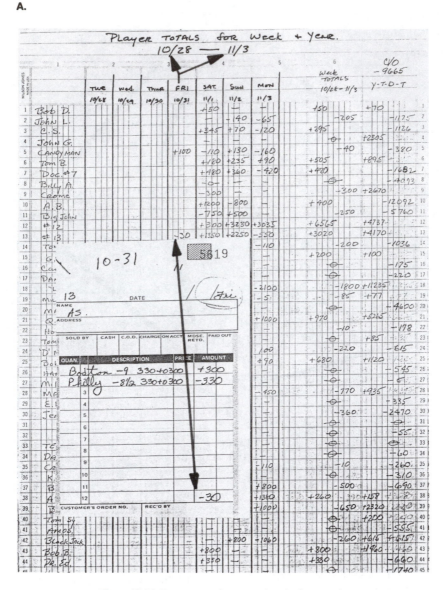

Figure 18.17. Demonstrates how to analyze betting records.

License Plate Numbers

License plate number(s) obtained at the target location will determine ownership of vehicles. If another address is listed, then you also need to run a background check on the second location. Remember, each vehicle or property involved may become forfeitable in the future; therefore, obtain as much information as possible on other locations involved for assets.

B.

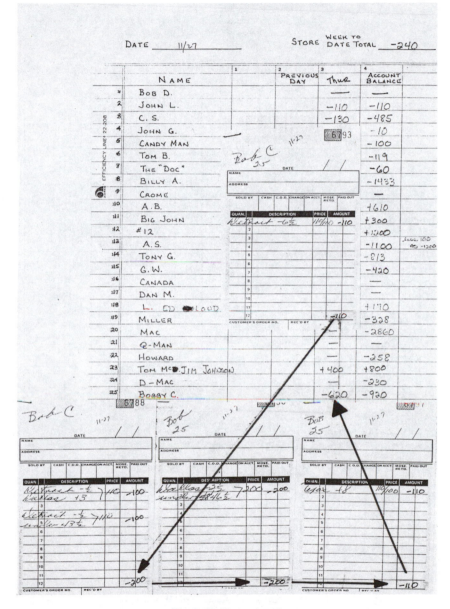

Figure 18.17. (continued)

U.S. Post Office

Request that a mail cover be placed on mail entering the target location. A mail cover will give information about all the mail that enters your location (see Chapter 2).

C.

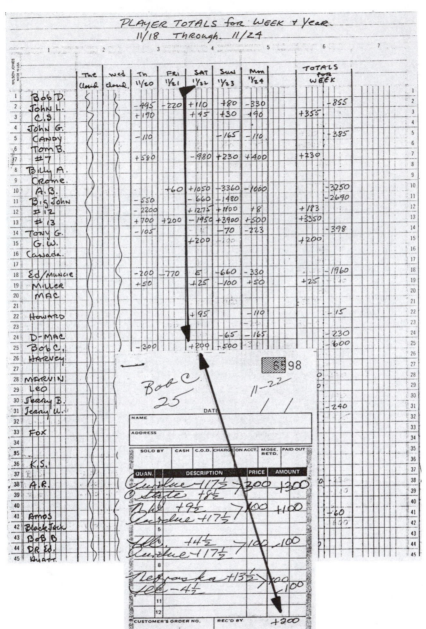

Figure 18.17. (continued)

D.

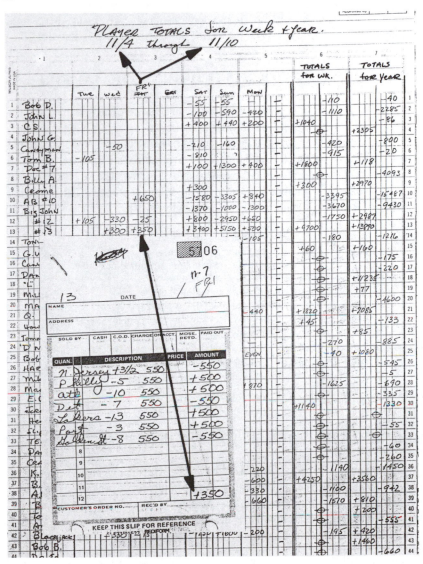

Figure 18.17. (continued)

Department of Natural Resources

Keep in mind that if there is a boat, there is much information that can be obtained from the registration number.

Telephone Company

Besides requesting subscriber information, you may want a couple of months of toll records. Toll records will list any long distance numbers charged to your target telephone number. This is how you can find out whether the subject is calling a national line service.

As you can see, starting from just a telephone number you can gather a large quantity of information. What you do with it is the subject of this chapter.

SPECIAL GROUPS TARGETED BY BOOKMAKERS

In the back of every bookmaker's mind is the question of how to make money and avoid going to jail, or worse, losing the money to the IRS. They have developed many creative ways to limit their chances of being investigated by targeting certain groups of people. By compromising a person who is in an important profession, the bookmaker can, in the end, own that person. The key is the person must fear exposure to the public more than the criminal charges. The following are some of the groups that are targeted and why:

Policemen	—	Protection
Judges	—	Protection against jail time
Doctors	—	Free medical treatment and sometimes drugs
Lawyers	—	Free legal representation
Politicians	—	Interference and control of the police
Coaches	—	Inside information and game fixing
Athletes	—	Point shaving, inside information, and game fixing

Important: Once an athlete takes money, he is owned for life. Sometimes a bookmaker will target players in high school.

Now that you have a general idea of terms and targets of bookmakers, we will describe the phases of an investigation.

RECEIPT AND VALIDATION OF INFORMATION

Information is received on a daily basis by investigators from a variety of locations, both within the law enforcement community and from the outside. Each piece of information you receive must be checked for its truthfulness and accuracy. Remember that the credibility of the investigator and the agency he or she represents is at stake, not to mention the liability that is attached if the investigator fails to do a complete background check before he or she acts on the information received. You must always keep in mind that your actions could place a limit on officers all over the United States if a court rules on your errors. *If you are not sure, do not do it!*

Anonymous Complaints

In many cases, you will receive your first indication that there is a problem at a specific location either through an anonymous letter or telephone call (Figure

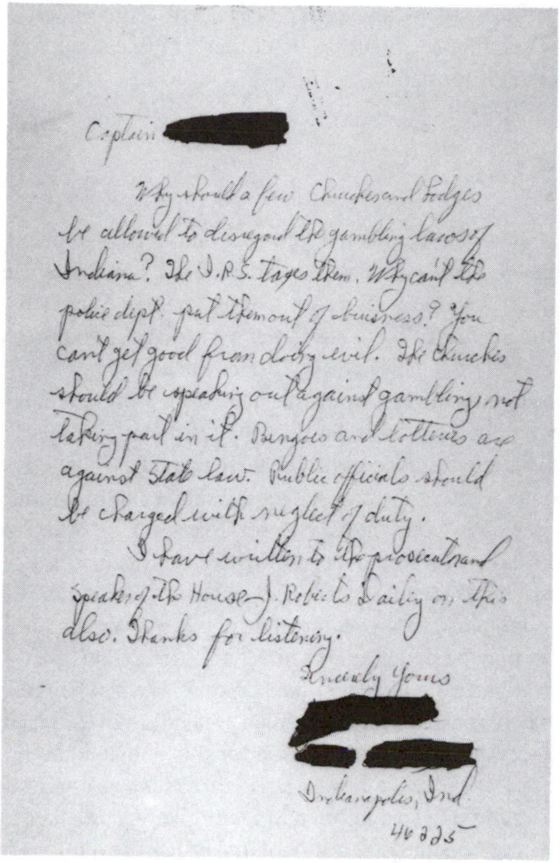

Figure 18.18. An example of a complaint.

18.18). As a general rule, information received in this manner can be validated. There is a wide range of reasons for letters and calls, but the most frequent reason in gambling cases is that a member of the family of a bettor has reached his or her limit in enduring what he feels is an addiction of a loved one. He or she is crying for help.

Once a complaint is received, you should utilize the background check techniques taught earlier in the book to attempt to validate the information. This is a very important step and must be taken to identify bad information as quickly as possible. You cannot afford to waste time on bad complaints.

Remember Your Checklist

In establishing the background for a case, you should investigate these sources: computer check, records check, interviews, traffic record checks, communications, Vice Branch record checks, informants, other police agencies, court records, telephone company, ownership of property, corporations, financial statements, utilities, intelligence branches, Recorder's Office, mail covers, trash, bank records, and credit information.

SURVEILLANCE

Once you have gathered some information on your targets, you should be ready to conduct some surveillance to reinforce your probable cause. Initial surveillance should cover the bookmaker's daily routine. Whether the bookmaker takes bets at a residence or bar, your initial surveillance should cover him during betting hours. Your first objective is to determine whether he is in fact at the location you were informed he would be. This is very important when your target is a residence and the bets are taken over the telephone.

If no one is at the residence when bets are taken over the telephone, then you need to determine whether the bookmaker is using a call forwarding setup to take bets. If this is the case, you will have to set up a track on your bookmaker prior to betting and follow him to the location where he is actively taking bets. If this occurs, you must try to identify where he will be on the day you serve your search warrant. If he is not present on your target date, you may not get the documentation you need and it may be better to take him on settle up day.

Initial surveillance should cover the bookmaker when he settles up with bettors and other bookmakers. This surveillance should cover the time before and after he is to meet the bettors. The reason for this is that some bookmakers will go to a bank and make withdrawals prior to settling up and some will make deposits after settling up. This information will give you another location to look for records. Do not be surprised if a bookmaker uses several banks. The importance of this information is that you can immediately show a connection between the gambling activities and the bank where the withdrawal or deposit was made.

If possible, put a covert officer inside the location where settling up occurs. Determine whether they just leave and pick up envelopes or meet in person. If they meet their bettors, use this as a way to gather witnesses for your future court testimony. Have the outside surveillance identify, if possible, the vehicles and plate numbers of the persons who meet with your target. Remember, you also want to identify whether any of the businesses where settling up occurs are involved in the activities. You should identify any and all vehicles used by your bookmaker to conduct business. Identify any and all locations that your bookmaker uses to conduct his bookmaking operation. This will come in handy for any future forfeiture hearing.

When conducting initial surveillance, you should have a form designed to provide a simple way to make sure that the person keeping notes on what is observed will not inadvertently miss an item of importance. A simple license plate log should be designed and records should be kept on all persons arriving and leaving the location being observed. Remember to use a recorder in this situation. Accuracy is very important.

Case Example

The investigation began with a complaint from a police officer who gathered information that directed his attention to a white male who owned a tavern in his district. His investigation and information demonstrated that Mr. James Doe was actively involved in sports gambling. The officer provided information with the hope of preventing the bookmaker from carrying out threats that Doe had communicated to several of the bookmaker's bettors who were behind in their payments. The officer stated that Doe was known to drive a blue Lincoln Continental.

After checking old complaints and finding that an informant had provided prior information that James Doe had borrowed a large amount of money in the past to cover major gambling losses, the informant was contacted and an update on James Doe was requested. The informant stated that James Doe was conducting his bookmaking operation out of his residence and tavern. The informant further stated that James Doe was threatening physical harm to any bettor who failed to meet a payment deadline. Due to the imminent threat of harm to bettors, much time was devoted to this case.

A computer background check was run on James Doe and revealed the following:

- James Doe had prior arrests for gambling-related offenses.
- James Doe was arrested for a firearms violation.
- James Doe had a prior arrest for assault and battery.

This information was convincing enough that James Doe was, in fact, capable of inflicting physical harm on his bettors.

We continued with a computer background check on the address where James Doe had his tavern. Search warrants had been served at the business on previous occasions, and professional gambling was central to the search warrant.

A computer check of the area of James Doe's residence was done, and we were unable to locate any complaints or reports. Continuing the search, we examined the Bureau of Motor Vehicles files and located a blue Lincoln Continental registered to James Doe at the address indicated as his residence. In addition to the Lincoln, a brown station wagon was listed to James Doe and his wife.

The informant was contacted and we requested that he frequent the tavern owned by Doe and attempt to warn us of any threats that might be carried out by Doe. The informant began to go in the tavern around lunch time and within 2 days had obtained the telephone number that James Doe was using to take bets when he was not at the tavern. The telephone company was contacted, and we found that this was a nonpublished number; thus a subpoena was obtained for subscriber information. Toll records for the last 3 months were also requested. The subscriber information was received the same day, and the telephone was listed to James Doe at the residence that the information had indicated. The toll records were received the next day and indicated that Doe was placing a large number of calls on a regular basis to Las Vegas.

Once this point was reached, we needed to identify the ownership of the two properties involved. The County Assessor's Office was contacted and found that both the residence and the tavern were owned by Doe. The Alcohol Beverage Commission (ABC) was also contacted, and we found that the permit to sell liquor was listed in both Doe's and his wife's name.

Keep in mind that businesses are prime for the laundering of money. During the whole background procedure, there was the possibility of the bar being used as a location to launder the illegal gambling income. A lookout for distributors of goods and services to the tavern would be used later as a way to identify discrepancies in what appeared to be sold and what was actually ordered.

During the course of the investigation, the informant overheard that Doe was to meet a bettor who was behind in his payments. The informant stated that Doe felt he had to make an example of this bettor to stop future problems. Doe stated that the bettor was to meet him in the bar at noon on the next day. A law enforcement partner was inside the bar on the next day to observe and intercede, if necessary, if Doe became violent. Shortly after arriving, the partner observed the bettor having a heated conversation with Doe. The bettor handed Doe a partial payment, and it appeared that it was not good enough for Doe. Doe proceeded to beat the bettor. At this time, the partner interceded and arrested Doe for battery, implying that his presence was just a coincidence. We attempted to get the bettor to assist us in the investigation, but he feared for his life if he cooperated.

For the next few days, the informant continued to frequent the tavern while we conducted our surveillance of the residence and Doe himself. A trash search was conducted and we were rewarded with a large amount of gambling paraphernalia. The contents of the trash included:

- A torn up bettor total sheet with numerous indications of "paid" on it
- Shredded records indicating that Doe was, in fact, taking bets at his residence
- A handwritten note requesting time to pay a debt
- Mail addressed to Doe and his wife at their residence
- A football schedule with lines from several sources indicated in pencil; games listed were for the day before the trash search
- Several receipts for cashier's checks listing "self" as remitter

With the information discovered and with the imminent threat that was perceived toward Doe's bettors, an infiltration of Doe's organization could not wait before we obtained warrants. Our informant contacted Doe on the telephone number provided and requested the lines on that evening's games. Doe provided the lines on seven games and asked if our informant wanted to get a bet down. Our informant stated, "Not at this time." The information we had was added to the information provided by the informant, and a search warrant was obtained for Doe's residence. On entering the residence, the following items were seized:

- 37 envelopes containing daily betting records, total sheets, and bets (Figure 18.19)

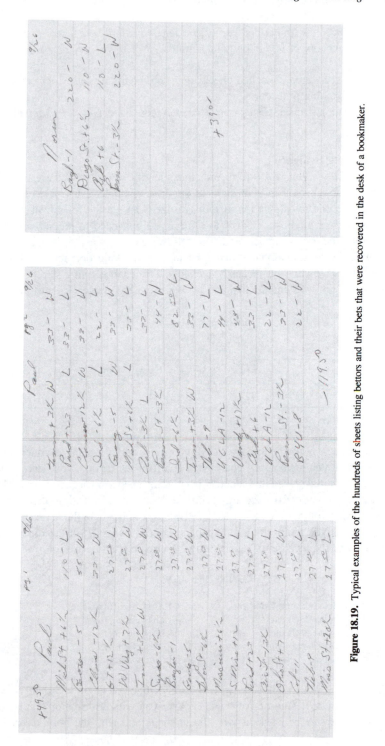

Figure 18.19. Typical examples of the hundreds of sheets listing bettors and their bets that were recovered in the desk of a bookmaker.

- A Rolodex file with bettors' names and telephone numbers listed
- A large quantity of gambling paraphernalia

We also recovered cancelled checks and noted bank accounts, and made a probe of his banking procedures.

As a result of this investigation, Doe was convicted and we forfeited his business.

Organizing the Evidence

In most cases, you will find records that identify bettors, and these records are very valuable to you in your case. In our case example, a list of 40 bettors with addresses and telephone numbers was seized. To get the full effect and to be able to present the best evidence to a jury, you will need to prepare another chart that will be easy to understand. The following chart is a simple one which begins with the organizational structure of the bookmaking operation and then lists the bettors by whatever means is available. This chart is a first step in determining whom you will contact first and who presents the greatest interest to you.

Investigation No. 1
John Doe
?

Steve	Fred	Micky	Mike	Wind	Tim	Jim	Bob	Gary
763	721	756	7777	235	421	817	993	924
tc aw	cc	sn	dd	wa	tr	ym	er	ik	ll

Whichever way the bettors are listed, you must find a system to understand the information you have. Once you have a chart for the bettors, you need to go through the material seized and identify what items show up for the bettors. The first place to start is the Rolodex file or address book. Look for listings that match the bettor codes. If initials are used, such as LK, look under K in the address book for a match. As you look through the papers you have seized, you need to chart each bettor and the location of his identifier. A simple chart to use follows:

BETTOR INFORMATION

Bettor name listed on	**Banking information**
Bettor total sheet	Bank name
Address sheet	Check numbers
Telephone listing	Dates of checks
Betting records	From and to whom

All this information will come in very handy when you begin your interviews of potential witnesses. Charting also will provide you with information that is not apparent on the surface, such as who the bettor is and who the bookmaker is.

Whenever possible, put your information on a chart. A visual chart is easier to understand than a page of typing.

Summary of the Investigation
- Received a complaint from a uniformed police officer
- Checked old complaints in reference to Doe
- Contacted an informant who had provided information on Doe before
- Conducted a computer check by name, address of business and residence, and license number
- Subpoenaed telephone records for subscriber information and tolls
- Had informant frequent tavern
- Obtained ownership information for the tavern and residence from county assessor
- Contacted ABC for information on liquor permit
- Looked for possible laundering of money
- Sent detective in as patron to observe settling up
- Conducted a trash search
- Obtained line information over the telephone from Doe
- Obtained a search warrant for Doe's residence

THE INFILTRATION OF SPORTS BOOKMAKING OPERATIONS

When your investigation reaches the point where it becomes necessary to introduce an undercover operative into the illegal organization, special consideration should be made to protect against leaks.

Preventing Leaks of Information Is Vital to the Success of Your Mission

Information about ongoing investigations should be handled with the utmost care, so as not to jeopardize the life of any covert operative. Leaks of information may come from any number of sources, both within and outside your organization. The love of gambling runs deep in American society; and as long as you have to involve people in your investigation, you will have leaks. Remember you were told earlier in this book the major professions that bookmakers want to target, and you will realize that you must limit the number of people you trust. Be ever on the alert for those people who attempt to gain protection by working within the system. They may sponsor police softball teams, fire department teams, cater food to political functions, or donate money to your favorite charities. These people are cultivating sources of information that they can use later. As you conduct your investigations, you should remember who the mouthpieces for these people are and never give them any chance to obtain information.

Other Information That Is Valuable to Bookmakers

Intelligence information about your investigations is not the only information of value to a sports bookmaker. He will pay a lot of cash for pictures of those individuals who work gambling investigations. If your branch has a policy of taking pictures of investigators on a yearly basis, you need to find a way to avoid having your picture taken. Be aware of freelance photographers who take pictures of investigators as they leave police headquarters. Keep in mind how much your investigation will cost the bookmaker, and then you can understand that his spending $500 for a picture is not much to keep the police out of his operation.

Other information that has and will be sold includes home addresses, home telephone numbers, names of your wife and children, and their place of employment or school. Never underestimate the intelligence a bookmaker has at his disposal and the information that a person is willing to sell.

FORMATS FOR ARRESTS

During the planning stage of your investigation, you should consider the format that will be used for the arrests of the bookmaker and other persons involved in the organization. The purpose of the format for arrests is to provide direction and an explanation as to why and how a person is to be processed once he or she is arrested. The point you need to keep in mind is how you explain treating people with the same involvement differently. The way you do this is to establish two areas of involvement. Area 1 is for the bookmakers and sub-bookmakers, and Area 2 is the aggravated bettor profile.

Area 1: Active Involvement

Area 1 is self-explanatory. It covers any persons whom you identify as being actively involved in the day-to-day operation of a bookmaking organization. These include the bookmaking operation you are investigating and any persons involved in the layoffs or operations of any other organization, such as bookmakers, sub-bookmakers, telephone men, and runners, and any other employees of the operations you uncover.

Area 2: Aggravated Bettor Profile

The purpose of the aggravated bettor profile is to establish a procedure and some guidelines to follow when considering which bettors should be prosecuted and which should be offered the chance to be a witness.

In most jurisdictions, police agencies very seldom go after the bettors involved in an operation. When you do, you will be bombarded with questions as to why you are doing so and why you have selected or singled out specific persons

Area 1

1. Bookmakers

2. Sub-Bookmakers

3. Employees of Operation

Culpability of Participants

1. Felony Charges

2. Misdemeanor Charges

Figure 18.20. Sample format for aggravated bettor arrests.

to prosecute. You should be able to provide a format for arrest of an aggravated bettor and demonstrate how and why the bettor was targeted for prosecution (Figure 18.20).

Persons who fit into any of the following areas will be classified as aggravated bettors, and considerations should be made as to their possible prosecution.

Prior Involvement

Prior convictions: The bettor has prior convictions for gambling and or other related offenses.

Prior involvement: The bettor has prior involvement in other gambling offenses, but to date no convictions are noted.

Volume of Betting

The total amount of money bet is excessive, and the total number of bets placed by the bettor is excessive.

Association With This Organization

Is the bettor located within the community of the bookmaker? Is the bettor located outside the community of the bookmaker and placing bets long distances?

Criminal Activities Other Than Gambling

- *Recruitment:* Is the bettor actively recruiting bettors for the bookmaker?
- *Financial investments:* Has the bettor invested money in the bookmaking operation?
- *Location:* Is the bettor providing the location for the bookmaking operation?
- *Inside information:* Is the bettor in a position to provide information to the bookmaker that could affect the lines on a given event (coach, player, trainer, etc.)?
- *Compromising position:* Is the bettor in a profession or does he hold a position which by the nature of his involvement could be compromised or controlled by the bookmaker (lawyer, doctor, police officer, etc.)?

- *Culpability:* Is the bettor profile of a nature which requires a *misdemeanor* charge? Is the bettor profile of such a nature which requires a *felony* charge?

Area 3: All Other Bettors Involved

You may consider having a third area which would contain all the other bettors involved. This list of bettors would become your pool of witnesses whom you need to interview and prepare for court. Again, their ability and willingness to cooperate is essential to your use of them in court proceedings.

The following are some actual examples from cases where bettors fit the aggravated profile and the reasons for concern:

1. *A professional athlete* calls long distance from another state to place bets with your target subject.
   Concerns: Is the player passing information to the bookmaker? Is the player shaving points on the games he is involved in? Why is he calling from one state to another to bet? Why can't he bet in his community?
2. *A doctor* is betting a large amount of money with your target subject.
   Concerns: Is the doctor in the department enough to provide an avenue for the bookmaker to obtain prescription drugs for narcotics operations?
3. *An attorney* is found to be a bettor on a book that is being run by his son-in-law. The volume of bets is large.
   Concerns: Has the attorney compromised his position as a criminal attorney? Has the attorney invested money in the operation?
4. *A retired police officer* is found to be a bettor of some size on several bookmakers' lists.
   Concerns: Is this person providing information on who and what is being investigated? Is he providing pictures and information about investigators involved in the investigation of bookmaking operations?
5. *A public official* is involved in a daily betting routine with the bookmaker. The size of the bets is not large, but the number of bets is large.
   Concerns: Has the official compromised his position by passing information about bids and contracts? Is the official attempting to deter investigation into bookmaking?
6. *A bank official* is involved in betting with a high volume bookmaker who is known to have influential political friends.
   Concerns: Is the bank official involved in laundering illegal money? Is the bank official issuing unsecured loans to bookmaking sources? Is the bank official in debt to the point where embezzlement is a possibility?

CASE EXAMPLE 1

November 9, 19XX: I received information that a bookmaker named Doe was attempting to set up a bookmaking operation in the area. The informant stated that the bookmaker was from Florida and he was trying to take over a large amount of the sports gambling by offering a greater variety to the public. I received a flyer that was printed for distribution by the bookmaker. Doe was offering over and unders, parlays from 2 to 6 teams, 7-point teasers, special 9- and 12-point teasers, and a 48-point scramble. Doe was brazen enough to put the hours and his two telephone numbers at the bottom of the $8\frac{1}{2} \times 11$ sheet. The informant also provided the address where Doe was working. On receiving this flyer I checked the crisscross and determined that the two telephones listed were nonpublished. I requested a subpoena for subscriber information and the last 2 months of toll records. I conducted a computer check on John Doe and determined that he had a brother living with him at the address provided by the informant. The brother had a traffic ticket issued the previous month. His name was James Doe and he held a current Florida driver's license.

November 10, 19XX: I went to the address provided and found that it was an apartment. I observed several vehicles parked outside. I obtained plate numbers from all the vehicles present and returned to the office where I conducted a computer check. I found that three vehicles were listed to the Doe brothers: Chevrolet Impala with Florida plates, Oldsmobile 88 with Florida plates, and a Jeep with Indiana plates. I obtained a copy of the lease for the apartment from an inside source and found that the Doe brothers had, in fact, just recently moved into the apartment. Their previous address was the one listed on their vehicle plates in Florida. I conducted a records check on the location and both Doe brothers, but I was unable to locate anything. I contacted several informants in the area and found that there was some concern developing in the bookmaking community about the new upstarts trying to take over the business. At this point in time, it was decided that an infiltration needed to be conducted to determine who was behind this operation.

November 11, 19XX: I received the subscriber information and toll record from the telephone company. The two telephones were listed to John Doe at the address provided by the informant. There was another telephone in the apartment that was listed to a third subject. The toll records contained a large number of long distance calls to what I found to be line services. I also located calls to numbers in several other states which appeared to be during the hours that the bookmaking telephones were open. Due to the fact that the bookmaking community was upset with the new boys on the block, it was relatively easy to get an introduction into the Doe operation. I needed a cover that would be hard to check on, so I decided to tell Doe that I drove a shuttle for a video store. If he needed to get a hold of me, he could call and leave a message. The video store owner was advised that anyone calling for me should be told that I was on the road and to take a message.

November 13, 19XX (1830 hours): I contacted John Doe by calling the number listed on the flyer. The number dialed was 222–3333. I introduced myself and told Doe that another bettor had given me the number and I was interested in getting a bet down. Doe proceeded to explain that the telephones would be open during the week until 6:30 P.M. and that settle up day was on Wednesday. Doe stated that he had a route on Wednesdays that took him to P's Restaurant at 7:00 A.M. until 7:30 A.M., B's Restaurant on the north side from 8:00 A.M. to 8:30 A.M., and M's Restaurant from 11:00 A.M. to 1:00 P.M. Doe stated that we could settle up at any of these locations. Doe requested that I provide him with information on myself so he could fill out a 3 × 5 card for his files. This was the first indication that he did in fact maintain files on location. I explained my cover to him and provided him with the telephone number of the video club. Doe informed me that until we met, he would have to put me on a $500.00 limit. I asked whether I could get a bet down now, and John Doe stated yes. John stated that his brother James would handle it. The next voice I heard was James Doe. He asked if I wanted the lines for the night's games, and I said yes. They were as follows:

NY Jets—5½ and 215
San Antonio—4½ and 217
Utah Jaz—8½ and 209½
Golden State—3 and 229½

James Doe then took my bet:

NJ—5½ for $200.00
NJ above 215 for $200.00

James Doe repeated my bet to me and said thanks and hung up. Just prior to hanging up, James informed me that when I called in, I should use my bettor identifier which would be no. 49. This information meant that the Doe brothers also had to keep records as to who each number was assigned to. In most departments, there is a limited amount of money that can be spent on an investigation. To limit our potential losses to 10%, as soon as I got the bet down with the Doe brothers, I contacted an informant and had him bet the opposite bets. This in effect would guarantee that on this bet my loss would only be the vigorish, which was $20.00 on each bet or $40.00 total.

November 14, 19XX: I obtained a newspaper and cut out the section on the sports page that listed the game I had bet on. I had won the first bet and lost the over and under bet. This newspaper article became part of my file.

November 14, 19XX (1715 hours): I called the Doe number, 222–3333, and John Doe answered. We talked for a couple of minutes about what he was doing and then he passed me to another subject whom John stated was Gary. John asked that I bear with him a bit because Gary was new and was trying to learn how to do the telephone work. Gary provided me with the lines on the games and I placed a bet:

Boston—+6 for $200.00
Boston over 216½ for $200.00

November 15, 19XX: I obtained a copy of the newspaper which listed the game I had bet on. Again I had won one and lost one. As I had done earlier, after I had talked to Gary and placed a bet, I called my informant and placed the opposite bet.

November 15, 19XX (1430 hours): I dialed 222–3333 and identified myself as no. 49. James stated, "What can I do for you JJ?" I asked for the lines and he began reading them to me. James finished the lines and said that John wanted to talk to me. John Doe got on the telephone, and I asked, "Is there a problem?" John said no, but he wanted to change my bettor ID number to 23 instead of 49. I asked, "Why the change?" and John stated that he wanted to keep the numbers from one on full. This gave me the indication that John had at least 48 bettors. At this time, John asked if I wanted to get a bet down, and I said yes. He took my bet.

Temple—+22½ for $200.00
Penn—4½ for $200.00

After my conversation with John, I contacted my informant and bet the opposite bet. Keep in mind that once you get bets down with a bookmaker, the more conversation you get the better your case will be. From this point on, I attempted to get in-depth conversation about how to bet different ways.

November 16, 19XX: I obtained a newspaper and found that I had won both games. Prior to this I was at −40, but with the $400.00 win, I was now at +360. My cover bets were at −$480.00. My total losses were $120.00.

November 17, 19XX: I called 222–3333 and identified myself as no. 23, and Gary asked what he could do for me. I referred to his flyer and asked for an explanation on how to bet a teaser. Gary asked me to hold and got John to explain it to me. After several minutes of explanation, I asked for the lines on that night's games. John passed the telephone back to Gary who read off the lines. In Indiana it is legal for me to record my conversation with the bookmakers. If it is legal in your area, it is recommended that you record all activities. I placed these bets with Gary:

Washington—−2 for $200.00
Washington—over 45 for $200.00.

I then asked Gary what my total figure was, and he asked James for my total. I could hear James in the background say +360. Gary repeated it to me. I said thanks and hung up. Again, I contacted my informant and had him place the opposite bets.

November 18, 19XX: I obtained a copy of the newspaper for my file. I had won one and lost one bet from the 17th. This put me at +$340.00 with James and −$500.00 with the cover bets.

November 20, 19XX (1710 hours): I dialed 222–3333 and stated, "This is no. 23." John asked what I needed. I asked for the lines and he gave them to me. I asked John if he could explain the 48-point scramble that was listed on his flyer. He went into a long explanation and then asked if I wanted to get a bet down. I told him the lines on the game I was interested in were too great, so I did not place a bet. Remember the conversation is the key at this stage. You do not have to bet each and every time you call.

November 24, 19XX: I dialed 222–3333 and talked to John; he gave me the lines on NY vs. Miami, as a pick and 53. I did not make a bet, but John stated that he would be at P's Restaurant from 0900 to 0930 hours, at S's Restaurant from 1000 to 1030 hours, and M's Restaurant from 1200 to 1300 hours if I wanted to settle up. Since I was concerned that Doe might identify me if we met, I said that we could carry my total over until Thursday; John agreed.

November 25, 19XX (1810 hours): I dialed 222–3333 and identified myself with my bettor ID number. John answered the telephone and gave me the lines on the NY vs. Houston game. I bet NY +4½ for $200.00. New York won 102 to 93 over Houston. I discussed where to meet John and we set it up to be at S's Restaurant between 10:00 and 10:30 A.M. on November 26, 19XX. I asked John to describe himself and his vehicle. He did so without any hesitation.

November 26, 19XX (1015 hours): Since I was concerned that John Doe would know me, I attempted to alter my appearance by putting on an old jumpsuit and a farmer's hat. I finished it off with a pair of my son's glasses. I entered the restaurant and observed a person matching the description of John Doe. I proceeded over to the table and introduced myself. Sitting at the table with Doe was a white male subject, dark skin, and about 50 years old. He was introduced as Black Jack. John Doe pulled out a list and looked up no. 23 and then pulled out a roll of bills. He counted $340.00 and handed it to me. I asked about the rest, and he informed me that the rest was on the next week's total. We sat and talked about the different games that we had bet, and Black Jack talked about a system that he had created. Doe left the location, and I observed him getting into the Olds 88 that we observed at the apartment. Black Jack got into a red Firebird with an Indiana plate, which I recorded. Again, this is legal in Indiana, but before you wear a recorder make sure it is legal in your area. As of this date John Doe owed me $400.00.

November 27, 19XX (1200 hours): I called 222–3333 and gave my bettor ID number, and John asked me how I was doing. I asked for the lines, and John read them off to me. I requested the following bet:

Green Bay—+6½ for $400.00

John read the bet back to me, and I hung up. I called the informant and had him place a bet that was the opposite of the one John had taken.

November 28, 19XX: I obtained a newspaper for my file which showed that Green Bay beat Detroit 44 to 40. My total with John was now +$800.00.

November 28, 19XX: I called 222–3333 and Gary answered. I gave my bettor ID number and asked for the lines. Gary read them off to me, and I then asked for my total. Gary had James Doe look it up for me. I could hear James Doe in the background tell Gary that my total was +$800. Gary relayed what James had said. I decided not to bet, so I told Gary that maybe I would tomorrow.

November 29, 19XX (1235 hours): I called 222–3334, which was the other betting line listed at John Doe's residence, and John answered. I gave my bettor identification number and requested the lines. I bet the following:

Georgia—10½ for $400.00

November 30, 19XX: I obtained a newspaper and found that the Georgia bet was a loser. I lost $400.00 which left me with a total of +$360.00.

November 30, 19XX (1150 hours): On this date, I called 222–3334 and requested the lines. James Doe read them off to me. The line on the Colts game was +8 and 44. I bet the following:

Colts under 44 for $400.00

The next day I again obtained a newspaper for the file. The final score in the Colts game was the Colts 3 and San Diego 17. The bet from the night before was a winner, and my total was raised to +$760.00.

December 1, 19XX (1715 hours): On this date I called 222–3333 and asked for the lines. Gary provided them to me, and I said that I would call back. A few minutes later I called back on the other line, 222–3334, and got James Doe. I placed the following bets:

Giants +4 for $400.00
Giants over 40½ for $400.00

This was the first time I had placed a bet of $800.00 on one night.

December 2, 19XX: I obtained a newspaper for the file and found that I had won one and lost one. This left my total at $320.00.

December 2, 19XX (1825 hours): On this date I dialed 222–3333 and John answered. I gave my bettor identification and requested the lines. John gave me to his brother James, who read the lines to me. At this time, I placed the following bet:

IU—5 for $400.00

After betting I talked to John, and he told me where he was planning to be to settle up and what times he would be there. I told him I would probably meet him at his last stop. As it turned out, I never met John to settle up because we were going to take him down on December 3, 19XX. (This bet resulted in a push or tie.)

December 3, 19XX: All during the time I was betting with the Doe brothers, the rest of the team was conducting the background check and surveillance that were necessary to identify the other persons involved in the organization. On the date that I met with John, the rest of the team was set up to cover all the settle up locations at the time when Doe was to be there. We videotaped and documented everyone who met with Doe. The team then had to perform background checks on all the license plates and people involved. Because of this background investigation, we were able to identify 15 bettors and two banks used by John Doe. A decision was made to take them off after John's last pickup so as to get as much information and currency as possible. As John Doe left the last location and approached his residence, we stopped him and served a search warrant that covered his vehicle, residence, and himself. I kept clear of Doe because we wanted him to wonder who had infiltrated his organization. The two detectives assigned to stop Doe were charged with the responsibility of conducting an interview with Doe on the spot. A search of John Doe turned up a list of bettors and a large amount of money. John Doe gave a confession and willingly accompanied us to his residence, where we were surprised to find that John Doe and his brother had a very large number of gambling documents in the residence.

Items recovered: We recovered records showing daily, weekly, and year-to-date totals for all the bettors. We recovered a large number of betting records and 13 90-minute cassettes, which were filled with betting transactions. We recovered the 3 × 5 cards that John had used and a sheet with the identifiers and names of all bettors. In addition to the gambling records, we also recovered a large amount of marijuana. Records recovered with the marijuana established that the Doe brothers were using the bookmaking operation to subsidize their other business, which was the importation and distribution of marijuana (Figure 18.21). They called it Doe's Investments. From the records seized, we determined that the Doe brothers were using an overnight mail delivery service to bring in the marijuana from Florida. There were several notations where a female had made trips from Florida as a courier. We discovered that the house telephone was a speed dial type with seven numbers listed. The first three numbers were local and the last four were out of state. The first two of these were for New York and a notation next to them was "Al Dimes Only." The next two were for Detroit and the notation was "Joe 2 Dimes." Additional documentation discovered described a computer program for sports bookmakers called "Soap." When we reviewed the cassette tapes, we discovered that a reference was made to the fact that they needed an open telephone so that "Soap" could use the line. From a review of the records, we discovered that numbers 10 and 12 on the bettor list were in fact running Doe's book and two others. We prepared two other search warrants for their

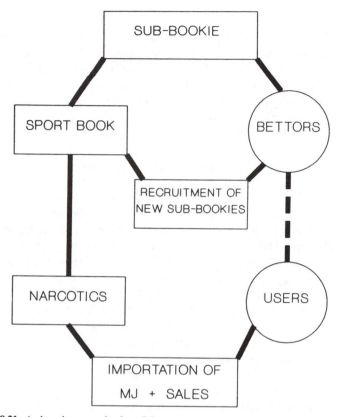

Figure 18.21. A chart demonstrating how John and James Doe set up their bookmaking business to promote the importation and distribution of marijuana.

residences and served them. We found that we missed a computer at one location and the suspect at the second had skipped town.

   End results: We targeted 10 bookmakers ranging from local people to people who were laying off from out of state; using the aggravated bettor profile, we targeted 17 bettors; we conducted 52 interviews and took statements; and those arrested ranged from athletes, attorneys, a doctor, and several very good golfers. To give an idea of the volume of business that was done by the Doe operation, one bettor risked $230,000.00 in 70 days.

CASE EXAMPLE 2

   November 14, 19XX: I received information from an informant who stated that a Mr. Doe and his wife were actively involved in both sports bookmaking and horse betting in this area. The informant further stated that the Doe couple also ran a large number of parlay cards in the area. The informant could not get me directly into the organization, but he did provide me with a location where one of Doe's runners would be gathering bets during the week around lunchtime. I conducted a background check on the information that the informant had provided. Both Doe and his wife had no prior arrests, but I did locate information showing that they did own their residence and a tavern in the area. I also determined from the background check that they had a 20-year-old son living at home and he had a prior arrest for possession of a controlled substance. With this information, I decided to attempt to infiltrate the operation by working a case on the runner and trying to "flip" him against the Doe family.

November 16, 19XX: I entered the tavern where the runner was supposed to be doing business. At approximately 1155 hours, a white male who matched the description provided by the informant entered the tavern and sat down next to me at the bar. He began to converse with the female bartender about how he had lost his ass on the horses the day before. The bartender laughed and said that he owed her for her bets too. The white male then pulled out a sheet of paper, checked the totals on it, and handed the bartender $72.00 and some change. He then said, "Now we are even." At this time, the bartender pulled out a current racing form and began to go through the races offered at the different tracks around the country. She conversed with the runner about several horses and then she placed three bets on horses with the runner. The bartender then asked whether the runner had any cards for her this week. The runner reached into his inside jacket pocket and pulled out about 40 parlay cards. The runner asked her how many she needed and she said about 30. The runner gave her a handful and stated that he would be around to pick them up on Thursday night or Friday morning. Then the runner prepared to leave and I followed him out. He got into an older model Ford pickup with Indiana plates. I wrote down the plate number and proceeded to the office, where I conducted a background check on the plate and its owner. When I ran the plate number, it came back to a Mr. Jones with a local address. Mr. Jones had two prior arrests for gambling-related offenses, both of which were minor unlawful gambling charges.

November 17, 19XX: I again entered the tavern at approximately 1100 hours and sat at the bar. I began talking to the same bartender who was present the day before. She was looking through a racing form at the time. I mentioned that I could never figure out how to use the form. She began to explain the form and its contents to me. As we talked, she explained how to determine what horse to bet on and how to figure out how much you won. As we were talking, Mr. Jones entered the tavern. He sat next to me and listened to her finish her explanation. He stated that all he needed was for her to teach other people her system. He asked her whether she was trying to put him out of business. I told him that he did not have anything to worry about with me, because I never win horse bets. I continued by saying that I did pretty well on football, but I could not get the hang of horse betting. He began to explain how easy it was to place a bet and how he figured the payoffs on a winner. He asked me whether I was interested in betting. I asked, "Football or horses?" He said either one. I asked the bartender to help me figure out what horse to bet. She did and I placed a bet on one to win. Shortly after this, I left the tavern.

November 20, 19XX (1105 hours): I entered the tavern with the intent of observing Mr. Jones pick up the parlay card stubs. The plan for that day was to observe Mr. Jones and then after he left the area to stop him and see whether he wanted to cooperate. Prior to this action, I had contacted a deputy prosecutor and obtained permission to offer Mr. Jones a deal for his help. Mr. Jones entered the tavern, picked up the parlay cards, and left. Approximately six blocks away from the tavern, we pulled Mr. Jones over. I went through all the charges that we had against him and asked whether he wanted to cooperate. Mr. Jones stated that he would help any way he could. At this time, we transported Mr. Jones to the office where we read him his rights and asked him to sign a waiver of rights form. We informed Mr. Jones that we would charge him if he failed to cooperate or if he leaked the fact that we were investigating the Doe operation.

Statement by Mr. Jones: The following information was obtained in the statement by Mr. Jones:

- The Does were involved in football, basketball, and horse betting. They did not take baseball bets.
- The two telephone numbers used were 234–5678 and 234–5679.
- The normal hours were during the week from 5:00 P.M. until 6:30 P.M. On weekends, bets were taken up to 1 hour before the games started.
- The Doe operation ran close to 4,000 parlay cards a week.
- Doe's wife handled the telephone work, and Mr. Doe did the pickups and settling up himself.
- Doe would pay Jones 25% of the profit that he brought in on bets.
- Jones gave several other locations that Doe had on his route.

During the conversation that followed the statement, Mr. Jones agreed to place bets with the Doe operation for us. At this time, I took Mr. Jones into my office and I dialed the number he provided as being that of Mr. Doe. The number, 234–5678, was answered by a female who Mr. Jones recognized as Mrs. Doe. I had Mr. Jones place several bets with Mrs. Doe and then get the lines on the next day's games. She provided them, and Mr. Jones thanked her and hung up. Mr. Jones was allowed to leave, but we reminded him to not let anyone know what was happening. After Mr. Jones left, I obtained a subpoena for the two numbers that had been provided as being the betting lines for the Doe operation. I requested both subscriber and toll information.

November 23, 19XX: I received the subscriber information and tolls from the telephone company. I found that the telephones were listed to Mr. Doe at the address we were provided by Mr. Jones. I also found that the toll records showed that Mr. Doe was calling line services on a daily basis. I proceeded to the residence, obtaining a good description of the property for my search warrant and three license plate numbers from vehicles that were parked there.

November 23, 19XX: I set up a surveillance on Mr. Doe's residence to track him on his rounds as he dropped off the parlay cards. We observed Mr. Doe driving his Cadillac to several parking lots around town. At each location Mr. Doe would stop in the outer lot and sit with his motor running. As we observed, several vehicles would pull up next to Doe and he would hand them packages wrapped in white. This is typical of the way parlay cards are wrapped from the printer. We made note of the vehicles and the plate numbers and tracked Mr. Doe until he returned to his residence.

November 24, 19XX (1730 hours): I met with Mr. Jones and chose an event to bet on. I dialed telephone number 234–5679, at which time Mrs. Doe answered and asked what we needed. We asked for the lines on that night's games, and then we placed a bet. We requested our totals, and Mrs. Doe provided them. We thanked her and hung up. During the time of this phone conversation, I had members of my team at Mrs. Doe's residence to verify that she was in fact taking the calls there and not using call forwarding. The surveillance team reported that Mrs. Doe was at the residence when the bet was placed.

November 25, 19XX (1745 hours): I dialed 234–5678 and Mrs. Doe answered. We requested the lines and Mrs. Doe read off what she had. We informed her that we did not want to get a bet down at this time, but we would call tomorrow. Again, team members were at the Doe residence to verify that Mrs. Doe was at home when she provided us with the lines.

November 27, 19XX (1800 hours): We observed Mr. Doe leave his residence in his blue Mazda and proceed to a parking lot on the west side of town. After a short wait a car pulled up next to Doe, and the driver of this car handed Mr. Doe a small brown paper sack. They talked for a short time and the other vehicle then left. While we observed Mr. Doe in the lot, we noted that seven vehicles pulled up to Doe at which time the drivers of these vehicles would hand Doe small paper sacks. After about 45 minutes, Doe left the parking lot and proceeded home. We contacted Mr. Jones and told him what we observed, and he stated that Doe picked up the parlay cards when he went out each Friday. Jones stated that Doe preferred to meet in parking lots so that he could see whether he was being followed.

November 26, 19XX (1130 hours): On this date I dialed number 234–5678, and Mr. Doe answered the telephone. We inquired about the lines on all the games for that day, and Mr. Doe read them off to us. We asked what our total was, and Doe looked it up and gave it to us. We then placed a bet on a football game played that day. Mr. Doe thanked us and hung up. After this bet was made, we decided to terminate the investigation, agreeing that the best time to hit the location was on Saturday morning. By doing so, we would get a large amount of parlay cards from Friday's collection and a large amount of bets from Friday night, and the telephones would be open so that we could take bets over Doe's telephones when we arrived. We continued to call and get the lines and place bets during the week. The last bet was on December 4, 19XX. We obtained a search warrant for Doe's residence and two of his vehicles. Our target time for the raid was 1100 hours on Saturday, December 5, 19XX.

December 5, 19XX (1100 hours): We served the search warrant at Doe's address. Mr. and Mrs. Doe were present. After reading the warrant to them, a member of the raid team placed a recorder on the telephone and began taking bets. Again, in Indiana this is legal, but I suggest that you get the okay from your legal advisor before you do this type of activity in your area.

Items recovered: As we first entered the residence, we observed Mr. Doe slip a book behind the couch and come to the door. After we read the warrant to him, I recovered the book. It contained sheet after sheet of both football and horse bets. During the search, we seized several bags of gambling records, line sheets, and gambling paraphernalia. We seized a small quantity of controlled substance from the son's room and 4,841 parlay card stubs for that week. It was projected that Mr. Doe's gross income from parlay cards was $10,000.00 per week, or $160,000.00 for the whole football season. Doe's sports betting operation was projected to be at least twice the parlay business.

End results: In a situation such as this, you may want to contact the FBI and request assistance in figuring out what the seized records represent. In this case, we arrested the Doe family for racketeering and filed a civil forfeiture. In keeping with our procedures, we included the state IRS in this case, which filed both criminal and civil charges. Keep in mind that once you serve the search warrant, you are not finished. Each person implicated should be examined. All vehicles and people involved in the parlay business need to be identified and a determination made as to whether an investigation should be done on them. We subsequently found that Doe had 29 people running parlay cards for him and 15 people functioning as sub-bookies.

CASE EXAMPLE 3

There are times when out of necessity you will have a case where you observe the activity and you have to take action right away. If possible, you should have what information you have typed up in a search warrant form so that you can lessen the time it takes to get a warrant signed. You may consider checking into anticipatory search warrants.

May 15, 19XX: I received information that a co-owner of the Dregs Bar, located at 98 West 7th, was going to be taking bets on the Preakness Horse Race on Saturday, May 16, 19XX. Post time for the race was 1640 hours. The co-owner, Jane Doe, was going to have a party at the bar starting at 1000 hours. I conducted a background check on the bar and the co-owner and found that there had been two prior investigations at the tavern. Both investigations were involving illegal poker machines. I obtained ownership information on the tavern and found that Jane Doe and her husband, John, were the sole owners of both the property and the tavern. I checked the reports that were filed on the earlier investigations and found that both times there were several handguns seized from the bar. John Doe was listed in both cases. I contacted the detective who had conducted the prior investigations and requested any information that could help our investigation. He provided me with a floor plan and made note of several hiding places he had found in his search. He also informed me that Mr. Doe was tied to some powerful people in the area.

May 16, 19XX (1015 hours): We arrived at the Dreg Bar. Prior to our entry, we made a sweep of the area and wrote down all the license plate numbers and descriptions of vehicles close to the tavern. The night before we had prepared a search warrant for which we could fill in the blanks if we needed to get a warrant in a hurry. At 1100 hours we entered the tavern and sat at a table that gave us a clear view of the bar area. We ordered lunch and began our observation. We noted a Double D Poker Machine sitting in the northeast corner of the room. There were several people in line waiting to play the machine. We observed a large number of empty quarter rolls on the floor and a lot of wear and tear of the machine. We saw patrons putting a large number of quarters into the machine. At the bar, we observed two females, one of which fit the description of the co-owner of the tavern. We overheard several patrons call her Jane. We saw the other female, a waitress, going from table to table taking what appeared to be horse bets. We overheard conversations such as, Snow Chief for $10.00 across the board and Ferdinand for $15.00 to win. As the waitress came closer, we observed her writing the bets that were being requested on a small pad. While we watched the waitress, the co-owner of the tavern came out of the back room and began taking bets at our end of the room. We overheard patrons joking with Jane Doe about their bets. One stated that if he did not win, he was going to have her arrested for being a bookmaker and he would throw in the illegal poker machine in the corner for good measure. Jane Doe laughed and continued her rounds of the tables taking bets. Jane Doe approached our table and informed us that she could not take a bet from us because her husband had told her if she did not take bets from any strangers, then the police could not arrest her. She apologized and went to the next table and took their bets. At this time we decided to have my partner go to the office and fill in the blanks of the warrant and return as soon as it was signed. He left and I continued to document the activities that were going on around me.

1300 hours: My partner returned and entered the tavern. He sat back down with me and we mapped out how we wanted to take the place down. By now there were about 70 people present, and we decided that we would need four district cars for the initial take down. We called from the pay telephone and had the cars come in. Just prior to their entry, I moved up to the bar so I could observe any activity that the co-owner would do to dispose of the betting records. My partner positioned himself so that he had a good view of the main body of patrons and could see their reaction when the police entered. He was to key on people whose reaction might indicate they were wanted or holding. As it turns out, we both got lucky. When the uniformed officers entered, my partner observed two people drop handguns and one drop an ounce of cocaine. I observed the co-owner gather up a large quantity of records and start to move to the back room. As it was, she walked over to me (and I said thanks). I then identified myself and read her the search warrant.

Items seized: Included were 40 sheets of paper with horse bets on them, several racing forms, payoff sheets for the poker machine and bingo machine, a box labeled Preakness betting box, one poker machine with a remote knock off switch, one bingo machine, and over $1,000.00 in cash.

CASE EXAMPLE 4

September 7, 19XX: I received a complaint from a subject who had eaten at Joe's Family Restaurant located at 123 W. 431. The complainant stated that while he and his son were at the restaurant, he observed a subject standing in the hallway by the bathroom using the telephone. As the complainant passed the suspect, he heard him talking about sports betting and observed that the suspect was writing down bets on a small notepad. The complainant hesitated as he passed, and the suspect turned on him and his son and told the complainant to keep on moving or he would "beat the shit out of him." This upset the son to the point where he began crying. The complainant further stated that the suspect drove off in a brown 1986 Chevy. This incident had occurred between 1700 and 1800 hours on September 6, 19XX.

September 8, 19XX (1700 hours): I went by Joe's Restaurant and observed a brown 1986 Chevy in the parking lot matching the description that had been provided. I obtained the plate number and had it checked. I had little or no information on who the bookmaker was, so I decided to make a soft entry to verify the information that I had received. I entered and sat at a table where I could observe the hall and telephone. I ordered a sandwich. After a short time, a white male subject went to the pay telephone and began making calls. The subject had a notebook in his hand. Shortly after the subject made his call, the telephone began to ring on a regular basis. The subject would answer and make notes on his pad. I noticed that anytime anyone walked by the subject, he would turn and glare at them. I decided to go to the bathroom so that I could get a closer look at the subject. I timed it so that the subject had just answered the telephone and was talking. As I passed, I overheard the subject say, "That was Indiana +5 for $100.00, right Jim? OK. I've got you down." At this time the subject turned and gave me a hard look, and I entered the bathroom. As I left the bathroom, I again overheard the subject refer to betting. I went to the register and paid my bill and left. Since I had no information on who the subject was, I did not want to take him off just yet. As I left, I walked by his vehicle and observed several betting sheets on the seat of his car. I also observed a large number of sports schedules in the back seat. I returned to the office and conducted a background check on the subject and found that he was a small-time bookmaker who had been convicted before for sports bookmaking. I decided to pay another visit to the restaurant on Wednesday. If he was still conducting business, I would confront the subject and see what happened.

September 9, 19XX (1700 hours): I again went to the restaurant and observed the subject's car in the lot. I walked by his vehicle and again observed gambling paraphernalia in the vehicle. I entered the restaurant and sat where I could observe the hall and the telephone. As I had found the previous day after the subject went to the telephone and made a call, the telephone began to ring off and on. Each time the telephone would ring, the subject would answer and write in a small notebook. He continued this activity for several minutes before I decided to do a walk by. As before, I waited until the subject had just answered the telephone before I walked down the hall to the bathroom. As I passed the subject, I heard several references made to lines and I overheard the subject say, "That's Miami over 32 for $100.00." I entered the bathroom and shortly thereafter I returned to my table. I continued to watch the subject until 1830 hours when the subject hung up and left the location. I followed and watched the subject enter his car and drive east. I contacted communication and requested a car with uniformed officers to assist. We stopped the subject just out of the area to limit the number of people who would see the stop. As soon as we stopped the subject, he began to "go off on" the uniformed officer. The subject was arrested for promoting professional gambling. I turned him in to the IRS and we seized his vehicle. My intent was to offer this subject a chance to cooperate, but instead we had to arrest him. Keep this in mind when you are trying to work from a low level person to an upper level bookmaker. Some of the people you want to "flip" will not cooperate. Never let them know whom you want to target, but instead ask them what they can do in the way of introductions. If they do not mention the person you want, do not bring it up unless you want to risk your target being warned.

CASE EXAMPLE 5

Remember, information that you receive and the documentation that you seize from a given location may be used in a probable cause against another target. The following is an example:

September 22, 19XX (1430 hours): I served a search warrant at 234 W. Lyn, under case no. XYZ012. During the search, I discovered documentation that Jim Doe was actively involved in sports bookmaking at 90 E. Tenth. The documentation consisted of several checks written to the bookmaker on Lyn Street; numerous betting records with Jim Doe listed along with his home telephone number; and Jim Doe's name, address, and telephone number on a description sheet describing Jim Doe as a large bookmaker with a $10,000.00 limit.

December 3, 19XX (1430 hours): I served a search warrant at 987 W. 11th, under case number XYZ123. During this search, I seized a large quantity of gambling records and 13 90-minute cassette tapes with a large number of recorded wagers. Within the records that I seized, I discovered that Jim Doe of 90 E. Tenth was laying off bets to the subject at 987 W. 11th. The following are some examples of layoff bets from Doe to this location on October 11, 19XX:

Colorado	$-7\frac{1}{2}$ for $800.00
Miami	$- 4$ for $800.00
Denver	$+9$ for $1,100.00
Rams	-6 for $1,200.00

Above the written bets was a notation "layoff." When I received the cassettes, I discovered several conversations between the bookmaker at 987 W. 11th and Mr. Doe. Doe would call and ask for the other bookmaker's lines, and they would discuss how their individual bookmaking operations were doing. In several of the conversations, Doe would provide the other bookmaker with his home or office telephone number. One number in the records was listed to J&C Construction at 11 W. West Street.

December 8, 19XX: I requested the subscriber information from the telephone company and the toll records from October and November 19XX. I checked the crisscross and found that the telephone number found in the seized records, 123–4567, was listed to J&C Construction. I contacted the State Corporations Division and found that there was no listing for a J&C Construction at 11 W. West Street. I also contacted city licensing and found that there had never been any permits issued to any organization named J&C Construction.

December 9, 19XX: I went by the address provided in the seized records and found that the building in question housed several small business entities. I located the office space which had J&C Construction listed on it. The time was 1400 hours. I observed that it appeared to be a small one room office with no windows. While I was in the hall just outside the door, I got the feeling that this was a vacant office. I obtained a description of the office building and the exact location of the door to J&C Construction. I looked around at the other offices in the building and discovered one striking difference between them and the office occupied by J&C Construction. Each of the other offices had interior windows, either in the walls or in the door, and each office had outside windows which provided a variety of views of the outside areas. In the case of J&C Construction, it appeared that the door had been replaced with a solid door so that a person could not see in, and the location where the exterior window had been was covered by a large piece of exterior siding. At this point in time, I decided to return to this location during betting hours to see whether there was any activity. In the meantime, the rest of the team assisted in the background check on the subject, the business, and the residence. While we conducted the background search on Mr. Doe, we discovered that he had two prior arrests for promoting professional gambling. One charge showed that no affidavit had been filed by the prosecutor, and the second was reduced from a felony to an unlawful gambling charge. Both charges listed the home address of Doe as the arrest location.

December 10, 19XX: I contacted several informants and requested information on Jim Doe. I found that it was common knowledge in the gambling community that Jim Doe was active in illegal sports bookmaking. Each one of the informants gave the information that Doe no longer worked out of his house for fear that we would seize it under the RICO Act. They further stated that Jim Doe had set up a business front from which to run his bookmaking operation.

December 10, 19XX (1730 hours): I returned to the address of J&C Construction and observed two vehicles in the lot that had not been there on the previous occasion. I made note of the plate numbers on those vehicles and then proceeded into the main entrance of the building. I walked down the hallway toward the door marked J&C Construction. Within two doors of J&C, I heard telephones ringing and two male voices. The closer I got to the door, the clearer the conversations inside J&C Construction were. From the conversations that I heard as I walked by, I realized that the two male voices were taking bets over the telephone. I overheard one male say, "Okay, Bill, that's Denver −5 for a nickel and Penn State pick for 300." I continued down the hallway and exited the building at the rear. I proceeded to the parking lot and walked by the two vehicles. Inside the blue Mazda, I observed a stack of football schedules and a piece of brown paper with the notation, "Jim, Chi +$100.00." I continued on through the lot and returned to my vehicle. I drove to my office and ran a check on the license plates that were on these vehicles. The blue 1989 Mazda was registered to Jim Doe at his residence; the other vehicle, a red Chrysler New Yorker, was registered to John Smith. I ran a background check on Mr. Smith and located one prior arrest for gambling-related charges.

December 11, 19XX: I received the subscriber information and toll records from the telephone company and found that there were three telephones listed to J&C Construction at the address listed. I also found that the bill for the telephones was being sent to A. J. Smith at 246 E. 73rd. The 73rd address is the same address listed to the red Chrysler New Yorker that was located in the lot. The toll records showed that the company was calling line services on a daily basis, and there were calls to seven other states including Michigan, Nevada, New Jersey, and Florida.

December 12, 19XX (1700 hours): I arrived at J&C Construction and observed the same two vehicles as before parked in the lot. I set up a surveillance on the parking lot and waited for the two males to exit the building and get into their vehicles. At 1920 hours, both subjects came out of the building and walked toward the vehicles. As I took photos of the two subjects, I noticed the subject known as John Smith was carrying a yellow trash bag in his left hand. Mr. Smith made a slight detour to a dumpster and dropped the bag in it. Both subjects stopped at the rear of their vehicles and talked for a short time and then left. I waited a few minutes and then went to the dumpster and retrieved the yellow bag. I noted that there was no other yellow bag in the dumpster. I left the location and proceeded to the office where I opened the bag of trash, after putting on rubber gloves and a mask. Inside I discovered envelopes that has passed through the U.S. mail with J&C Construction and the address 11 W. West Street. Some of these letters were from people outside the area. In addition to the above, I discovered several sports schedules which had the lines written in next to them. One sheet of paper I located had notations such as Denver +3½ for $100.00 and Illinois −7 for

$600.00. Each one of these notations had what appeared to be a bettor identifier number listed before the bet.

December 15, 19XX (0600 hours): I set up a surveillance on Mr. Doe's residence with the intent of following Mr. Doe as he made his rounds to settle up with his bettors. At 0600 hours, Mr. Doe left his residence and proceeded to Don's Deli, located at 765 W. First. He entered the deli and took a seat just inside the door. My partner entered the deli and positioned himself so that he could photograph anyone who met with Mr. Doe. We were using a 35-mm camera hidden inside a gym bag to obtain covert photos. My partner was wired with a body wire and as people would meet with Doe he would call them off, and I was responsible for getting the license plate numbers from their vehicles. Our main reason for the surveillance was to obtain a list of potential witnesses to counteract any political clout that Mr. Doe might try to employ. During the 30 minutes that Doe was at the deli, he met with seven people, two of whom through conversation were determined to be bookmakers. My partner kept records of all the conversations that he overheard. In each case the discussions centered around gambling activities. At 0630 hours Doe left the deli, drove to a truck stop on the south side, and sat in the parking lot. We observed five vehicles exit the interstate and pull up next to Mr. Doe. The occupants would converse for a short time and then they would pass an envelope. Three of the people passed Doe an envelope with Doe passing the envelope to the other two. From here Doe went to a donut shop on the west side, arriving at 0730 hours. Doe entered the shop and began making calls on the pay telephone. Doe completed several calls, then sat down and had coffee. We had another member of the team enter the shop and again position herself so that she would be able to photograph the activity involving Doe. In this situation we used a 35-mm camera inside a handbag for the photos. Doe met with nine different people in the next hour, all of whom were dressed as construction workers. Each time Doe would refer to a sheet of paper in his shirt pocket, and money would exchange hands between Doe and the other subject. As before, each conversation centered around gambling activities. At 0845 hours, Doe left the donut shop.

0900 hours: Mr. Doe arrived at the DORP National Bank, located at 5678 North Vernon. Mr. Doe entered the bank and went to a teller, making what appeared to be a deposit. Then Mr. Doe returned to his residence where he pulled his vehicle into the garage and closed the door. While part of the team maintained the surveillance, one member went to the office and prepared a subpoena for information from the bank as to the number of accounts and the volume of business conducted from the accounts listed to Mr. Doe. Since we intended to ''take off'' Mr. Doe's operation within 2 days, the bank information was necessary so that when the warrant was served, we could also freeze the bank accounts. When we received the information from the bank, we found that Doe had a checking and savings account with a total of $120,000 in them.

1100 hours: Mr. Doe opened his garage door and left the residence with the surveillance team following. Mr. Doe drove to the Italian House located at 11th and Main. Mr. Doe entered and went into the back room for a short period of time. When he came out of the back room, he was observed putting an envelope into his inside shirt pocket. Mr. Doe then sat down at a table and had lunch. When Doe finished lunch, he returned to his residence, and the surveillance team broke off the track.

December 15, 19XX (1500 hours): I received a call from an informant who had been checking into the background of Jim Doe. This informant stated that Doe was going to leave town on December 20, 19XX, and would not return until after the first of the year. The informant further stated that he had obtained a business card that Jim Doe and John Smith used for their sports bookmaking operation. I set up a meeting at 1545 hours to pick up this card. The card that I received from the informant was a tan business card with the name Jim in the lower left-hand corner and the number 123–4567 above the name. In the lower right-hand corner of the card was the name John and above it was a second number 123–4568, which is listed with the telephone company to J&C Construction. In the middle of the card was a football player, a basketball, and a horse. Due to the fact that the informant had found out that Doe was leaving on the 20th, we decided to serve search warrants on the 18th. In order to keep our information fresh, we decided to check the business each night during the time that betting was being conducted and do a trash search, if possible.

December 16, 19XX (1730 hours): We set up a surveillance at J&C Construction. We observed Doe's and Smith's vehicles parked in the lot. We walked through the hallway outside the business to verify that the office was in fact occupied. As I walked by, I again heard two male voices inside conducting business. The conversation I overheard was "Okay, Mark, you want the numbers, okay. Penn +4½, Navy −3, Ill +7, and Army −8." I continued to walk down the hallway and exited the building. I returned to the surveillance site and waited to observe the subjects leave.

December 16, 19XX (1900 hours): We observed both Mr. Doe and Mr. Smith exit the building. As previously, Mr. Smith was carrying a small yellow bag. Mr. Smith proceeded to the dumpster and dropped the trash bag into it. Mr. Smith and Mr. Doe then got into their vehicles and left the location. At this time, we recovered the trash bag from the dumpster, taking it to the office where we did an inventory. Inside, we found U.S. mail that had been addressed to J&C Construction at the target address and a large number of betting sheets which had been torn up. When we put them together, we discovered that the betting records were dated December 15, 19XX.

December 17, 19XX (1700 hours): We again set up surveillance on J&C Construction. We observed the two vehicles which we had identified as belonging to the subjects. Again the subjects dumped trash into the dumpster located there. We recovered the trash and inventoried the contents. As before, we recovered U.S. mail with the business and the address listed, and also betting records and other documentation consistent with sports bookmaking.

December 18, 19XX (1740 hours): We arrived at the target location. We deployed the team and proceeded to the hallway outside the business where we again heard the two males actively involved in sports gambling activities. We knocked and Mr. Doe came to the door and asked us what we wanted. We identified ourselves and secured the two subjects as we read the warrant to them. Two of the team members placed recorders on the telephones and began taking bets over the telephone. When we concluded the reading of the warrant, we began to videotape the location as we found it. We followed up the video with 35-mm pictures of specific items of interest. We discovered a large number of bets with bettor total sheets and bettor identifiers. We located a stack of 30 envelopes which had been preaddressed and stamped for the mail. The names on these letters matched the names on the bettor total sheet that we obtained from Mr. Doe's right front shirt pocket. We discovered several checkbooks with notations in them as to checks written to the people on the bettor total sheet. We seized documentation as to who several bookmakers in the area were. Two members of the team went to the parking lot and searched the two vehicles listed on the warrant. They discovered two boxes of football schedules and several betting records in Doe's car and several line sheets and bets in Smith's car. Both vehicles were seized and forfeited.

December 19, 19XX: On this date, we began the job of correlating the information we had obtained the night before. We attempted to match up each bettor identifier number with a name and address. We were able to identify 22 of the bettors on the list. At this time, team members began contacting the bettors and seeing whether they wanted to cooperate. Each contact was made by telephone and each was recorded. As I said before, you should check with your legal advisor to be sure that you can record your conversations in your area. The reason for telephone contact and recording is because when a person is contacted out of the blue, he is likely to give himself up out of surprise. This way, if he later denies what he said earlier, you will have it on tape. It is also nice to have his voice on tape so that you can compare it to the voices that called in to you and placed bets while you served your warrant.

Questions asked: Keep in mind that another goal of your investigation is to develop intelligence information and informants. With each individual we interviewed, we developed a set of questions that would elicit responses which would assist us not only in the criminal trial, but also in determining how the illegal organization functioned. We were interested in how they met the bookmaker, where they met, and how the bookmaker approached the bettor. Questions were asked such as, "Were there any perceived threats involved in the collection of debts and who else was involved in the day-to-day workings of the organization?" You should always ask the person, "Are you now or ever have been involved with another bookmaker?" In many cases, a bettor will have several bookmakers with whom he can place bets. This is how you will develop introductions into other illegal organizations. In the case listed, we ended up with seven bettors who helped us infiltrate other operations.

CASE EXAMPLE 6

November 9, 19XX: I served a search warrant at 765 N. Waldow on a subject named Robert Doe. During the search of the location, I discovered a large quantity of gambling records. Among these records we found line sheets, bettor total sheets, individual bets, and a large amount of receipts which established that Mr. Doe also had an illegal poker machine business. In addition to the above records, we also recorded numerous bets over the telephone located at 765 N. Waldow. Some examples of these bets are as follows:

Mike N.D.　　−6 for $400.00
Tim J. In　　+4 for $200.00
Vill　　　　 +7 for $200.00
Ill pick for $200.00
Ill over 30 for $200.00

Charges were filed on Doe. The case proceeded through the court system where, with no advance notice, Mr. Doe was brought in and pleaded guilty to a misdemeanor. He received a $60.00 fine and walked. Needless to say, I began to conduct a background check to determine who Mr. Doe's power base was and determine whether my case had been enough to make Mr. Doe stop bookmaking.

December 7, 19XX: I received a call from an informant who stated that Doe was still bookmaking. In fact, he had never stopped. The informant further stated that Doe was bookmaking at the same location on Waldow that I had hit before, and he was still using the same telephone numbers. The two numbers were 123–4567 and 123–4569. During the next several weeks, I conducted a background check to determine who his power base was. I located records showing that Mr. Doe sponsored a FOP softball team and a fire department softball team and had purchased a tavern which was a favorite hangout for undercover detectives. I also determined that Mr. Doe had numerous friends in the legal profession, including a few judges. From the look of things, it appeared that Mr. Doe was using the tavern to launder money from the illegal bookmaking operation.

January 4, 19XX: I decided that I had enough information on Mr. Doe's power base to begin another investigation, this time in such a way that I would be able to take the case into a higher felony court which was not affected by Mr. Doe's manipulation. I began gathering information on how Mr. Doe was running the book, and I attempted to determine whether he had any changes in his operation. Due to the sensitivity of this case, I limited the number of officers involved to myself and one partner.

January 5, 19XX: I received a call from an informant who stated that Doe was still actively involved in sports bookmaking using telephone numbers 123–4567 and 123–4569. I contacted the telephone company and requested by subpoena the subscriber information and toll records for the last 3 months. Because of the sensitivity of this case, I delivered the subpoena to the head of security of the telephone company (I had identified him as reliable) and requested that he conduct the search and have no contact with anyone on this case except me. He agreed. I reviewed my prior case with the intent of using it as a point in time where I could show that illegal activity was being conducted by Doe. I needed to show the continuing enterprise covered several months. With information from informants and prior family involvement in bookmaking, I could show that the illegal activity spanned several years. I determined that two brothers assisted in the day-to-day running of the sports bookmaking. They were James and John Doe. I further found that when they assisted with the telephone work, Robert would transfer the telephones by using the call forwarding feature.

January 6, 19XX: I conducted a check on each of the three residences where the brothers lived to update the information I had from the prior investigation. I established that the three still lived at the same locations and their vehicles had remained the same as had been found in the first investigation. In the previous investigation, I had determined that during football season Doe would settle up on Tuesday morning, and during basketball season when there was no Monday night football he would settle up on Monday. I also determined that his last stop was his tavern, The Duce, located at 321 W. 71st.

January 7, 19XX (1100 hours): I set up a loose surveillance of the tavern in an attempt to identify whether and when any law enforcement officers frequented the location. I had to determine a time of day when I could enter the location and conduct my investigation. Based on several days of surveillance, I decided that from 1100 hours until around 1200 hours was the best time to enter without being "decked." Each time I observed the tavern I obtained plate numbers from vehicles and kept a license plate log on the location.

January 10, 19XX: I set up a surveillance on Robert Doe's residence. The purpose of this surveillance was to determine whether Doe had changed his pattern of settling up debts. At 0700 hours, Mr. Doe left this residence, got into his 1990 Buick, and proceeded to Joy's Deli, located at 1070 IB Avenue. Mr. Doe entered and ordered coffee. For the next hour, Doe greeted nine people and with each one an envelope was exchanged. Two of the nine sat with Doe, and they in turn also greeted several other subjects. They also exchanged envelopes with the people who approached them. While Mr. Doe was inside, we were taking videos of the activity and we also obtained license plate numbers from the vehicles of the people who entered the deli and approached Mr. Doe's table.

January 10, 19XX (0800 hours): Mr. Doe left the deli, and as in the past he drove to the Brown Restaurant, arriving there at 0820 hours. He entered and sat with his back to the wall in the southwest corner. As at the deli, several people entered and an exchange of envelopes occurred. Each person who approached Doe was videotaped, and the plates on their vehicles were recorded. At 0930 hours, Mr. Doe left the restaurant and went to the Dyno Doughnut Shop, located as 123 E. Elvin. At this location Mr. Doe entered, walked up to the owner, and handed him several envelopes. The owner in turn reached behind the register, pulled out several envelopes, and handed them to Mr. Doe. I made note in the file that this location should be checked much closer in the future. Doe left this location and proceeded to the Tye Auto Auction. Mr. Doe left his vehicle, went inside, and was observed looking at a vehicle on the lot. Doe then left the auction and returned home.

January 10, 19XX (1200 hours): Doe left his residence, drove to the Greek Isle Restaurant, and parked in the lot. Mr. Doe entered the restaurant and sat at a table with several other subjects. Currency exchanged hands between several of the subjects, and then they began to eat their lunch. Lunch was concluded, and the subjects left at 1330 hours.

January 11, 19XX (1100 hours): I entered the Duce Tavern located at 321 W. 71st. As I entered, I observed that the bartender was in the process of turning on all the electronic devices located within the tavern. Among these items were several poker machines. There were three patrons inside the tavern, and I sat at the bar next to them. I requested the lunch special and ordered a drink. When my meal arrived, I took it and the drink and moved to a table close to the door. I positioned myself so that if anyone came in, I could see them first. If they could deck me, I would be able to leave before being seen. As I sat there, I observed one of the patrons get a roll of quarters from the bartender and approach one of the poker machines. The patron deposited all the quarters into the machine, and I observed that the right to replay was located on the face of the machine. As he dropped coins in, the number was displayed in the upper left-hand corner. As he pressed the bet button, the total was reduced and the amount of the bet showed up in the lower right-hand corner. The patron pressed the deal button and five face cards were displayed on the face of the screen. The patron decided which cards he wanted to keep and pressed the discard button under the cards he did not want. When he pressed the deal again, the discarded cards were replaced with new ones. When a winning hand was obtained, the option was given to double up or take the score. When a winning hand was obtained and taken, the numbers were added to the total. While present, I overheard conversations with the bartender in reference to paying off on the poker machines. I also heard reference to betting on different sporting events. Since it was approaching noon, I felt I had to leave rather than risk the chance of being decked. I left the tavern and obtained plate numbers from the vehicles in the tavern lot. I returned to the office and noted in the file the descriptions of the patrons in the tavern. I conducted a background check on the plates and identified the person playing the poker machine through the files located at the Bureau of Motor Vehicles. From this point on, it was decided that we would serve warrants on both the residence and the tavern. We intended to file RICO charges and civil forfeiture, and give the rest to the IRS.

January 12, 19XX: I was contacted by an informant who could provide me with a card that was passed out by Robert Doe. The card in question listed the betting lines on it and the names Robert, Jim, and John. I met with the informant and obtained the card. During the conversation that I had with him, I discovered that this informant could place bets with Robert Doe. I set up a meeting with the informant for 1730 hours, at which time we would attempt to place a bet with Mr. Doe.

January 12, 19XX (1500 hours): We went to the tavern and without being seen, we placed a large piece of cardboard inside the dumpster which was used by the tavern. The purpose of this cardboard was to separate the trash that was already inside the dumpster from that thrown out on this date. This would assist us in placing a time and date on the records we discovered.

January 12, 19XX (1700 hours): I met with the informant and we discussed the procedures that were being used by Robert Doe. I found that Doe used a number system to identify his bettors. I dialed Doe's number, 123–4567, and a male voice answered. The informant gave his bettor identification number and asked who he was talking to. The male stated, "This is James, what can I do for you?" The informant asked for the lines and James proceeded to read them off to us. After the lines were read, we requested the informant's totals. The total owed by the informant was substantial, and this is why the informant had come forward to assist us in the investigation. The informant placed a bet for $400.00 and then hung up. I set up another meeting with the informant at 1700 hours the next night.

January 13, 19XX (0300 hours): We returned to the tavern and set up a surveillance. At 0325 hours an employee exited the tavern and placed three black trash bags into the dumpster at the rear of the tavern. At 0400 hours, all employees left the bar and we recovered the three trash bags shortly thereafter. We did an inventory on the trash when we arrived at the office. The following items were recovered from the trash: several letters with postmarks on them addressed to the tavern; several tip boards and assorted paper gambling items; and nine pieces of paper with notations on them such as Tim G., P.M. $20.00, and Mark N.P. machine $25.00. These notations are indicative of payoffs on poker machines. In addition to the above items, we also discovered register receipts from the bar.

January 13, 19XX (1700 hours): We met with the informant and had him call 123–4569. When it was answered, the informant gave his bettor identification number and asked the name of the person answering. He stated that he was Robert. We asked for the lines and our totals. Robert provided them and we placed a bet on a sporting event. Robert informed us that the telephones would not be open on Friday night, but they would be early on Saturday.

January 16, 19XX: We met with the informant, called 123–4567, and talked to Robert Doe. We obtained the lines and placed a bet. Robert Doe informed us that he would be at the following locations to settle up on Monday the 17th:

Joy's Deli	0730 to 0800 hours
Brown's Restaurant	0830 to 0930 hours
Dyno Doughnut	0945 to 0955 hours, just to drop off envelopes
Duce Tavern	1200 to 1330 hours

January 17, 19XX (1130 hours): We decided to take a chance and enter the Duce Tavern at 1130 hours to observe the informant settle up with Robert Doe. Again, our intent was to determine all illegal activities that occurred at the bar and the residence and to use them in a RICO case. We arranged for the informant to enter the tavern at 1145 hours to settle up with Doe. We were unable to get all the money that the informant owed, so we were going to make a partial payment. The informant entered the tavern and sat where we had told him to. His location was directly across the room from where I was stationed. At 1155 hours, Robert Doe entered the tavern and walked up to the bartender. The bartender reached under the bar by the register, pulled out several envelopes, and handed them to Mr. Doe. They had a short discussion about some messages that were left for Doe, and then Doe went over and sat with the informant. The informant was wired and my partner was monitoring the conversation. Doe and the informant discussed the amount that was owed; when the informant told him that he would give him half that day, Doe got very upset. Doe grabbed the informant by the shirt and verbalized his displeasure. The informant stated that he would have the rest of the money for him on Thursday. Doe informed the informant that if he did not have it, his brothers would be real upset. At this time, the informant got up and left. I stayed for a few minutes and observed Doe. As soon as the informant left, Doe went to the bar and began laughing. He told the bartender that he loved "scaring the shit out of people who were born with a silver spoon in their mouth." Doe then handed the bartender several envelopes and told him to hand them out as the people listed on the outside of the envelopes entered. At this time, I felt I had stretched my visit long enough, so I left. The time was 1220 hours.

Mid-January, 19XX: During the time we were tracking this case, we had requested that a mail cover be placed on the residence of Robert Doe. By the middle of January, we had discovered where Doe was banking and we also identified where some of Doe's bettors lived outside the area. We began to work up a file to cover the freeze and seizure of the currency held within these bank accounts. With the information we obtained from the banks, we began pulling records that showed the checks written to bettors and the different places where these checks went. By this time, we were nearing the time when we would be ready to hit the residence and the tavern and freeze the bank accounts.

January 18, 19XX (1100 hours): I entered the Duce Tavern and after a short while began to play one of the three poker machines located within the tavern. Over the next 30 minutes I played and marked two of the machines. Each of the machines that I played had the components characteristic of an illegal video gambling device. In addition, I observed a large number of paper quarter rolls torn up and discarded in the trash can next to the machines. I left the tavern at 1145 hours.

January 19, 19XX (1730 hours): We had the informant call 123–4567 and ask for the lines. We had no intention of betting on this date, but instead we had a surveillance at Doe's residence to determine whether he was there conducting his bookmaking business. We found that when we made the call, Doe was in fact at the residence.

January 20, 19XX (1730 hours): I had the informant call the betting line and ask for Robert Doe. He answered and the informant stated that he had Doe's money. Doe said that he was tied up until Monday, so Doe requested that they meet on Monday and settle up then. The informant agreed. Again, we asked for the lines, but no bet was placed. After the conversation, we felt that we had to do the raids prior to settling up on Monday, the 24th. At this time, we informed the rest of the team of our intention to serve warrants, but we still did not inform them as to where the targets were located.

January 21 and 22, 19XX: The selection of the teams and the equipment needs were addressed, and the process of raid preparation was followed. We set it up so we would get a bet down with Doe at his residence on Sunday, the 23rd, and I would go in and again play the poker machines in the tavern on the 23rd. This would give us the fresh information we needed to add to our probable cause.

January 23, 19XX (1100 hours): I met with the informant and we placed a call to Robert Doe at 123–4567. Robert Doe answered and we requested the lines for the day's games. Doe read them off and we placed a bet on one of the events. We verified the fact that Doe would be at the Duce Tavern by noon on Monday. Doe stated yes and we hung up. We again verified that Doe was at the residence when the informant called him.

January 23, 19XX (1430 hours): I entered the tavern with the intention of verifying that the two machines I had played before were still there. I also wanted to play the third machine and determine whether it had the same components as the first two. After a short time in the bar, I approached the poker machines and began to play the first two. I verified that they were the same ones that I had played before. As I got ready to check the third, I observed a police officer in civilian clothes come through the door. At this time, out of necessity, I left the tavern.

January 23, 19XX (2330 hours): Since I was unable to do the verification of the third poker machine, it became necessary for me to return before the tavern closed. At approximately 2300 hours, I entered the tavern and observed an elderly white male playing the third poker machine. I walked up to him and began watching him play. From my position, I observed that the machine did have the components characteristic of an illegal gambling device. The subject playing the machine was on a run and before long he had accumulated 130 points. I began talking to him and made the comment that I could not believe he was going to keep on playing. The subject played a few more hands and seemed to think about what I had said. He called to the bartender and said, "Herb, cash me in." The bartender came over and looked at the total on the machine, which was now 120 points. Then he proceeded to the cash register where he got out $30.00 and made a note on a sheet of paper which was located in the register. The bartender returned to us and handed the subject the money. The bartender then pulled a remote control box out of his pocket and with the push of the button, the total on the machine was erased. Since the patron was finished, I began to play the machine. As I played, I marked the machine and finished out the quarters that I had deposited.

Then I sat down for a short time. When the patron got up to leave, I followed and got his license plate number from his vehicle. After the completion of this task, I went to the office and made the necessary entries to the two search warrants that we intended to serve.

January 24, 19XX (1000 hours): With the search warrant completed and signed, I conducted a briefing, leaving out only the target locations addresses. My partner had the packet for the tavern, and I had the one for the residence. At 1145 hours we proceeded to the targets and waited for Doe to show up at the tavern. When he arrived, my partner advised me by radio. At this time, we hit the tavern. After Doe was read the warrant for the tavern, he was requested to accompany one of the officers to my location where we read him our warrant and requested the keys to enter the residence. Mr. Doe complied and was present during the search.

Items recovered: We recovered a large amount of gambling records and paraphernalia at the residence. We discovered records noting the split of money which had been obtained from the illegal poker machines at the tavern. At the tavern, we recovered records of payoffs on the poker machines and several envelopes which contained money from bettors. We also discovered records which showed that the illegal money was being run through the tavern. With the expectation of Robert Doe trying to pull a power play, we did not arrest Mr. Doe at the time of the warrant. Instead, we continued to work the case, obtaining statements, analyzing records, and developing an even stronger RICO case. When we finally arrested Mr. Doe, it happened to be on the day he was settling up with his bettors.

February 19XX: On the first Monday in February, we served arrest warrants on Mr. Doe as he left a tavern and got into his vehicle. On his person, we found several bettor total sheets, numerous bets, a line sheet, and a large amount of currency. This documentation was included with additional charges that were filed against Mr. Doe.

19

Other Gambling Interests

Over the past 15 years there has been an explosion in the number and complexity of video poker machines. This is due in part to the perfection of the minicomputer. Prior to this, most gambling devices were patterned after the slot machine. In the early days when laws were passed to stop the spread of slot machines, manufacturers incorporated changes within the devices in an attempt to skirt the laws. They added stop buttons to demonstrate an element of skill and some delayed payment until the next play.

The modern day video gambling device manufacturer has learned that diversion and evolution are very important to their future. The new machines include features which attempt to hide the real nature of the device. The diversions used may be as simple as a disclaimer stating "for amusement only" to a complex diversion such as a poker machine with two programs: one that is not illegal and one that can only be displayed after a sequence of buttons is hit, which is illegal. Remember that the only limitation to the diversions that are employed is the creativity of the programmer.

In today's video gambling device market, an investigator must be part bloodhound and part computer wizard. You must be able to sniff out characteristics of the gambling device and at the same time not do anything that would eliminate evidence needed for court. As in other investigations, law enforcement officials have a tendency to go step by step through a situation, which makes them very predictable. The manufacturer will use this predictability against the officer. In the past, toggle switches were used as knock off switches on many machines, and it was common practice for the police to flip this switch to see whether it was a knock off feature. The programmers took this knowledge and installed an erasure feature in this switch, which when flipped would cycle the poker machine into a legal video game. The officer would find himself with a legal device and nothing to show in court. Keep this in mind when conducting your investigation. If possible, you should video the device and its legal components before you attempt to seize it.

TERMS

When you start in the field of poker machine investigations, I recommend that you get a copy of the *FBI Law Enforcement Bulletin* for March and April 1985. In it Special Agent William L. Holmes wrote about the complex elements of video-gambling devices. The title is "Video Games Concepts and Latent Influences."

Agent Holmes presents a historical account of the development of slot machines and a comparison of amusement and gambling video display devices. Agent Holmes names and defines the terms that are used in the identification of illegal gambling devices. Two of the terms that he defines follow:

1. **Knock-off feature:** This is found only on a gambling device. It allows a way to eliminate accumulated credits on the machine, and forces a subsequent player to deposit additional coins to continue to play.
2. **Meters:** One meter records the number of coins dropped in the machine, and the other records the number of credits knocked off the machine.

For information about video poker machines, contact:

FBI Documentation Section
Laboratory Division
Washington, D.C.

HOW TO CONDUCT A POKER MACHINE INVESTIGATION

Normally, each case will start with a complaint of payoffs on a machine at a specific location. You should begin your investigation with a determination as to the validity of the complaint. Then if you feel that the complaint is valid, you should start a background check on the location provided.

Identify the Location

- Check for prior investigations at the location.
- Check the ownership information and determine whether the owner has a prior arrest for gambling-related offenses.
- Identify the types of patrons that frequent the location.
- Identify the employees and determine whether they have any prior involvement in gambling-related activities.
- Attempt to determine the ownership of the video device and conduct a background check on this subject.

Make Entry to Identify the Machine

Gain information about the types of patrons who frequent the location and adapt your appearance to fit in. Use work clothing, hats and glasses, scarring techniques, or casts and braces.

The best thing about this type of infiltration is that you do not need the elaborate role camouflage that is necessary in sports bookmaking investigations. You simply need a way to enter the location and observe the machine in its natural setting.

Entry Techniques

The use of ploys to make entry are effective when dealing with a local bar with a closed circle of patrons. Some entry ploys are as follows: traffic stops outside the location, uniformed employee such as telephone company or mechanic for a dealership, salesman, and male-female team.

After entry determine the type of machine and its description. Identify any features that you can see from your position in the location. Remember, you will need a good description of the machine for the search warrant.

Locate Any Signs of Gambling

- Look for empty quarter rolls on or around the machine. This is indicative of illegal gambling.
- Look for excessive wear of the machine or the floor around it. More often than not, there will be signs if the machine pays off.
- Look for patrons dropping large amounts of money into the machine. You may observe the patron obtaining rolls of quarters from the bartenders. You need to note this type of information. When you do your search warrant, you want to seize the money from the machine and the supply from the bar.
- Look for multiple poker machines on site. If a location has several machines, you can almost bet that they are illegal gambling devices.

Attempt to Identify the Components of the Machine

Watch players as they drop quarters into the machine. Take note of any indicator on the face of the machine that shows the total number of coins dropped. As the player bets, see whether the number of coins bet are subtracted from the number of coins deposited. If the player wins a hand, see whether the amount won is added to the number of coins deposited.

You want to be able to establish that there is a right to replay. A right to replay is nothing more than a total number of plays that the person has left on the machine. This is the figure that is wiped out when a knock-off switch is employed.

Observe the patrons play the machine and key on anyone who is winning. If the machine pays off, the patron will eventually notify the bartender that he wants to get paid. When this occurs, you need to identify where the bartender gets the money, whether the bartender writes down the payoff and where, and what the bartender does to employ the knock-off feature. This information will be necessary in your search warrant. You want to obtain as many records as possible which indicate that the bar is actively involved in illegal gambling.

If, while you are present, no one plays the machine, you should go ahead and play it. Again, your intention is to determine whether the machine contains components that are characteristic of an illegal gambling device. Refer to the *FBI Bulletin* by Agent Holmes. The chart that he uses contains features such as: multiple coin feature, two or more meters, knock-off features, and power interrupt circuit.

As you drop in quarters, search the front of the machine for a total being listed. If you are wired with a recorder, you should give a verbal description of the machine and its condition. As you go through the process of playing the machine, you should continue to describe it. Once you have deposited your coins, you should locate the bet button. As you hit the button to bet, you should scan the screen and determine whether the number of credits bet are deducted from the total deposited. It is a good idea to have a second person with you working the machine. This person can look out for you as you talk into the recorder and also can try to identify where the knock-off switch is.

There are many types of knock-off switches. The following are a few: toggle switches; sequence of buttons; key feature on machine; remote control feature; remote push button (wired from the machine to the back of bar); push button that is inserted into a hole in the machine; built in push button (in the side speaker of the machine); and two screws (set in the side of the machine—touching something metal to both screws erases the right to replay). As you can see, the people who design these machines are very creative. You and your partner also must be creative to be able to locate the components necessary to prove the machine is an illegal device.

Observe a Payoff

It is always best to observe a payoff and identify the people involved so that they can be afforded the opportunity to be a witness or a defendant. If you have witnesses that were paid off on the machine at the direction of the owner, you ease the necessity of proving the machine is illegal in and of itself. If you observe a payoff and you intend to return with a search warrant for records of this transaction, you will need to mark the machine before you leave. This can be accomplished by holding a quarter in your hand when playing and placing a mark on the side that can be identified. You need to be able to say this was, in fact, the same machine on which you observed the payoff.

Remember, there are three observations that need to be made when a payoff occurs. They are

1. Currency is obtained from somewhere—the register, a cash box, etc. Attempt to identify the source of the payoff money.
2. The bartender normally makes a notation as to who was paid and how much was paid. Identify where the paperwork for the payoff is kept.
3. When the bartender pays off a patron, the credits on the machine must be eliminated. Watch what the bartender does. This will indicate what type of knock-off is used and where it is located.

Remember to make sure the machine is marked!

PROBABLE CAUSE FOR A POKER MACHINE SEARCH WARRANT

Affiant for a fact:

I, _____ , received a complaint that payoffs on illegal poker machines were occurring at 1234 Barns, this being in violation of Indiana law.

Affiant for a fact:

On January 7, 19XX, I entered 1234 Barns, Indianapolis, Marion County, Indiana, and observed a poker machine against the southwest wall of the bar. This poker machine was a Double D Poker Machine, which is an electronic closed circuit television device. This machine is approximately 4 feet tall and 2 feet wide. On the face of the machine are the words "Double D."

While I was present, I observed a quantity of empty quarter rolls. I observed that the floor around the machine had excessive wear compared to the rest of the floor. While I was present, I observed a white male subject depositing a large number of quarters into the machine. As he deposited the quarters, I observed on the face of the machine a number located in the upper left-hand corner of the TV screen which counted the number of quarters that the patron deposited. I observed the patron depress a button marked points. Each time he depressed this button, one credit was subtracted from the total. The patron then depressed the deal button and a series of cards appeared on the screen. The patron decided which cards he wanted to keep and then pressed the discard button under the cards he didn't want. New cards appeared and the poker machine made a noise that indicated a winning hand. The poker machine indicated that the patron had the option to take the score or take a chance to double up the points. As I watched the patron, he pressed the high button and won the double up. He then pressed the take button and the total won was added to the total score on the face of the machine.

After about 30 minutes of playing the machine, the patron waved at the bartender and said, "I want to cash in now." On the face of the poker machine, I observed that he had built up 40 credits. The bartender came over, looked at the total, and went to the cash register and took out a $10.00 bill. The bartender pulled a small piece of paper off a pad and wrote something on it and put it in the register. The bartender proceeded to the poker machine and handed the patron the $10.00. The bartender then reached behind the right rear of the machine, there was a click, and the total credits on the face of the machine went to zero. At this time, the patron left the bar and one of our team followed. We obtained the plate number from the vehicle that the patron was driving and he was followed so we could identify his residence.

Affiant for a fact:

As soon as the patron left the bar, myself and my partner approached the poker machine. I began to play the machine and found that the machine had the following characteristics of an illegal gambling device:

- The machine accepted multiple coins.
- There was little or no skill involved.
- Time of play was very short.
- The payoff method was credits.
- A knock off switch was located on the back.

As I was playing the machine, I marked the machine by placing my initials on the left side of it. In addition to my initials, I also observed a city registration sticker on the left side of the machine. This sticker had the number 1123 on it.

Once you get to this point, you have enough to get a search warrant. The key point to remember is that you also want any documentation showing payoffs on the machine and any documentation as to ownership of the machine. The search should include all areas where that type of information may be concealed. Remember to check records for the laundering of this currency through the tavern account.

If you want to get additional information for the search warrant, I recommend that you do a trash search and look for payoff slips in the trash. In most cases, the bartender only keeps the slips until their accounts are balanced, and then the sheet is discarded. To make the trash easy to separate from one day to the next, lay a piece of cardboard in the dumpster so that you can say that all the trash on top of the cardboard came out of the tavern on the date of recovery. You should also attempt to locate mail or other items that have the tavern's name on it.

CASE EXAMPLE 1

April 1, 19XX: I received a call from an informant who stated that Jane Doe was paying off on illegal poker machines at her tavern located at 123 W. 11th. In addition to the illegal gambling activities, Miss Doe buys and sells stolen property using the business as a front. This informant could not get us into the gambling side of the business, but he did introduce us as thieves.

April 5, 19XX (1100 hours): A member of our team, Mike, entered the tavern and was introduced to Jane Doe. Mike informed Jane Doe that he had two VCRs that he wanted to sell. Jane Doe asked him how hot the VCRs were, and Mike told her that he had ripped them off at a department store. Mike further stated that the store did not keep numbers on them, so they could not be traced. Jane Doe asked how much Mike wanted and he said, "It's up to you." Jane Doe gave Mike $75.00 for both. Since the only way we could get into the tavern was by posing as thieves, it was decided that we would work a case that would include the buying and selling of stolen property, illegal poker machines, and money laundering. Our intention was to include all illegal activities in a Racketeer Influenced and Corrupt Organizations (RICO) case.

April 6, 19XX (1100 hours): Mike entered the tavern and walked over to the poker machine and deposited ten quarters. As he did, the total number of coins deposited showed up as credits on the screen. The machine was described as a small, bar-top type of poker machine. The outer case was of black plastic and the machine featured six buttons on the front. The buttons, from left to right, were *bet, start, take score, double, small, and big.* On the left side of the machine there was a coin slot that took quarters and just below it was a slot that took $1's, $5's, $10's, and $20's. The face of the machine displayed *fruit, bells, bars, and sevens* when it was plugged in. As coins were deposited, the total showed up in the lower left-hand corner of the screen; when the bet button was pressed, the points bet were deducted from the total credits and showed up in the lower right-hand corner as points bet. When the start button was pressed, the fruit and other items, which were in three rows, started to spin like that of a slot machine. When they stop, you have won if you get three in a row and you had bet that there would be that combination. The winning points are added to the total credits at this time if you decide to take the score and not double up. If you double up and win the score, it is again added to the total credits. Mike looked for a knock off switch while playing, but the only features he noticed were two key slots on the rear of the machine. While Mike was playing the machine, Jane Doe approached him and asked whether he had anything for her. Mike asked her if she was interested in clothing. Jane asked to look at it, so Mike finished the game and went out to get the clothing. Mike told Jane that he had stolen the items, but he had torn off the stickers so they could not be traced. Jane offered to buy all the clothing that Mike had. Each time we set up a sale, Mike was wired with a body wire and a mini-cassette because we wanted to get evidence on tape. We decided that Mike should keep playing the machine. Each time he went in with the hope that Jane would pay him off and reveal where the knock off switch was. If nothing else, we wanted some conversation as to the function of the machine.

April 8, 19XX (1120 hours): Mike entered the tavern, proceeded over to one of the two poker machines, and deposited $20.00 worth of quarters. Mike had brought more clothing to sell as stolen. It was our hope that Jane Doe would cash in Mike's points before he left. Jane Doe came out of the office and walked over to Mike. After a brief conversation, Mike said that he had some more clothing items. Jane said, "Let me see them." Mike left and went to the car and returned with them. Again, he told Jane Doe that he had ripped off the clothing. Jane bought the items and she was observed by Mike getting the money out of the register located behind the bar. Mike asked Jane what other items she needed him to rip off for her. Jane stated that she would take anything he could get. Mike asked her to write him a list, and at this time Mike began to play the machine again. Jane said that the machine Mike was on was very tight and that he would have a better chance on the other machine. Mike told her that he felt lucky and was going to make her eat her words. Mike continued to play for a short time when he hit for 30 points. Mike had accumulated 100 credits on the machine. Mike asked whether Jane would cash him in, and she could not believe he had won. She went to the register and took out $25.00, and made a notation on a sheet of paper which she placed in the register. After she handed Mike the money, she used her ring to touch two screws at the same time on the rear of the machine. The credits on the front of the machine disappeared. Mike took his money and left the tavern. Just prior to leaving, Mike had marked the left side of the poker machine so that he could identify it in the future.

Analysis of case: At this point in time, we had enough to take the tavern down. We felt, however, that if we could get a better feel for how much the owners were buying in the way of stolen property, we might be able to get a more substantial penalty. Again, our goal in this case was to put the suspect out of business for good. We continued to make sales of stolen property to the owner for about 2 more weeks, during which time she began going through catalogs and writing down item numbers, pages that the items were on, sizes, and colors. We determined that the owner of the tavern was buying items from burglars and selling the items at the bar. Each time that Mike entered the tavern, he played the poker machine and verified that it was the same machine he had played before.

May 1, 19XX: We served a search warrant on the tavern. We wrote the warrant up as a financial search warrant and searched for records of both payoffs on the poker machine and records of purchase and sales of the stolen property. We discovered that the tavern owner was listing the money from the poker machine as commissions on her income. She was only reporting one shift of workers to the IRS, thereby under-reporting her income by $500,000 in 2 years. We filed criminal RICO charges and civil forfeitures of the bar, a house, two cars, and other assets; the state IRS filed in excess of 30 criminal charges.

Reminder: Remember that the narration listed in these examples does not include all the work done by the support teams. You need to follow the steps outlined elsewhere in the book pertaining to backgrounds, infiltrations, team assignments, and research in order to have a successful investigation.

CASE EXAMPLE 2

October 9, 19XX: I received a complaint that the tavern at 123 W. 5th was paying off on a small table-top poker machine. I conducted a background check of the bar and the owner and found nothing. I contacted several informants who stated that the bar was clean and a nice place to go for a quiet drink. Due to this, I decided to make an entry and if I observed a violation, I would address it at that time.

October 9, 19XX (2130 hours): I entered the Glove Tavern and observed a poker machine on the bar at the east end of the building. I was wearing a telephone company shirt and I had a belt with telephone lineman equipment attached to it. I sat at the bar and talked to the bartender for a few minutes until he was at ease with me. I watched one patron drop three quarters into the machine and walk away after his play. The machine was clean and the area around it seemed to be the same as the other areas in the bar. I told the bartender that when I was in a few weeks ago, they did not have a poker machine. The bartender said that a guy came around the other day and said they needed it to compete with all the other bars in the area that have them. The bartender stated that the owner of the machine guaranteed that the bar would double its business, and the bar's cut of the money from the machine would be at least $250 per week. I walked over to the poker machine and dropped several quarters into it. While I played it, I observed several components that are characteristic to those found in an illegal gambling device. I accumulated 80 points on the machine and requested that the bartender cash in my points. He did so, handing me $20.00, which he got from a box under the bar. He then wrote the amount in a small book that was next to the register. At this time, I identified myself and seized the machine, the box with the currency, and the book with the payouts in it. Due to the fact that this was not the normal situation, I did not make an arrest or do a search warrant. Instead, I interviewed the bartender and the owner of the bar, and obtained valuable intelligence information which I used in subsequent cases. In addition, I took the poker machine apart and identified how it worked. This was also important in future cases.

Chapter
20
The Raid

One of the most difficult decisions that a covert officer must make is deciding when you have enough to "take down" the target or location. As you get into the investigation, you worry more and more about the chance that you will be burned and lose everything you have worked for. The decision to terminate the investigation should be a team decision and it should be based on whether you have enough to arrest and convict your subject. In reality, in most locations you have little or no control over when the case will be terminated. No matter at what level the decision is made, you must be prepared to conduct the raid of the location at a moment's notice. It is recommended that as the investigation is progressing, a member of the team should be assigned to do the research that is necessary to conduct a successful raid.

RAID LOCATION INFORMATION

Prior to conducting a raid, background information should be obtained about the raid location. The best place to start is with the covert officer and his case file.

Note: As you go through your case you should be looking for issues that will need to be addressed when you plan the raid. Remember that safety is your first priority.

The following information is required to conduct a successful raid.

Historical Background on the Target Location

As in the past, you should start with a computer check of the specific address in question and then branch out to a two or three block canvass. When reviewing prior radio runs and reports:

- Key on facts such as violent acts, weapons, and relatives of the target.
- Consider each report, whether it seems tied to the target or not, as background. Look for any ties to the target no matter how remote.

- Identify the type of people in the area and attempt to predict the type of reaction you may face when a warrant is served.
- Identify ownership of property and background of the subjects.

Obtain Photographs And Descriptions

Neighborhood
The use of an aircraft is very helpful in identifying problems to be faced by the raid team members.

Photographs of Raid Location
Pay special attention to:

- The location of all exits and defenses
- The location of all windows and if they are covered to prevent entry
- Descriptions of adjoining buildings and common grounds
- Estimated number of people in the immediate area (attempt to determine the number of apartments or rooms that may have to be secured)
- What the exterior of the building is made of and what type of cover the walls of the target location will provide
- All limitations that are placed on the entry team, such as burglar bars, steel mesh, etc.
- What type of doors are in the target location: whether they open in or out, and whether they are wood or steel-reinforced doors and frames
- Whether there are entry ways inside the outer doors and whether there are additional doors that must be passed through to gain entry
- Whether there are portholes or gun ports around or near any entry point
- The location of any and all stairs in the target location
- The presence, type, and number of dogs or any other animals at the target location
- Any body traps used by the subjects, such as

    - Glass fragments on walls and in window sills
    - Treble hooks on monofilament line hanging head high
    - Razor blades embedded in walls, window sills, banisters, and door handles
    - Use of caustic agents and irritants
    - Openings in the floors just inside the outer doors
    - Any other type of trap. Remember that the only limitation on the number and types of traps that are set by the suspect is his creativity. *Always expect a trap!*

- Lookouts—determine what signals are being used, whether handheld radios are being used, and if possible what frequency they are on (accomplished by having a marked police car pull up front and using a scanner to lock in the frequency they broadcast on)

THE SUSPECTS

A second area of importance besides the location itself is obtaining in-depth information about the suspects themselves. Some of the information gathered about the location will cross over and fit into the suspects' backgrounds. You should list the information twice, once under the location and then again under the suspects. This will guarantee that the information will not be missed by any team member. The following is a sample of the type of information that is necessary to fulfill this requirement.

Number of Suspects

An estimate of the number of suspects that can be expected to be on site when the raid is conducted is necessary to be able to properly staff the raid team positions. The team needs to know the number of males and females they will encounter and their descriptions and look at pictures, if possible. The pictures can be obtained from surveillance photographs or arrest pictures.

Background on Each Suspect To Be Encountered

Any suspect that may be present on the day the raid is conducted must have a background check done on him. You should look for:

* Prior arrests, keying on tendencies toward violence
* Prior military training, identifying anyone with prior military experience and the type of specialty he may have had (attempt to isolate any suspect who may pose an added threat to the raid team)

Weapons Known To Be on Site

Attempt to identify through informants' surveillance any weapons that are known to be at the target location. If possible, the exact location must be known so precautions can be taken.

Vehicles Accessible to the Suspects on Site

Attempt to identify any and all vehicles that are under the control of or are accessible to the suspects at the target location. This information must be taken into consideration in the raid briefing to eliminate any escape of key suspects. A good surveillance may find that the suspect has a vehicle he normally does not drive placed in the neighborhood so that if things go bad, he can ease out of the area.

Who and Where the Lookouts Are

Attempt to identify who and where the lookouts are. This knowledge will provide you with information that you may not have obtained in other ways. The lookout also can be afforded the opportunity to be a witness or a defendant. Have a uniformed officer drive through the area so that you can identify the lookouts.

Pictures and Descriptions of Family Members in the Area

A detailed description of family members who live in the area should be obtained. The bookmaker may shift his operation from one place to another by using call forwarding. You need to know any and all potential locations.

Information on Known Associates in the Area

You should attempt to identify known associates in the area. Obtain criminal histories and known tendencies toward violence.

Daily Patterns of Suspects

You should utilize surveillance to determine the daily patterns of the suspect. This information can assist you in many ways. You may be able to anticipate his actions when the raid begins and you also can tell whether you have been discovered before the raid based on the suspect's actions.

PLANNING RAIDS

Throughout the United States each year, there are thousands of search warrants served, and it seems at times that police officers have a tendency to be complacent and not recognize the dangers involved. The backgrounds on the previous pages may not be easy to follow because of time constraints, but it is recommended that you at least review the procedures each time and assess the dangers involved.

When you begin to plan your raid, you should first begin with defining the purpose of your raid. The purpose of the raid is to:

- Capture and control suspects
- Recover contraband
- Obtain evidence for court presentation

Remember that the first and foremost priority of law enforcement in a raid situation is the safety of the officers. This priority can be accomplished by making plans to ensure that the initial stages of the raid are swift, they contain the element of the surprise, and they are very simple to conduct.

Prior to conducting the raid, you first must plan each and every facet of the action to be taken. Planning a raid begins with the selection of raid team personnel. *All selections should be made based on skills, not rank or seniority!* When planning begins, you should first consider the following.

Raid Team Commander Skills

The skills of the raid team commander should include the ability to communicate clearly and experience planning and executing raids. The raid team commander should maintain control of the team members and oversee their functions.

Entry Team Member Skills

Entry team members are the ones that face the greatest threat of injury. They must have the ability to work closely with other team members and be well trained in the many different entry techniques used today. They must have extensive training in weapons usage and specialized training in specific areas of entry and containment. In most cases, large departments utilize their SWAT team to do the entry and containment. In any case, the members of any entry team should have some sort of psychological profile done before joining the team. This psychological evaluation should continue throughout their membership on the team.

Search Team Skills

For the purpose of the court presentation, the search team is the most important component of the raid team package. The team's job begins only after the entry has been made and all threats neutralized. The search team must be trained in search and evidence recovery methods. The recovery and processing of the evidence is a very important aspect of the case and can lead to a discharge of the case if handled improperly. You cannot afford to assign a "cowboy" type to conduct your search.

Outer Security Skills

One area that is often missed when the important assignments are given is appointing a team to handle outer security. From the beginning you have attempted to identify the threat level of the neighborhood, the relatives in the area, and all other potential threats. It should not be difficult to assign someone to cover you when you are preoccupied with your search. It is not uncommon to have someone show up well after the search has begun and attempt to disrupt the target location. Without someone assigned to outer security, you could find yourself looking into the barrel of a shotgun.

Support Personnel Skills

Support personnel are those members of the raid team who have both specialized and general duties. The members with general duties are, for example, those officers who are going to transport the prisoners in a wagon. The specialized members may be K-9 officers, evidence technicians, crime lab personnel, or any other member you feel is necessary to support the case.

Responsibilities

There are many different responsibilities that go along with the assignment to a raid team including:

Entry Team

The entry team is responsible for the entry, securing the suspects, and isolating all weapons. The secondary responsibility is to prevent the destruction of evidence. In this tactical situation, the safety of the team takes precedence over the recovery of evidence.

Search Team

The search team responsibilities are many, including photographing or taking videos of evidence as it is found; and identifying, recording, and recovery of the evidence and documents that are to be seized. The search team members are responsible for gathering all evidence and documents for transportation to the holding facility. The types of documentation they may seize are items that indicate assets, currency from illegal sources, identities of associates and co-conspirators, and records that can be used to determine income from the illegal enterprise.

Pre-Raid Briefing

Prior to the actual raid, you should have a formal briefing. At this time, you should have team assignments and a description of what each person's responsibilities are. You should go over each and every item that has been provided in the background check of the target location and all the potential threats that may be present. You should use, when possible, photographs to explain the locations of each team and their duties. You must explain the limits of the search warrant so that everyone will understand. If you are looking for a truck, you cannot look in a desk drawer. You must emphasize where you can search and what you are seeking. If you stretch the scope of the search warrant, you risk the chance that a judge will throw out your case or, worse yet, that you will set a precedence that will haunt the law enforcement community in the future.

In most cases, you will be searching for items that can fit anywhere, no matter how small. You should provide the searchers with locations where they should look for evidence.

RESIDENCE OR BUSINESS SEARCHES

The following are some examples of where searchers should look. When you consider the search of a room, you should begin by taking time to evaluate the room to determine the best way to get the job done. You may want to begin by evaluating the floor for potential hiding places, for example, under carpet, in air ducts, or behind baseboards. Move up the walls and evaluate the fixtures, wall coverings, electrical outlets, and baseboard heating. Evaluate the doors that are present. Determine whether they have hollowed out areas that are hidden behind slats held in place by magnets or Velcro, or if the door frame itself is hollowed out and disguised in a similar manner.

As in everything else you do, you are competing with the creativity and imagination of the bad guy. If you are more creative, you have a much greater chance to win the battle of wits. Each room you face should be evaluated, and the best way to proceed should be determined. Once this is done, the best thing you can do is proceed slowly and never get distracted.

These are other places where items may be hidden: false walls; inside pillows; in crawl spaces; inside interior walls; inside fluorescent light fixtures; behind pictures and other wall covers; inside electric dryers; behind pullout medicine cabinets; above false ceilings; in air vents over stoves; inside plastic Ziplock bags in toilet tanks; inside seat cushions; in laundry chutes; behind and under dressers, shelves, beds, and other furniture; inside TVs; in flower pots; in chimneys and stoves; under attic insulation; inside openings in window sills; inside vacuum cleaners; in the bottom of boxes filled with trash; inside cat litter boxes; under mattresses; under dirty clothes; and at a separate location, when evidence is computer generated. The best way to search is to check each and every square inch and *never get in a hurry*.

When conducting an evidentiary search warrant, there are several points that should be remembered, such as:

- Limit the number of searchers. The fewer the better. It may take longer, but the results will be fewer mistakes and fewer persons who have to testify.
- Have one person assigned to recover all evidence. This person will be the key person in court.
- Photograph and videotape all evidence as it is found prior to seizure.
- *Never, never get in a hurry!* If it takes all day to do it right, take all day.

- Attempt to maintain a tight chain of custody. Again, limit the number of people who have to testify as to where the evidence was found and where it went.
- Once entry has been made and the suspects are secure, avoid the desire to rush to the most likely place for evidence. Begin a thorough search of all areas covered by the warrant.
- Stop at each room and look around, evaluating the best procedure to follow.
- Mark all items seized. It is best to assign a person to accompany the seizing officer who will have the responsibility of taking notes and assisting.
- Identify items that require an immediate response, such as papers identifying a safe deposit box or bank accounts. This information should be provided to your prosecutor right away if you intend to search the safe deposit box or freeze the bank account.
- After the search warrant is concluded, walk back through the area and pause in each room to see whether you are comfortable with the search that was conducted. Inevitably you will discover something that you have missed.

What You Search For

You should determine what can be seized under your search warrant, and then explain it to the search team. It is recommended that you write your search to cover the seizure of the following items.

All Financial Documentation
This shows purchase of assets, maintenance of the illegal enterprise, income, co-conspirators, and any financial documentation that will identify witnesses.

Any Credit Card Receipts
Credit card receipts reveal locations of trips and the dates and times that your target was in a specific city or location, identification of assets, names of associates, and additional expenses for your income analysis. In addition to receipts, you should also copy the numbers of any credit cards found so that you also will be able to track those accounts.

Other Receipts
- *Utilities.* Identify assets, income, and expenses.
- *House payments.* Identify assets, income, and expenses. If the house is a rental, you may also be able to identify co-conspirators. You may want to track the ownership of a residence to the bank official who handled the purchase and identify whether he is involved.
- *Lease information.* Identify the company involved and the item leased and determine whether it is leased to hide income.
- *Any receipt.* Identify any transaction that denotes an asset, a purchase, or any expense.

Telephone Lists

Telephone lists are important for many reasons. They can identify co-conspirators, bettors, money laundering locations, banking involvement, assets, and layoff locations. When you recover telephone numbers, you need to track each and every number as soon as possible to determine the total picture of the illegal enterprise. Telephone numbers will provide you with other targets, and often they will provide you with valuable information and witnesses.

Deeds and Titles

If possible, seize all deeds and titles to property or other assets. A determination as to how they were purchased and whether they were obtained with money from the illegal organization needs to be made. You may find some interesting facts such as the transfer of property for $1 from the original owner to the criminal. This situation is common, and it normally demonstrates a major loss in the gambling enterprise where the bettor is forced to sign over the asset to the bookmaker. You need to pull the original owner in to determine whether this is the case.

Photographs

If possible, you need to seize any photographs that can be used to show the target and any co-conspirators. You may also find pictures of assets, other criminal activities, and locations.

Computers and Other Related Electronic Equipment

When dealing with the automated area of a criminal enterprise, it is recommended that, if you have any idea at all that a computer is being used, you should take steps to ensure that an expert is available to assist you in the seizure of the items involved. Expect that the criminal has safeguards in place to protect the information in the computer from police seizure. In some recent cases, the bad guy established a magnetic field in a doorway; when someone left with the computer disks, the magnetic field erased the information on the disk. In another case, a computer program allowed the criminal to push a code button that would erase all the information in the computer.

Audio Tapes and Equipment

In several cases, it has been found that the bookmaker has kept audio tapes of all transactions conducted over the telephone. In fact, we arranged to have a bookmaker record transactions because we continually argued that we bet the opposite way than what the bookmaker had us listed as. The bookmaker began to tape the bets so that he could play it back when there was a question. We ended up with 13 90-minute cassettes of recorded wagers when we did the search. Remember, another reason why a bookmaker would record wagers is because there is someone above him who does not trust him.

Items That Establish Occupancy

Establishing occupancy is important because you need to eliminate any debate in court about whether your subject did in fact either reside or maintain control over the location you have targeted. Any items, such as mail to or from the target location with your subject's name on it and any other documentation that the subject is using the location for the illegal operation as his own are very important in establishing his control over the location. Again, the use of utility bills and lease details and the fact that the subject was found in possession of keys that fit the doors at the target location are the types of information that must be noted to establish dominion and control over the property.

Weapons Found in the Possession of the Suspect or at the Targeted Location

If the seizure of weapons is covered under your search warrant, you should attempt to confirm that your subject did in fact handle the weapons. It is recommended that prints be taken and a determination be made as to whether your subject had prior convictions that would preclude his or her legal ownership of the seized weapons. The aim of this seizure is to establish to a jury that the subject was armed while he conducted his illegal activities. This type of information may assist you in obtaining a conviction before a judge and jury. Throughout your investigation you should develop information about your subject being in possession of and utilizing weapons in his or her illegal operation.

Any and All Items That Are Evidence

Your search should be for any and all items that are evidence or tend to support the facts that your subject is in fact involved in the illegal activities you are investigating.

Currency and Other Valuables

Criminals have a tendency to attempt to hide their wealth in objects such as rare coins and jewelry and other items that they feel will hold value. You need to address this in your warrant so that you will be able to seize any of these items. Your warrant should also include large amounts of currency that you locate at the target location.

What to Do with All This Documentation When It Is Seized

Once you have seized documentation as described above, you need to analyze it and plug it into your case. You need to demonstrate the day-to-day workings of your subject and his or her operation. Most subjects will attempt to move their money and liquidate assets as soon as possible after a warrant has been served. You need to get court action to freeze the subject's assets and then conduct a thorough analysis of the operation itself.

Who Can Help Conduct an Analysis of the Records

If you, or your department, do not have the personnel or staff able to conduct a good analysis of the records, you can turn to the FBI Laboratory for assistance. The services of the FBI Laboratory are available to all duly constituted state, county, and municipal law enforcement agencies in the United States for criminal investigative matters only. The FBI Laboratory can provide the following services:

- The examination, analysis, and interpretation of criminal records
- The examination, analysis, and interpretation of number operation records
- The analysis and interpretation of legally obtained telephone conversations
- The analysis and interpretation of gambling devices to include: slot machines, electronic devices, casino tables, cards and dice, and carnival games

In addition to the analysis of the records, the FBI is willing to provide you with expert witnesses to testify in regard to the evidence submitted. All the expenses including travel and lodging are paid for by the FBI.

How to Send in Your Records

If the records are small enough to ship, the following steps are recommended:

- Pack the records securely inside a box.
- Seal the box and mark it as evidence.
- Place a copy of the transmittal letter in an envelope and mark it "invoice".
- Stick the envelope on the outside of the sealed box.
- Wrap the sealed box in outside paper and seal with gummed paper.
- Address to: Director
       Federal Bureau of Investigation
       10th & Pennsylvania, N.W.
       Washington, D.C. 20535
       Attn: FBI Laboratory Documentation Section

How to Write the Transmittal Letter

The transmittal letter is nothing more than a request in writing for the services described above. You need to address the letter to the Director of the FBI Laboratory. Identify what items you have enclosed and explain what you need to have done. It is recommended that you specify the trial date and the defendant's name in the body of the letter. You should finish the letter with a telephone number and an address where you can be reached. Have it sent from your chief or other lead officer.

All of the above information plus several examples are provided by the FBI Laboratory in a small booklet that can be obtained on request. It is recommended that you contact the FBI Laboratory and make sure of the current procedures for the shipment of documents prior to sending them.

EXECUTION OF THE SEARCH WARRANT

Timing

As we said before, timing of the search warrant service is very critical. You should combine speed, surprise, and simplicity to ensure success. Another fact to keep in mind is that in most jurisdictions, the time between getting the warrant signed and serving it is limited. It is recommended that you plan to serve the warrant as soon after it is signed as possible. This limits the chance that the information will be leaked, and it also limits the court's chance to rule on a staleness issue. If possible, search warrants should be served in daylight hours when you have better control of the location and the surrounding areas.

Entry

In most cases, police officers are locked into a knock-and-announce routine that is mandated by the court. You must first knock, identify yourself as police officers, and state that you have a search warrant for this specific location. You must then give the occupants a reasonable time to respond. Be sure the persons at the front who are assigned the initial entry have a specific announcement such as, "Police—we have a warrant for the search of your residence. Open the door or we will be forced to make entry." The need for this kind of statement is crucial in a situation where a suspect fires on the officers and then claims that he did not know they were the police. In addition to this statement being yelled aloud, each officer on the entry team must be clearly marked as a policeman. You never want a police officer to have to debate before a jury about whether the suspect knew he was a police officer.

These are the two exceptions to the knock-and-announce rule:

1. There is imminent danger of serious injury to the officers.
2. Evidence could be destroyed if notice is given.

Unless you can explain one of these exceptions to the court you must knock and announce.

Use of Trickery or Deception to Gain Entry

The use of a trick or deception to gain entry to a targeted location is permissible. Before you use a ruse to make entry, you should consider first how it will look in court in front of a jury. It is recommended that if you are going to use a ruse, you should use it in such a way as to isolate the suspect, either at or away from the target location. In this way, you can read the suspect the warrant and then with his knowledge make entry. The following are a few ways that a ruse can help get the suspect outside so as to limit the destruction of evidence:

Flower Delivery

This technique has worked very well, especially when you find that the subject has a girlfriend or wife. Deliver flowers to the target location in her name. In most cases the subject will not answer the door. Place the flowers on the ground several steps from the door and turn them around so a card with his girlfriend's or wife's name is visible to the person inside. As you leave the location, you should locate two officers outside by the entry way. The subject will become jealous and step out to see who is sending his girlfriend or wife flowers. At this time, you have your team members identify themselves and read the warrant to the subject.

Pose as a Deliveryman

In an attempt to isolate the subject so that the destruction of evidence is limited, pose as a deliveryman, phone man, etc.

Pose as a Lawn Mowing Service

Obtain an old lawn mower and cut the muffler off so it is loud. Add some oil to the gas so the mower will smoke a lot; remove the blade. When you arrive at the location with a helper who looks as if he is going to trim the hedges, pull out the mower and start it as though you are going to mow the lawn. It is guaranteed that the subject will come running out to see what is happening. You then identify yourself and read him the warrant.

Fake Car Trouble

Fake car trouble and ask to use the telephone. This is especially effective when you use a young looking female or an elderly woman.

Use a Smoker Machine

In most cases, the subject wants to have a view of the outside of the operational location. He will check the outside on a regular basis. Use this to your advantage. If your department has a tear gas smoker machine, use it in conjunction with ordinary smoke. Smoke pots will also work. Have the smoker provide enough smoke so that the subject will come outside to see what is on fire. You then identify yourself and read him the warrant.

Use a Meeting to Settle Up

If you meet with the bookmaker to settle up during your investigation, you may want to use a settle up time to stop the bookmaker away from the target location.

Consent Searches

Consent searches are those where the person in charge of the premises gives permission to search. In order for this to be valid, the consent must be voluntary and the person must have the right to give permission to conduct a search. The burden of proof in court that the consent to search was free and voluntary is on the state. The sum total of the surrounding circumstances will be taken into account when the determination is made. Facts such as the number of officers present and the manner in which the request to search is made will affect the court's decision as to whether the consent was voluntary.

To determine whether the person had the right to give the consent to search, you need to prepare some questions that will draw out the information necessary to prove the person you are dealing with is in lawful possession.

Even though there is no requirement to provide the Fourth Amendment rights before the consent, it is recommended that the person consenting be informed so that he or she may refuse. In any case where you request a consent to search, it is recommended that you obtain this consent in writing and, if possible, record the way it is requested on tape. In most agencies, there is a form that covers both "in custody" and "not in custody" consents to search. Examples of each form are provided in Figure 20.1.

Control of the Premises and Persons During the Search

When you serve a search warrant, you as a police officer have absolute control of the location to be searched. The occupants have no right to refuse or impede the search in any manner. It is recommended that once the entry team has secured the location and the subjects inside, the search team should request that all subjects be moved to one central location while the search is conducted. Persons found on the scene may be frisked if there is reasonable suspicion that they possess a weapon. However, unless they are particularly described in the search warrant, you may not search them for evidence described in the warrant.

Scope, Duration, and Intensity of the Search

The scope of the search is directly related and controlled by the objective of the search. The search may extend to all areas where the evidence could be reasonably concealed. The search must stop when all the items described in the warrant are located. In most cases, your search warrant will not be concluded until all areas described in the warrant are covered because you will be looking for an unknown quantity of records of betting activities. Be ever mindful that your actions will be judged in court; thus it is recommended that you attempt to keep the unnecessary damage to the property of the bookmaker to a minimum. It is also recommended that if you feel there will be a problem, you should videotape the location after you complete the search so as to protect yourself from claims that you caused unnecessary damage.

A.

CONSENT TO SEARCH
(In Custody)

Place _____

Date _____

Time _____

ADVICE OF RIGHTS

YOU ARE HEREBY INFORMED THAT YOU HAVE THE FOLLOWING CONSTITUTIONAL RIGHTS:

1. You have the right to require that a search warrant be obtained before any search of your residence, vehicle or other premises.

2. You have the right to refuse to consent to any such search.

3. You have the right to consult with an attorney prior to giving consent to any such search.

4. If you cannot afford an attorney, you have the right to have an attorney provided for you.

CONSENT

The above statement of my RIGHTS has been read to me and I am fully aware of those RIGHTS and do fully understand those RIGHTS.

I hereby CONSENT TO A SEARCH WITHOUT A WARRANT by officers of the _____ _____Police (Sheriff) Department of the following described residence (motor vehicle) (premises): _____

_____

_____located at

County, _____ State of: _____

I hereby AUTHORIZE those officers to SEIZE any article that those officers may deem as evidence or pertinent to their investigation.

THIS STATEMENT IS BEING SIGNED BY ME WITH FULL UNDERSTANDING OF MY RIGHTS AND OF MY FREE WILL WITHOUT ANY THREATS OR PROMISES HAVING BEEN MADE TO ME.

Signed: _____

Age: _____

Witnessed:

_____

_____

Figure 20.1. Consent-to-search forms.

B.

PERMISSION TO SEARCH
(Not In Custody)

Place _____

Date _____

Time _____

I,_____, residing at_____

_____, County, State of, do

knowingly authorize officers of the_____ Police (Sheriff) Department

to search the following described residence (motor vehicles) (premises) over which I have control, to wit: _____

_____

_____ located at _____

County, _____ State of: _____

I further knowingly and voluntarily authorize said officers to SEIZE any article that they may deem as evidence or pertinent to their investigation.

THIS PERMISSION IS GIVEN KNOWINGLY AND VOLUNTARILY UPON FULL KNOWLEDGE OF MY RIGHT TO REFUSE SUCH PERMISSION.

Signed: _____

Age: _____

Witnessed:

_____

_____

Figure 20.1. (continued)

Inventory, Receipt, and Return

When the search is completed and you have located all items of contraband and records to be seized, you should conduct an inventory of the items and provide the person in charge of the premises a receipt and an inventory sheet. In most states this is a requirement. Once the inventory is completed and the items are transported to the holding facility, you then must inform the court as to what you have seized. The format is different in many areas, but in most cases you fill in a return area on the warrant with a list of items and then return it to the court or clerk's officer for filing.

C.

CONSENT SEARCH AUTHORIZATION

DATE _____

TIME _____

LOCATION _____

BEFORE ANY SEARCH IS MADE YOU MUST UNDERSTAND YOUR RIGHTS.

    1.   You may refuse to consent to a search and may demand that a search warrant be obtained prior to any search of the premises described below.

    2.   If you consent to a search, anything of evidentiary value seized in the course of the search can and will be introduced into evidence in court against you.

I _____, HAVE READ THE ABOVE STATEMENT OF MY RIGHTS AND AM FULLY AWARE OF MY RIGHTS. I HEREBY CONSENT TO A SEARCH WITHOUT WARRANT BY OFFICERS OF THE _____ POLICE DEPARTMENT OF THE FOLLOWING: (Describe premises or automobile).

_____

_____

_____

I HEREBY AUTHORIZE THE SAID OFFICERS TO SEIZE ANY ARTICLE WHICH THEY MAY DEEM TO BE OF VALUE AS EVIDENCE.

THIS STATEMENT IS SIGNED OF MY OWN FREE WILL WITHOUT ANY THREATS OR PROMISES HAVING BEEN MADE TO ME.

Signed: _____
                          (Person Giving Consent)

Witness: _____

Witness: _____

Figure 20.1. (continued)

APPENDIX 1: RAID TEAM CHECKLISTS

You should provide each team with a checklist of the items that will be necessary to accomplish the mission. Each team should be required to check off each item before entering the field. The purpose of this list is to make sure that everyone has what is required and that you do not look unprofessional when conducting the raids.

Raid team instructions: Raid team instructions are nothing more than a list of procedures to be followed in the event of arrests. These instructions should be accompanied by a raid packet and a list of its contents. The following is an example of raid team instructions:

- All raid packets will be checked prior to leaving. They will contain arrest slips, rights waivers, property room slips, report forms, affidavits (charging), copy of the search warrant/arrest warrant, tape recorder/telephone attachment and tapes, 35-mm camera and film, video unit with film, flashlights, black markers, and assorted packaging, paper sacks, plastic bags, etc.
- All arrests shall have the name of the lead officer on them.
- Make all reports in his name and place the property in the property room under his name and case number.
- Transport your prisoners, if possible (no telephone calls).
- Locate and search all vehicles listed; seize all personal telephone books.
- Seize all cash and hold it for forfeiture.
- Seize all electronic equipment used in the operation.
- Attempt to record any bets coming in while the search is in progress.
- Photograph and videotape all gambling evidence as it is found, prior to removal.
- Seize all weapons and turn them in for processing.

All you want to do with these instructions is to eliminate questions. You may want to list the channel and car number to contact for answers.

Supplies: These may include paper sacks (25 each), arrest slips (10 each), property slips (10 each), envelopes (paper and plastic) (25 each), 35-mm cameras (2 each), videocameras (2 each), 35-mm film (4 rolls, ASA 400 and 4 rolls ASA 1000), videotapes (5 each), tape recorders (4 each), 90-minute recording tapes (8 each), power source (batteries and electric) for 4 recorders, incident reports (25 each), black markers and tape (10 each), flashlights (4 each), rights waivers (10 each), receipt books (4 each), tow-in slips (4 each), rubber gloves (30 each), paper masks (10 each), carbon paper (10 each), and boxes (10 large and 10 small). This is a short list of supplies necessary to conduct an effective search. You should have a discussion with the other team members to determine exactly what will be required.

Vehicle equipment: Equipment that should be stocked in each vehicle used in the raid should include

- Emergency medical kit
- Flashlights and power sources
- Both handcuffs and plastic strip cuffs
- Body armor and helmets

- Field glasses
- Information packets on the target location (pictures and drawings)
- Information packets on suspects (with pictures)
- One radio per person in vehicle, charged and set on the right frequency
- Packaging, such as boxes, sacks, plastic bags, etc.
- Extra ammunition and weapons, if necessary (shotgun)
- Flares
- Rubber gloves and outer clothing, such as raid suits or jumpsuits
- Rope and crime scene tape
- Any other equipment deemed necessary

When it comes to the planning stage, you should always be prepared for the injury of an officer or citizen. Always have emergency medical care standing by if possible.

APPENDIX 2: CHAPTER SUMMARY

Raids: Information required about raid location includes

- Background on target location
- Photographs and description of location
- Neighborhood makeup

Give special attention to:
Exits
Windows
Adjoining buildings
Construction of building
Bars on doors, windows
Door frames
Inside layout
Doors, open in or out
Stairs
Dogs
Booby traps
Lookouts
Walkie talkies

First priority is officer safety!

Raid team selected by skill, not rank!
Team leader
Entry leader
Search team
Outer security
Support personnel

The search:
Explain limits of search warrant
Limit number of searches
Photograph all items seized

Required information about suspects:
Number of males and females
Background on suspects
Prior military experience
Weapons present
Known associates
Habits
Family members in the area
Vehicles

Purpose of raids:
Capture and control suspects
Recover contraband
Obtain documents and evidence for court

Never hurry!

Identify items that need action:
Safe deposit box
Bank accounts

Identify how to involve the FBI in the analysis of records:
Raid packets
Raid checklists
Vehicle equipment list

Use of trickery to gain entry: The purpose is to isolate the suspect away from the evidence. Examples include making flower deliveries; posing as a deliveryman or lawn mowing service; faking car trouble; using a smoker machine; or settling up as a ruse.

Control of the premises and persons during the search: Officers have absolute control of the premises.

Scope, duration, and intensity: Scope—cover all areas where items listed can be hidden. Duration—stop when all items listed are located. Intensity—limit the damage caused by the search.

Consent to search: This must be voluntary, and the person must have the right to give consent.

Formats for arrests: If you intend to make a variety of arrests with some suspects being charged with a lesser offense, you need to be able to explain what decision making process was used and what factors were considered.

21

Interviews and Interrogations

In the field of criminal investigations, one of the most important skills that an investigator can develop is the ability to obtain information from a suspect through interrogation. Interrogation can, in fact, be fine-tuned to an art through training and experience. The only limitations are the investigator's personality traits and the laws of the land. There is very little that can be done about these laws, but through training and practice you may be able to dramatically increase the skills of interpersonal communication which are necessary to function in the area of interviews and interrogation.

Long before you are placed in a situation where interviews are necessary, you should take several different courses on interview and interrogation techniques. Within the courses you take, you should cover some of the following subjects: nonverbal communication, verbal communication, active listening, legal issues and limitations of interrogations, and preparing and conducting interrogations.

WHERE YOU BEGIN

To begin, you need to understand the difference between an interview and an interrogation:

Interview: In the strictest sense of the word, an interview is conducted when a person who is not a suspect is questioned to determine whether the person possesses information that is of value to the investigator's case.

Interrogation: The definition of interrogation is essentially the same as that of interview, except that the person being interviewed is a suspect in the case at hand.

For the purpose of your investigations and subsequent interrogation, it is recommended that you use the term *interview* when you refer to any conversation with a witness or a defendant. This is very important, especially while in court.

Expect the defense attorney to attempt to conjure up visions of bright lights and rubber hoses if you make the mistake of referring to your conversations with the defendant as an interrogation.

WHY YOU INTERVIEW A SUSPECT

The main reason that you interview a suspect is to obtain a confession. This may sound easy, but there are several procedures that must be done before you can even begin.

HOW TO PREPARE FOR AN INTERVIEW

The basic way you prepare for an interview is to gather information in three areas. They are

Case Information

- Review a copy of the report of the incident and make note of the date and time of occurrence.
- Review any and all photographs of the scene.
- Review the information obtained from any other interviews.
- Identify key information that is known about the case that can be used to verify whether the suspect is being truthful.

Remember that to be successful as an interviewer, you must have the answers to several of the questions that will be asked. In this way, you can confront the suspect about deception early on and make him believe that you have all the answers.

Background Information

- *Prior arrests.* You need to know what the suspect's past involvement has been. Focus on prior techniques used by the suspect and associates. Most people maintain the same habits; thus, if possible, use this knowledge against them.
- *Arresting officers.* Interview officers that arrested the suspect on prior occasions and identify information that could be useful.
- *Prior interviews.* If possible, obtain copies of any of the prior interviews conducted with the suspect. Look for mannerisms and defenses that the suspect uses. If possible, use the audio tapes from the interviews of prior cases to prepare you for the new case.

Personal Information

You need to obtain information of a personal nature about the suspect. This information may give you some insight into what technique will be most effective. You will need to:

- Know age, date of birth (DOB), and where the suspect was born and information about where the suspect has lived and the conditions under which he has lived
- Identify the suspect's likes and dislikes, incorporating this information into your planned interview
- Identify marital status, the number of children and their names, if possible, and parental information

WHAT IT TAKES TO BE A GOOD INTERVIEWER

- Careful preparation is the key to a successful interviewer.
- A good interviewer must have the ability to maintain complete control of both himself and the direction that the interview is taking at all times. The interviewer must be able to act sympathetic and nonjudgmental, no matter how upsetting the crime is.
- The interviewer must be a good listener. You need to read the suspect and his verbal and nonverbal messages and tailor your attack accordingly.
- A good interviewer maintains a personal appearance that does not adversely affect the interview.
- A good interviewer is mentally alert, patient and not pushy, and flexible in his attack.
- A good interviewer is a good actor, as well as a good listener. He is self-confident and maintains a professional image.

WHERE YOU SHOULD CONDUCT YOUR INTERVIEW

The location of the interview can be as important as the content of the discussion in some cases. The most important feature of an interview location is the absence of distractions. The location should not have windows or wall coverings that will allow the suspect to wander from the discussion at hand. The interviewer should choose a location that is foreign to the suspect and places the suspect in a situation where he feels he has little or no control. The interview location also should be free of items that could be used as a weapon against the interviewer.

Always keep in mind that you as the interviewer must always be in control of the interview and that you also must avoid distractions.

LEGAL ISSUES THAT APPLY TO CONFESSION

In order for a confession to conform to the guidelines prescribed by law, you must establish the following:

- That the confession was given freely and voluntarily
- That the suspect was not forced to confess and was not threatened or promised anything to obtain the confession
- That you not only provided the suspect with the Miranda rights, but also that he knowingly and intelligently understood and waived his rights
- That the suspect understood the charges against him and the consequences
- That the suspect was not under the influence of any drugs
- That the detention which resulted in the confession was legal according to law

The failure to establish the above facts renders the product of the interview (confession or admission) subject to exclusion.

WAIVER OF RIGHTS

The law requires that before a suspect can be interviewed, law enforcement officials must warn the suspect that he has the Miranda rights. Subsequent to this, before the government can enter a statement by the suspect into court, the government must prove that (1) the suspect understood the warnings and (2) the suspect freely decided to answer the questions posed by the investigator.

Although these two points seem simple, the burden for the government is very heavy. To attempt to lighten the burden for the prosecutor, it is recommended that you try to get the waiver of rights in writing (Figure 21.1). The waiver of rights forms used by most agencies simply gives you documentary proof of providing both the warnings and the waiver to the suspect. You can increase the value of this document even more if you record, either on cassette or videotape, the explanation and signing of this waiver.

INTERVIEW LOGS

Interview logs are nothing more than logs that are maintained by someone present in an interview session. It is recommended that an interview log be kept whenever a waiver of rights is necessary or any time a suspect is interviewed who is not under arrest at the time of the interview. This log should be handwritten by the officer assigned and it should note and record the following information:

- The name, DOB, and other descriptive information of the person being interviewed

CUSTODIAL INTERROGATION

Place _____

Date _____

Time _____

ADVICE OF RIGHTS

BEFORE WE ASK YOU ANY QUESTIONS YOU MUST UNDERSTAND YOUR RIGHTS.

1. You have the right to remain silent.

2. Anything you say can be used as evidence against you in court.

3. You have the right to talk to a lawyer for advice before we ask you any questions and to have him with you during questioning.

4. If you cannot afford a lawyer, one will be appointed for you before any questioning.

5. If you decide to answer questions now without a lawyer, you will have the right to stop answering questions at any time. You also have the right to stop answering questions at any time until you talk to a lawyer.

WAVIER OF RIGHTS

The above statement of my RIGHTS has been read to me and I am fully aware of those RIGHTS and do fully understand those RIGHTS.

I hereby WAVIER my RIGHTS and state that I do not want a lawyer at this time and that I am willing to make a statement and answer questions.

This WAVIER of my RIGHTS has been KNOWINGLY and VOLUNTARILY made by me without any promises or threats having been made to me and further without any pressure or coercion having been used against me.

Signed: _____

Age: _____

Witnessed:

_____

_____

Prosecutor's Office 1982   Form No. 10-1-37

Figure 21.1. Rights waiver.

- The officers present during the interview
- The date and time of the interview and where the interview is being conducted
- The date the subject was arrested and the charges filed, if applicable
- The time when the suspect was advised of his rights, and the name and identifier of the officer who informed the suspect

- The time that the suspect either waived or refused to waive his or her rights
- The time the interview was completed
- The time that preparation of the statement began, by whom, and the time completed (remembering that if you take a recorded statement, get a copy made and use it to transcribe the statement from instead of the original and to always secure the original for court)
- The time the suspect reviewed and corrected the statement and the time the suspect signed it
- All requests that are made during your contact with the suspect and what actions were taken, including any complaints that the suspect makes

This log plus any other information you use should become a permanent part of the case file.

HOW YOU BEGIN YOUR INTERVIEW
OF A SUSPECT

You begin your interview of the suspect by taking charge of the situation: You direct the suspect where to sit and then inform him as to who you are, your title, and your rank. Your introduction should inform the suspect that you have total control of the investigation and how it is to be handled. Inform the suspect that there is a prosecutor who is assigned to the case and that the prosecutor depends on you for direction as to how the suspect is to be prosecuted. Throughout this introduction, you should be friendly and relaxed. You should attempt to put the suspect at ease.

Advise the suspect of his rights: Make sure that you cover all of the rights that are mandated and then ask the suspect whether he understands his rights. In most cases, it is recommended that you provide the rights waiver to the suspect and have him read along as you read his rights off to him. Keep in mind that if your suspect only has a second grade education, do not expect the court to believe that he read and understood his rights. You need to determine, before you read him his rights, whether he has the mental capacity to intelligently waive his rights. If he understands his rights, you then ask whether he wants to waive his rights and talk to you. If the answer is yes, obtain the necessary signature on the form. Be sure that you check the signature and note that he did, in fact, sign his name and not some animated character's name.

Charges pending: If there are charges pending against the suspect, you need to explain each charge and the consequences that may result from a conviction. Do not appear to be in a hurry. Take your time and do not push the suspect. As you are talking to the suspect, you may want to ask him whether he is comfortable or needs anything. You should be gaining the suspect's confidence and steering the suspect toward a general discussion about the case in question. Never jump in and attempt to get a confession right away. You should peck away until you first get the information that the suspect was there and then work into a general admission that the suspect was involved in the crime. The first time through, it is suggested that you do not take notes, but instead just sit back and listen. While the suspect talks, attempt to show that you are interested, but try not to interpret. If the suspect stops or starts to get off track, you may want to try to steer him back toward the subject at hand. *The key is to not be in a hurry!*

Let the suspect talk: Once the suspect finishes, you should inform the suspect that you would like him to go through it again. During this narration, you should feel free to ask questions, clarify comments, and seek additional information. Once you have obtained the information necessary to make your case in court, you should attempt to get the suspect to allow you to get the statement on tape or video.

DEFENDANT'S STATEMENT FORM

Figure 21.2 is an example of a form that may be used for a defendant's statement. You can see that this form is nothing more than a format to follow to make sure that you ask specific questions and cover specific areas. It is recommended that you have a form approved by your legal advisor so that you can cover all the items in a statement that he feels is necessary.

PROCEDURES FOR REVIEW OF STATEMENTS

Once a statement has been reduced to typewritten form, there must be a procedure set up to allow the person who gave the statement to review it and make sure it is correct. The following is an example of the procedures that could be used:

- Once the statement is returned, make sure that the original tape of the statement is placed in a secure location.
- Have the witness or defendant read along while you read the statement to him or her. Remember to make note as to whether the subject can read. If there is a problem, you may want to videotape the review of the statement.
- As you go through the statement, you should make corrections for spelling and content errors.
- Have the person who gave the statement initial and date each page. You may want him or her to initial each correction that is made.
- Once the statement has been reviewed, have the subject sign and date the statement.
- Have another detective witness the signature of the subject.

This is a defendant statement being given to _____ & _____.
who are police officers of_____. This statement is being
given by _____ who is _____/_____/_____, and lives at _____
_____. This statement is being given in reference to
_____ which occured at _____ on
(day, date & Time)_____. This statement is being given
in room number _____, in the police wing of the City-County Building on (day, date & time)_____.

Before asking any question, state "Question"
Q. State your name, age and date of birth
Q. What is your home address
Q. Are you employed and if so what is your job and where are you employed
Q. What is your social security number
Q. How far did you go in school
Q. What school did you last attend
Q. Can you read and write the english language (if no)
   a. ask: do you understand what I am saying to you now
   b. if, while we are talking, you do not understand somthing I say, will you stop me and ask me to explain
Q. Do you understand that we are police officers
Q. Do you understand that you are under arrest for _____
Q. Again I will like to explain your rights to you
   1 - You have the right to remain silent
   2 - Anything you say can be used against you in court
   3 - You have a right to have an attorney present now, before any questions are asked of you
   4 - If you do not have the money for an attorney one will be appointed for you by the court
   5 - If you decide to answer questions now without a lawyer present, you will still have the right to stop answer-
      ing at any time. You also have the right to stop answering at any time until you talk to a lawyer.
Q. Knowing all of your rights do you wish to give this statement at this time
Q. Do you understand that everything we say is being recorded on this tape recorder. If making a video tape also,
   explain this to defendant.
Q. On (day, date and time) _____ an incident occured at
_____ in which (describe incident) _____
_____. Will you in your own words tell us what
   you know of this incident:

Allow the defendant to give a narrative, in his own manner and words, as to his actions in the incident. Do not interrupt him during this phase of the statement. While he is giving this statement you should take notes of some
questions that you may ask to clarify the statement. (full names of persons he mentions, correct dates and times,
correct locations, etc.)

Occasionally, during the questioning part of the statement, ask the defendant if he wants to stop talking, if he feels
he is being treated fairly, if he needs to take a break for refreshments or if he has to go to the bathroom.

To end the statement:
Q. Are you under the influence of any drugs or alcohol at this time
Q. Was this statement been given truthfully to the best of your knowledge
Q. Have there been any force, threats or promises made, by me or any other person, to induce you to make this
   statement, or any other statement to the police
Q. Subsequently this statement will be reduced to typewritten material, after reading it and having it read to you
   will you sign this statement
Q. Has this statement been given voluntarilly and of your own free will
Q. Do you have anthing to add or retract from this statement at this time

Sign off by stating:

This is the end of the statement being given by _____.
It is (day, date and time) _____.
End of statement

Figure 21.2. Interview format.

APPENDIX 1: CHAPTER SUMMARY

Training Needs of Interviews and Interrogations

- Nonverbal communication
- Verbal communication
- Active listening
- Legal issues involving interrogations
- How to conduct interrogations
- How to prepare for an interview/interrogation

Purpose of Interviews
Obtain information leading to the arrest and conviction of the perpetrator.

Preparation for an Interview

- Be prepared
- Maintain control
- Be a good listener
- Maintain good appearance
- Be alert
- Be patient
- Be flexible

Location for Conducting an Interview

- Should have no distractions
- Should have no windows
- Should be foreign to suspect
- Should be free of weapons

Legal Issues of Confessions

- Confession must be given freely and voluntarily.
- No force, threats, or promises should be used.
- Suspect understood rights and waived them.
- Suspect understood charges and the consequences.
- Suspect was not under the influence of drugs.
- Detention was legal.

Interview Logs Needed

- Necessary when a waiver of rights is required
- Necessary when a suspect is interviewed who is not under arrest

Defendants' Statements

- Form provided
- Procedures for review of statements provided

Chapter

22

Court Preparation

Your preparation for court begins the day you receive information and you start your case. You need to understand that the documentation you gather today must be clear and concise, because it is from this that you will be required to construct your testimony in the future. Your objective when you gather this information is to be able to present the facts of the case to the court in a complete and convincing manner.

Once the investigation is completed and an arrest is made, you need to concentrate on consolidating all the information you have and provide it to the prosecutor in charge of your case.

You should provide the following:

- The date and approximate time the original information was received
- The names and addresses of all witnesses
- A brief summation as to what the case consists of
- All statements given by the witnesses
- Copies of all defendant statements
- Diagrams, charts, and any pictures of the operation (provide copies)
- Any detective notes
- A copy of the investigator's file
- Any videotapes that were taken (provide copies)
- Any audio tapes of transactions and conversations (provide copies only)
- A list of the sequence of events that led up to this point
- Any and all observations
- A list as to what each witness can testify to
- A summation as to what you feel is still to be done
- An approximate date when you feel that the case will be completed

MEET WITH THE PROSECUTOR IN CHARGE

Once you know who the prosecutor is, you should attempt to set up a meeting where you can provide the above items and give him a complete explanation as to what comprises the case. As in any line of work, you do not find many people who are willing to let some outsider tell them how to do their job. When dealing with prosecutors, this is especially true.

In most cases involving criminal and civil actions, you will have to work with the prosecutor very closely. He will need you to explain the in's and out's of the type of case in which you are involved. Remember, most persons on prosecutor staffs are not experienced in investigating your type of operation. Work with them.

Before the prosecutor can be effective in court, he or she must:

- Understand the terms used by your subject in the day-to-day operations
- Be able to explain the terms to the jury
- Understand the process used by your subject
- Know the process that was used to track assets
- Understand the process used to track bank records
- Know the process used to track and identify co-conspirators
- Understand the format used for arrests
- Understand the forfeiture process
- Understand the statute which covers the crimes you are investigating

Once you have reached the point where the prosecutor is comfortable with the terms, such as those of a sports bookmaking network, you need to turn your attention to your expected testimony in court.

PREPARE FOR COURT TESTIMONY

You as an undercover officer need to understand that the only way a defendant can win in court is to attack you on the stand. The defense attorney will analyze everything that was done during the investigation and attempt to make it appear that you committed a violation of law or some other indiscretion. You must be prepared for this type of cross-examination. The most important thing to keep in mind is to never lose your cool on the stand. The defense will come at you with a myriad of cross-examination techniques and each will have a different purpose. The best way to prepare for the attack is to go over the techniques that have been used in the past. The following are some examples of what to expect:

1. Watch for the defense attorney who acts as if he is your friend. He will attempt to get you to relax and then hit you with a question that will shake you. Remember, think before you answer any question.

2. Watch for the defense attorney who will ask you the same question over and over again, each time changing the words. If you answer differently, he will attack your recollection of the case.
3. Watch the defense attorney who attempts to use intimidation as a tool. He will stare a hole in you after he has posed a question. If you recognize his game, he will not be effective.
4. Watch for the defense attorney who continues to attack you as if he hates you. His reason for this is to shake you enough so that you lose your professional appearance. If you get angry on the stand, you dramatically increase the chances of the jury siding with the defense.
5. Watch for a defense attorney who demands a yes or no answer. The prosecutor should step in and help when this technique is used. The purpose of this attack is to limit the explanation of an action by the officer. The prosecutor should note the question and return to it to give the officer a chance to explain his answer.
6. Rapid fire questions are used to limit the time that an officer has to think about his answer. The chances are that if you allow the defense to continue, you will make a mistake. Remember, you can control the time of each question by hesitating before you answer.

The following are some actions that you can take to increase the value of your testimony:

1. Hesitate each time before you answer a question.
2. Always look at the person asking the questions and then direct your answer to the jury or judge.
3. If terms are to be used that are not common to the community, you should explain their meaning. If possible, limit the use of police terminology.
4. When answering a question, be brief but be sure the jury understands.
5. Speak loudly and clearly and use proper English.
6. When you are questioned, allow time for objections by the prosecutor.
7. Be courteous to both the prosecutor and the defense. Attempt to demonstrate that you are impartial and professional.
8. Expect to be attacked by the defense. React professionally and show no anger. The jury will side with you.
9. Your courtroom demeanor should demonstrate good manners and respect for the seriousness of the situation.
10. Your appearance should be clean, well-groomed, and presentable at all times. Wear a uniform or suit and tie. Contact the prosecutor for his suggestions.
11. Maintain a good posture while on the stand.
12. Answer all questions in a positive way. The stand is not a place to voice your opinion. Never try to sneak in information. You will pay dearly in the eyes of the jury.

13. Never set yourself up as an expert in your own case. Have someone else testify, if possible, as to the documents. This will separate you from any attack on credentials.

FINAL REVIEW PRIOR TO COURT

Prior to his court appearance, the investigator should conduct a review of all his notes. He should go over any charts, photographs, reports, and any other information on the case to refresh his memory of the specific dates and times when specific incidents occurred. The investigator should review the tapes of all transactions for which he is accountable and view all debriefing of the above transactions. The investigator also should be able to describe each detail of every step taken in the investigation. If there has been a substantial time lapse between the arrest and the trial, the investigator should refresh his memory of the location either by a photographic review or by revisiting the location in question. The documentation to be used in court should be in the possession of the investigator and should be arranged in such a way as to guarantee easy retrieval of any information requested.

THINGS TO REMEMBER WHEN TESTIFYING

* Never take the stand without being prepared. This will lead to disaster.
* Always maintain a professional appearance while in the court and surrounding area.
* While testifying, you should maintain good posture and attempt to avoid body language that detracts from your testimony.
* Speak loudly and clearly and use good grammar.
* Review all case information.
* Never lose your temper, no matter what the defense tries.
* Be fair and impartial to both the defense and the prosecutor.
* Never joke or be a "wise guy" on the stand. This will reduce your professional appearance.
* Never volunteer information. Make the defense draw it out through questioning.
* Direct your answers to the jury and judge.
* When answering, delay a few seconds before answering.

It is recommended that anyone who testifies on a regular basis should be trained in the art of testifying. There are several courses offered around the country which can be very effective. In addition to this, it should be common practice to review and critique each court appearance.

APPENDIX 1: FORMS USED IN CASE WORK

A.

```
                           AUTO THEFT
                GYPSY WRECKER ACTIVITY REPORT

                                    C.A.T.#_____

ON DATE_____ I CONDUCTED AN INVESTIGATION OF A GYPSY WRECKER

AT LOCATION_____ AS A RESULT OF_____

_____.  THE PURPOSE OF THIS INVESTIGATION WAS TO

OBTAIN THE NAME OF THE DRIVER AS WELL AS THE OWNER OF THE WRECKER.

THIS INVESTIGATION WAS ALSO CONDUCTED SO THAT THE CORE AUTO THEFT UNIT

CAN MAINTAIN AN UP-TO-DATE FILE ON ALL KNOWN GYPSY WRECKERS, THEIR

DRIVERS, OWNERS AND BUSINESS LOCATIONS.

RESULTS:

    1. NAME OF WRECKER_____

    2. BUSINESS LOCATION_____

    3. TELEPHONE NUMBER_____

    4. DRIVER'S NAME_____

    5. ADDRESS_____

    6. D.O.B._____

    7. OWNER'S NAME_____

    8. ADDRESS_____

    9. D.O.B._____

    10. LICENSE PLATE #_____

    11. VIN #_____

    12. WAS AN ARREST MADE?  YES____  NO____  IF YES, EXPLAIN:

        _____

    13. WAS UTT ISSUED?  YES____  NO____  UTT#_____

    14. WAS THIS IN RESPONSE TO A COMPLAINT?  YES____  NO____


                    RESPECTFULLY SUBMITTED,


                    SIGNATURE_____

                    RANK_____IDENT_____
```

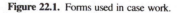

Figure 22.1. Forms used in case work.

B.

```
                           AUTO THEFT
                   SEARCH WARRANT ACTIVITY REPORT


                                        C.A.T.#_____


ON DATE_____, DETECTIVE_____

FILED A SEARCH WARRANT UNDER IPD CASE NUMBER_____.

THIS SEARCH WARRANT WAS SERVED ON_____.


TARGET INFORMATION:

        Name_____

        Address_____

        _____

        D.O.B._____

        Evidence or property sought_____

        Information generated from_____


RESULTS: _____

_____

_____

_____

_____

_____

_____

_____




                        Respectfully submitted,




                        Name_____

                        Rank_____Ident_____
```

Figure 22.1. (continued)

C.

AGREEMENT TO ASSIST THE INDIANAPOLIS POLICE DEPARTMENT

I _____, date of birth _____, age
   Printed Name
_____, who resides at _____ agree that in the
course of my assistance to the Indianapolis Police Department (IPD)
that:

1] I will not represent to anyone that I am a police officer or an
employee or agent of the IPD or that I have expressed or implied
authority to commit or obligate the IPD.

2] I will not engage in illegal conduct of any kind including but not
limited to the sale, delivery or possession of drugs or stolen
property.

3] Criminal acts performed by me will be prosecuted without any
special consideration of my status as an informant.

4] I will not induce or solicit any person to commit a criminal act
unless I know that person to have been previously involved in that
activitiy and I have cleared the activity with an authorized
representative of the IPD in advance.

5] I will not use force, threats or any type of sex or the promise of
sexual relations of any type to induce or persuade any person.

6] Only a deputy prosecuting attorney has authority to bind the State
of Indiana to prosecute or decline to prosecute a criminal charge or
to agree to specific terms to resolve a criminal charge by plea or
dismissal. Officers of the Indianapolis Police Department cannot
bind or limit any such a decision to be made by a deputy prosecuting
attorney.

7] Information on criminal activity I provide may be used in both
civil and criminal actions against wrongdoers and I may be called
upon to testify completely and truthfully in any legal action that
results from these activities.

8] I will at all times be completely truthful in all my dealings with
officers of the IPD, deputy prosecuting attorneys and counsel for any
accused person as well as in any testimony in court.

9] The terms of this agreement represent the entire agreement between
the IPD and me and may be modified only by a subsequent written
memorandum specifically referring to this agreement and signed by me
and an authorized agent of the IPD.

By my written signature below I confirm that I have read this entire
document and that I fully accept and agree to each of its terms without
any express or implied qualification or reservation.

                              _____
                              Signature

                              _____
                              Printed Name

                              _____
                              Date of Signature

Accepted on _____ of 19_____
  for the IPD and witnessed by:

_____
Signature

_____
Printed Name

Figure 22.1. (continued)

D.

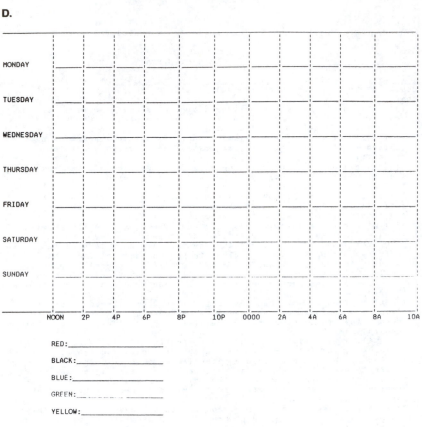

RED:_____

BLACK:_____

BLUE:_____

GREEN:_____

YELLOW:_____

Figure 22.1. (continued) Charting patterns.

E.

AUTO THEFT
RECOVERED RE-TAGGED STOLEN VEHICLE – NO ARREST

C.A.T. #_____

ON DATE _____ I RECOVERED A VEHICLE REPORTED AS STOLEN ON DATE

_____ UNDER IPD CASE #_____. AT THE TIME OF

RECOVERY, THE VEHICLE HAS VIN #_____. THIS NUMBER

IS REGISTERED THROUGH B.M.V. TO _____

WITH AN ADDRESS OF _____,

HOME TX _____, WORK TX _____.

THIS VEHICLE WAS RECOVERED FROM (NAME)_____

ADDRESS _____ HTX_____ WTX_____.

::

THE TRUE VIN # IS _____ REGISTERED TO _____

ADDRESS OF _____ HTX_____ WTX_____

THE TRUE OWNER OF THIS VEHICLE IS $_____. INSURANCE LOSS IS

$_____ INSURANCE COMPANY, AGENT & TX_____

_____

NO ARREST CAN BE MADE AT THIS TIME FOR THE FOLLOWING REASONS:_____

_____

_____

_____

_____

RESPECTFULLY SUBMITTED,

SIGNATURE_____

RANK_____ IDENT_____

Figure 22.1. (continued)

F.

AUTO THEFT
SURVEILLANCE ACTIVITY REPORT

C.A.T. #_____

ON DATE _____ SURVEILLANCE WAS CONDUCTED ON THE FOLLOWING

PERSON(S) OR LOCATION(S). THIS SURVEILLANCE WAS IN RESPONSE TO IPD

CASE NUMBER _____ OR ON INFORMATION RECEIVED FROM

_____.

DATE_____ OFFICERS_____ BEGIN_____ END_____

DATE_____ OFFICERS_____ BEGIN_____ END_____

DATE_____ OFFICERS_____ BEGIN_____ END_____

DATE_____ OFFICERS_____ BEGIN_____ END_____

DATE_____ OFFICERS_____ BEGIN_____ END_____

DATE_____ OFFICERS_____ BEGIN_____ END_____

DATE_____ OFFICERS_____ BEGIN_____ END_____

DATE_____ OFFICERS_____ BEGIN_____ END_____

RESULTS:_____

_____

_____

_____

_____

_____

RESPECTFULLY SUBMITTED,

NAME_____

RANK_____ IDENT_____

Figure 22.1. (continued)

G.

SPECIAL TASK TEAM
COMPLAINT/INFORMATION FORM

DATE:_____   CONTROL NUMBER_____

TAKEN BY:_____

TYPE OF COMPLAINT:_____

WHERE OCCURRING:_____

BUSINESS OR RESIDENCE:_____

SUBJECTS INVOLVED:_____

_____

_____

VEHICLE DESCRIPTION:_____

_____

NUMBER OF SUBJECTS INVOLVED:_____

COMPLAINT'S/VICTIM'S NAME:_____

PHONE NUMBER:_____

WILL COMPLAINT/VICTIM ASSIST IN INVESTIGATION:_____

NARRATIVE OF INCIDENT:_____

_____

_____

_____

_____

RETURN INFORMATION:_____

_____

_____

Figure 22.1. (continued)

H.

SPECIAL TASK TEAM
CRITIQUE/DEBRIEFING FORM

CONTROL #:_____

LOCATION:_____   INCIDENT TYPE:_____

DATE/TIME:_____   SIGNATURE:_____

1. MANPOWER USED:_____

    ADEQUATE:_____YES _____NO   IF NO, EXPLAIN:_____

_____

2. EQUIPMENT USED:_____

    ADEQUATE:_____YES _____NO   IF NO, EXPLAIN:_____

_____

3. DID CASE GO AS PLANNED?:_____YES _____NO

4. VARIATIONS USED:_____

_____

_____

5. COULD CASE HAVE GONE MORE EFFICIENT?: _____YES _____NO   IF

    YES, EXPLAIN:_____

_____

6. INADEQUACIES OF CASE:_____

_____

_____

7. DO YOU FEEL CASE WAS A SUCCESS?: _____YES _____NO   WHY:_____

_____

_____

8. COMMENTS/SUGGESTIONS:_____

_____

_____

Figure 22.1. (continued)

BIBLIOGRAPHY

1. Organized Crime: 25 Years After Valachi, hearings before the permanent Subcommittee on Investigations of the Committee on Governmental Affairs, U.S. Senate 100th Congress, 2nd Session, April 11–29, 1988.
2. **Drug Enforcement Administration (DEA),** DEA Investigator's Manual, U.S. Department of Justice, Office of Training, Quantico, VA.
3. **Drug Enforcement Administration (DEA),** Introduction to Asset Removal Investigations, U.S. Department of Justice, Office of Training, Quantico, VA.
4. **Drug Enforcement Administration (DEA),** Documentary Warrants, U.S. Department of Justice, Office of Training, Quantico, VA.
5. **Boyd, K. T.,** Gambling techniques, *FBI Laboratory Technical Suppl.,* FBI Laboratory, Washington, D.C., revised March 1981.
6. **Harker, R. P.** Sports bookmaking operations, *FBI Laboratory Bull.,* September 1978.
7. **Holmes, W. L.,** Baseball, wagering and line information, *FBI Law Enforcement Bull.,* June 1979.
8. Laboratory Examination of Clandestine Business Records, Racketeering Records, Analysis Unit, FBI Laboratory Documentation Section, Washington, D.C.
9. Facts on Sharing, Legal Forfeiture Unit, Legal Counsel Division, FBI, U.S. Department of Justice, Washington, D.C., 1990.
10. **Sirene, W. H.,** Surveillance Photography Guides, FBI, U.S. Department of Justice, Washington, D.C., January 1979.
11. **Fiatal, J. D.,** Lights, camera, action — Part 1, *FBI Law Enforcement Bull.,* FBI Academy, Quantico, VA, January 1989.
12. **Fiatal, J. D.,** Lights, camera, action — Conclusion, *FBI Law Enforcement Bull.,* FBI Academy, Quantico, VA, February 1989.
13. **Florez, C. P. and Boyce, B.,** Laundering drug money, *FBI Law Enforcement Bull.,* FBI Academy, Quantico, VA, April 1990.
14. **Dipietro, A. L.,** Anticipatory Search Warrants, *FBI Law Enforcement Bull.,* FBI Academy, Quantico, VA, July 1990.
15. **Sauls, J. G.,** Curtilage: the Fourth Amendment in the garden, *FBI Law Enforcement Bull.,* FBI Academy, Quantico, VA, May 1990.
16. **Wade, G. E.,** Undercover violence, *FBI Law Enforcement Bull.,* FBI Academy, Quantico, VA, April 1990.
17. **Goldsmith, M.,** Civil forfeiture: tracing the proceeds of narcotics trafficking, Bureau of Justice Assistance, Washington, D.C., November 1988, no. 1.
18. **Booth, F. R.,** Public record and other information on hidden assets, Bureau of Justice Assistance, Washington, D.C., November 1988, no. 2.
19. **Gallagher, G. P.,** The management and disposition of seized assets, Bureau of Justice Assistance, Washington, D.C., November 1988, no. 3.
20. **Stolker, R. S.,** Financial search warrants, Bureau of Justice Assistance, Washington, D.C., February 1989, no. 4.
21. **Bryant, W. G.,** Disclosing hidden assets: plea bargains and the use of the polygraph, Bureau of Justice Assistance, Washington, D.C., February 1989, no. 5.
22. **Morley, C. H.,** Tracing money flows through financial institutions, Bureau of Justice Assistance, Washington, D.C., February 1989, no. 6.

23. **Murphy, T. G.,** Uncovering assets laundered through a business, Bureau of Justice Assistance, Washington, D.C., May 1989, no. 7.

24. **Ferris, J. E.,** Starting forfeiture programs: a prosecutor's guide, Bureau of Justice Assistance, Washington, D.C., July 1989, no. 8.

25. **Holmes, C. H.,** Developing plans to attack drug traffickers' assets, Bureau of Justice Assistance, Washington, D.C., July 1989, no. 9.

26. **Stolker, R., Sadighian, J., and Lenck, W.,** Profile factors after Sokolow, Bureau of Justice Assistance, Washington, D.C., September 1989, no. 10.

27. **Lenck, W. L.,** Tracking drug proceeds: bank Secrecy Act reports, Bureau of Justice Assistance, Washington, D.C., September 1989, no. 11.

28. Training Program Background and Reference Manual, Police Executive Research Forum, Washington, D.C.

29. Using Photography for Surveillance, Eastman Kodak Company Publication no. M-10, Rochester, NY, 1984.

30. **Hammer, R.,** *Organized Crime: An Illustrated History,* Running Press, Philadelphia, 1989.

31. **McWeeney, S. M.,** The Sicilia Mafia and its impact on the U.S., *FBI Law Enforcement Bull.,* February 1987.

32. The New Face of Organized Crime, *U.S. News and World Report,* January 18, 1988.

33. **Stoler, P.,** Crackdown on the Mafia, *Time,* October 15, 1984.

34. **Powell, S., Emerson, S., Kelly, O., Collins, D., and Quick, B.,** Busting the Mob, *U.S. News and World Report,* February 3, 1986.

35. **Rowan, R.,** 50 biggest Mafia bosses, *Fortune,* November 10, 1986.

36. **Keene, L. L.,** Asian organized crime, *FBI Law Enforcement Bull.,* October 1989.

37. **Rowan, R.,** How the Mafia loots JFK airport, *Fortune,* June 22, 1987.

38. Mafia on the run, *American Legion,* February 1987.

39. Mob-busting a union, *U.S. News and World Report,* July 11, 1988.

40. **Clarke, P. C.,** Twilight of the mob, *American Legion,* February 1987.

41. **Hedges, S. and Witkin, G.,** The great Mob roundup, *U.S. News and World Report,* April 16, 1990.

42. **Rowan, R.,** The Mafia's bite of the big apple, *Fortune,* June 6, 1988.

43. Indianapolis Police Detective School Manual, Indianapolis Training Academy, Indianapolis, IN.

44. **Milam, R.,** *On Evidence for the Law Enforcement First Responder,* South Carolina Criminal Justice Academy, Columbia, SC.

Index